Asmat Art

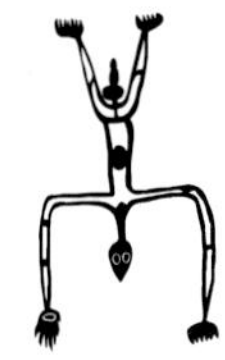

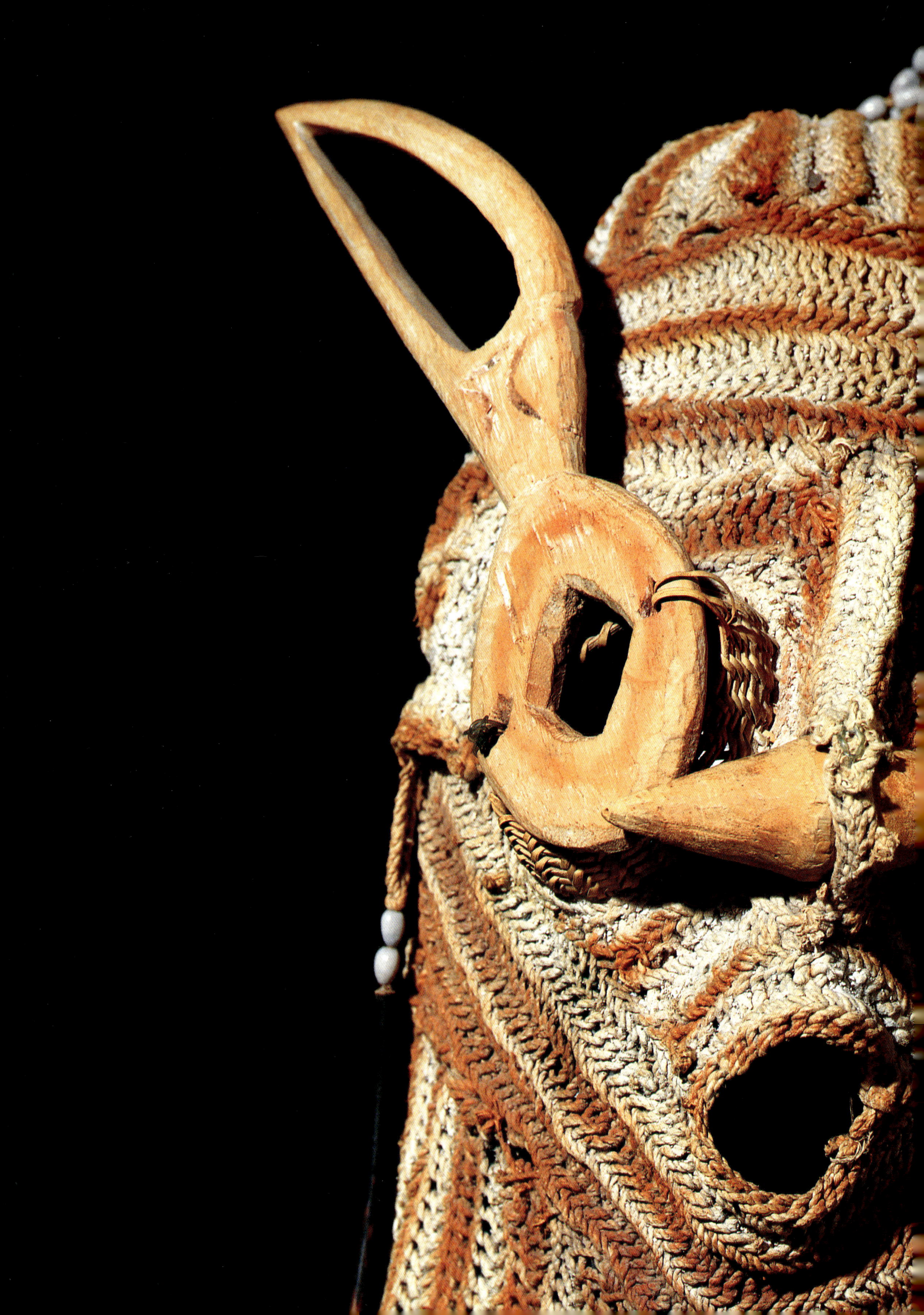

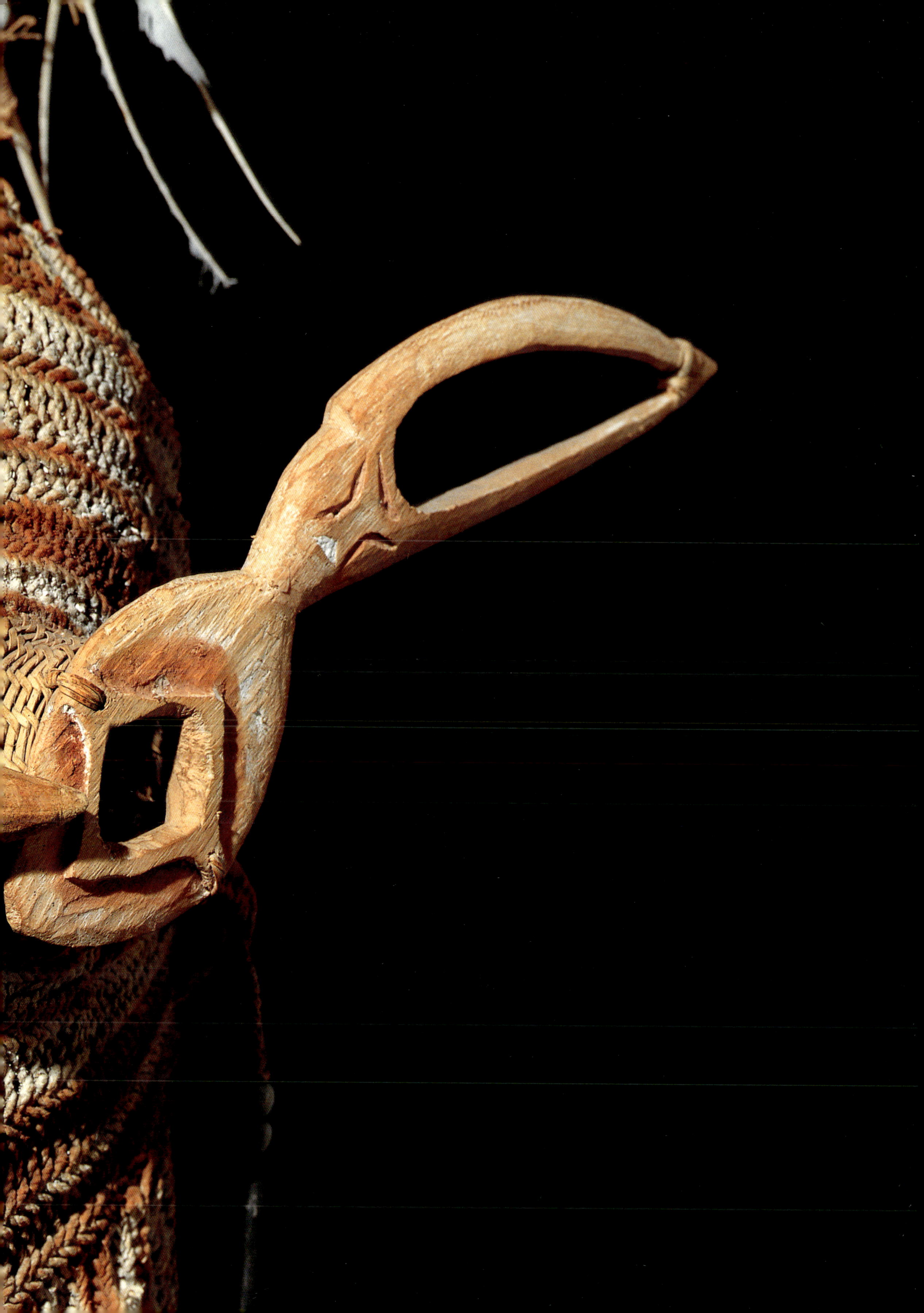

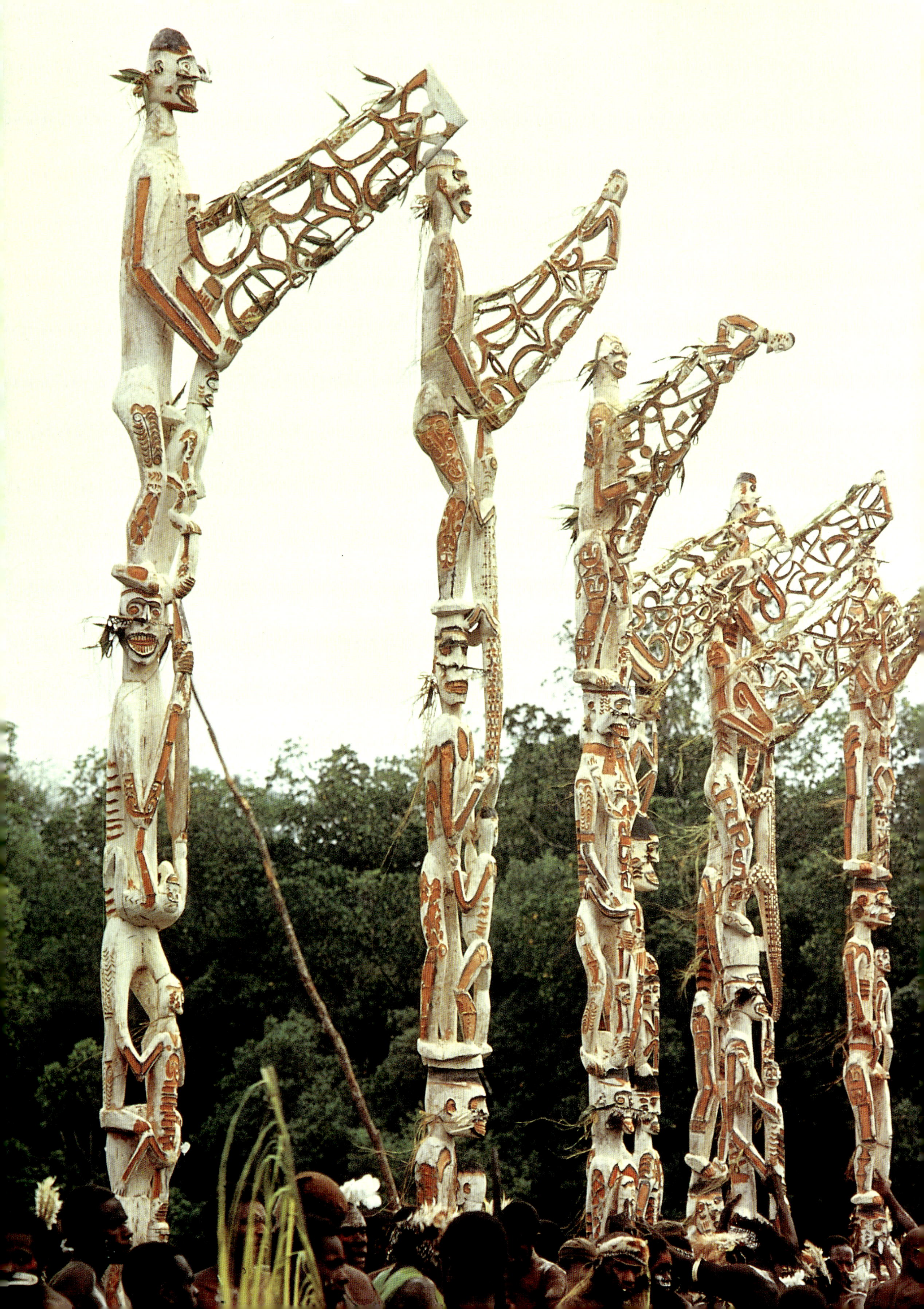

Asmat Art

WOODCARVINGS OF SOUTHWEST NEW GUINEA

Edited by Dirk A. M. Smidt

with contributions by

Adrian A. Gerbrands
Gerardus A. Zegwaard
Gunter and Ursula Konrad
Jac. Hoogerbrugge
René S. Wassing
Adriaan Lamme
A. F. M. Tigges
Dirk A.M. Smidt

GEORGE BRAZILLER, NEW YORK
in association with
Rijksmuseum voor Volkenkunde, Leiden

First published in the United States in 1993 by George Braziller, Inc.

For information, please address the publisher:

George Braziller, Inc.
60 Madison Avenue
New York, New York 10010

Library of Congress Cataloging-in-Publication Data

Asmat art : woodcarvings of southwest New Guinea / edited by Dirk A. M. Smidt : with contributions by Adrian A. Gerbrands ... [et al.].
p. cm.
Includes bibliographical references and index.
ISBN 0-8076-1299-5
1. Wood-carving, Asmat—Indonesia—Irian Jaya. 2. Wood-carving, Primitive—Indonesia—Irian Jaya. I. Smidt, Dirk A. M.
NK9780.A3I743 1993 92-36172
730'.089'9912—dc20 CIP

Production Editor: David Pickell
Design and production: David Pickell
Cartography: David Pickell
Museum Photography: Isaäc C. Brussee and Ben Grishaaver

Jacket photographs: Isaäc C. Brussee

Frontispiece: *Bisj* poles, Buepis village, Fajit River, Casuarina Coast. Photograph: Tobias Schneebaum.

Contents

Introduction

Dirk A.M. Smidt

The Asmat woodcarver's art is a form of communication between the living and the dead, between the community of human beings and the complex and pervasive world of the spirits. In the coastal swamps of southwest New Guinea, deceased relatives, the many birds and animals that share the land with the Asmat, and even the whirlpools and channels of the great brown rivers have a spiritual life. It is in this context that Asmat art must be understood. Despite differences in style from one carver to the next, or from one region to the next, all these grand works serve the same function: to make the spirit world tangible. In doing this, the artist helps bring his community into balance with the world of the spirits.

In a flat land of thick jungle and muddy rivers, where even a stone was a trade object from the highlands, the Asmat turned to the forest for their art materials, using a variety of woods and rattan and sago fiber for construction, and the seeds of the Job's tears grass and the crab's-eye vine for decoration. The color scheme is always the same: red, white and black. The red comes from ocherous clay, the white from calcined clam shells, and the black from charcoal. These pigments are applied without a binder, which results in flat, earthy tones.

Asmat art was never designed to be preserved in a museum, and the vicissitudes of time have faded the colors of some of the objects displayed here. Keep in mind when looking at these plates that when first made and used, these items were usually brilliant with color.

As with other Melanesian cultures, a purely professional group of artists does not exist among the Asmat. Every man has learned how to work wood: to fell a tree, to make common utensils like a canoe paddle or a small cup. But special items, such as shields or statues, were traditionally created by the master carvers, the *wowipits* (*wow* means "woodcarving" and *ipits* means "man"). These men were, and in some cases still are, well-known personalities, famous for their work. They are amateurs, in the strict sense of not earning a living from their carving, but their talent has earned them considerable prestige.

The scope of this book

This book presents a full range of Asmat woodcarving art, but emphasizes the rare early shields and figure sculptures in the collection of the Rijksmuseum voor Volkenkunde, the National Museum of Ethnology in Leiden. Drums, canoe prowheads and the larger, more dramatic "objects" be shown. [1]

Together with *bisj* poles, war shields are perhaps the most famous creation of Asmat artists, and these were carved throughout the region. It is in the design and construction of the shields that the variations in style region can most clearly be seen. Figure sculptures, of varying styles, are also well represented here, and a limited number of the huge ceremonial carvings, such as *bisj* poles and *basu snakus*, have also been included.

The cultural context in which these items play their part is described in detail in the introductory chapters. But it is not the intention of this book to be an ethnography. The focus is on the art pieces themselves.

Chapter 1 offers an overview of the physical and cultural world of the Asmat. Aspects of day-to-day life in southwest New Guinea, as well as the impressive ceremonies in which works of art feature so prominently, are described here. Perhaps most importantly, the crucial spiritual and cultural role of head-hunting is outlined. This article, by Dirk A.M. Smidt, is condensed from his earlier writings.

Chapter 2 is a brief history of the region, beginning with the Asmatters' first contacts with outsiders, and emphasizing the period of Dutch colonial rule. This is written by René Wassing, who until recently curated the Oceania department of the Museum voor Volkenkunde in Rotterdam, and who spend several years in Dutch New Guinea in the early 1960s, working for the Office of Native Affairs.

Chapter 3 is a detailed look at the *jipae* festival, based on previously unpublished notes by Father Gerard A. Zegwaard. The costumes worn during the *jipae,* though not woodcarvings as such, are dramatic examples of Asmat art. Zegwaard explores the cultural meaning of the

---

1. The word "objects" has been set in quotation marks to indicate that what are being referred to are not simple physical objects. Though material constructions of wood and pigment, the more important carvings have been created in a ritual setting, and are imbued with the spirit of ancestors or recently deceased relatives. Indeed, such an "object" even bears an ancestor's name.

jipae, and details the specific context and circumstances in which he acquired an extraordinary mask costume for the Leiden museum, which is included in this publication. Father Zegwaard was the pioneer Catholic missionary in the Asmat region, spent decades among the Asmat, and is the author of the seminal article on the significance of head-hunting among the Asmat.

Chapter 4 devotes itself to the artists themselves, the woodcarvers or *wowipits*. Editor Dirk Smidt examines the social position and status of Asmat artists, and the materials, techniques and tools they use.

Chapter 5 examines the four identified style regions of Asmat art: Northwest Asmat, Central Asmat, Citak and Brazza River. Although many motifs, types of objects, and materials can be found in all these regions, the style of carving in each of these areas is distinct. A comparative survey of representative shields from each of these areas, based on nine style characteristics, introduces the differences among art pieces hailing from these distinct areas.

Motifs in Asmat art are also examined in chapter 5. Traditional motifs—the flying fox, the whirlpool, the stingray, the shell nose ornament, and many more—are analyzed here, with some thoughts on their significance in Asmat art. Editor Dirk Smidt discusses the regional appearance of certain motifs, and their abstraction into almost purely geometric forms.

Chapter 6 discusses the art of the people of the Brazza River area. This region, east and north of the Asmat region proper, has only recently been explored. Gunter and Ursula Konrad, who have collected extensively in the region and written on the art of the people of the Brazza River, have contributed this chapter. It is illustrated by some of the fine shields in the Konrad Collection of the Museum of Ethnology of the Josefine and Eduard von Portheim Foundation in Heidelberg.

Chapter 7 is the catalog, the heart of the book. Here a number of shields, sculptures, monumental carvings, drums and prowheads from the Leiden museum's collection are displayed. They are arranged in series showing a specific connection: similar characteristics of style with variations, the same region of provenance, the same period of collecting, the same themes (for example, animal figures) and, sometimes, the same collector. The arrangement here approximates that used in the Asmat shows at Leiden (1990) and Breda (1991).

In the text of this chapter, written by Dirk Smidt, the context and meaning of the shields, drums, prowheads and larger carvings are described. A.F.M. Tigges, based on extensive comparative research on the collection of the Leiden museum, offers the current state of curatorial knowledge of the function and meaning of ancestor carvings, perhaps the most poorly understood genre of Asmat carving.

Chapter 8 focuses on a unique, coherent group consisting of seven figures and seven shields from the village of Atjametsj, Central Asmat, collected by Dr. Adrian A. Gerbrands in 1961. The figures in particular are special, both for their individual style and large size. Some of these represent two people in relationship, such as man and wife, which rarely occurs in Asmat sculpture with the exception of small figures of a couple engaged in sexual intercourse (see, for example, Plate 7.35, pg. 95). Despite heavy collecting in the region after 1961, no figures comparable to those shown here have surfaced.

These figures and a few shields can be seen *in situ* in this chapter, as well as in the 1967 book *The Asmat of New Guinea*. This book, out of print for years, was edited by Adrian A. Gerbrands from the journals of Michael C. Rockefeller, who disappeared in the region while collecting art in 1961. *The Asmat of New Guinea* contained little information on the sculptures and shields of Atjametsj, however, and it is in the present volume that the collector reports for the first time on how these items were acquired, and on the meaning of the arrangement of the sculptures, and their motifs.

As Gerbrands' account shows, these figures aroused great admiration among fellow woodcarvers from the neighboring village of Amanamkai. The European museum community was equally impressed. I witnessed this reaction myself during the installation of a group of figures from the Atjametsj collection in the exhibition "Wow-ipits, man and art among the Asmat" ("Wow-ipits, mens en kunst bij de Asmat") which was held in the Royal Academy of Fine Arts (Koninklijke Academie voor Schone Kunsten) in Antwerp in 1969, and in the exhibition "The Seasons of Humankind" ("De jaargetijden van de mens") in the Leiden museum in 1987. During the inauguration of the latter exhibition, organized for the museum's 150th anniversary, the Queen herself admired these figures.

Chapter 9 offers a historical survey of the Leiden museum's Asmat collection, which includes more than 3,500 objects. Special attention is paid to the collection's main components:

the Gooszen Collection (1907–1913), the "Kooijman shipment" (1953–1954) and the Gerbrands Collection (1960–1961).

Of great importance historically and artistically is the Asmat section of the Gooszen Collection. This includes some 900 Asmat pieces (more than 6,000 in all) collected by Captain Antony Jan Gooszen during the first military exploration of South New Guinea by a detachment of the Dutch East Indies Army in the period 1907–1913. Though several Asmat ethnographic items had already been collected for the museum in the 19th century (as shown by the Von Siebold collection—Series 1—on the basis of which the museum was founded in 1837), the Gooszen Collection includes the earliest collected Asmat carvings that we could call "art"; in this case, figure sculptures and shields. The museum thus has irreplaceable material at its disposal.

An important part of the Gooszen Collection is now presented to the public for the first time (Group of Shields I, pages 72–75). Moreover, thanks to Adriaan Lamme's recent archival research, light is shed on Gooszen as an individual, his motives, and the circumstances under which he collected.

Having acquired the Gooszen Collection at the beginning of the century, only an occasional shield or figure was added to the museum's collection until after World War II. But special mention should be made of two fine shields collected in 1910 by H. A. Lorentz through the Society for the Promotion of Natural History Research in the Dutch Colonies (Maatschappij ter Bevordering van het Natuurkundig Onderzoek der Nederlandsche Koloniën), and acquired by the museum in 1913. (See Plate 5.6, page 61, and Plate 7.12, page 79.) The two female sculptures collected in 1937 by Police Commissioner R.R. van Ravenswaay Claasen also stand out. (See Plate 7.31 and Plate 7.32, page 93.)

Shields and figures displaying high artistic quality and interesting motifs were also collected after World War II. These include the shields the businessman C.C. Verhey van Wijk and then Resident J.J. Spijker collected from the Northwest Asmat region in 1953. They were acquired by the museum through Dr. S. Kooijman, at that time Curator of the Department of Oceania (Group of Shields II, pages 76–78.)

Chapter 10 is an examination of Asmat art today. Author Jac. Hoogerbrugge, who worked for the United Nations sponsored Asmat Art Project in the 1960s, describes the new influences in Asmat art brought by the rapid growth in trade and tourism in the past three decades. Following a slump in carving and festivals in the late 1960s because of an Indonesian government ban on these activities, Asmat art re-emerged in the 1970s in both traditional and changed forms. Hoogerbrugge examines the changed materials, motifs, and context for contemporary Asmat art.

Collections of Asmat art

For a number of years, sponsoring governments, journalists, and members of the museum community have questioned the "overcrowded" storage rooms in the ethnographic museums of Europe. As curator of the Asmat collection at the Leiden museum, I was asked several years ago by a journalist from the weekly *Vrij Nederland* to defend the collection's, at first sight, large number of shields. One hundred and fifty shields, in the layperson's eyes nearly all the same. Why keep so many?

"They hail from *different* areas and from *different* periods and are all made by *different* artists. Even if they were made by a single artist—does not the Rijksprentenkabinet own numerous etchings made by Rembrandt, too? What hangs here you can never again collect—they hail from a time past.... [T]his museum does not exist for this generation only. One can never know how they will produce new information through scientific research. One also does not know how they will be exhibited again in some form or other—if not by our then perhaps by a next generation." (Pollman 1987:15.)

At that time I could not yet know how well this collection would serve the Asmat exhibitions in Leiden and Breda,[2] and how the very fact of having extensive series of shields at my disposal would prove essential for these exhibitions.

In recent times comments have been made on the best, or most important, Asmat collection in the world. In 1989, during the opening of the Asmat House at the Heidelberg Ethnological Museum, one of the official speakers suggested that the most important Asmat collection is the Heidelberg's Konrad Collection. Moreover, in a book on the masterpieces of the Rotterdam Ethnological Museum (Museum voor Volk-

2. The exhibition "Asmat Shields and Sculptures" took place at the Rijksmuseum voor Volkenkunde in Leiden from June 23 to December 30, 1990. An elaborated version of the exhibition with the same title was held at the branch museum in Breda, May 3 to October 7, 1991.

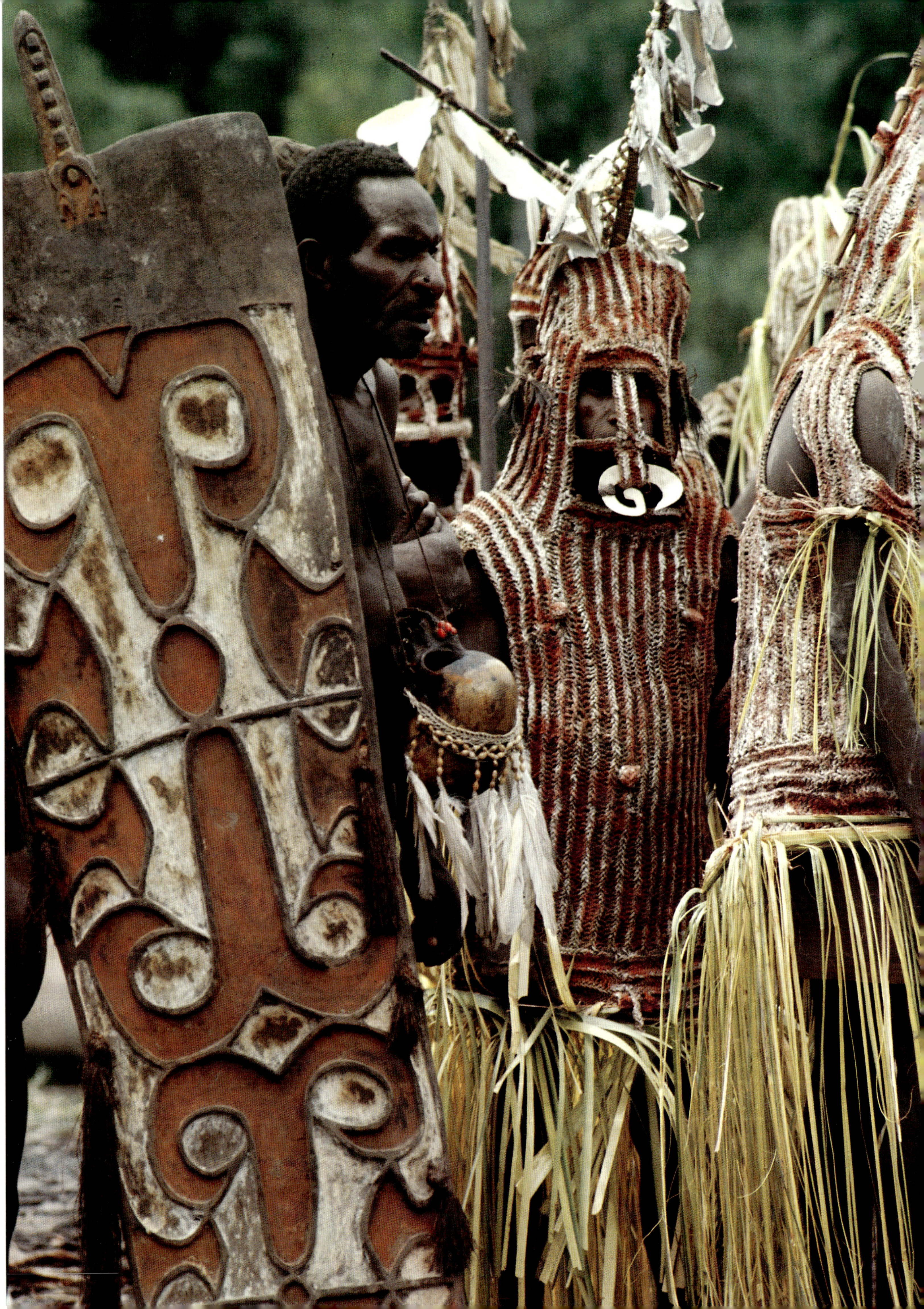

CHAPTER 1

The Asmat: Life, Death and the Ancestors [1]

Dirk A.M. Smidt

Some 64,000 Asmat live on the coastal swampforest of southwest New Guinea (see map pages 16–17). This area was the easternmost reach of the former Dutch East Indies, and is now part of the province of Irian Jaya, in the Republic of Indonesia. Although the Dutch colonial government, the Catholic and Protestant missions, and the Indonesian government have brought many changes to the Asmat, most still live in a rather traditional manner, gathering sago, the region's staple, and hunting and fishing.

The residential area of the Asmat is one wide, muddy plain, covered with tropical rainforest and intersected by countless winding rivers and streams. The largest of these rivers empty into the shallow Arafura Sea, which separates the island of New Guinea from Australia.

Tides here reach 5 meters, and at their low ebb, wide mudflats appear along the coast. Because of this, and the unbroken flatness of the land, it is difficult to make out where the sea ceases and the land begins. Even far inland the difference between low and high tide is noticeable on the rivers, and travel is timed to incoming or outgoing tides.

The Asmat area, bordered on the north by the towering central highlands of New Guinea, and on the south by the Arafura Sea, is even today hard to enter, and local travel is still difficult. Today, an average of a single regularly scheduled flight a week, by a small, twin-engine aircraft, lands at the airstrip in Ewer, near the regional capital of Agats. It is thus unsurprising that it was not until the 1950s that the area came under Dutch government control, and head-hunting ended. During the Second World War, the region was a no man's land of sorts located between territory held by Japanese and by Australian troops.

The waterways are the only traffic arteries here. Indeed, all transport takes place by means of dugout canoes. In the past, war parties went on raids in huge numbers of these canoes. Later, mock raids were staged for government holidays such as the Queen's birthday, and today some villages put on such shows for tourists.

The weather is uniformly hot and humid, and some 5 meters of rain falls in an average year. Although rainfall is heavy, it is also erratic, and the weather can be dry for weeks at a time. Along the coast, the rivers are always strongly brackish, and finding a reliable source of drinking water is a recurrent problem. The small springs in the forest are often unreliable. Only when one gets as far inland as Sawa-Erma, Ayam and Atsj, does the groundwater usually run fresh.

Village life

In much of this muddy region, there is not a stone to be found. Although the Asmat had long used stone tools, these were acquired from the foothills and highlands through trade networks. Pottery, until quite recently, was unknown. All food was grilled on a small open fire. This is still a very typical way to cook, but aluminum pots, as well as steel axes and chisels, *parangs*—the Indonesian machete—and metal tools are fairly widespread now, having been brought in by the first Europeans beginning in the early 20th century. These conveniences spread rapidly after the Second World War.

The most important subsistence food is sago flour, an almost clear starch extracted from the pith of the sago palm, *Metroxylon* spp. New Guinea has the largest stands of sago palms in the world. The sago (*sagu* in Indonesian, *amos* or *ames* in Asmat) is a tall, stately palm, somewhat like a coconut palm but carrying its fronds more upright. Sago has the distinction of being the most efficient source of staple starch. Although cutting down the tree, breaking up the tough pith, and washing out the starch is hard work, a couple working together for half a day can extract 25–50 kilos of sago starch from a single tree. And, of course, sago trees are not planted or tended.

The sago palm is also the source of a very important ceremonial food, the larvae of the Capricorn beetle. (See Plate 1.6, page 20.) These grubs are considered a great delicacy, and 30–40 days before a festival is scheduled, tens or even hundreds of sago trees are felled and punched full of holes so that the beetles will lay their eggs in

Plate 1.1 Men at a *jipae* festival in Buepis village, Casuarina Coast. The *jipae* ceremony serves to encourage the spirits of the recently deceased to leave the vicinity of the village and journey to Safan, the realm of the spirits. For more on the *jipae*, see Chapter 3, page 33. Note that one of the men wears an ancestor skull. 1976. Photograph: Gunter Konrad

---

1. This chapter is largely based on two earlier published articles (Smidt 1970 and 1987).

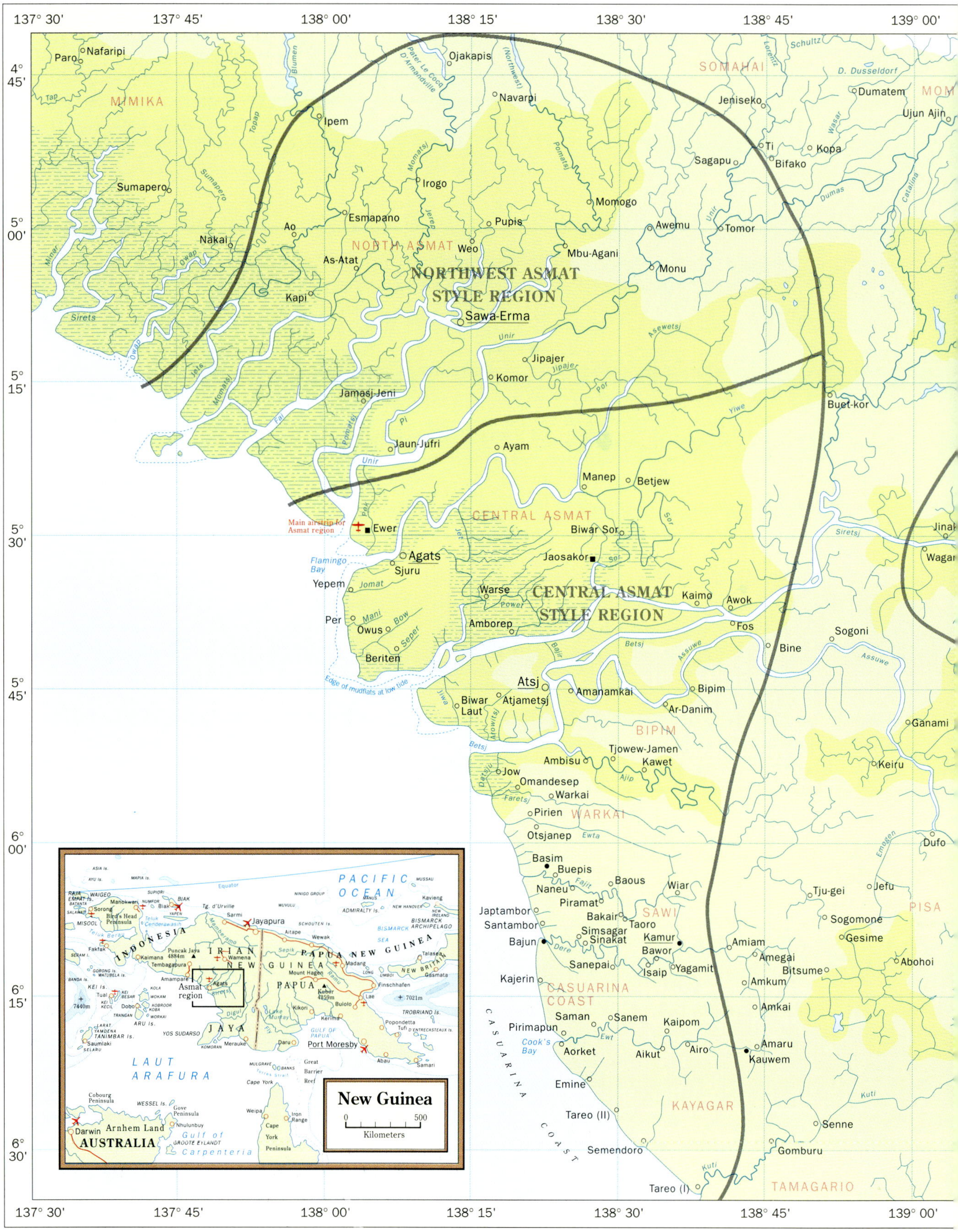
137° 30'
137° 45'
138° 00'
138° 15'
138° 30'
138° 45'
139° 00'
4° 45'
5° 00'
5° 15'
5° 30'
5° 45'
6° 00'
6° 15'
6° 30'
MIMIKA
SOMAHAI
NORTH ASMAT
NORTHWEST ASMAT STYLE REGION
CENTRAL ASMAT
CENTRAL ASMAT STYLE REGION
BIPIM
WARKAI
SAWI
CASUARINA COAST
KAYAGAR
TAMAGARIO
PISA
Paro
Nafaripi
Ojakapis
Navarpi
Jeniseko
Dumatem
Ujun Ajin
Ipem
Ti
Bifako
Kopa
Sagapu
Sumapero
Irogo
Momogo
Esmapano
Pupis
Awemu
Tomor
Nakai
Ao
As-Atat
Weo
Mbu-Agani
Monu
Kapi
Sawa-Erma
Jipajer
Komor
Jamasj-Jeni
Buet-kor
Jaun-Jufri
Ayam
Manep
Betjew
Main airstrip for Asmat region
Ewer
Biwar Sor
Jinak
Agats
Sjuru
Jaosakor
Wagar
Flamingo Bay
Yepem
Warse
Kaimo
Awok
Per
Owus
Amborep
Fos
Sogoni
Beriten
Bine
Edge of mudflats at low tide
Atsj
Amanamkai
Bipim
Biwar Laut
Atjametsj
Ar-Danim
Ganami
Tjowew-Jamen
Kawet
Ambisu
Jow
Keiru
Omandesep
Warkai
Pirien
Otsjanep
Dufo
Basim
Buepis
Baous
Wiar
Neneu
Piramat
Tju-gei
Jefu
Japtambor
Bakair
Taoro
Santambor
Simsagar
Sinakat
Sogomone
Bajun
Kamur
Amiam
Gesime
Bawor
Amegai
Sanepai
Isaip
Yagamit
Bitsume
Abohoi
Kajerin
Amkum
Amkai
Saman
Sanem
Kaipom
Pirimapun
Amaru
Cook's Bay
Aorket
Aikut
Airo
Kauwem
Emine
Tareo (II)
Senne
Semendoro
Gomburu
Tareo (I)
CASUARINA COAST
Sirets
Unir
Betsj
Assuwe
Sor
Blumen
Lorentz
Schultz
D. Dusseldorf
Topap
Momats
Pomatsj
Jipajer
Yiwe
Asewetsj
Jomat
Mani
Bow
Seper
Ewta
Faretsj
Kuti
Dumas
Catalina
Wasar
Ewt
Dere
New Guinea
PACIFIC OCEAN
INDONESIA
IRIAN JAYA
PAPUA NEW GUINEA
Jayapura
Biak
Asmat region
Agats
Port Moresby
LAUT ARAFURA
AUSTRALIA
Darwin
Arnhem Land
Gulf of Carpenteria
Cape York Peninsula
Kilometers
0
500

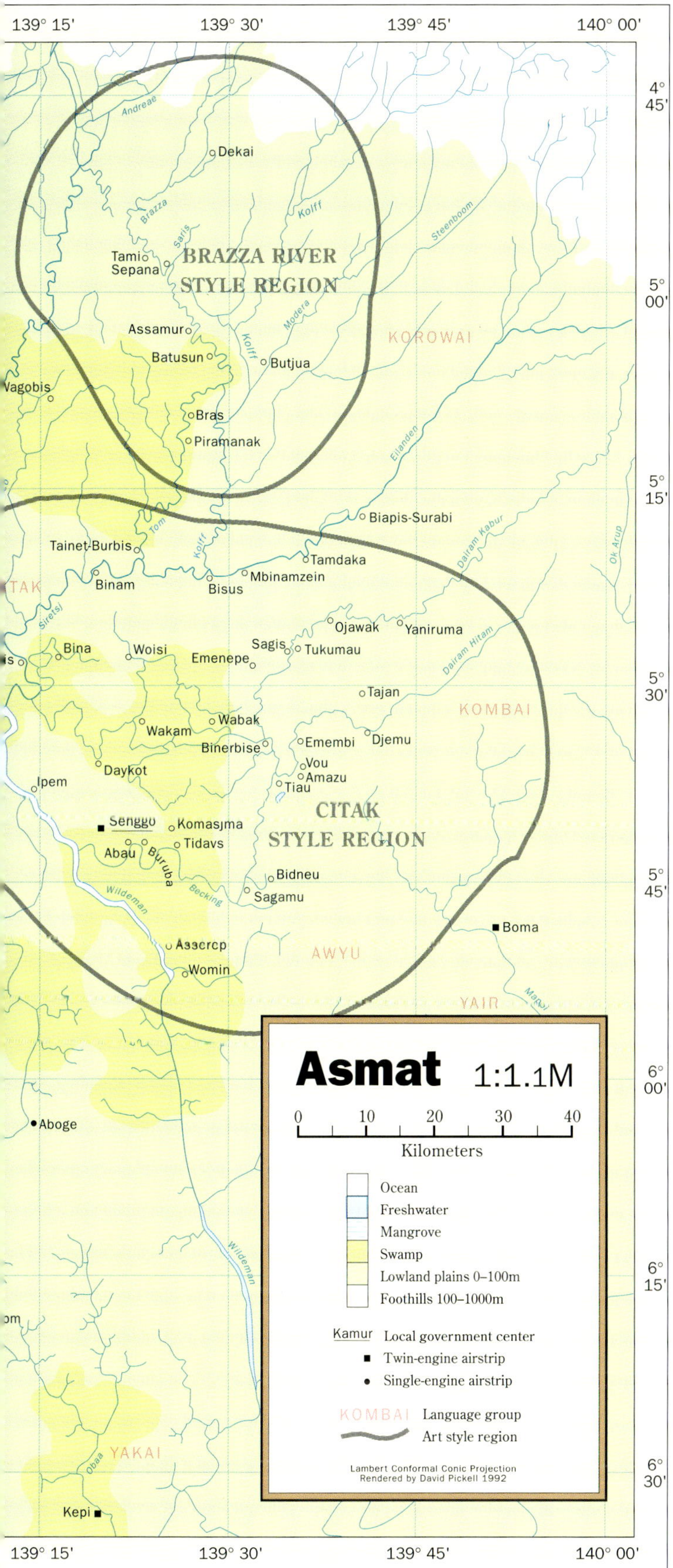

them. Just before the celebration the mature larvae are collected and eaten in great quantities out of specially carved wood bowls.

The Asmat supplement their staple sago, which is rich in calories but rather nutrient poor, by netting prawns and small fish in the saltwater creeks, collecting crabs and clams, and by hunting for birds, wild pigs and other game in the forest. Inland of Ayam, villages often have some well-drained soil where manioc, yams and other vegetables can be grown. The same is true of the Casuarina Coast area to the south—named for the distinctive Australian pine (not a true pine) found here in great stands, the feather-leaved *Casuarina equisetifolia*—where the sandy coast provides enough drainage to grow vegetables.

In the past, when it was still necessary to protect against enemy attacks, the Asmat lived in shifting villages, often far inland on tributaries and smaller streams. Because these small rivers ran dry at low tide, it was almost impossible for a potential enemy to approach the village through the mud. At high tide one could easily blockade such a river by letting a few logs fall over it.

A larger village might locate at the bend in a river, where oncoming war parties could be easily seen. Today, since there is no longer any danger of raids, for convenience's sake most villages have moved to the banks of the large rivers. The Dutch and Indonesian governments in turn have encouraged this move, as it makes the villages much easier to administer.

Asmat villages have 35 to 2,000 inhabitants, although this latter figure is unusual. Currently Atsj is the largest village, with a little more than 2,000 people. Most villages have a population of about 350. In 1961, the population of the region was 30,000, distributed over 76 villages. Current estimates vary from 50,000 to 70,000.

In general, villages consist of one or more rows of houses lining the river bank. The houses are built on short poles, and made of wood, bamboo, rattan and sago palm leaves. Traditionally, houses were shared by a number of related nuclear families, such as several brothers with their wives and children, or two parents with the families of their married sons. In such a family house each family has its own fireplace. Currently, however, more and more single-family houses are being built.

The men's house

The ceremonial life of the village revolves around the large men's house or *jeu*. The *jeu* is both a

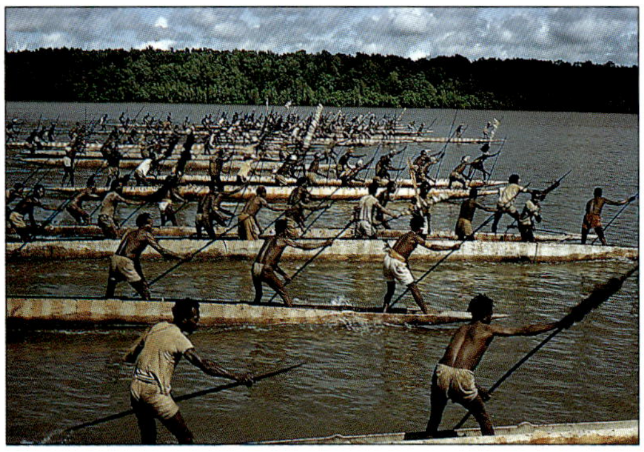

ANONYMOUS

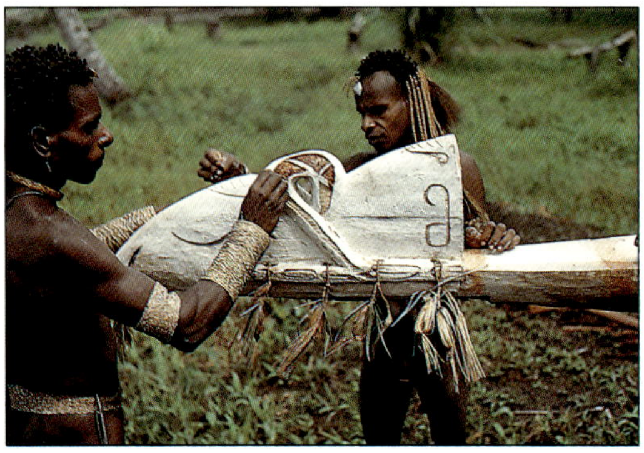

ADRIAN A. GERBRANDS

physical structure, and the basic unit of political affiliation. A large village will have a number of *jeus*; a small village just one. Tensions between *jeus* in a large village can lead the members of a *jeu* to split off and resettle elsewhere.

The *jeu* is a long, narrow, raised building, where community matters are discussed, ceremonies are planned and held, and woodcarvings are made. Important carvings like drums and statues are stored in the *jeu*. In the past, the *jeu* is where head-hunting expeditions were planned. The interior layout of the *jeu* is arranged around a central, "public" fireplace: this is where the leaders meet, important guests are welcomed and the drummers and singers sit during the feasts. On either side of the central fireplace are fireplaces for each head of a household in the *jeu* (see the diagram on page 121).

The *jeu* also serves as a kind of school, where boys gradually acquire the knowledge an adult man must possess to function in Asmat society. Here the boys listen to the stories of the older men, who in the past told of feats of heroism in head-hunting expeditions, and today talk about the world of spirits and ancestors. Many *jeus* have ancestors represented in permanent carvings in the posts supporting the building, or in those surrounding the central fireplace.

Thus the *jeu* is the place where the world of the living meets the world of the dead and the contact between both worlds is kept alive. Although such distinctions are breaking down, women still rarely enter the *jeu*. They do so only when a new *jeu* is being inaugurated or during the ceremony held when villages make peace.

Death and head-hunting

Death holds a special meaning for the Asmat. Without death there is no life; the two are inextricably connected. This is not such an extraordinary idea to a Judeo-Christian society. The martyrdom of Christ is an essential part of Christian doctrine, and through the rite of communion, Christians even engage in a symbolic act of cannibalism, eating the "body" and drinking the "blood" of Christ. The Asmat did not restrict themselves to symbolic actions. They considered actual heads to be necessary for the spiritual well-being, fertility and survival of the community. As a practice, head-hunting may seem shocking; but the doctrine underlying it is not so foreign to the Judeo-Christian tradition.

In its day, a head-hunting expedition was a very powerfully charged event, a time of great

Plate 1.2 (above, top) Men paddling their war canoes in Flamingo Bay, near Agats, circa 1960.

Plate 1.3 (above, bottom) Men painting the prow of a new dugout canoe. The man at right is Tamtjie, the maker of the canoe. Omadesep village, Casuarina Coast, 1961.

Plate 1.4 (opposite) A new canoe is heated over a fire to dry out the wood, seal cracks and kill insects. This makes the canoe water-tight. Basim village, Casuarina Coast. 1979.

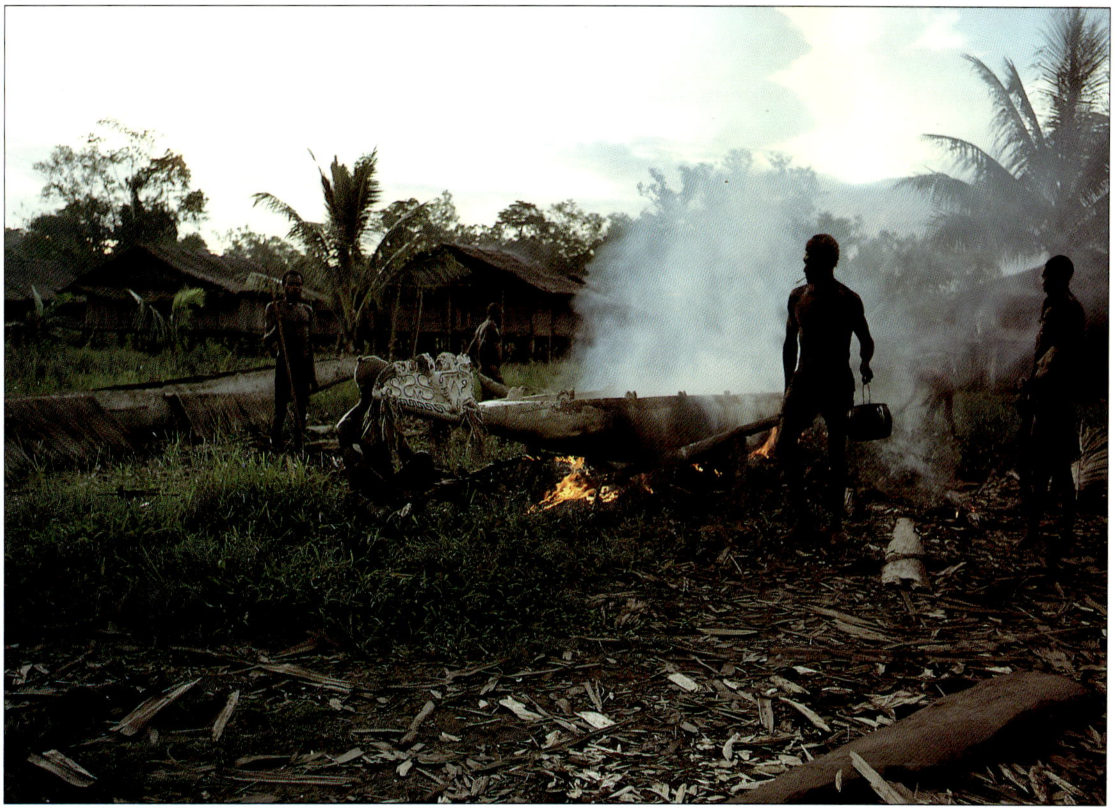

GUNTER KONRAD

danger and great reward; a time when the spirits seemed most present. The Dutch colonial government, and later the Indonesian government frowned on head-hunting and the practice has been formally banned since the first Dutch presence in the region. However, head-hunting still persisted among the coastal Asmat up until perhaps the early 1960s, and among the Asmat of the more remote areas, until perhaps quite recently. Even today, there are areas in the foothills between the Asmat area and the highlands where head-hunting is likely still going on among unacculturated groups.

The life cycle has for the Asmat, as it has for us, moments of joy and sorrow. The arrival of a child is a case of the former; a death, the latter. The Asmat react strongly to a death in the community. An adult, dying in his old age, is surrounded by lamenting and weeping relatives. He is treated with the greatest care, supported, fanned and given cool drinks. When he finally dies, the community mourns for hours on end. Relatives shave their heads. Women, overcome by grief, strip and wallow in the mud.

In the coastal villages, men and woman are buried in front of the men's house, although the bodies of little children are laid in the branches of trees. The bodies of women who have died in childbirth are buried in the forest away from the village, because such a premature and unnatural death is much feared, and, of course, their spirits will live on. Important men and war heroes receive special treatment: their bodies are wrapped in mats of palm leaves and placed on a platform in front of the men's house, or in a spiritually charged tree and left to slowly decompose. After the corpse has disintegrated, the skull is then decorated and kept inside the men's house.

There is no such thing as dying a natural death among the Asmat. Even if death comes about because of illness or through an accident, the event is always determined by magic or the spirits. A person dies because he or she has fallen victim to the evil intentions of someone else, someone who through magic and supernatural power has weakened the body and spirit of the deceased. In other words, an enemy. If every death is caused by the spear or black magic of an enemy, then the importance of vengeance for the Asmat becomes more clear.

Community members who have died are immortalized in sculpture, one of the reasons

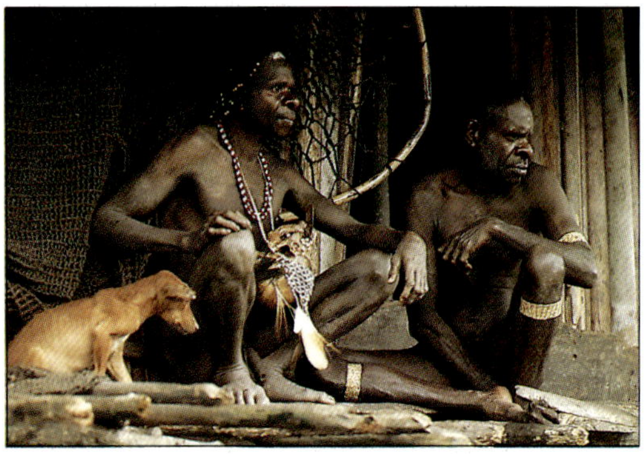

GUNTER KONRAD

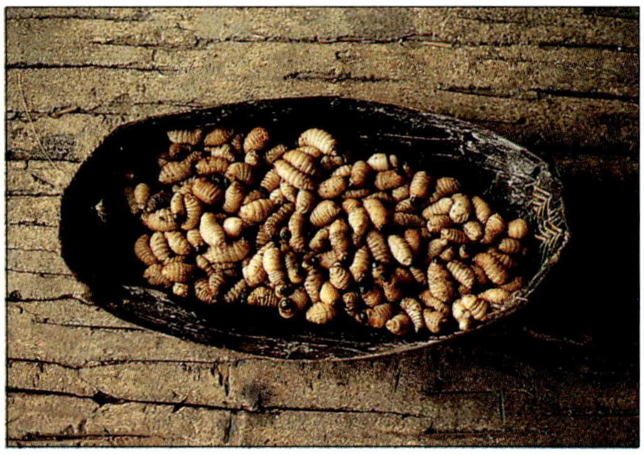

URSULA KONRAD

Plate 1.5 (above, top) Two men on the porch of a *jeu.* One man wears a decorated ancestor skull. Naneu village, Fajit River, Casuarina Coast. 1976

Plate 1.6 (above, bottom) Sago grubs in a wooden bowl. Amborep village, Central Asmat, 1975. Sago grubs, the larvae of the large Capricorn beetle, are an important ceremonial food.

Plate 1.7 (opposite) Decorated ancestor skull. Baous village, Casuarina Coast. Human skull, feathers, Coix seeds, Abrus seeds, shell. 21 cm. Collected in 1971 by Gunter and Ursula Konrad. Konrad Collection, Völkerkundemuseum der Josefine und Eduard von Portheim-Stiftung für Wissenschaft und Kunst, Heidelberg I0125. Photograph: Rolf Bulmer, 1980.

In contrast to trophy skulls, ancestor skulls are kept with the jawbone attached, and the decoration suggests the festive attire a living person might wear.

being to serve as a constant reminder that the death needs to be avenged. Men have been known to carve the likeness of an unavenged relative into the knob on the end of their canoe paddles, so with each stroke the reminder is staring them in the eye.

There were strong social pressures as well. Women would urge the men to avenge the death of a husband, father, brother or son. If a man did not yield to this pressure, he became the object of derision, was proclaimed a coward, and all sexual favors were withheld from him. On the other hand, a successful warrior saw his prestige—both sexual and social—increase tremendously.

The cycle of revenge was fueled by social pressure, prestige, fear—of the souls of the unavenged dead, who wandered unhappily, causing trouble—and even simple anger. But the underlying justification for head-hunting was to maintain the life force of the community. For the Asmat, this life force was tied up with the fertility of the crops, particularly the stands of sago, on which one depended for food. For example, if the sago grounds were producing poorly, or game was scarce, then the community leaders might decide to hold a head-hunting raid.

Enemies were killed in battle, or captured, and killed at special points on the river. The enemy skulls were pierced at the sides with the sharp edge of a stone or a special axe, and the brain was removed. Cooked, either by itself or with the ritually important sago grubs, the brain was eaten to share in the victim's power. After the brains were eaten, enemy skulls were often decorated. The lower jaw was a traditional trinket given by a warrior to his wife or some other woman to wear as a necklace.

The skull of a deceased relative was given much more attention. The head, complete with jawbone attached with rattan, was carefully cleaned and decorated. (See Plate 1.7, page 21.) The eye-sockets and nasal cavities were filled with a sticky mixture of beeswax and sap, and set with the shiny gray seeds of the Job's tears grass (*Coix lachryma-jobi*) and red and black seeds of the crab's-eye vine (*Abrus precatorius*). A splendid head-dress of cockatoo feathers was often placed round the brow, as if the deceased was about to take part in a dance feast.

A relative of the deceased will at times wear the skull around his neck (see Plate 1.5, page 20), or even use it as a kind of pillow. Such intimate contact with this most powerful talisman insures that the spirit of the deceased will always be

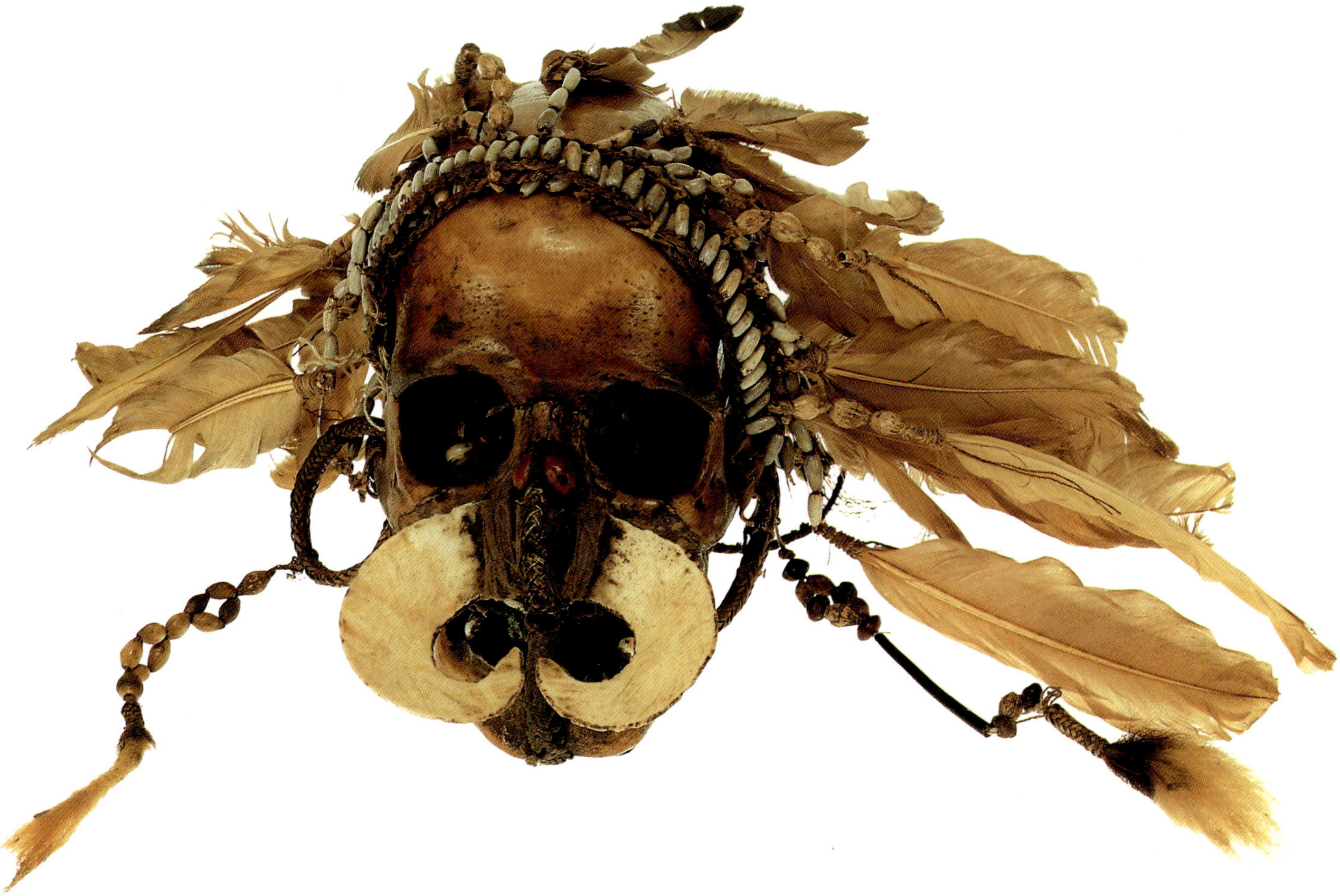

around to help the living.

The initiation ritual

The importance of captured heads in traditional Asmat life is clearly demonstrated by the role they played in male initiation. It was impossible for boys to become men without taking a head. A man's vital strength is said to be particularly present in the skull, and the life force of another provided the energy necessary for a boy to make the jump to manhood. Initiation traditionally took place not long after the boy's first head-hunting raid. At one stage in the group ceremony, each of the boys held a recently severed skull in front of his crotch, and meditated on it. At this stage, the young man was given the head-hunted enemy's name, and his vital strength was assimilated into the group. To ensure the identification between initiate and victim was as close as possible, the boy meditated on the head for two or three days, and was also rubbed with the victim's blood and his burned hair. These acts were a tribute to the power of the enemy.

The initiation continued with a ceremony in which the young man symbolically dies, and is born again. Still carrying the fresh head, the boy was taken in a canoe towards the setting sun—that is, toward Safan, the realm of the ancestors. As the canoes got further and further out, the boy began acting as if he were getting older, until finally he collapsed as an "old man." One of his maternal uncles then lifted him up, and immersed him and the skull in the water. When he came to the surface again, he was "reborn," and acted the part of a newborn baby.

The canoes then turned back to the east. As they got closer to the village, the boy grew up slowly, gradually becoming wiser. By the time they reached the village, he was an adult. The skull he held between his legs and which had accompanied him on his journey, was presented to a female relation. Later, the skull would be hung near banana trees, coconut palms or in the sago swamps, in order to stimulate their growth.

Relationship between humans and trees

The ceremonial life of the Asmat is chiefly aimed at appeasing the spirits of the dead. As part of this ceremonial cycle, and in keeping with the basic themes of Asmat culture—head-hunting and ancestor worship—an impressive woodcarving art has developed. These carvings depict

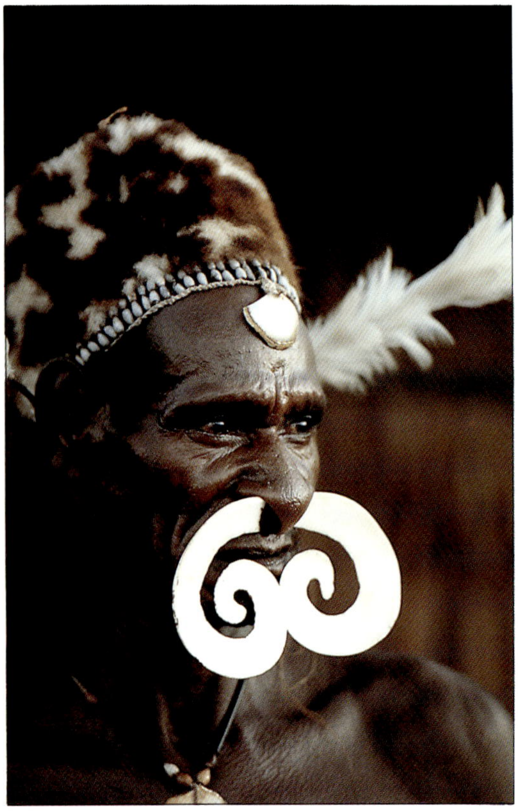
URSULA KONRAD

deceased ancestors, and a variety of head-hunting symbols: the praying mantis, and the hornbill bird and black king cockatoo.

The praying mantis—the female of which eats the male's head during mating—seems an obvious head-hunting symbol. The importance of the birds, both impressively large, is that they eat fruit. Fruit-eating birds are important head-hunting symbols because of the Asmat identification of human beings with trees. In this analogy, the tree's fruit is equivalent to a man's head.

The identification of tree and human, and the importance of carving figures from trees, is made more clear in the Asmat myth of creation. The Asmat primeval hero or god of creation is Fumeripitsj. After a period of vicissitudes and wanderings, Fumeripitsj built the first *jeu*. However, there were no human beings yet to live in it. So he then carved wooden images of human beings and placed them in the men's house.

They were merely lifeless wooden figures, however, and their elbows and knees were connected. (See Plates 7.28 and 7.29, pages 90–91.) Fumeripitsj then made a drum, started playing it, and the figures came to life. He kept playing, the elbows and knees of the now flesh-and-blood figures came unstuck, and they stood up and began to dance. This story reinforces the deep connection between human beings and trees. The parallels are these: the tree's branches are arms, the roots are legs, and the fruit is the skull.

In this context the importance of fruit-eating birds—and mammals, such as the flying fox bat and the cuscus, or phalanger—as symbols of head-hunting becomes more clear. As an animal eats the fruits of a living tree to stay alive, likewise a human being hunts another human being's head in order to "stay alive"; that is, to strengthen his own vitality through the life force of the dead.

Today, when a new *jeu* is inaugurated in a *jeu pokmbu* ceremony, the Fumeripitsj story is reenacted. As the drummers drum and sing, men slowly stand up and dance, wiggling their knees to symbolize the transformation from wood to flesh, and the breaking of the bond of elbows and knees.

Woodcarvings and ancestors

Practically every carved object the Asmat touch bears a name. Canoe prows, paddles, paint vessels, sago bowls, drums and head rests and other more pedestrian objects are often named after ancestors. They are also sometimes carved with

Plate 1.8 (above) Portrait of a man wearing a *bipanew*, a shell nose ornament. Sjuru village, Central Asmat, 1986. Stylized representations of the *bipanew* are important motifs on shields.

representations of specific ancestors, or schematic motifs representing specific ancestors. But the symbolically most important depictions of the ancestors are in ancestor sculptures, shields, and monumental carvings like the great *bisj* poles.

Sometimes feasts are held to commemorate deceased ancestors. For these, sculptures of the dead are carved and placed in the *jeu*. (See Chapter 8, page 115.) These figures, which can be two meters high, represent relatives of the makers' own generation, as well as relatives going one or two generations back.

Such ancestors are also often depicted on shields. Sometimes a human figure representing the dead relative is carved at the top of the shield. In this case the shield bears the dead person's name. The pattern carved on the front of the shield often refers to various ancestors—often three—related to this dead person. Grandfather, grandmother, mother, father, brother, sister are the relatives depicted on the shields, sometimes in the form of seemingly abstract motifs.

Such shields were traditionally made at the *jamasj pokmbu*, the shield festival, which served as the preliminary to a head-hunting raid. During the raid, the deaths of the shields' namesakes were avenged. The naming, and consequent presence of the ancestors' spirits in the shield, gave the warrior supernatural support in battle.

Perhaps the most famous of the Asmat carvings are the *bisj* poles, carved in the Bisjmam villages of the central coast (see Plate 1.12, page 25). These spectacular carvings, often more than five meters in height, consist of several human figures, one above the other, the uppermost one having a large open-work, pennant-shaped protrusion rising up from the body. This segment, the *tsjemen* (literally "penis") is in fact one of the buttress roots of the mangrove tree from which the pole is carved. Small figures representing dead children are often carved into the *tsjemen*.

Even the making of the *bisj* mimes the taking of a head. Once a tree is chosen, the carver confronts the tree as if it were an enemy he wants to decapitate. He cuts it down as he would an enemy, and strips off the bark. At this stage the tree releases a blood-red sap, resembling the blood of a man being skinned.

The tree is then brought to the village, where the women welcome it, shouting with joy in the same manner they would welcome a slain enemy. The tree is then taken to a separate workroom, or laid down in front of the men's house. Then the woodcarvers begin their work.

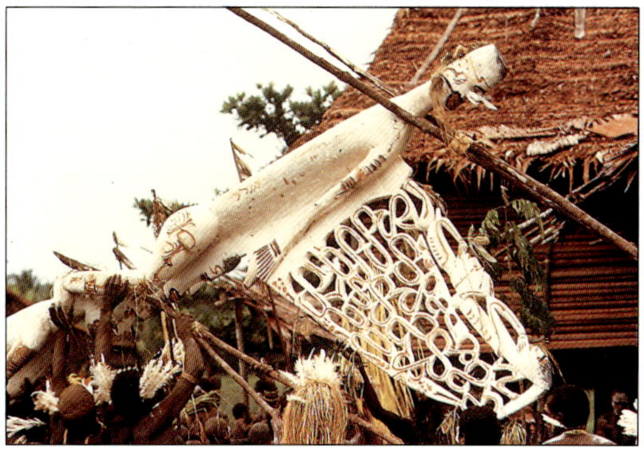

TOBIAS SCHNEEBAUM

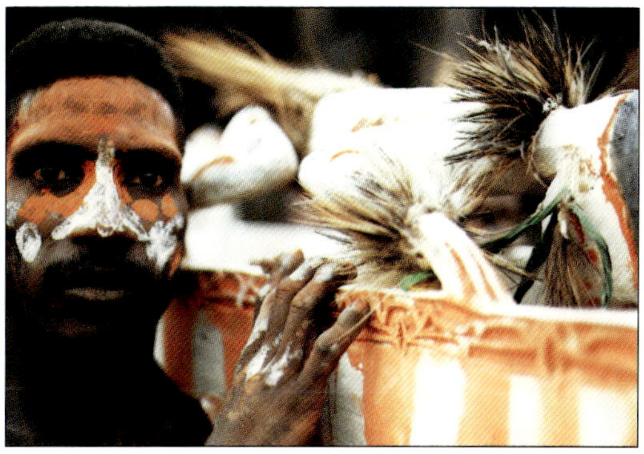

ALPHONSE A. SOWADA

Plate 1.9 (above, top) Men carrying a *bisj* or ancestor pole. The openwork *tsjemen*, or "penis" of the *bisj* is most prominent in this photo. Buepis village, Fajit River, Casuarina Coast. 1977.

Plate 1.10 (above, bottom) Man carrying a *wuramon*, or soul canoe, during an initiation ceremony. Jamasj village, Pomatsj River, Northwest Asmat, 1989.

The *wuramon* ceremony takes place during the *emak cem* feast, held to celebrate the initiation of boys and, to a lesser extent, girls.

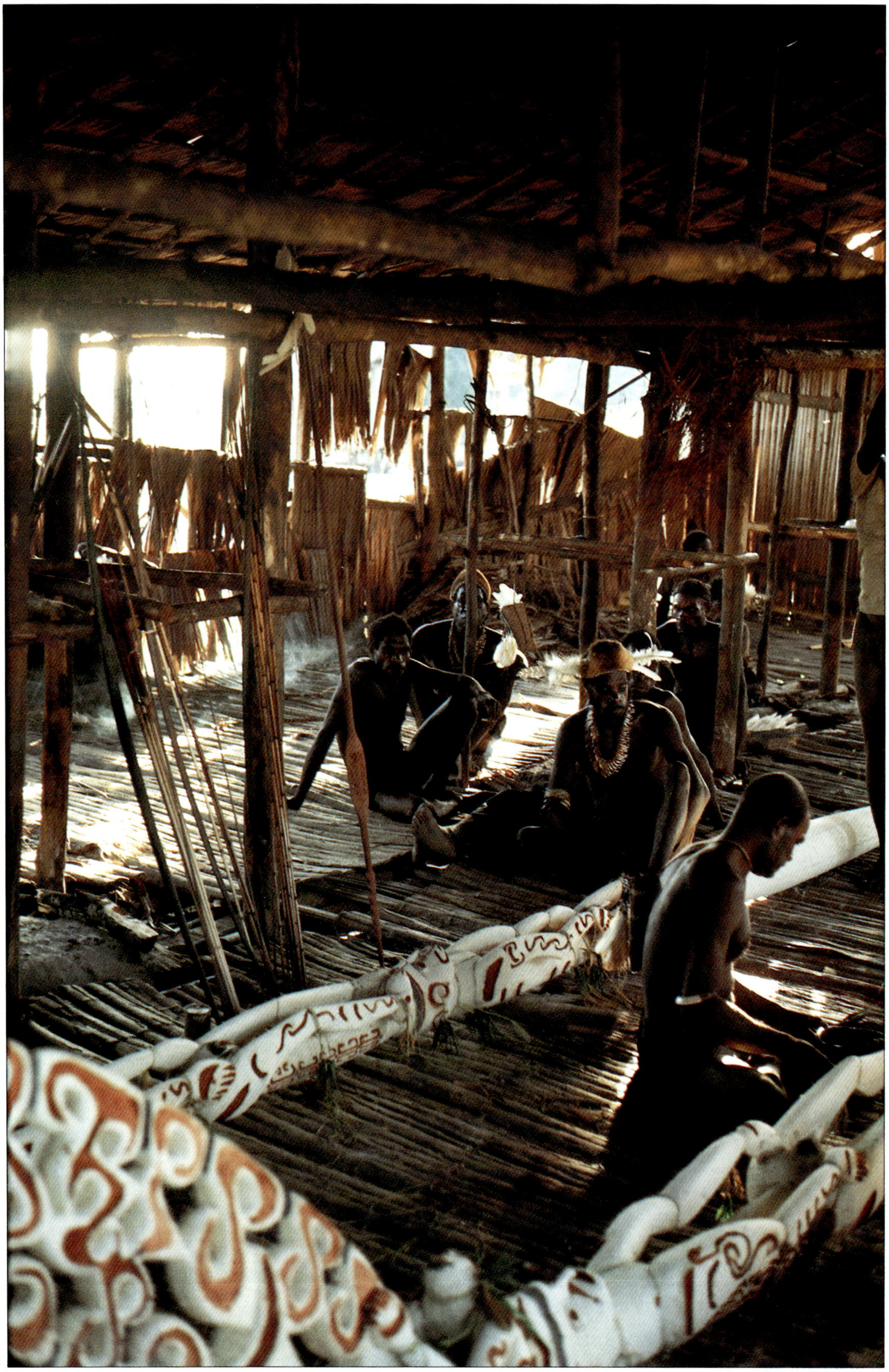

The *bisj* are made for a festival called the *bisj mbu,* on the occasion of which a number of such poles are placed in front of the men's house (see Plate 2.2, page 29). The *bisj* ceremony serves as a tangible promise by the living to avenge the death of the people carved into the poles. During the festival the men boast about their heroic deeds and engage in mock battles. They want to make it quite clear that they are capable of avenging the dead, thus convincing their spirits that it is safe to travel to Safan, the realm of the dead.

During the ceremony the *bisj* stand facing the river. (The dead are buried with their feet toward the river.) The river, of course, is the road to the sea, and behind the sea is the realm of the ancestors. Thus the deceased require a canoe to reach the realm of the ancestors. The *bisj* serves as a kind of ritual canoe, to take the souls of the deceased to Safan. This is why the bottom of some *bisj* have the shape of a small canoe. In that receptacle food is placed for the journey of the dead to the other world.

After the ceremony, the *bisj* are taken into the sago swamps and allowed to rot; their supernatural power is transferred to the sago palms whose growth is thereby stimulated. Smaller, more permanent *bisj* are also sometimes carved. These stand in the *jeu,* near the fireplace, and seem to function like ancestor sculptures. (See Plate 2.1, page 26.)

Plate 1.11 (left) Men in *jeu* with *bisj.* Amborep village, Siretsj River, Central Asmat. 1986. Photograph: Ursula Konrad

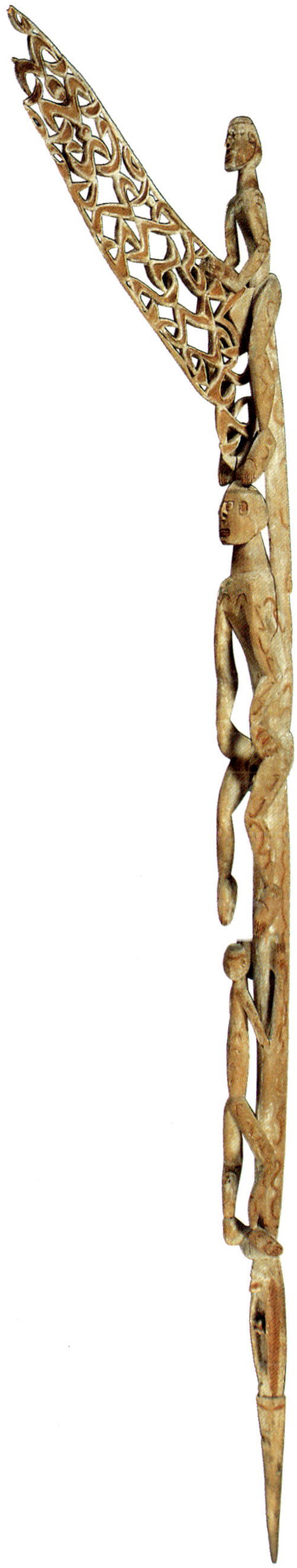

Plate 1.12 *Bisj.* Amborep village, Siretsj River (formerly Eilanden), Central Asmat. Wood, lime, red ocher and charcoal. 508 cm. Collected in 1954. RMV 3242-2. Photograph: Ben Grishaaver.

This *bisj,* together with the *bisj* illustrated in Plate 7.46, page 103, was carved for a ceremony celebrated in Amlaorep in 1954. From top to bottom, the *bisj* shown here consists of two male figures on top of each other, and a third male figure facing towards the pole. Because of its position and the shape of the arms, the upper part of the bottom figure bears some resemblance to a praying mantis. Underneath the lowest figure a small canoe is carved, with a figure sitting inside. In the openwork pennant or *tsjemen* (literally "penis"), of which the tip is damaged, some S-shaped motifs and other curvilinear motifs are carved.

It is interesting to note some differences between this *bisj* and the other one from Amborep (Plate 7.46) in the placement of the *tsjemen* in relation to the upper male figure. In the former, the figure's literal penis is visible because the *tsjemen* is placed about midway along the thighs of the uppermost figure. The *tsjemen* of the *bisj* in Plate 7.46, in contrast, displaces the literal penis of the figure.

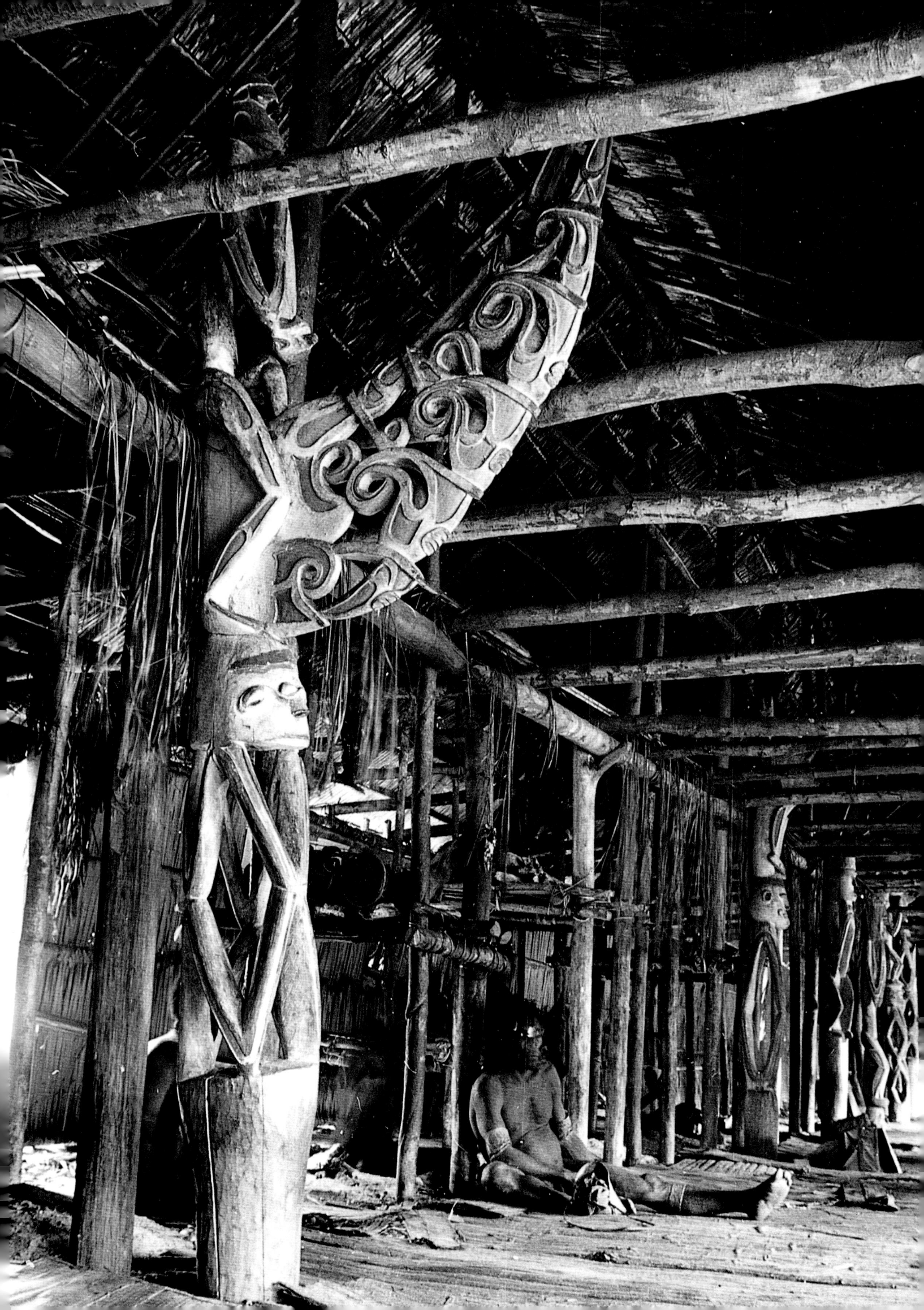

CHAPTER 2

History: Colony, Mission and Nation

René Wassing

The Asmat region first appears in written history as part of a great, unnamed blank on the map, an ominous island east of the fabled "Spice Islands" of the Moluccas. The first European to set foot in New Guinea was Jorge de Meneses, the Portuguese governor of the Moluccas, who was blown off course and landed on the north coast of the island's Bird's Head Peninsula in 1526. Throughout the 16th century, Spanish explorers touched here and there on the island, hoping to find gold. (New Guinea, thoroughly unknown at the time, was rumored to be "La Isla de Oro.") In 1545, The Mexican-Spanish captain Ynigo Ortiz de Retes gave the island its name—"Nueva Guinea"—while claiming it for the Spanish king.

By the early 17th century, however, the Dutch came to dominate commerce and exploration in the East Indies. The Spanish claim lasted only until the 1714 Treaty of Utrecht, when it was relinquished to Holland. Dutch navigator Willem Jansz, still looking for gold, touched land at several points along the south coast, including the mouth of what is now called the Digul River. Jan Carstenz, another Dutch captain, passed the southwest coast of the island in 1623, and sighted the snow-capped peaks around Puncak Jayakesuma in the interior highlands. These mountains—the highest between the Himalayas and the Andes—were named after Carstenz in 1913, but in his own day people simply refused to believe there could be snow-capped mountains in the tropics.

In 1770, the famous English explorer James Cook, passing the southwestern coast of the great island, stopped in Asmat territory near the Casuarina Coast in search of fresh water. The encounter was brief, and unpleasant. As Cook and several of his men approached the forest, a small party of men emerged. Judging them a threat, Cook's men fired upon the Asmat and they retreated, but the explorer decided to return to his boat. As the Englishmen did so, some 60–100 Asmat followed them. In 1913, the bay and river where this encounter took place were named after Cook. (See map pages 16–17.)

The Dutch Indies

Holland's initial control of the Indies was based on a trade association, the Vereenigde Oostindische Compagnie (Dutch East India Company) or V.O.C., which in its prime, earned a fortune in cloves and nutmeg from the Spice Islands. By the end of the 18th century, the company was going bankrupt, and its "estate" was inherited by the Dutch government. Part of this was the "Papuan Islands" of Cenderawasih Bay north of New Guinea, and the western half of the island itself, which were (optimistically) specified in an old V.O.C. treaty as vassal lands of the Sultan of Tidore, one of the original clove-producing islands of the Moluccas. Thus western New Guinea became a Dutch colony.

The Napoleonic Wars in Europe resulted in an interregnum (1811–1816), during which Britain managed the Dutch colonies. After this period the Dutch became aware of possible British interest in New Guinea, and strengthened their claims to the western half of the island. Thus in 1828, as a stated matter of policy, the Dutch government proclaimed sovereignty over that part of New Guinea west of the 141°E longitude line.

A new treaty with the sultan of Tidore signed in 1872 stipulated that the Dutch government henceforth acted as a sovereign, and could thus take over direct rule of the feudal state of New Guinea whenever it so desired. Meanwhile, political and economical activities beyond the border, both in German New Guinea (Kaiser Wilhelmsland) in the north and British New Guinea (Papua), in the south, compelled the Dutch government to take measures to protect their territory. At this time, the Dutch still had no significant administrative presence on the island.

The British had complained several times about head-hunting raids across the 141st meridian into British New Guinea, undertaken by Dutch subjects, Marind-anim people from the Dutch side of the border. At long last, in 1898, administrative posts were established at Fakfak and Manokwari, followed in 1902 by Merauke, in the far southeast, near the border. At this time south New Guinea became an autonomous department in the colonial administration, put under the direct control of the Governor-General. The early 20th century began a new era of exploration in New Guinea, at the time perhaps the last unknown place on the globe.

Plate 2.1 Interior of Jeu Amman, in Amanamkai village. The *bisj* in the foreground was made by the woodcarver Matjemos. 1961. Photograph: Adrian A. Gerbrands.

The chief goal of the early explorers was to find a route to the Central Highlands, particularly to Puncak Jaya, then called Carstenz Top. In 1904 and 1906, surveys were conducted up the rivers of the far north of the Asmat region. The big push, however, was given to a series of government-sponsored military and scientific expeditions during the period 1907–1915. These expeditions yielded a range of important topographic, geographic and anthropological data. The records of these expeditions added greatly to Europe's knowledge of New Guinea in general, and the Asmat region in particular.

First Dutch contacts with the Asmat

The initial contacts between members of these expeditions and the Asmat were brief. But already the first ethnographical objects had found their way to museums in Holland, stirring great interest in the people who made these items. The Leiden museum, founded on the collection by Ph. F. von Siebold, received a few ethnographic objects in 1838 that probably were of Asmat origin. (See Chapter 9, page 137). Many more came to the Leiden museum later.

In 1907, the Annual Report of the Museum voor Land- en Volkenkunde at Rotterdam refers to an exhibition of newly aquired objects from the Asmat region. Through the intervention of J.W. van Nouhuys (who had joined some of the expeditions before being appointed director of the museum in 1915), the objects were presented to the museum by J.H. Hondius van Herwerden, who had visited the Asmat coast in April 1906 as commander of the government steamship *Valk*. Van Herwerden's journal—here he is heading northward from Yos Sudarso Island (then callled Frederik Hendrik)—paints a quite recognizable picture of the Asmat:

"More rivers were encountered after the Eilanden River, all wide and easy to enter, probably of an extended course, perhaps branches of the same river; here too the crew of the *Valk* made contact with the population, crowds that were not ill-natured, but were obtrusive and noisy. Sailing up northwest, the steamship reached the river Utumbuwe ... flowing into Oost Bay [now Flamingo Bay], familiar from the reports of the Snow Mountain expeditions. Here too the natives came alongships in order to start trading by barter. All were stark naked with the exception of an occasional rattan band around the lower or upper arm...

"It became obvious that these inhabitants of the Utumbuwe hitherto have been saved from foreign slurs... iron was completely unknown to these Utumbuwe people; and also other objects such as mirrors, usually the forerunners of civilization into unknown territory, were literally unknown on the Utumbuwe. Up till now they lived in the stone, bone and shell age. That it is possible to achieve fine results without iron utensils is demonstrated by the open-work lances present in the Van Herwerden collection. Most curious of all are perhaps the ornamented bamboo tubes used as shell-trumpets for blowing far reaching audible signals.... More unmanageable material than the smooth bamboo surface to be worked up with flint stone, shell or boar's tusk, does not exist."

We easily recognize the Asmat from this effective, if typically colonial, early description. But their proper name was unknown at the time.

The first Dutch post in Asmat

The Dutch colonial government presence in the area was in the Mimika region, northwest of the Asmat. Here officials first began to learn of the Asmat, particularly their fierce reputation. The Mimikans called the Asmat *wé mana wé,* literally "men who eat men." For want of the correct name, the Dutch called the Asmat "Manowe."

The Dutch in the Mimikan area soon learned that the Mimikan dread of the Asmat was not imaginary. In a famous raid in 1928, 10 canoes with more than 100 Asmat landed at the village of Atuka, near Kokonao, the Dutch headquarters. The Atukans fled to the forest, and the raiders stripped the village, taking everything, particularly anything made of steel. The Asmat tore apart the desks and benches in the Atuka school, and pulled out the nails. (A nail, stuck into a wood handle and with the head flattened into a chisel, is still a popular carving tool for fine detail work.) The police retaliated, but unsuccessfully. Then, in 1931, an Asmat raiding party was caught in a trap set by Dutch police and angry Mimikans. All but 17 were killed, and raids into the area stopped.

In 1939, the Asmat area finally got its first official post: it was established on Flamingo Bay next the village of Sjuru, and dubbed Agats. This post did not last long, however. In 1942, it was abandoned when the Japanese finally reached southwestern New Guinea. During the war, a few Japanese troops were stationed in Asmat territory, at the villages of Kapi, Ao, As-Atat and Jamasj. Many more—1,000—occupied the Mimikan area.

After the war, perhaps because of a crisis

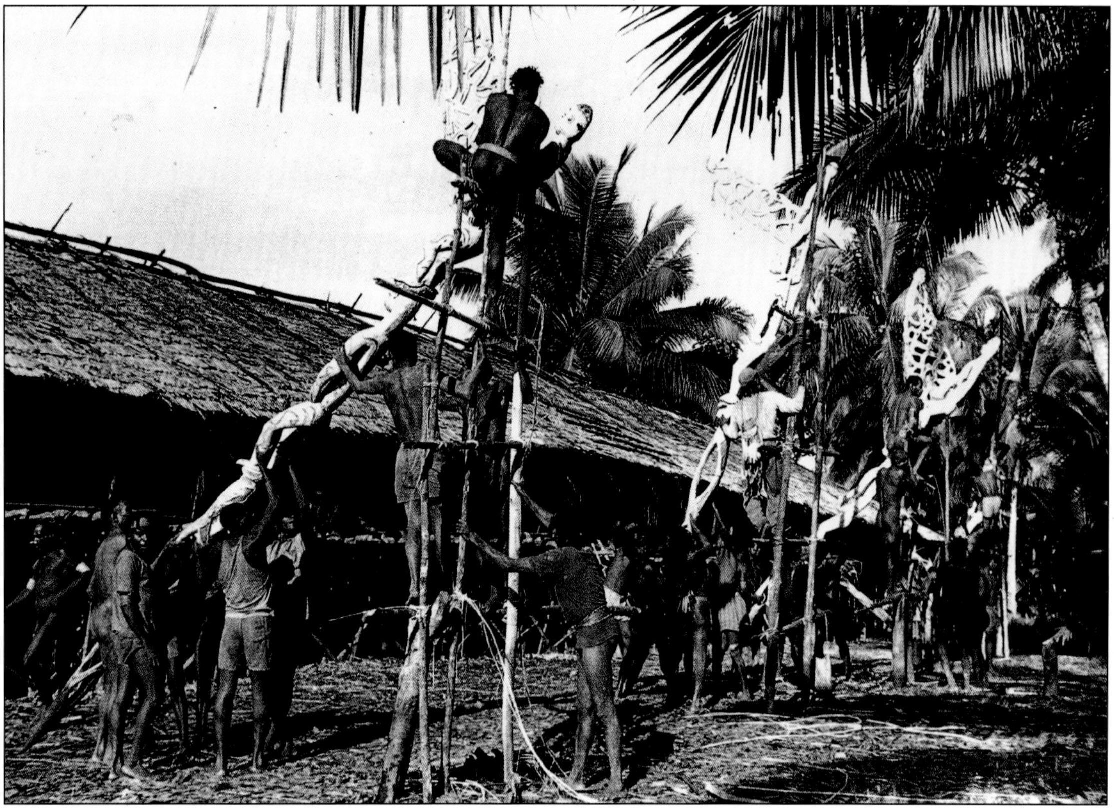

ADRIAN A. GERBRANDS

brought on by the disruption of foreign presence in the area, widespread raiding broke out in the Asmat lands, driving many villages to self-imposed exile. Warse and Amborep fled to the Digul River area to the south. Ewer, Sjuru, Ajam, Jamasj-Jeni, Juferi, Jaun, Kapi, Ao, Nakai, and As-Atat fled to Mimika. All told, between 1946 and 1948, some 6,000 Asmat exiled themselves to the Mimikan areas to the north, perhaps one-fifth of the total population at the time.

The Catholic mission

The first European authority to return to the area after the war was the Roman Catholic mission. Catholic missionaries had, albeit briefly, visited the Asmat since 1912. Before the war, regional mission activities were directed from Langgur on the Kei Islands, and Father Munster patrolled the area in his "White Boat." Some Asmat had come to Mimika in the late 1930s, and there Father H. Tillemans set up a school for them, and even sent a few Mimikan teachers to Asmat villages. This, however, ended with the war.

The post-war mass exodus of Asmat into Mimika gave missionaries a chance to become acquainted with Asmat customs and the Asmat language. Father Gerard A. Zegwaard, M.S.C., worked with the exiled Asmat, and learned their language. It was at this time he learned the name "Asamat-ow," which in Asmat means "we people," in the sense of "we people, as distinct from spirits or animals." Soon, the presence of 6,000 Asmat in Mimikan territory—there were just 10,000 Mimikans at the time—led to tensions between the two groups, and began to seriously overtax food supplies. In late 1949, the government led the exiles back to their old villages. Soon after, Father Zegwaard was put in charge of all mission activities among the Asmat.

Throughout the early 1950s, Mimikan catechists were placed in Asmat villages, and Zegwaard attempted to extend the reach of the Church in the region. This was a difficult time for proselytizing. Tobacco, in those days, was liberally used by missionaries as both payment and a

Plate 2.2 Erecting four *bisj* and tying them to the scaffolding opposite Jeu Ndesep. During the *bisj* ceremony, people feast, and sing, drum and dance near the carvings to honor the dead depicted on them. Omadesep village, Faretsj River, Central Asmat, Casuarina Coast. 1961.

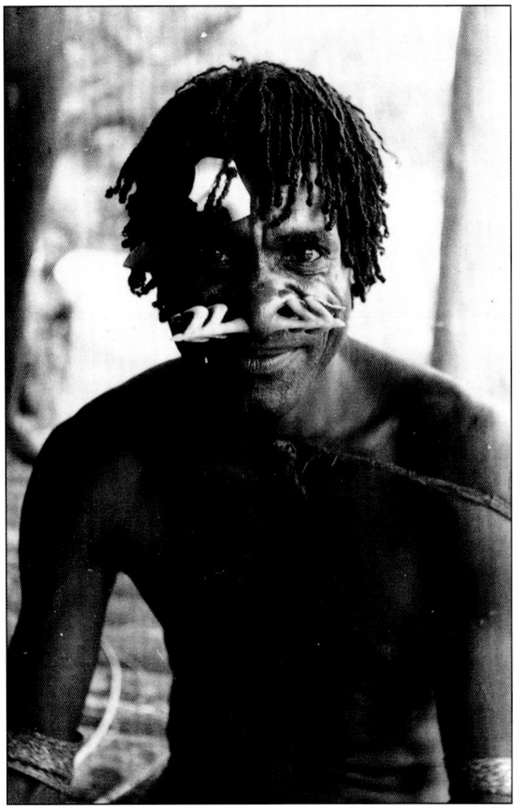

ADRIAN A. GERBRANDS

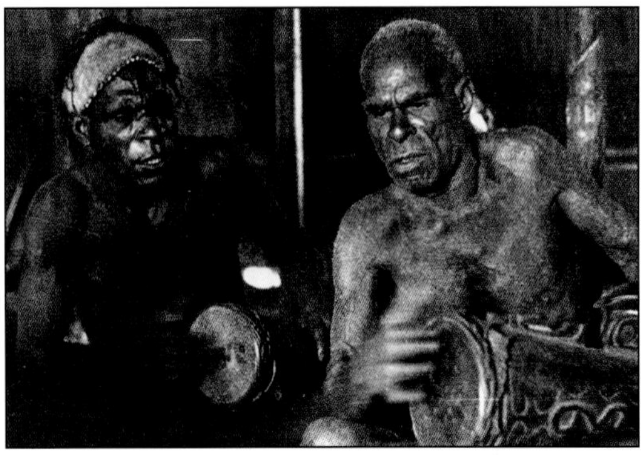

ADRIAN A. GERBRANDS

Plate 2.3 (above, top) Portrait of Jaobenem, of Jeu Awok in Amanamkai village. In his pierced septum, Jaobenem wears a nose ornament of pig's bone in the shape of a praying mantis, an important head-hunting symbol. 1960.

Plate 2.4 (above, bottom) The woodcarver Ndojokor (left) and Safanpo, singing and drumming during the inaguration ceremony of Jeu Amman in Amanamkai village. Safanpo is the religious leader of the village. Amanamkai village, Central Asmat. 1961.

kind of modest bribe. Soon the Asmat were hooked, and demanded tobacco at every turn. Supplies (particularly tobacco) were stolen, Zegwaard was on several occasions attacked, and the Mimikan catechists were gaining a reputation for having sexual liaisons with their host's daughters and generally carrying on in a superior manner. At one point, while Zegwaard and his partner, Father Wellington, were away from their quarters in Sjuru, villagers from Owus broke in and stole their vestments and a chalice.

Culture shock

In 1953, the mission set up a permanent headquarters at Agats, and in 1954 the Dutch government established a permanent post there. The Asmat became and administrative region. The influence of the outside world on the Asmat accelerated at this point. Schools, medical care and Christianity were provided. New crops—manioc, bananas, and especially, coconuts—were introduced to supplement the local diet of sago, and ducks and chickens were imported.

Economic development was encouraged by the lumber trade, which assured desirable goods and even money, in exchange for regular manual labor. This change took place over such a short period of time that culture shock was inevitable. The ban on head-hunting, in particular, caused disruption in Asmat society. (Although small-scale head-hunting did not really end in the coastal villages until the 1960s.)

Woodcarving flourished in this period, and soon the Asmat people discovered the economic value of their art. Museum representatives and private collectors came to the region to buy art. C.M.A. Groenevelt, licensed by the Dutch government and supported by the Tropenmuseum in Amsterdam and the Museum voor en Volkenkunde in Rotterdam, compiled representative collections for both museums.

Scientists and ethnographers were also attracted to the region. Adrian A. Gerbrands of the Rijksmuseum in Leiden came to Amanamkai to study Asmat art and artists. His collection was later donated to the museum. D. B. Eyde studied Asmat warfare and head-hunting, while C.L. Voorhoeve, following up on the work of pioneering missionary-linguist P. Drabbe, studied the coastal dialects of the Flamingo Bay area.

After accompanying the Harvard-Peabody Expedition to the Baliem Valley in the highlands, Michael C. Rockefeller arrived in the Asmat to collect art for museums in the United States. In

November of 1961, during his second trip to the region, Rockefeller's boat overturned at the mouth of the Betsj River, and when he tried to swim to shore he disappeared. Rockefeller's father Nelson, then Governor of New York, directed a much publicized search of the area. Rumors, fanned by the tabloids, that Michael was "eaten by cannibals," brought considerable bad publicity to the Asmat. Today, the collection that Michael amassed is displayed in the Rockefeller wing of the Metropolitan Museum of Art in New York.

Indonesian rule

Increasing international pressure, including a small Indonesian invasion, led Holland to relinquish its claim to Dutch New Guinea on October 1, 1962. The United Nations oversaw the brief transition to Indonesian rule, and on May 1, 1963, the Republic of Indonesia assumed full control of what was then called Irian Barat. Indonesian control of Dutch New Guinea was a very powerful nationalist issue in Indonesia, and the political career of the republic's current president, Suharto, began with the military campaign to wrest Irian Barat from Dutch hands.

Indonesian rule of Irian has been controversial, and sparked a guerilla resistance, the Organisasi Papua Merdeka ("Free Papua Movement") or O.P.M., which continues to seek an independent Papuan state. Because of the O.P.M. and Irian's importance as a symbol of national pride, Irian Barat—later renamed Irian Jaya or "Victorious Irian"—has a high Indonesian army presence, and even today there are areas that are off-limits to casual travelers.

Although things are better today, initially Indonesian policy toward the Irianese was clouded by apparent disdain for indigenous culture. For the Asmat, this meant the destruction of *jeu* buildings and some art, and a ban on ceremonies. Through the efforts of the Catholic mission, and a United Nations Development Project (see Chapter 10, page 149) the already world-famous art of the Asmat was again encouraged.

By the late 1960s, things were beginning to turn around, and in 1973 the American bishop Alphonse A. Sowada, with the help of the Crosier Mission and Tobias Schneebaum, opened an Asmat Art museum in Agats, the Museum Kebudayaan dan Kemajuan Asmat (the Asmat Museum of Culture and Progress). In 1982, an adept of the mission school, Yuven A. Biakai, became the first trained Asmat curator.

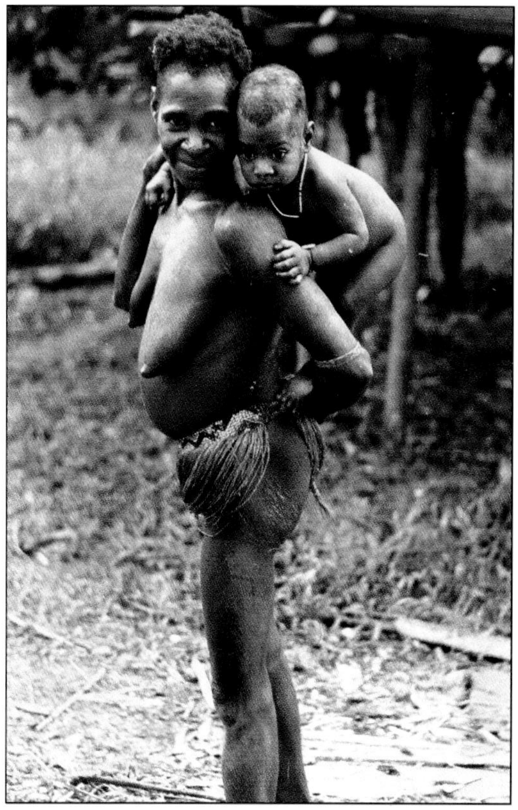

ADRIAN A. GERBRANDS

Plate 2.5 Jewejmenmaq and her youngest son, Ompaq. Ompaq is standing on the belt of her skirt, which is a typically Asmat way of carrying small children. Jewejmenmaq's skirt of sago leaf fiber is the standard clothing for Asmat women. Amanamkai village, Central Asmat. 1961.

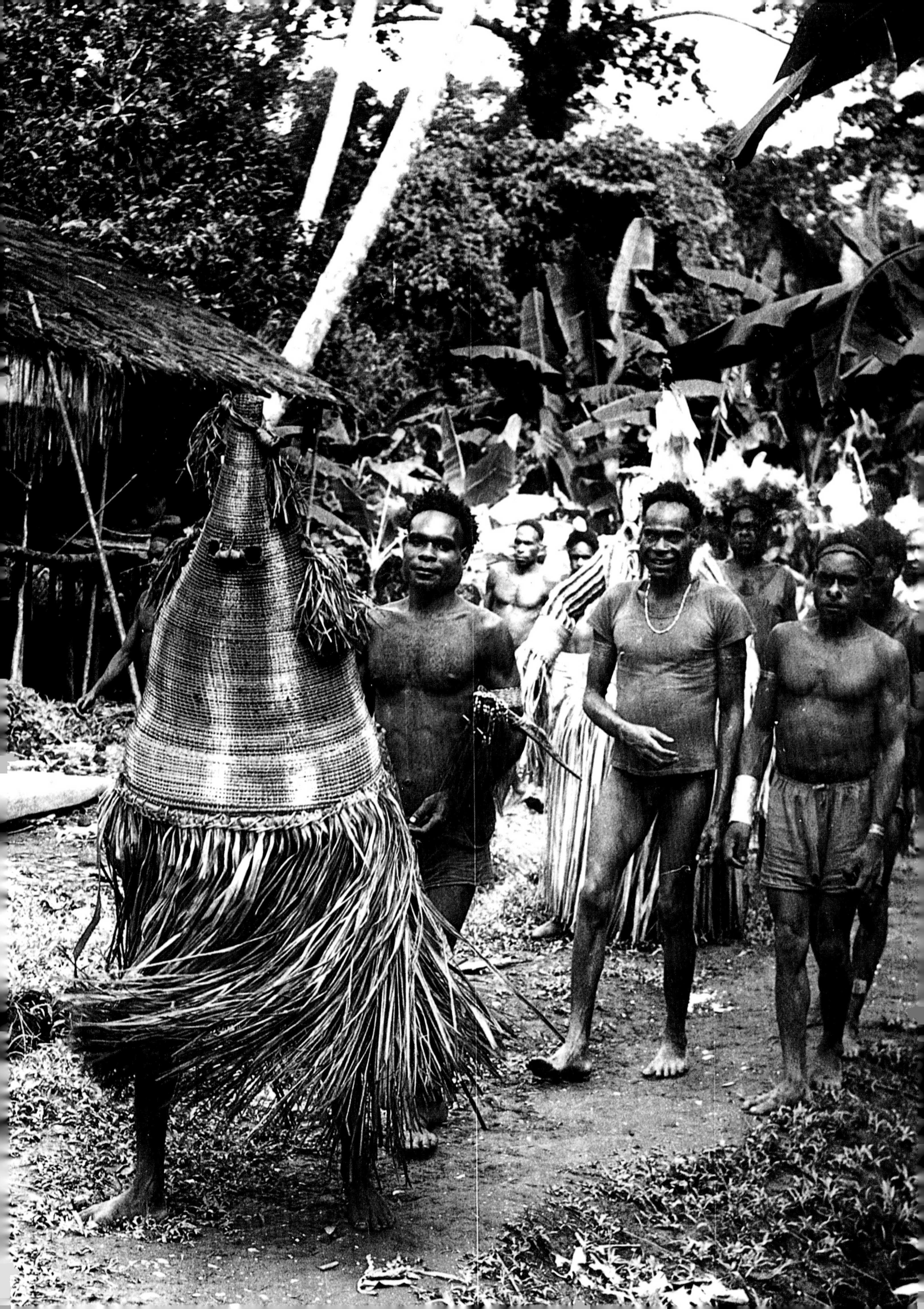

CHAPTER 3

Jipae: Festival of the Mask Costumes

Gerardus A. Zegwaard

Asmat mask costumes are less well known than war shields and sculptures, and have only been collected relatively recently. The costumes are dramatic, full-length suits of rattan, bark and palm fiber, striped with red and white, and decorated with shell nose-pieces, feathers and other accouterments, including small woodcarvings. The overall effect is decidedly eerie, especially the "face," which is distorted or even absent. The costumes are worn during the *jipae* feast, a celebration of the passage of the dead from the world of people to the world of the spirits. (The costumes are also called *jipae*.)

Though roughly similar in design, *jipae* costumes show an exuberant variety. Comparative studies of Asmat shields have led to the establishment of style regions; an eventual study of the masks will presumably result in a similar pattern, although the mask costumes are only known from the Northwest Asmat and Central Asmat style regions. (See Chapter 5, page 53.)

The same basic materials are used throughout the Asmat region for making the costumes: plaited rope made of bark, rattan and sago leaf fibers. The same pigments used on woodcarvings give color to the costumes: lime, red ocher, and charcoal. The face and head of the costumes are decorated with nose shells and nose pens, wooden hornbill beaks, parrot and cassowary feathers, and sago leaf tassels. This combination of human and animal characteristics suggests something otherworldly, and thus sacred.

As far as is known, the costumes only represent people who have recently died, and are not used to impersonate ancestors and culture heroes in general. According to the legends and songs of the culturally related population of the Mimika region, the masks were acquired by culture heroes from the spirit world. These heroes, who had been to the spirit world for only a short visit, had been given the costumes by their ancestors.

According to one story the Asmat traditionally tell, the *jipae* costume was invented by a desperate orphan boy who, on the brink of starving to death, created the costume to scare off some women so he could steal their food. In another, lesser-known story, two bachelors invent the mask to seduce young girls.

Every few years the people of Central and Northwest Asmat organize a *jipae* feast, during which the important and beloved persons who have passed away since the previous feast return for a single evening and a single night. After the festival, they take leave of the community permanently. Immediately after the celebration, their successors are installed, and the care of any children orphaned by the deaths is formally passed to new parents. The event extends over several months, the largest part of which is spent preparing for the actual feast, making the costumes and armbands. In 1954 I was able to witness the armband feast at close range in the village of Sjuru, on the coast near Agats. About the same time, I saw the mask feast in the village of Ajam, further inland on the Asewetsj River.

Making the rope masks

First it is decided which family group is going to organize the feast. A number of deceased people are chosen to be remembered during the feast, and the actors who will wear the masks are chosen. Politics and rivalry between family groups plays an important role in these decisions. In organizing the event, considerable attention is paid to encouraging the participation of all groups in the village.

Those who will wear the masks will also be the people who will take upon themselves the rights and obligations of the deceased, particularly raising the children and eventually arranging their marriage. Young men enjoying a certain prosperity—in 1954, for example, this often meant those who were working for the mission and thus paid in western goods—are the most likely candidates for this role. The men who are picked to wear the costumes must choose a few "followers" or assistants. The family of the deceased throws a lavish reception for these men, and they, in turn, honor their "followers."

As I observed in Sjuru, two distinct kinds of mask costumes are made for the *jipae* festival. These are called the "younger brother" and the "elder brother." The "younger brother" costume is made of rattan, and shaped like a basket. There

Plate 3.1 The mask costumes (*jipae*) tour the village during the jipae festival held by Jeu Awok. The "basket" costume is in front, followed by the two rope costumes. The tour is the culmination of the *jipae* festival, and for the previous day, in preparation, the costumes had been hung on display in the *jeu.* Amanamkai village, Central Asmat, 1961. Photograph: Adrian A. Gerbrands.

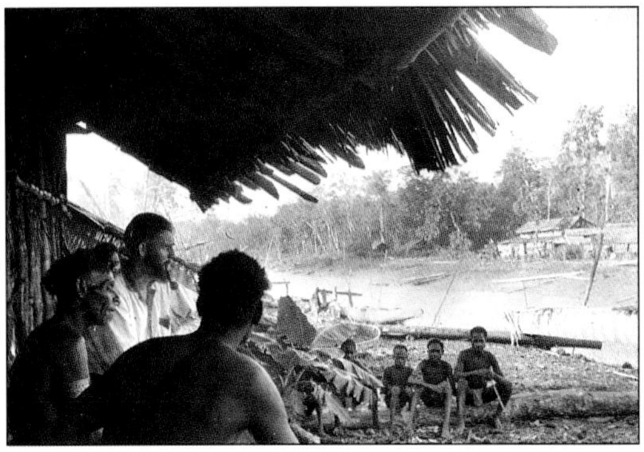

GIJS BERTELS

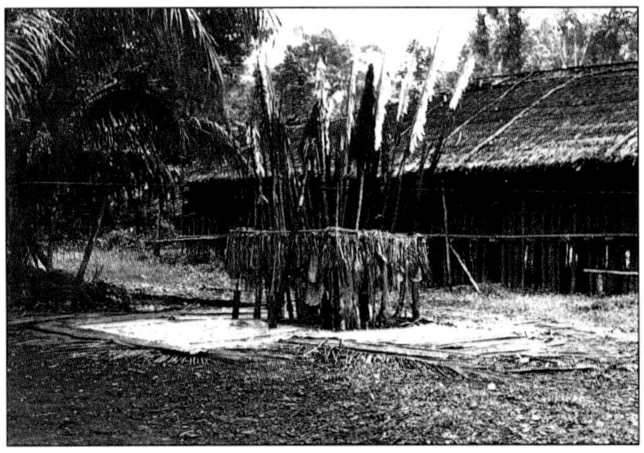

ADRIAN A. GERBRANDS

Plate 3.2 Above, top. Father Gerardus A. Zegwaard, m.s.c., at the time the parish priest, visits his parishioners at Amborep village, Central Asmat. 1953.

Plate 3.3 Above, bottom. The scaffolding in front of Jeu Awok, erected for the *jipae* festival. The guests of the feast have inserted their decorated spears, paddles and digging sticks into the structure. *Syrinx aruanus* shells, which serve as an insignia of social rank, are placed on top. Amanamkai village, Central Asmat, 1961.

are a few scanty references to the eyes and the mouth (see Plate 3.10, page 41), or none at all (see Plate 3.13, page 44). The open bottom of the basket is hung with sago leaf fiber, to form a kind of "skirt." The costume is pulled over the head and the upper part of the body, and the sago-leaf skirt covers the wearer's legs. This basket costume, or "younger brother" is not considered particularly sacred.

The rope costume or "elder brother" is the important costume in the festival. (See Plate 3.11, page 42, Plate 3.12, page 43, and Plate 3.14, page 45.) The rope costume is carefully stored away after the feast in a corner of the men's house. The basket costume lies around for some time, and is used as a toy by the children who—to the amusement of young and old—play "orphan boy."

The rope masks are made in the men's house or *jeu*. Skilled men make the actual masks in secret. Each evening they are stored away in mats. If one wishes to say something about the masks being made, one speaks of the "mats." Sacred matters are not directly referred to in public by name; they are referred to indirectly.

Adrian A. Gerbrands has studied the tools and materials used to make the masks, and described them as follows. First bark from *fum* wood is collected, and laid above the fireplaces to dry, which takes several weeks. Nobody ever says "fum" because it is considered sacred. The bark is stripped off the wood and then, using a splinter of wood (*tjow jokoss*) or a shell (*jètsj* or *fuij*), the fiber (*fum oss*) on the inside is pulled off in small strips. This fiber is made into rope (*fum semèn*) by twining it on the sole of the foot. To make the fibers stick to each other while twining, the rope-maker occasionally pulls them through his mouth to moisten them. The *fum semèn* may only be used for making rope masks. If one were unwise enough to use it to make, for example, a fishing net, anyone who ate the fish caught in such a net would fall ill. Fishing nets are made of sago fiber rope. (Gerbrands 1961).

The pieces that will be the chest, back and shoulder areas of the costume are made separately, and later sewn together. At the bottom, a skirt of sago leaf strips is attached. The costume is then painted, firstly in white stripes (Plate 3.4, page 35) and then in red stripes (Plate 3.5, page 35).[1] Finally, carved wooden eye-pieces in the form of

---

1. The field photographs in this chapter (except Plate 3.2) and the accompanying documentation were kindly made available by Adrian A. Gerbrands.

mirror-image pairs of bird bills—hornbill or black king cockatoo—are secured to the costume. A tip of an arrow may be attached to the costume, indicating that the deceased was killed by an arrow. Or a small bamboo shield may be attached to the back, showing that the deceased has cut off the head of an enemy with a bamboo knife. Sometimes a stick decorated with feathers is attached to the back of the head of the costume. Decorated in this manner, the *jipae* costume is hung up to dry (Plate 3.6, page 35; also, in color, Plate 3.11, page 42).

Meanwhile food has been collected to be placed on display in front of the mask. The "owners" of the masks will later divide these gifts of food between the members of their immediate family and fireplace group.

The *jipae* festival

While a few skilled men are busy making the masks, the rest of the village members play drums, sing and dance, almost every night. The mask-makers take their time with the work, as for the duration of their labors, the family of the deceased supplies them with excellent food. Day after day, at certain moments, people engage in horseplay, men and women romp in public, particularly the younger ones. The men stand together and shout insults at the women: "She has the small head of the tortoise!" "She has the broad nose of a *yuw* fish!" "She looks like a *nibung* palm!" (equivalent to "bean-pole"). The women are accused of having red eyes, long chins, wet noses, and pot bellies, or their manners are maligned: "She saves the best tidbits for herself!"

The women then jump out of their houses and run towards the men, brandishing weapons—pieces of wood, bundles of arrows, spears, bone daggers, or the toothed bill of the sawfish. They stab wildly, or at least pretend to. For their part, the men allow themselves to be stabbed, and when one of them runs off, he is chased by one or more women (Plate 3.7, page 36 and Plate 3.8, page 37). The women laugh and scream and call the men every name under the sun. The people call this game *faimutsj,* which means "peace." The game is clearly designed to release tension, creating an amicable atmosphere for the feast.

Evening after evening, the adventures of Kir are sung. Kir was a naughty boy—at that awkward age—who led the other children in teasing their grandmothers and stealing food from them. To keep from being punished, they sought refuge in a hollow tree. The tree, alas, floated off down

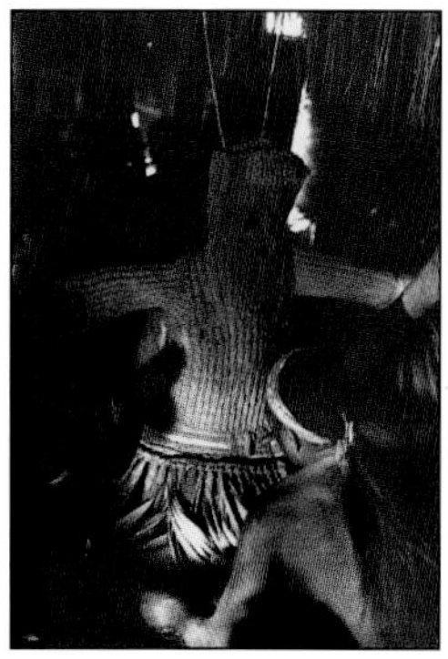

ADRIAN A. GERBRANDS

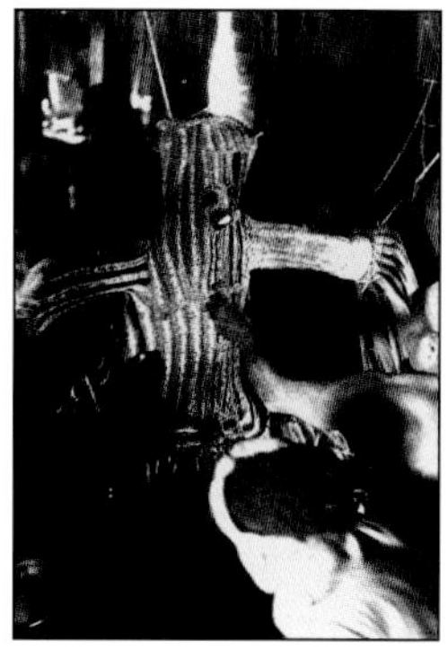

ADRIAN A. GERBRANDS

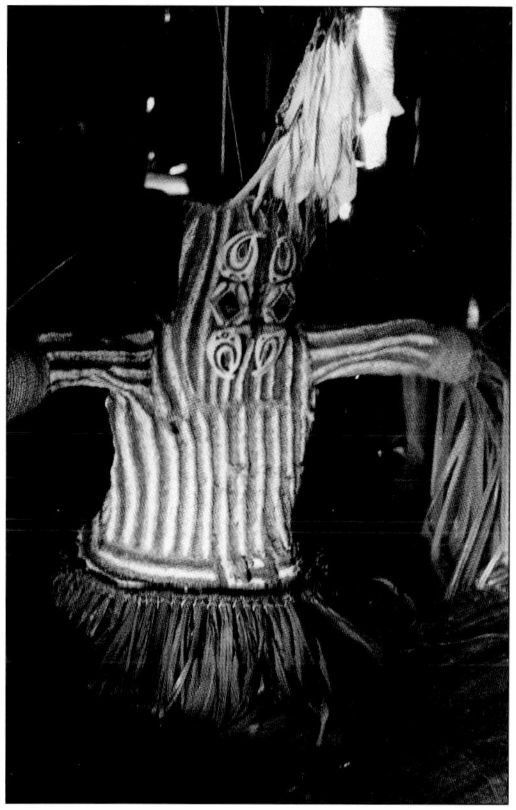

ADRIAN A. GERBRANDS

Plate 3.4 (above, top left) A newly made rope costume hangs in Jeu Awok. The costume is hung this way so that it is easy to apply the pigments. Using a small stick, shell lime mixed with water is rubbed into the grooves.

Plate 3.5 (above, top right) The alternate grooves are filled with red. The pigment comes from ocherous clay, which is mixed with water to produces a reddish-brown "paint" that is applied with a small stick.

Plate 3.6 (above, bottom) The completed *jipae* hangs drying. Two wooden eye pieces and a wooden nose ornament have been added. This *jipae* is now in the Leiden museum. See Plate 3-11, page 42. Amanamkai village, Central Asmat, 1961.

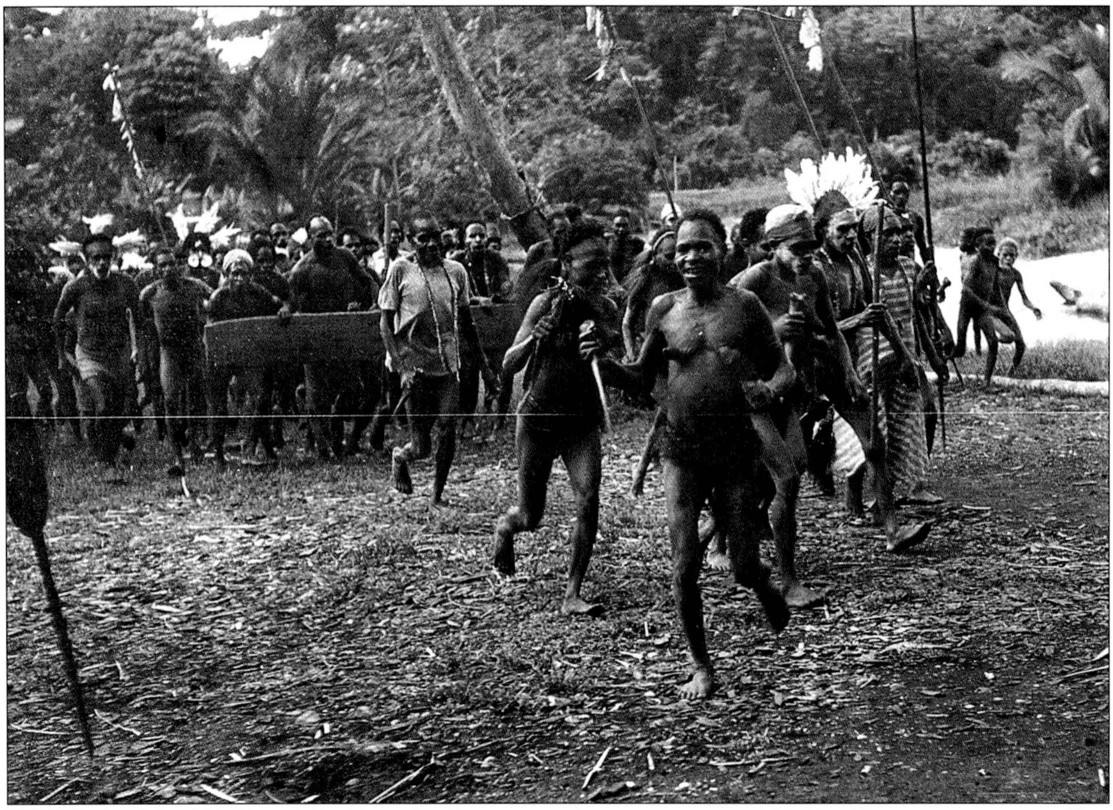

ADRIAN A. GERBRANDS

the river, finally ending up on a sand bank in the far West, near the horizon. Here lived a large colony of "women-without-men," who eagerly embraced the boys, who in the meantime had grown up into young men.

During the day people sing, too. The deceased are called upon to leave their hiding places, and to move out of the forest at the upper, mid and lower course of the river, and go towards the mangroves along the coast. As they sing, the varieties of trees, birds, bush animals and fish inhabiting those various areas are mentioned in turn. The dead are invited to hide near the village, inside hollow trees, under the prop roots of mangrove trees, and under clamshells. The spirits are asked to prepare for the upcoming feast.

On specific days, the big girls and younger women are scarified by their fathers and brothers. The scarifications, applied to the women's upper arms and thighs, in due course produce scars in the shape of a shell nose ornament, the figure of a frog or snake, or a disk—a symbol for the flat round stone used as a ritual object in initiation.

At dawn on the day the *jipae* feast takes place, the orphan boy Mbanma is spotted on the other side of the river, and a dug-out canoe sets out to collect him. He wears the rattan basket mask. When he arrives in the village, he is pelted by the children who, during the previous days, had for just this purpose carefully collected a large stock of the sturdy husks of *nipah* palm fruit, and broad *amo* leaves. The orphan boy starts running from one end of the village to the other, chased by the screaming children. As he runs, he shakes his head back and forth and waves his arms. At times he staggers, like one about to die. This game continues, with short interruptions, all day. Everyone laughs, and everyone is in a happy frame of mind. Not even the smallest children show any fear of the basket costume. Meanwhile, many guests have arrived to attend the mask feast.

Mbanma, the orphan boy

The actions of Mbanma are based on a well-known story. Once upon a time a small orphan boy lived all on his own. With no parents and family to take care of him, he had to scrape along. He went from house to house begging, but eventually the people got sick and tired of him, and sent him off empty-handed. Hunger forced him to start stealing. Gradually, he acquired more and more skill in stealing small quantities of

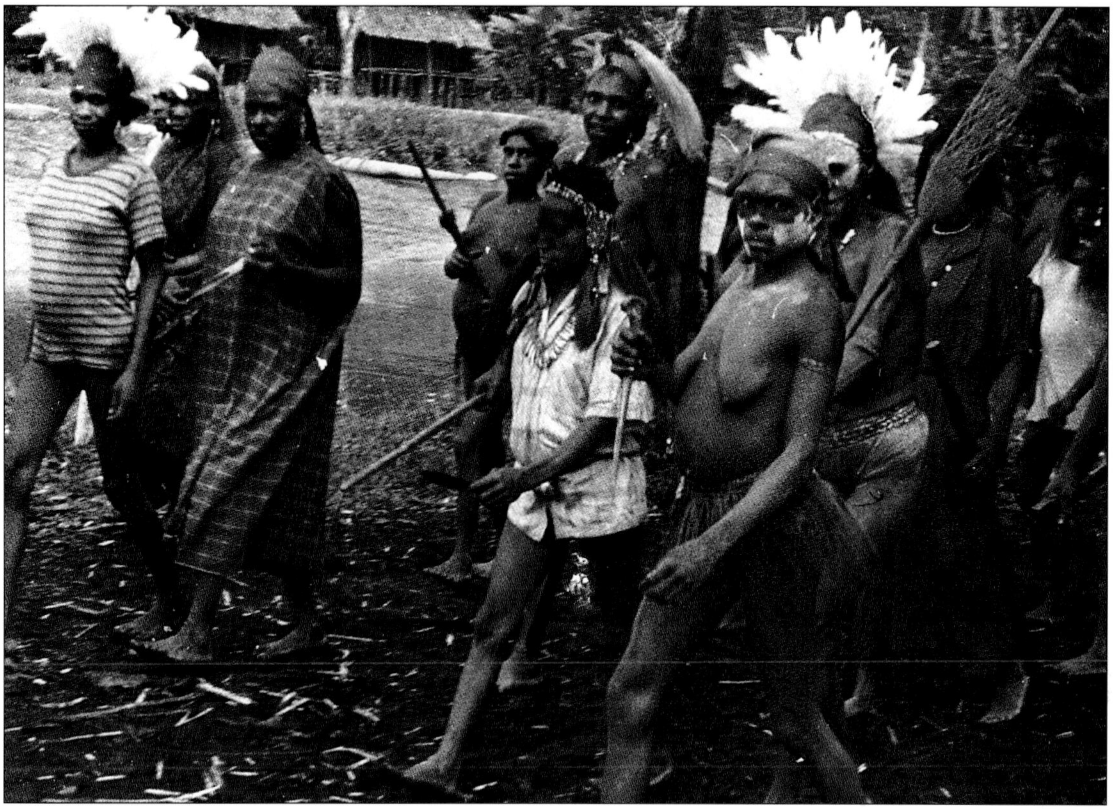

ADRIAN A. GERBRANDS

food. The people called him Mbanma (or Pokomban), which means "The Cunning Thief." Sometimes he was forced to scrounge at night for scraps of food that fell among the rubbish under the houses. When they caught him at this, people pelted him with garbage or bits of wood.

Nobody wanted him around. When he tried to join people who were fishing, they sent him across the river, where there were no fish. The other children of the village teased him relentlessly, and threw thick *amo* leaves at him and the husks of *nipah* palm fruit. His body grew weak, and eventually he became so feeble he stumbled and staggered. He would soon have died of hunger, had he not stumbled on a plan.

At irregular intervals he slipped into the forest and collected bark. When he had enough, he twined a rope from it, with which he made a mask costume. Wearing the costume, Mbanma hid himself behind a large tree near the sago swamps. When the village women, walking in a row with their loads of sago, set off for home, he jumped out, raised his arms in the air and shouted: "Hu!" "Hu!" In a panic, the women threw the sago on the ground and fled. Mbanma had enough to eat for a long time. Whenever he ran out of food, he repeated this trick. The women complained to their husbands, and accused them of being afraid to drive this ghost away.

The men took measures to catch Mbanma, and eventually they discovered the orphan boy's trick. They were very impressed with Mbanma's cleverness, however, and made an agreement with him: "We will not tell the women a thing, your secret will be kept private by the men." Since that moment, it is said, orphans were never left to their own devices again.

The arrival of the dead

In the late afternoon, the dead—called *ndat*—appear. Accompanied by Mbanma in the basket costume, they emerge from the bush at the edge of the village compound, wearing the rope cos-

Plate 3.7 (opposite, left) and **Plate 3.8** (above) Mock fighting between women and men is an important part of the *jipae* festival at Jeu Awok. This fighting, which can draw blood, serves to release any stewing tensions in the community, or between men and their wives. This insures a good festival. The plank carried by the men in Plate 3-7 serves as a dividing line between the two warring sides. Amanamkai village, Central Asmat, 1961.

tumes. The *jipae* are brightly painted and decorated. The living members of the village walk towards them and dust them with great clouds of powdered lime.[2]

The leader of the ceremony announces the names of the dead, and says that they have come from the Far West, that they are very tired from the long journey. He says they ask for food and lodging for the night, and they will continue on their way early the next morning.

A procession is formed, which sets off slowly, shuffling past the houses (See Plate 3.1, page 32). The procession halts at the houses of the deceased. Their living relatives cry, and ask all sorts of questions regarding the well-being of the spirits of the deceased. They emphatically declare they themselves are not short of anything and give the deceased handfuls of tasty sago grubs. When the procession finally reaches the front of the *jeu*, those who do not belong to the family organize mock fights with the dead. These are aimed at "embarrassing" them, and making them apprehensive of their safety, thus inducing them not to prolong their visit. At this point, the dead retreat into the bush.

When it has been dark for some time, the dead return, to begin dancing in the *jeu*. The dance lasts all night, during which time several men take turns wearing the costumes. While dancing, the men in the *jipae* move their upper body and shoulders, sweeping their arms the way a cassowary flaps its wings. Later in the night, the women of the celebrating group bring in large quantities of sago, and pile it up around the costumed dead. Those who have married into the celebrating family hand out sago to all present. At dawn, the dead disappear into the bush; it is now their turn to dust the living with clouds of lime. After the feast, the rope masks are carefully hidden, and the skirts of sago fiber are removed and burned.

The feast of the armbands

While the skilled men were making the *jipae* in great secrecy during the previous weeks, they used the same materials to make armbands, *kon*. These were wrapped in mats, and stored inside the *jeu*. The armbands that have been decorated with a plume of cassowary feathers are just as sacred as the mask costumes, and are given the names of the deceased. They are worn with pride for months after the feast.

After the dead have left, and moved on to travel through a kind of no man's land in search of the realm of the dead, the attention of the celebration shifts to the living. The positions left vacant by the departed must be filled. The children need new parents.

After a week has been spent in gathering the necessary food, the feast of the armbands is ready to be celebrated. At this feast, those who have been chosen to replace the deceased family members are ceremoniously installed as members of the new family.

The ceremony involves decorating the people who have performed in the mask costumes. The first stage takes place in the homes of the new family members. Each of their ritual children, brothers and sisters chooses a new member of the family to adorn. Men choose men, women choose women, boys choose boys. The new family members receive all manner of decorations. Tradition requires the men in the *jeu* to regularly exhort them to hurry up. Once decorated, the new family members are escorted by their spiritual relatives to the area in front of the *jeu*, where they stand in rows.

Now the second stage of adorning begins. First, the new family members are covered in red earth from head to toe. Then the new armbands, attached to a spear, are brought out of the *jeu* and, one by one, slid onto the upper right arms of the participants. As each armband is slid into place, the bystanders let out a yell. This is the community's confirmation of the adoption.

It takes some time before all the armbands are in place. Once they are, daggers made from the thigh bone of the cassowary are inserted into the bands. The adorning continues, everyone gets a second armband, and a second dagger, the men on their arm and the women on the band of their skirts. The decoration takes place individually, one after the other. Each time, the crowd yells.

At the conclusion of the adornment ceremony, there are exchanges of gifts in the houses of the participants. The family members of the deceased present their new fathers, uncles or brothers with stone axes and bundles of spears and arrows. The new fathers, uncles and brothers

2. The lime, made of burned and crushed clam shells, is kept in bamboo tubes. When the tubes are swung back and forth, the lime comes out in great clouds. In the days of head-hunting, lime was deployed in this same way to frighten and confuse the enemy, and lime-throwing was a common response to European boats. Lime is considered a hot, magical substance. In the practice described here, the lime functions to chase away the spirits of the dead (and evil influences), and to mark the separation between the living and the dead.

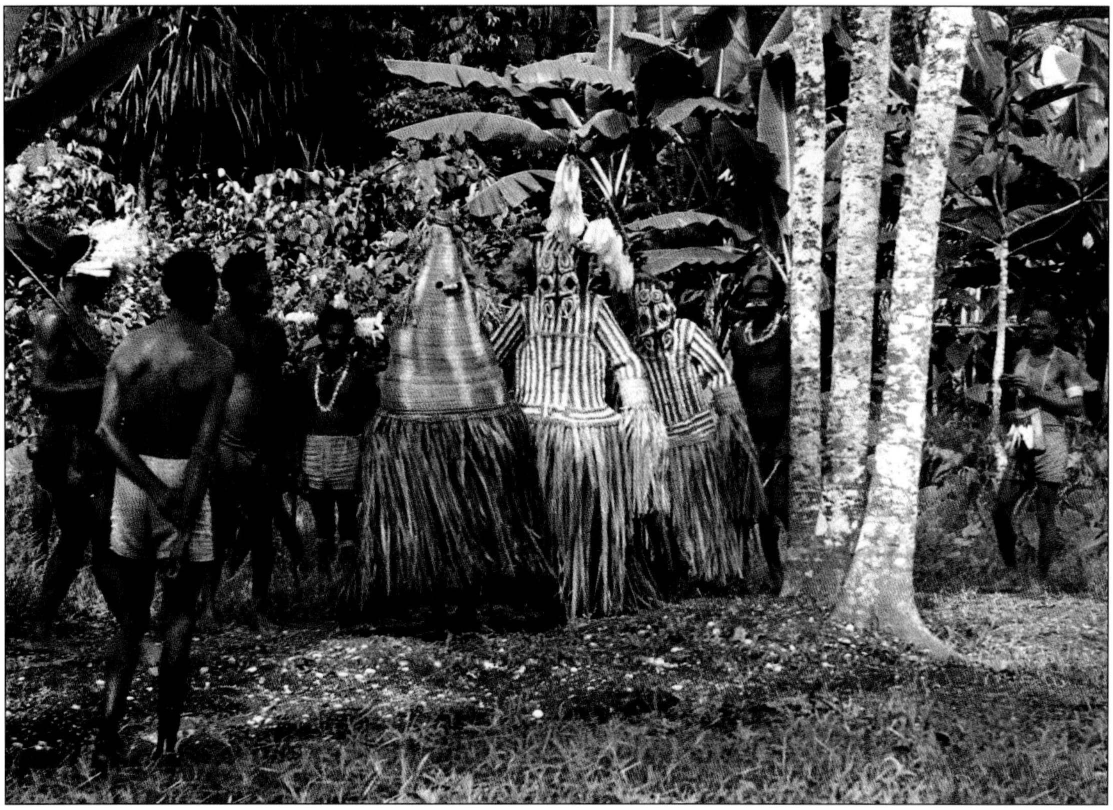

ADRIAN A. GERBRANDS

give the same presents to their children, nephews, brothers and sisters. The new family returns considerably more than it has received.

Now the families are united. Shortly after the feast, the new members accompany the family group to its sago swamps and fishing waters. For a period of time, they are addressed by the name of the deceased. Eventually, perhaps after a few months, they are addressed by their own name. The relationship, however, continues. When one of the children is in need of something, he or she makes the request by addressing the adopted relative by the name of the deceased.

Sacred ritual or public amusement?

Being a missionary in a recently opened region,* I was extremely interested in the rituals and the myths of the Asmat, to enrich my knowledge of their religious ideas and sentiments. I had high expectations of the *jipae* feast, but when it was over, I was left with the question. Was this a sacred, "religious" event? Or simply a folk celebration?

During the preparations for the feast, especially during the romping, much attention was paid to creating a peaceful atmosphere and a good mutual understanding. However, these games which I presume included sexual liberties—were the exact opposite of my picture of religious acts. Thus I focused my attention on the masks. The mask costumes were shrouded in an atmosphere of secrecy. Certain words associated with them were taboo. After the feast, the masks were to be stored in the men's house, in a place where the community kept special heirlooms. Cautionary stories were told of women who had accidently seen a mask, and died as a result.

I had hoped the *jipae* feast itself would render an explanation of the sanctity of the event, but this never happened. Most conspicuous during

* Editor's note: Father Gerardus A. Zegwaard, M.S.C. was the first missionary to work extensively in the Asmat region, beginning in the early 1950s. See Chapter 2, page 27 for more of the history of the Catholic mission in the Asmat region.

Plate 3.9 The *jipae* emerging from the forest, just before setting off on their tour of the village. The basket mask had earlier that morning toured the village on its own. Amanamkai village, Central Asmat, 1961.

the mask feast was the effort the celebrants made to bring the friendly, peaceful atmosphere to a climax. Everyone told everyone else what to do and what not to do. A delegation came to my house asking me not to interfere at all (for example in the mock battle) and to look on only.

Not a trace of fear was shown, not even among the women and children. The masked dead were treated with friendliness and somewhat exaggerated respect, but also with some amusement. The peaceful atmosphere was apparently meant to give the visiting dead the impression that the relatives led a very virtuous and impeccable life. This show was designed to convince the dead that their further presence had become completely superfluous. There was thus not a single reason why they should not move on to the realm of the dead. People call this *ndat tuw*, the moving (*tuw*) of the dead (*ndat*) to the otherworld, the domain of the ancestral spirits.

What I told myself at the time was: This is the Asmat version of the Dutch feast of Saint Nicholas. It is not a religious ceremony, but a public amusement in which everybody plays along for the sake of the communal festivity. I concluded that the *jipae* festival, which had been adopted by the Central Asmat people from the Northwest Asmat—where it had presumably been created by some distant ancestors—had in the course of time and translation lost its religious significance and been secularized into a mere popular amusement.

Researching the festival again, many years later, I am no longer sure of this conclusion. I think it is possible that, among the Asmat, religion can not be distinguished from a kind of collective well-being. And further, that the sacred is tangible, and can be seen and felt in the experiences of daily life, in ritual life, and in art. The *jipae* festival ritually stimulates the mutual solidarity of a community and its numerical strength (through the guaranteed care of children) which are both indispensable to the preservation of a small community.

Aipas's mask

An extraordinary mask depicted in this publication (Plate 3.12, page 43) is the mask the people of Atat in the Northwest Asmat region made and used in 1953 to pay the last respects to the village head Aipas, who died in 1949.

Aipas had moved from Atat to Kaokanao in September 1948, as part of the second large wave of post-war evacuees from the Asmat to the Mimika area (see Chapter 2). I became acquainted with him there. He was a friendly old man, of very small stature. We became close friends and addressed each other as "son" and "father." While on a fishing trip in January 1949, Aipas was assaulted by people from Ewer who had been evacuated from the region of Central Asmat. The villages of Atat and Ewer were enemies, but I do not know if any personal feelings of revenge played a role. The man who stabbed Aipas to death was Otamporé, and the police captured him without difficulties and took him to prison in Merauke. He was back within a year and the people from Atat had only one comment: "Otamporé is back but Aipas is not."

Having returned to their own living quarters for a number of years, the people of Atat celebrated the *jipae* ritual. The ritual lasted several months, and towards the end, the mask costume feast was celebrated. I did not witness the mask feast in Atat, but when visiting the village some time afterwards, I was allowed to see the mask costume that had already been stored away. Because of my friendship with Aipas in Kaokanao, and in return for a substantial compensation, I was allowed to take the mask to my presbytery in Agats.

Returning to Agats, I stopped at the village of Sawa-Erma, along the Pomatsj River, which at the time was by far the largest and most feared village in the region. My oarsmen, from Ajam village on the Asewetsj River, were terrified and wanted to travel at a safe distance around Sawa-Erma. However, I succeeded in bringing them along. Shortly before we arrived in Sawa-Erma, however, they begged me at the point of tears to allow one of the rowers to wear Aipas's mask. It was their intention to use the mask to intimidate the people of Sawa-Erma with it. To avoid difficulties, I refused their request.

My good relationship with Aipas was continued with his son Akum, who succeeded his father as village head. In 1978, after an absence of many years, I returned to Agats on the occasion of the Silver Jubilee of the Catholic Mission's presence in the Asmat region. During a speech in front of a full hall, filled with people I had never met, I mentioned (among others) Akum's name. The next morning a young man approached me, and introduced himself as Akum's son. He felt honored because I had mentioned his father as an old friend. When I told him about his grandfather Aipas, and the mask that was kept in the Netherlands, tears filled his eyes.

I. Group of Mask Costumes
Northwest and Central Asmat
Collected: 1953, 1961, 1978, 1979

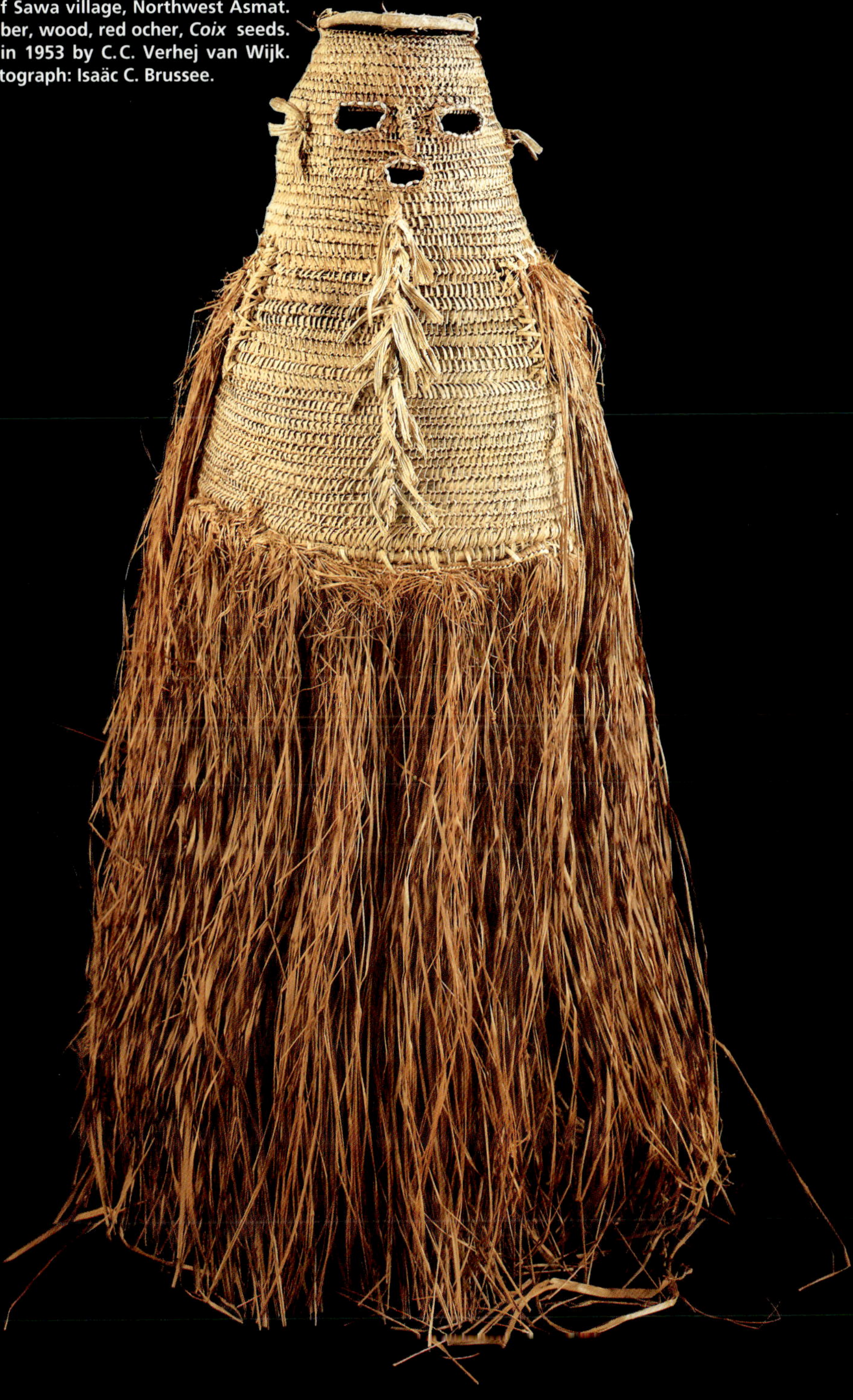

Plate 3.10 Rattan basket costume (*mbanembar*). From the vicinity of Sawa village, Northwest Asmat. Rattan, sago leaf fiber, wood, red ocher, *Coix* seeds. 150 cm. Collected in 1953 by C.C. Verhej van Wijk. RMV 3070-513 Photograph: Isaäc C. Brussee.

Plate 3.11 Rope mask costume (*jipae*). Amanamkai village, Central Asmat. Rope, wood, chalk, red ocher, sago leaf fiber, cassowary feathers and quills. 180 cm. Collected in 1961 by Adrian A. Gerbrands. RMV 3790-8. Photograph: Isaäc C. Brussee.

This mask represents Atekamekamat's spirit. This former head of Jeu Awok, Amanamkai village, was killed by men from Atsj. The costume was used during a *jipae* feast in Jeu Awok, held at the end of 1960 through the beginning of 1961.

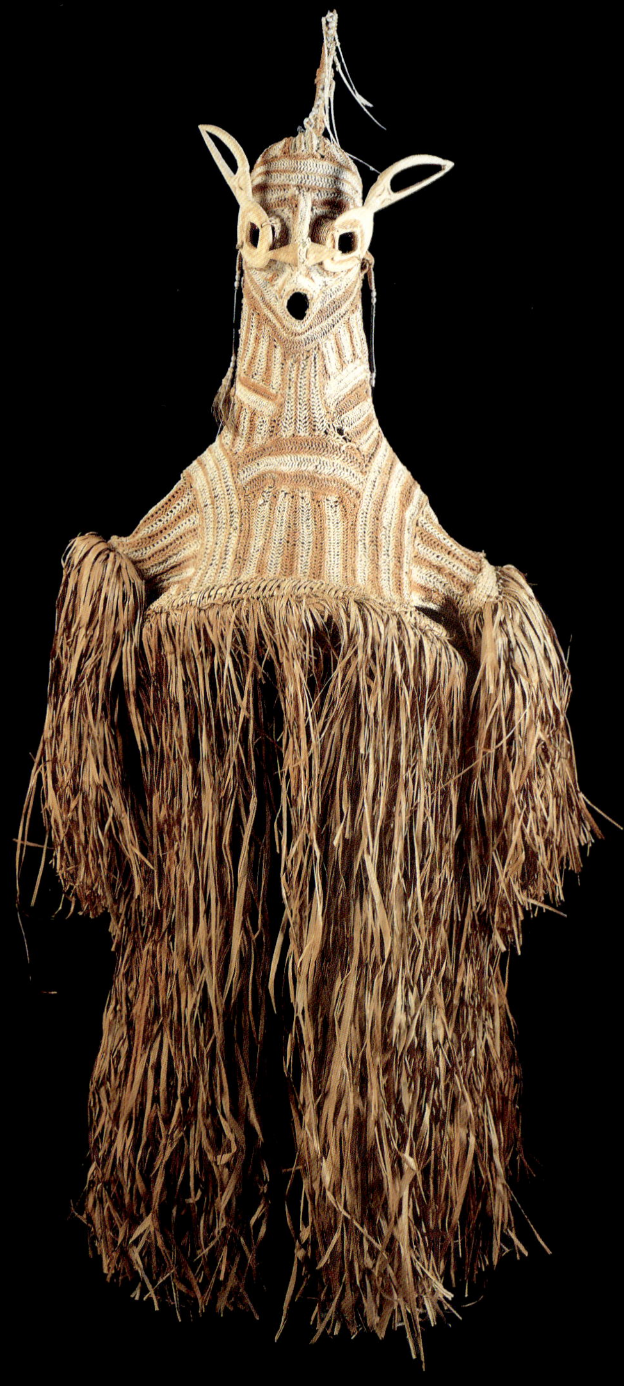

Plate 3.12 Rope mask costume (*jipae*). Atat village, Northwest Asmat. Rope, wood, lime, red ocher, sago leaf fibre, *Coix* seeds, cassowary quills, feathers. 175 cm. Collected in l953 by Gerard A. Zegwaard. RMV 3070-212. Photograph: Isaäc C. Brussee.

This mask was made in 1953 to commemorate the village headman Aipas, who died in a head-hunting raid. In his lifetime, Aipas was a respected warrior, and had taken many heads. The ear ornaments of cassowary feather quills and *Coix* seeds are worn by head-hunters.

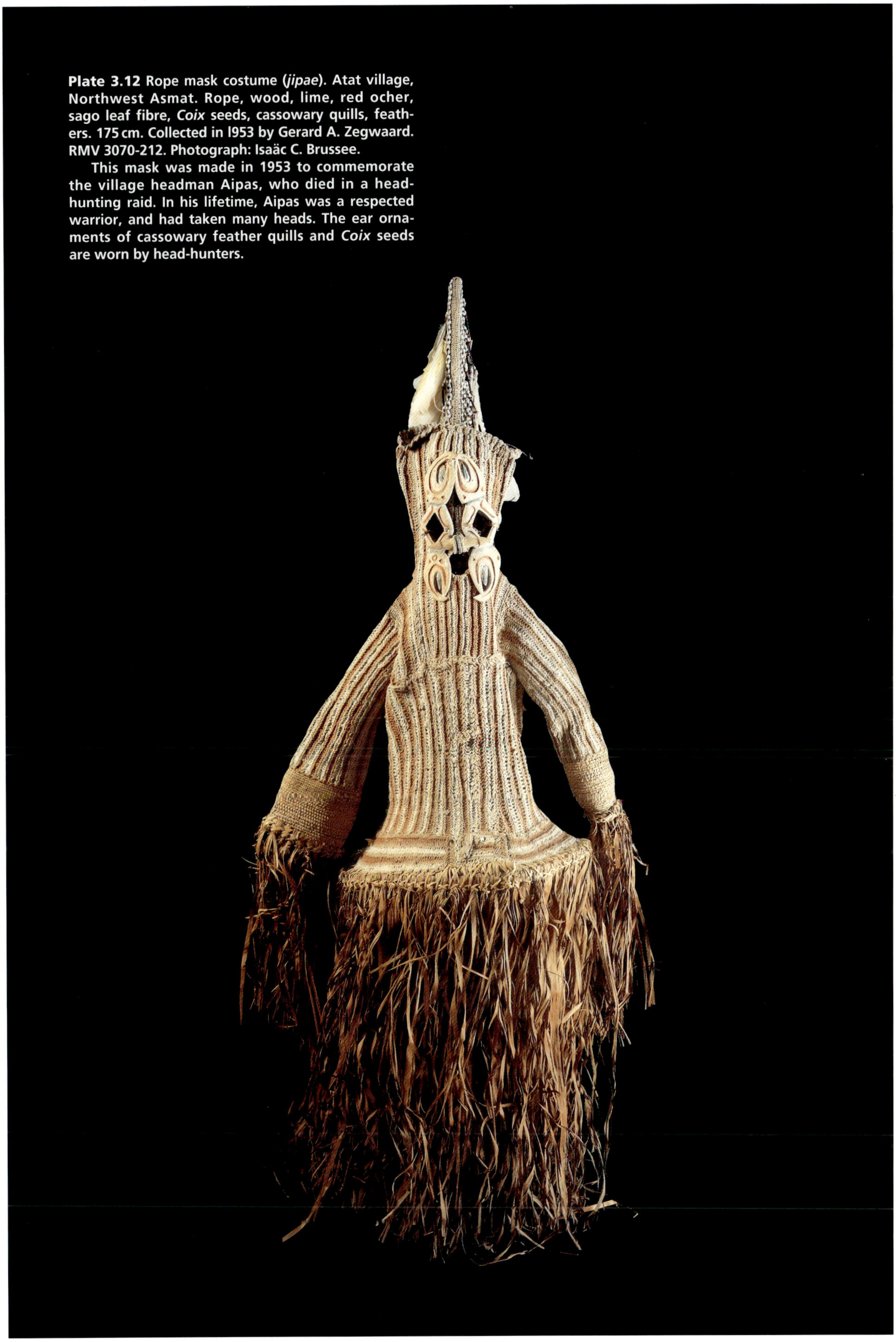

Plate 3.13 (B/W basket costume, Konrad. #M011)

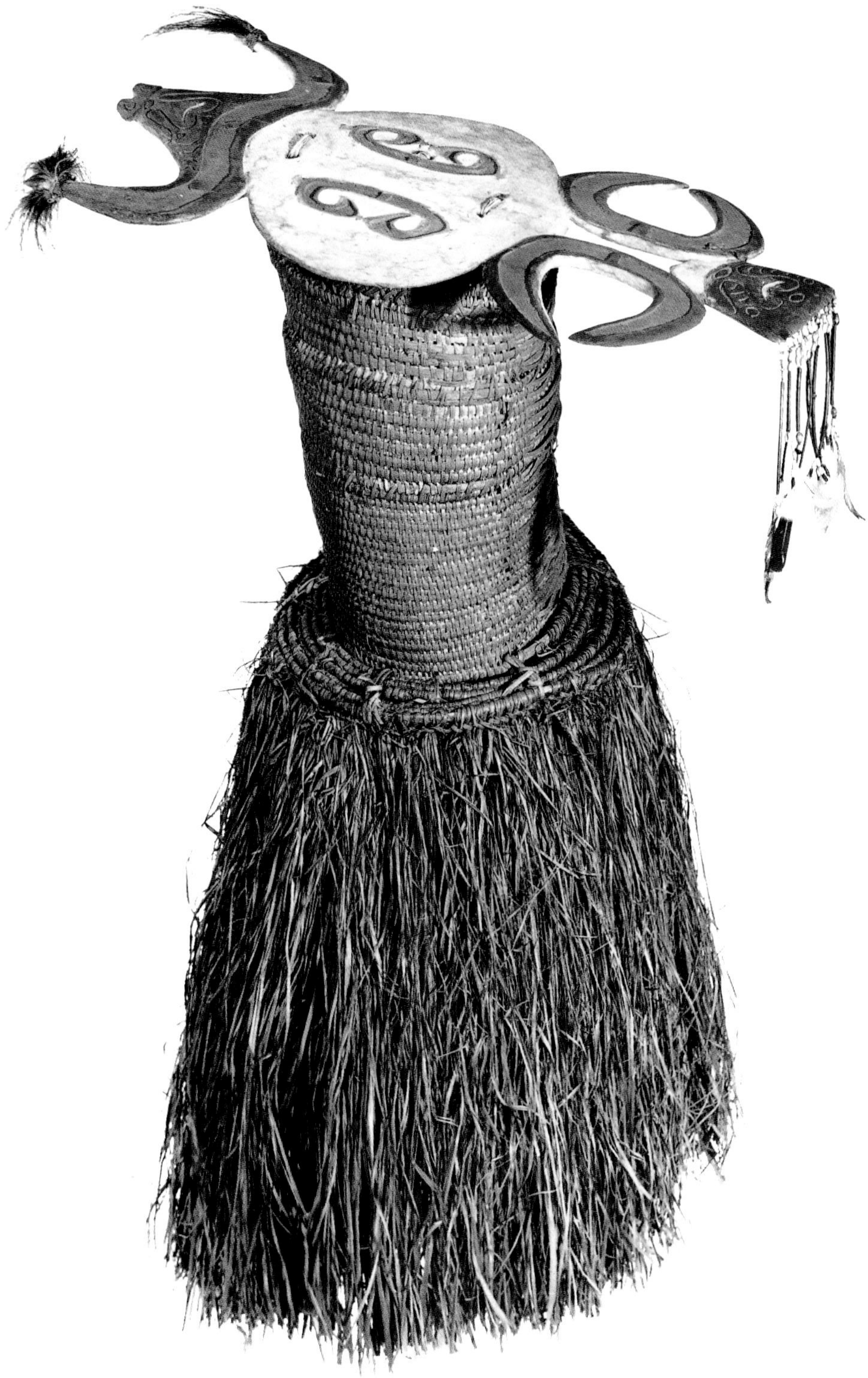

Plate 3.14 (B/W mask costume, Konrad. #M010)

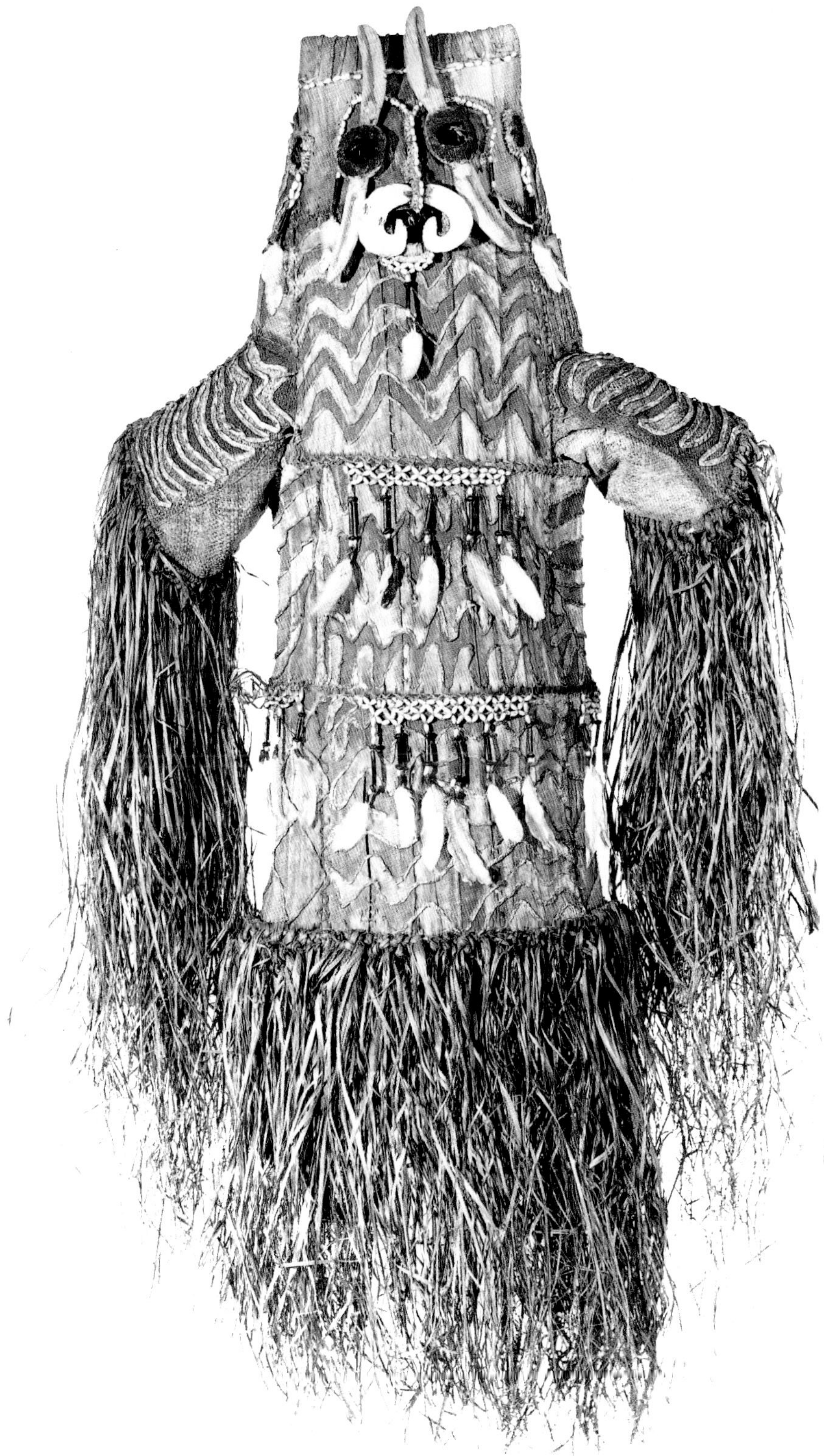

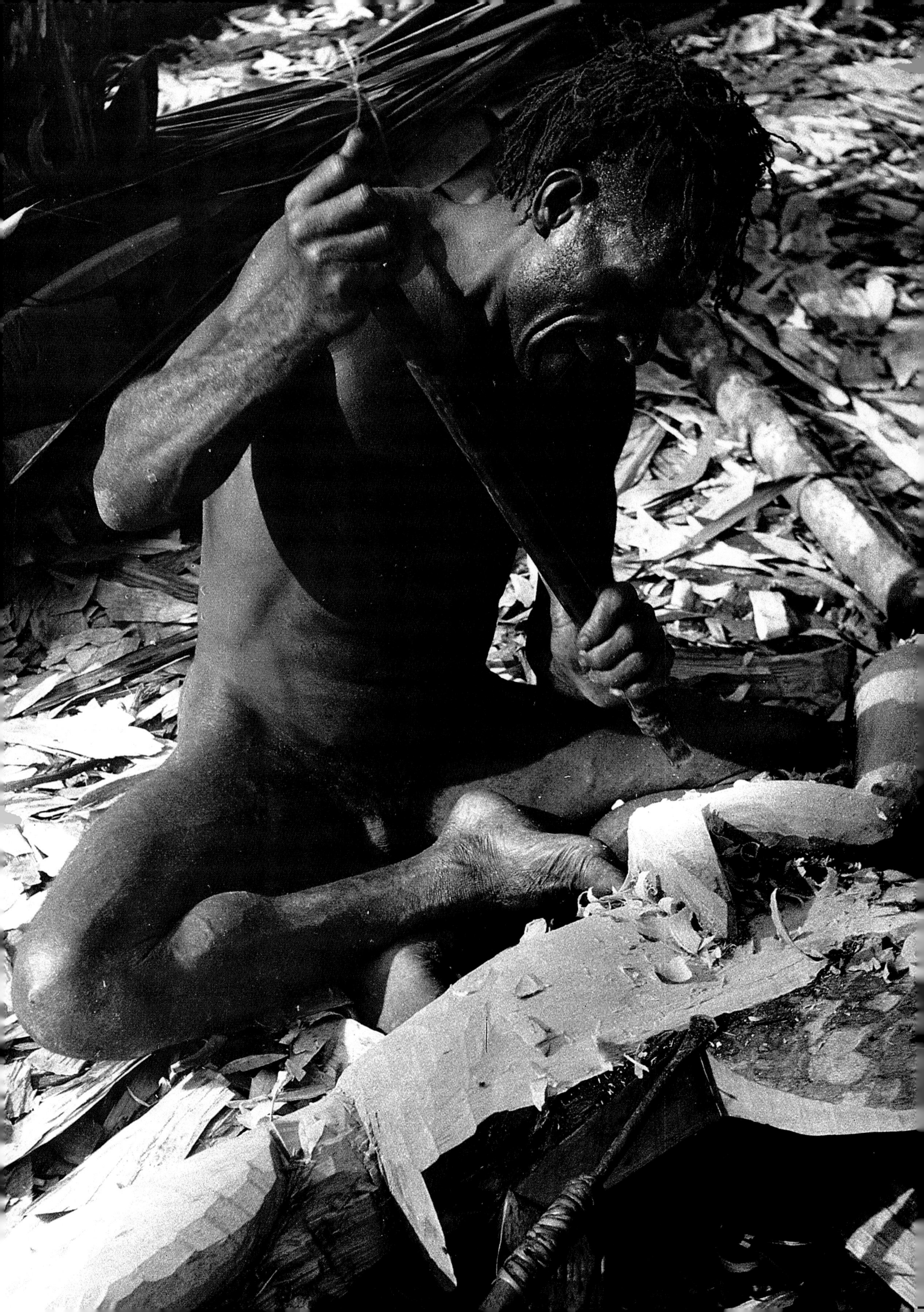

CHAPTER 4

Wowipitsj: The Asmat Woodcarver

Dirk A. M. Smidt

Every Asmat man can carve, and create various useful items out of wood, such as canoe paddles, bowls and similar utensils. But when a special object is needed, such as a shield, the Asmat approach the *wowipitsj,* the master woodcarvers. *Wowipitsj*—the word literally means "woodcarver"—do not represent a professional class of artists or artisans in a western sense. They are talented individuals who have gained a reputation for woodcarving skill, but they gather sago, hunt and perform the usual tasks of an Asmat man. Given the importance of woodcarving, however, the *wowipitsj* often enjoy considerable prestige in the community.

The status of the woodcarver

Adrian A. Gerbrands, whose research in the 1960s on the artists of the village of Amanamkai led to the book *Wow-Ipits: Eight Asmat Woodcarvers of New Guinea,* found considerable individuality in woodcarving styles (Gerbrands 1967). Although the artist expresses himself within the framework of a regional style, he leaves a very distinct individual stamp on every woodcarving he makes. The work of an individual woodcarver can easily be recognized as such both within and outside his own community. The collection in the National Museum of Ethnology at Leiden arranged according to artist (collected by Gerbrands) offers a unique opportunity to witness this:

"If sculptures by several different carvers are placed haphazardly on a table, it transpires every time that groups of students are able to rather quickly group together works by the same carver. Remarkable here—and one should check the illustrations in Gerbrands' book—is that the statues by any one artist can in no way be described as being copies of each other. Never does the artist repeat himself in every aspect, though there are, of course, similarities in conception and detail, like the shape of a nose or ear." (Smidt 1990:208.)

Master woodcarvers, although accepted as specialists, are villagers like everyone else and have to hunt, fish and pound sago in addition to their carving activities. Good woodcarvers indeed are respected for their artistic abilities, but that respect is expressed in the orders they receive rather than in material rewards. While working on an order, the client is required to provide the carver with food and tobacco, and this is considered sufficient. In the interest of encouraging the carver, he is usually given good food, but this cannot really been seen as the same as payment. Today, a woodcarver can also earn some money selling woodcarvings to dealers in tourist art, or to the Asmat Museum of Culture and Progress, established by the Crosier Mission in Agats.

Some woodcarvers have the same status as great war heroes, but in these cases, factors other than their talent as artists are present (Konrad, Konrad and Schneebaum 1981:33). To achieve such a status, it is certainly just as important to be socially and politically influential. This status comes after one has gained a history of experience in social intercourse, which can only be built up over the years.

Materials and techniques

The species of wood from which Asmat shields and sculptures are carved have not been thoroughly analyzed, making it impossible to describe them precisely. Traditionally, statues seem to have been carved of softer, more fibrous wood than shields. On the face of it, there does not seem to be much difference in hardness between the older statues and many of the newer ones.

Practical items such as paddles, spears, canoes and bowls are made of woods that possess the qualities needed in the item. For example, paddles and spears are made of very dense, flexible woods. Containers and horns are made of bamboo, a material that is extremely difficult to work. Canoes are made of *karamati* wood, a relatively soft wood, but one which resists rot and leaking.

War shields (*jamasj*) are made of fairly hard woods. Though one might at first think so, they are not made out of planks. They are carved out of the flat buttress roots of swamp trees (See Plate 6.4, page 65) which helps explain the somewhat free-form shape of particularly some of the larger shields. *Bisj* are also made from trees with these distinctive buttress roots. One root is selected for the *tjemen* or protruding "penis" of the carving, and the trunk of the tree itself becomes the pole

Plate 4.1 The artist Ndojokor carving a *bisj.* He uses a long-handled chisel to rough out the contours of the shape. Amanamkai village, Central Asmat, 1961. Photograph: Adrian A. Gerbrands.

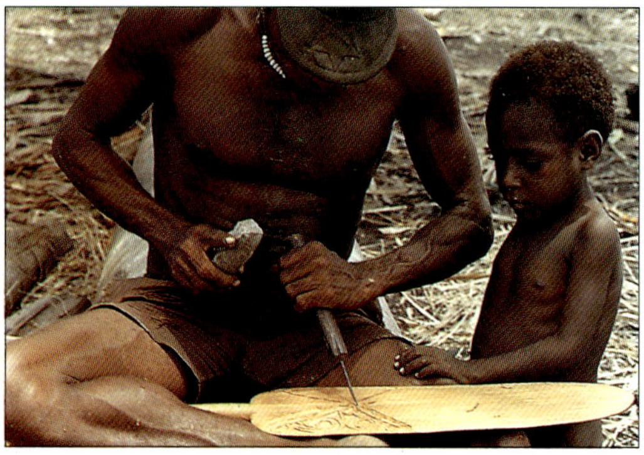
JAC. HOOGERBRUGGE

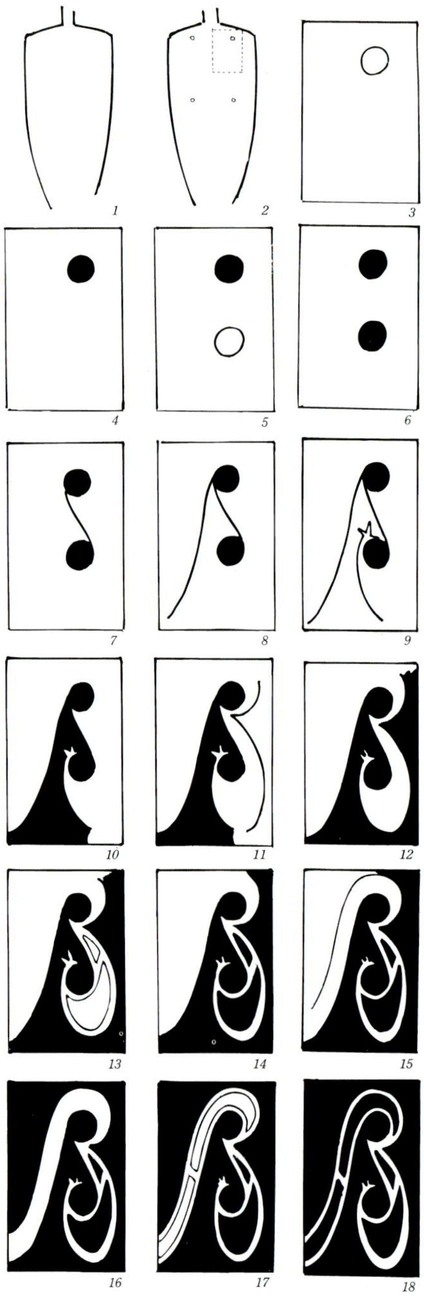

of the *bisj*.

Today, Asmat sculptures for the tourist market are often made out of "ironwood" (*Intsia* spp.), any of several species of attractive, rot-resistant hardwoods. Carvings made from these woods, which are an attractive yellow or red color when freshly cut, form a separate category. Ironwood was never used for carvings in the past. This dense, fine-grained wood can be smoothed to a high polish, which appeals to foreign tastes. However, the grain of the wood is not rough enough to readily accept pigment.

Making ironwood carvings presumably originated under the influence of the Catholic mission, for a much heard saying runs: "Ironwood is mission-wood." The mission set up the first sawmills in the region, where ironwood was cut into planks for local construction.

Tools and methods

In the past, stone axes, animal bone chisels and shells were the only tools available to the woodcarver. Stone axes and adzes were used to hack out the rough shape. Scraping and polishing was done with sharpened clam shells. These shells are still used for this work. For the finer work, such as carving the motifs in relief, the carver used bone chisels, sharpened boar's tusks, or the teeth of animals or fish.

After contact with Europeans and local traders, the Asmat started using iron tools. Iron nails were doubtless the first metal tools the Asmat used. For centuries, planks of wood containing nails, from shipwrecks, were known by the coastal people to wash up occasionally on the beaches or become trapped in the mangrove swamps. With the thick head flattened out and sharpened, and the tip stuck into a wooden handle, such nails made a fine small chisel for detail work. Today, of course, metal tools are known throughout Asmat, and much sought after.

When a woodcarver makes a statue or ancestor pole he first roughs out the form with an axe. For a shield, he does the same, sparing a bit in the middle of the back of the shield, which later will be carved into a vertical handle. After it has been roughly shaped, the flat "plank" of wood for a shield is touched up with an adze until it is the desired thickness, usually about one centimeter.

At this stage, a finer tool is employed. Using a long planing-chisel, the uneven cuts left by the axe are smoothed away. Such a chisel has a long wooden handle so that the woodcarver is able to apply ample force with both hands and arms (see

Plate 4.1, page 46). Finally, the more elaborate work is done with smaller chisels (see Plate 4.2, page 48 and 4.3, page 49). Such a small chisel made from a nail is driven through the wood using a stone as a mallet. Traditionally, these fine chisels were made out of bone, often the thigh bone of the cassowary bird (see Hoogerbrugge and Kooijman 1976: plates 44–46).

In this manner, details such as grooves in limbs are made to indicate the skeleton, eyes, nose and mouth. When making a large *bisj,* the labor with axe, adze and chisel can take several weeks, because the woodcarver can not work on it all the time. He usually has other obligations, such as beating sago, hunting or fishing, or participating in the ritual songs in the men's house. Once the woodcarving has been done, the *wowipitsj* can start painting it.

Pigments and decoration

The Asmat artist uses three colors: white, red and black. It is remarkable that even today artists rarely depart from this traditional color scheme. This is in contrast to other areas, such as the Sepik River region of Papua New Guinea, where artists have now taken to applying commercially prepared pigments, like shiny red paint, and where new colors such as green and blue have been added to the traditional palette.

The white pigment is lime, made from clam shells. The shells are calcined over a fire, and then pounded, using a spath of sago as a mortar, into a fine white powder of calcium oxide. This lime is then mixed with water and applied (see Schneebaum 1985: 44–45, figures 17a–d). This lime serves as the ground color on the statues. Lime is also used for personal decoration, and in the past was hurled from bamboo containers to confuse and intimidate enemies. In the Citak and Brazza areas, where clam shells are not available, white clay is used to produce a white pigment.

The color red is made of ocherous clay from the banks of rivers inland of the coastal regions. The color comes from the presence of iron oxide in the mud. For the coastal people, who live in brackish swamps, this material is a trade product. The clay, yellowish when fresh, is formed into lumps and burned over the coals of a fire. This changes the chemistry of the clay, resulting in a dark, brick-red color. This pigment is prepared by mixing the burned clay with water in a wooden cup, using one's hands and small shells to break up the lumps and mix the material evenly. On sculptures, this pigment serves to indicate limbs,

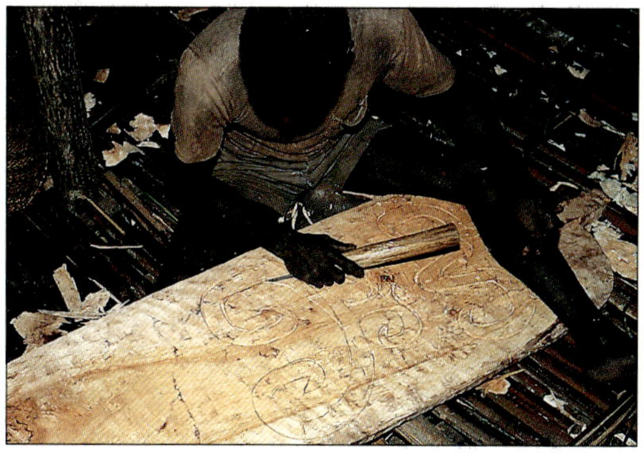

GUNTER KONRAD

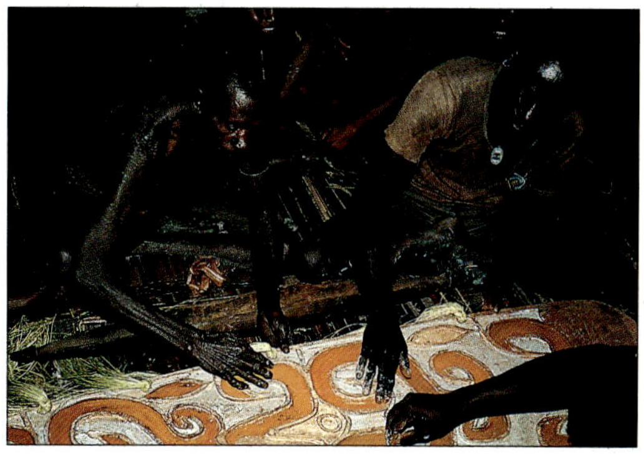

URSULA KONRAD

Plate 4.2 (opposite, top) Ekam, sitting on an overturned canoe, cuts a relief pattern into a new canoe paddle, while his son looks on. He uses a chisel made from a nail, which he taps into the hard wood with a piece of a broken stone axe. He uses his legs to keep the three-meter–long paddle under control while he renders the fine carving. Sawa-Erma village, Pomatsj River, Northwest Asmat. 1969.

Figure 4.1 (opposite) This is the approximate order of rendering of the design Ekam is applying to the canoe paddle above. Illustration based on drawings by Jac. Hoogerbrugge.

Plate 4.3 (above, top) The woodcarver Ndeize carving a shield. Basim village, Casuarina Coast. 1979.

Plate 4.4 (above, bottom) Ndeize applying paint to a shield. Basim village, Casuarina Coast. 1979.

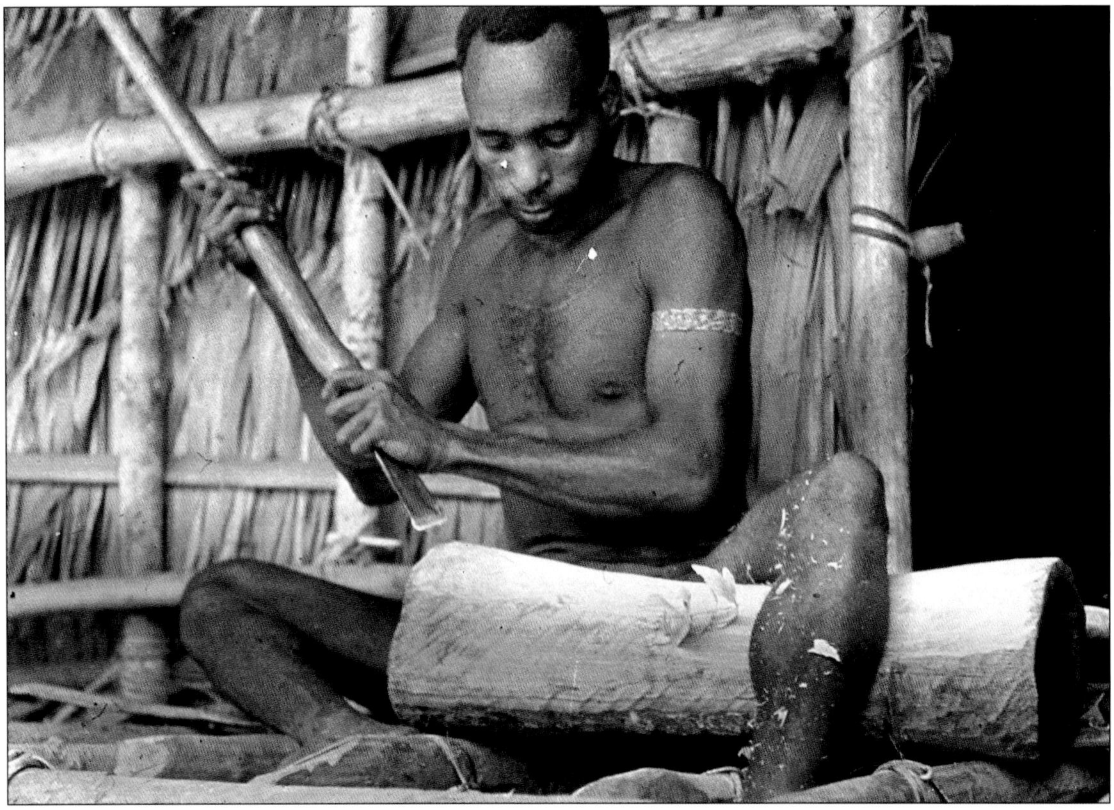

Plate 4.5 (above) The woodcarver Matjemos during the early stages of the making of a drum. Here he smoothes the outside of the drum with a long chisel. Amanamkai village, Central Asmat, 1961. For the finished drum, see Plate 4.6 opposite. For a *bisj* made by the same artist, see Plate 2.1, page 26.

Plate 4.6 (opposite) Drum. Amanamkai village, As River, Central Asmat. Wood, lizard skin, rattan. 63 cm. Collected in 1961 by Adrian A. Gerbrands. RMV 3790-425. Photograph: Ben Grishaaver.

This is the famous drum made by Matjemos in 1961. The whole process of the making of this drum was recorded by Adrian A. Gerbrands in his documentary film *Matjemos.* The main motif carved in the grip is a praying mantis. From the tail of the mantis to the bottom of the drum, the remainder of the grip represents two stylized heads of the black palm cockatoo and two hornbill heads, both head-hunting motifs.

bones or tattoos. On shields, it is used to fill in the motifs. A tuft of fiber serves as a paint brush (see Plate 4.4, page 49). In some areas, the red is intensified and made stickier by mixing it with red tree sap.

Black is made by mixing charcoal with water. There is nothing special about the wood used, simply burned firewood. The charcoal is used only to indicate hair, or to highlight the raised rims of the motifs carved into shields. The black paint is applied with small sticks, with tattered leaves or with the fingers.

Asmat carvings often receive some form of decoration, tassels of sago fiber, seeds, or feathers. Tassels of sago fiber are used in the Central Asmat style region (see Chapter 5, page 53) to decorate the perimeter of shields. The fiber is also tied to sculptures, for example serving as the skirt of female sculptures.

Two common seeds are often seen adorning Asmat woodcarvings. The smooth, grayish-blue seeds of a grass, Job's tears (*Coix lachryma-jobi*), are strung like beads on bits of fiber, and made into decorative tassels to adorn figure sculptures. *Coix* seeds are commonly used in the Asmat region to make necklaces and to decorate bags.

Also seen on woodcarvings are the seeds of the sága or crab's-eye vine (*Abrus precatorious*). *Abrus* seeds are shiny, and very hard. They are half black and half bright red. These seeds are sometimes set into sculptures or shields with wax and sap, to serve as "eyes." (See, for instance, the shields and sculptures in the Atjametsj collection, particularly Plate 8.1, page 114.)

Bird feathers are commonly used to decorate bags, and to make a decorative sleeve slipped over the end of canoe paddles during festive occasions, but they sometimes adorn sculptures. The large white feathers of the sulphur-crested cockatoo, are commonly seen, as are the brown, almost hair-like feathers of the large, flightless cassowary, endemic to Australia and New Guinea, and an important game animal for the Asmat.

Changes in the woodcarver's craft

As the way of life of the Asmat has changed, so has the subject matter, and to a lesser extent, materials of Asmat woodcarving. Presumably, some Asmat artists began to realize there was a market for selling carvings to travelers beginning in the 1950s.

In the context of his research into artistic individuality among Asmat woodcarvers in 1961, Gerbrands commissioned a number of different woodcarvings by way of an experiment (Gerbrands 1967). This approach resulted in several remarkable pieces.

Today, the woodcarver also makes use of motifs passed to him from the outside world, such as Christian motifs and Garuda, the mythical bird from the national seal of the Republic of Indonesia. (See Plate 10.5, page 152. For more on modern carvings, see Chapter 10, page 149.)

The Asmat woodcarver has also started developing sculptures which depict narrative scenes, such as a mother and child, a group of women busy with preparing sago, and men in a canoe. For examples see Hoogerbrugge and Kooijman (1976) and Konrad, Konrad and Schneebaum (1981: 120-133).

In addition to the changes in subject matter, the Asmat sculptor has also adapted to the physical requirements of tourists, who of course have no way of transporting a two-meter sculpture. The modern narrative style carvings described above are carved on a small scale, and the Asmat now carve rectangular plaques laced with motifs, thin openwork carvings (*ajour*), and miniature *bisj*-like carvings, all three of which are made of ironwood, and can easily be stowed in a suitcase.

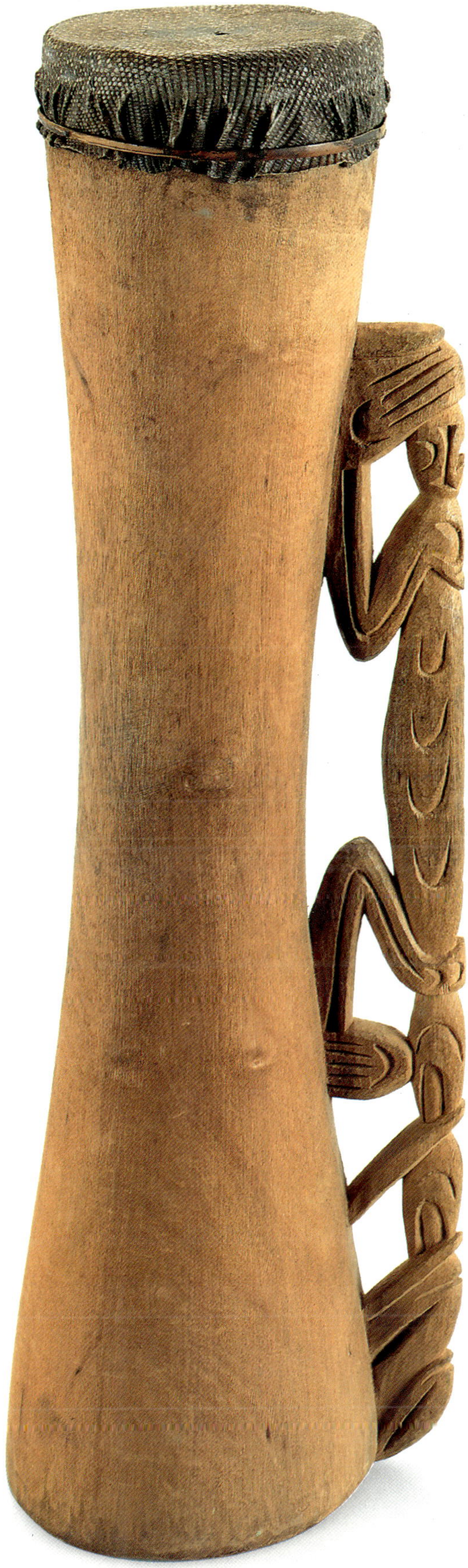

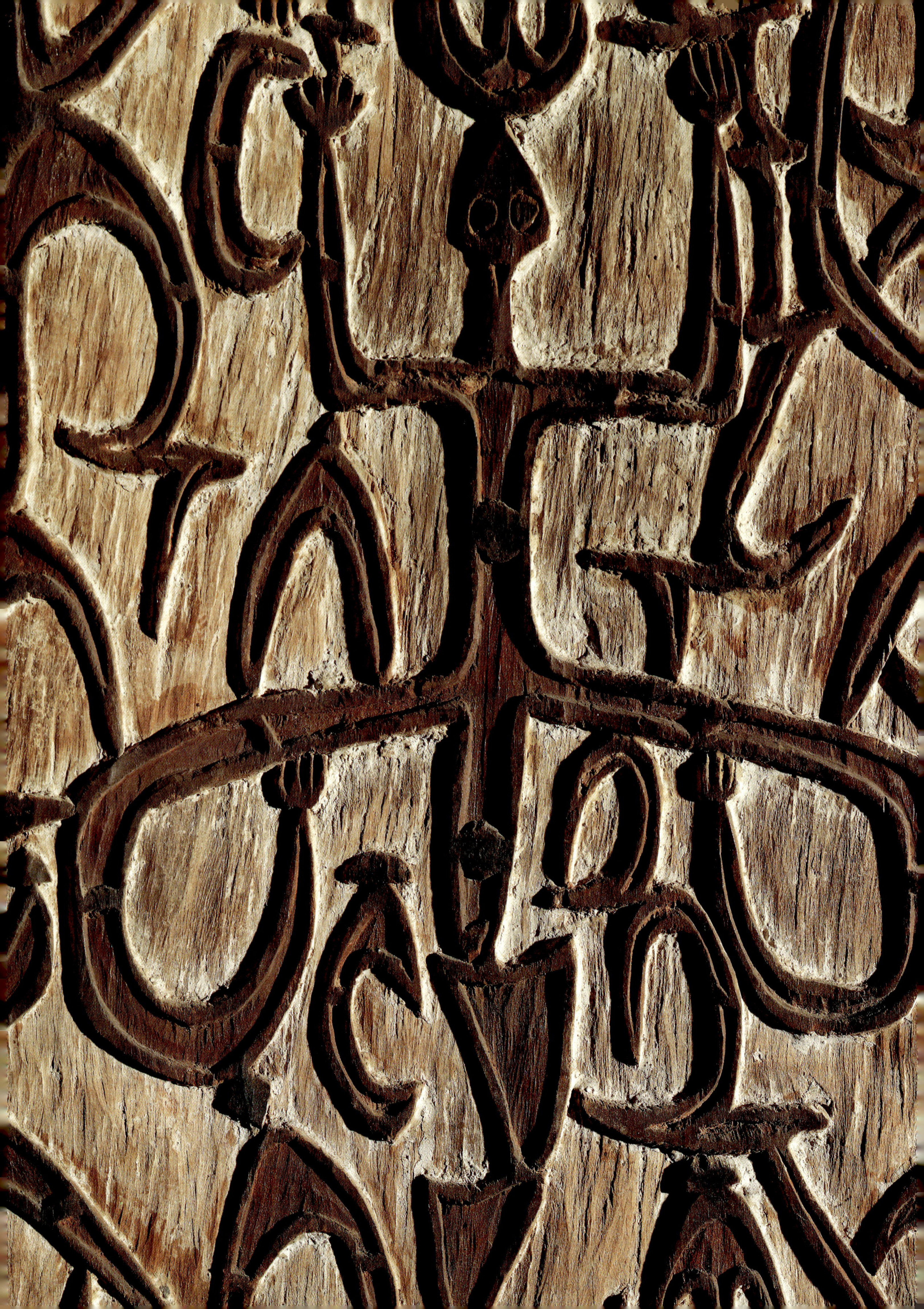

CHAPTER 5

Woodcarving Art: Style Regions and Motifs

Dirk A.M. Smidt

Four general geographical style regions have been identified in Asmat art: Northwest Asmat, Central Asmat, Citak and Brazza River. (See map pages 16-17.) These are broad categories, and in the case of some objects, important local variations can be discerned. But considering the space available, we will limit the discussion here to these four broad regional groupings.

We will also limit ourselves to shields. Style regions can be seen in other objects, but it is in the shields that they stand out most starkly. The near two-dimensional quality of shields allows the shapes and motifs to be analyzed in a more objective way, and allows them to be more accurately assessed from a photograph. But more importantly, there are more shields in museums than any other genre of Asmat carving.

In 1976, A.J.J.M. Boeren conducted a thorough stylistic analysis of 131 shields in the Leiden museum's collection, and using photographs of shields from other collections, expanded his sample to 318. The results of his research are laid down in an unpublished report (Boeren 1976) and summarized in two publications (Boeren 1985 and 1986).

Boeren's inventive analysis considers the motifs and the manner in which they are displayed in the frame. He describes the inherent structure of the designs of the motifs in rules of "combination," "transformation," "rotation," "inversion" and "transposition."

He has also found it fruitful to compare the rules governing the representation of motifs on the shields with other aspects of Asmat culture. For example, he sees parallels between elements of Asmat doctrine concerning head-hunting and the ways in which head-hunting symbols are displayed on the shields. Within the cycle of head-hunting, continuity between younger and older generations is insured by the obligation of the younger to avenge the deaths of the older generation. This continuity and obligation, Boeren argues, assumes a visual form in the shields in "the continuity of series of identical elements mutually connected by rules of mirroring and repetition." (Boeren 1985a: 185). He concludes:

"...Asmat wood-carvers as a whole translate in their creations the relations of continuity and interchangeability characterizing the ideas in relationship with head-hunting into spatial relations of combination and transformation between shapes of ornament. They hereby bring about not only a synthesis between different elements of form, but also between ways of thinking and ornamentation." (Boeren 1985a: 185.)

The underlying structure Boeren suggests exists in the two-dimensional art of Asmat woodcarving does not preclude the "dynamics" of woodcarving art, or artistic individuality:

"The artist has apparently a large freedom in experimenting with forms, and makes use of it in an inventive manner...this experimenting is indeed linked to a collection of rules on the basis of which elements are selected and combined." (Boeren 1985: 175.)

Boeren arrived at nine categories by which Northwest and Central Asmat shields can be usefully contrasted (Boeren 1985b: 4):

1. The shape of the shield
2. The ornaments that form the decoration of the front
3. Measure of symmetry in the ornamentation
4. The utilization of space in ornamentation
5. Types of borders
6. Sculptures on top of the shield
7. The use of color
8. Depth of the carved relief
9. Ornamentation on the back of the shield [1]

Boeren's conclusions are based only on Northwest and Central Asmat style regions. These are the shields most widely represented in European collections, and those that have by far the longest collection histories. On page 56, Boeren's categories are applied to representative Northwest and Central shields. On page 57, some general conclusions are outlined for Citak shields, and Gunter and Ursula Konrad list some of the basic design elements of Brazza River shields.

---

1. As Boeren, to a great extent, had to rely on black-and-white photographs, he was not always able to include characteristics 7 through 9 in his analysis.

Plate 5.1 Detail of an old shield from the Northwest Asmat region. Wood, lime, red ocher, charcoal. The colors have faded with age. 112 cm. Collected in 1908 or 1913 by A.J. Gooszen. Donated by Gooszen in 1919. RMV 1971-974f. Photograph: Isaäc C. Brussee.

The dominant motif on this detail stands midway between a human figure and a figure of the large fruit bat called a flying fox (*tar*). For the entire shield, see Plate 7.6, page 75.

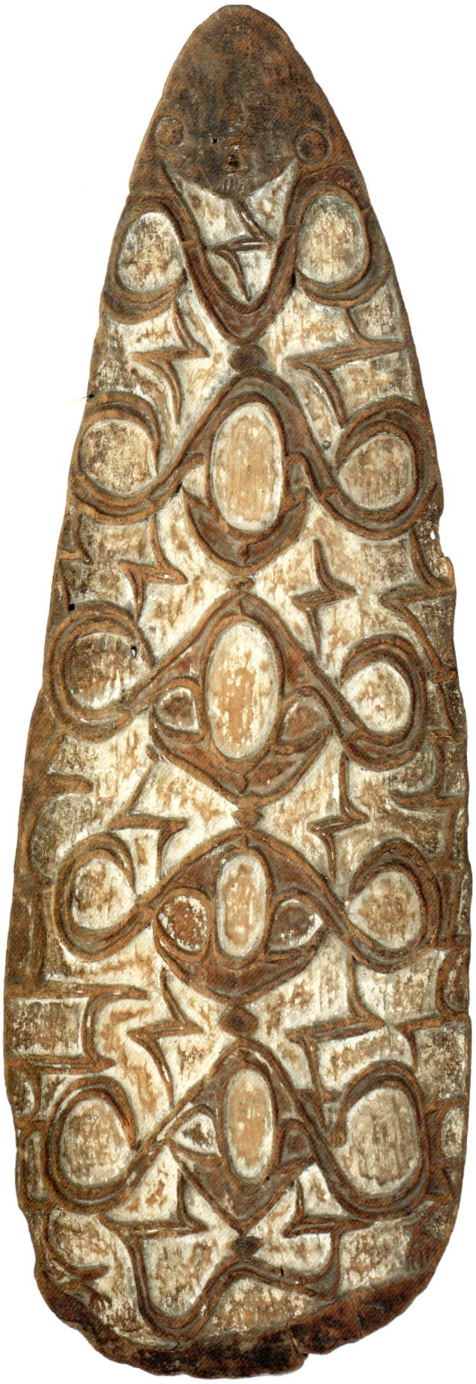

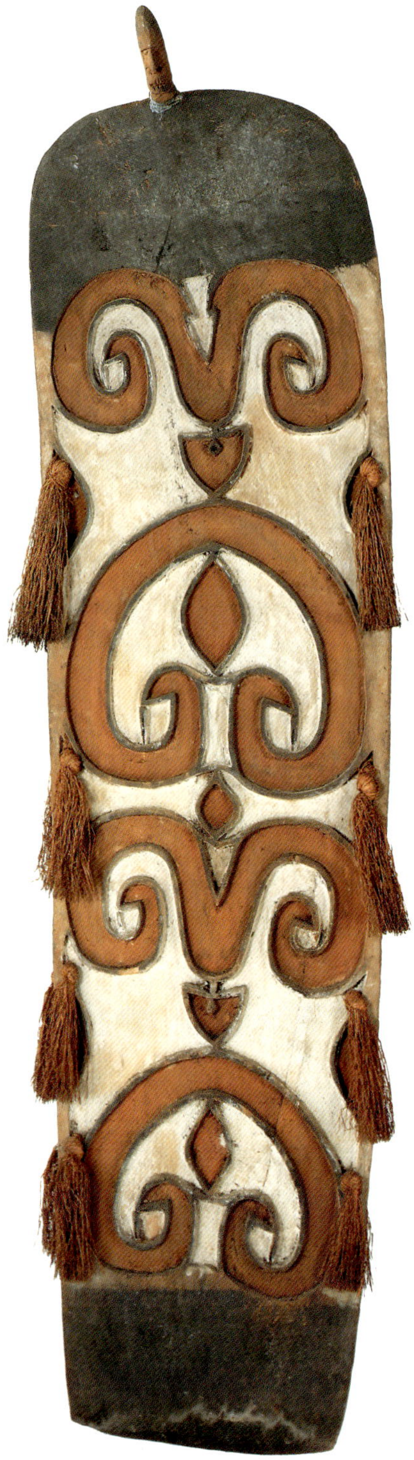

Plate 5.2 Northwest Style Region shield. Unir River (formerly Lorentz), Northwest Asmat. Wood, lime, red ocher, charcoal. 106 cm. Collected c. 1913 by the Maatschappij ter Bevordering van het Natuurkundig Onderzoek der Nederlandsche Koloniën. RMV 1854-442. Photograph: Ben Grishaaver.

The large motif with curved ends, which covers the width of the shield, is possibly a stylized rendering of a flying fox (*tar*).The style of rendering seems to be unique to this shield.
Illustrated: Fischer 1923, Taf. XX, fig. 120.

Plate 5.3 Central Asmat Style Region Shield. Wood, lime, red ocher, charcoal. 174 cm. Presumably collected by F.R.J. Eibrink Jansen, c. 1953. RMV B175-1. Photograph: Ben Grishaaver.

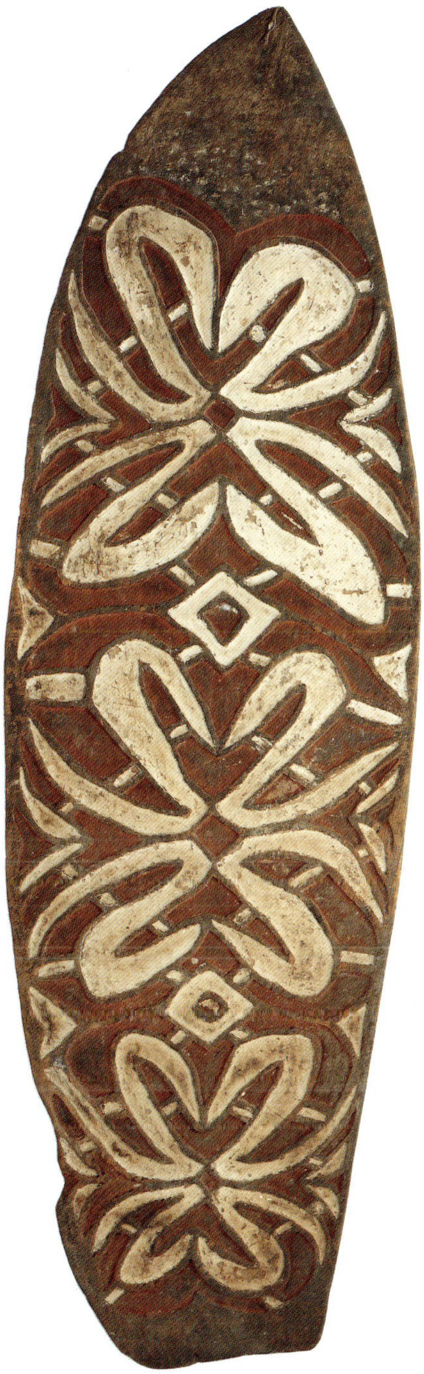

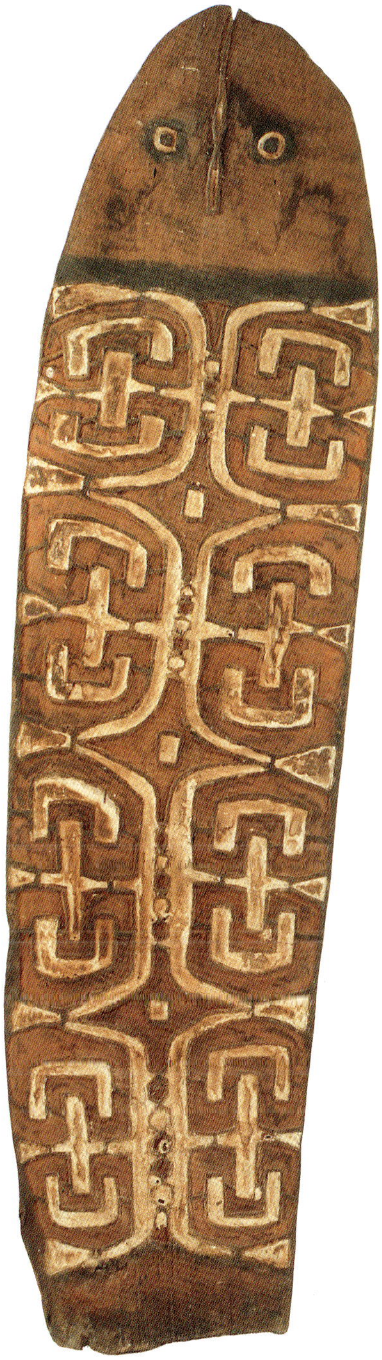

Plate 5.4 Citak Style Region shield. Urébi village, Wildeman River, Citak. Wood, lime, red ocher, charcoal. 178 cm. Collected c. 1954 by J.J. Spijker. RMV 3530-6. Photograph: Ben Grishaaver.

The basic pattern on this shield consists of three mirror-image pairs of strongly curved motifs. Each pair consists of two identical motifs that display both horizontal, and vertical symmetry.

Plate 5.5 Brazza Style Region shield. Tainet-Burbis village, Bras people, Brazza River, Northeast Asmat. Wood, lime, red ocher, charcoal. 184 cm. Collected in 1975 by Gunter and Ursula Konrad. From the Konrad Collection, Völkerkundemuseum der Josefine und Eduard von Portheim-Stiftung für Wissenschaft und Kunst, Heidelberg. Photograph: Ursula Konrad.

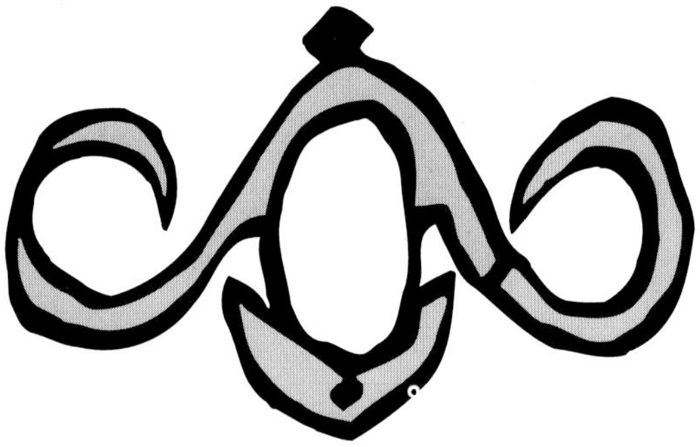

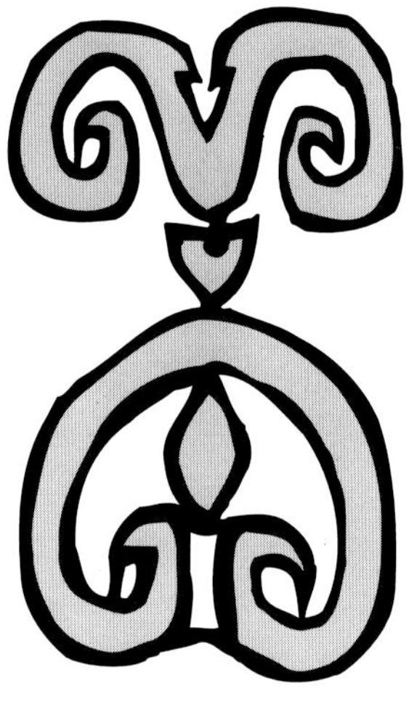

I. Northwest Asmat

Northwest Asmat shields tend to be roughly oval in shape, and covered with numerous, relatively small motifs. Most are large, although not as large as shields from the other regions. However, there is also a very small type (see Plate 5.6, page 61).

According to Boeren's categories, Northwest shields have the following characteristics:

1. Oval, to almost triangular in shape.

2a. Animal figures (basically recognizable) are present, especially flying foxes and birds.

2b. Human figures are almost never found.

3. There is bilateral symmetry along the vertical axis of dominant motifs; additional elements are set asymmetrically.

4. The motifs are slender, and the groove between the raised edge of the motifs is often narrow; there are a limited number of dominant motifs, and the rest of the plane is literally filled with small motifs.

5. A small frame is filled with small, identical motifs above each other.

6a. The top of the shield, is flat, triangular or oval, and is reminiscent of a face, often with carved eyes, mouth and scar-tattoos.

6b. Alternately, there can be a protrusion in the form of a small animal head at the top.

7. The motifs are rendered in red against a white background.

8. The motifs are rather shallowly carved (the newer examples are carved more deeply than the older shields).

9. There is no significant decoration on the back of the shield, apart from occasional vertical strokes of red and white.

II. Central Asmat

Central Asmat shields tend to be rectangular, decorated with a few large motifs, and often topped by a carved figure, the *tjemen* or figurative "penis" of the shield. They are usually large.

According to Boeren's categories, Northwest shields have the following characteristics:

1. Rectangular in shape, and tall.

2a. The motifs are chiefly abstract, geometric and curvilinear, although sometimes recognizable as heavily stylized flying foxes.

2b. Recognizable squatting human figures sometimes appear. (Note: Combinations of "abstract" and figurative motifs are rare; the motifs are either abstract or figurative.)

3. The shields display bilateral symmetry along the vertical axis.

4. The motifs are few and large, and stretch across the entire width of the shield. The grooves between the raised edges of the motifs are broad.

5. The frame of the shield does not incorporate small motifs; it is plain.

6. A point, a human or animal head, or a human figure projects from the top of the shield.

7. The motifs are red against a white background.

8. The motifs are deeply carved.

9. The back of the shield, on both sides of the grip and from top to bottom, is entirely covered with painted (but not carved) geometrical motifs, generally a zigzag pattern in white, red and black.

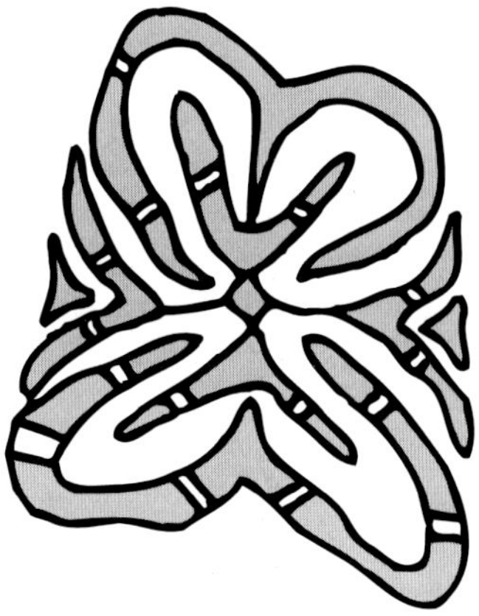

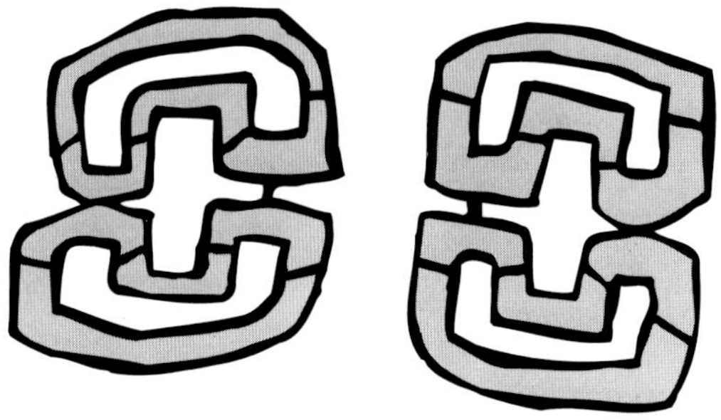

III. Citak

Shields from the Citak area, which lies east of the Central Asmat region, are very large, with a pointed top and flat bottom. They are generally covered with large geometric or "floral" motifs. Citak shields have only been collected relatively recently.

Typical characteristics of Citak shields are:

1. An overall "bullet" shape.
2. Great height, averaging almost 2 meters.
3. Thinness, which despite their size makes them light and easy to maneuver with in the bush.
4. The depth of carving is not as great as it is on Central Asmat shields.

Citak patterns have not been well-documented, although Schneebaum (1985) suggests that some Citak patterns are highly stylized representations of fish, swirling water, and sago pounders. The frequent interruption of the pattern by small white blocks or "bridges" is a common stylistic trait of Citak shields.

Citak shields with recognizable human elements (even with a full-standing human figure) do occur, although abstract designs are much more typical. At least some of the shields with anthropomorphic elements may represent a recent stylistic innovation.

No sculptures or other genres of carving are known from the Citak region.

IV. Brazza River

Shields from the Brazza River area, north of the Citak region, are similar to Citak shields in that they are generally large, and display abstract designs. Brazza shields tend to have a very recognizable "face" at the top.

Some characteristics of Brazza shields:

1. Quite noticeably divided into a "head," "body," and "foot"—the body represents about two-thirds of the total height of the shields.
2. The head tends to be round or pointed, colored red with a white tip.
3. Simply formed hooks, circles or spirals represent a "face" with eyes, nose and mouth. These carved elements are colored white.
4. Motifs consist of a rich variety of spirals, hooks, bows, circles, and rhomboids, sometimes linked together into a complex decoration.
5. There is clear bilateral symmetry in the layout of the motifs. At the center of the motifs is sometimes a small rhomboid or circle, often called the "navel" of the design. This marks the plane of symmetry.
6. The shields often have a noticeable "foot" area, lacking in carving and simply painted in the background color of the shield. Sometimes this foot section is of minimal size.

—Gunter Konrad

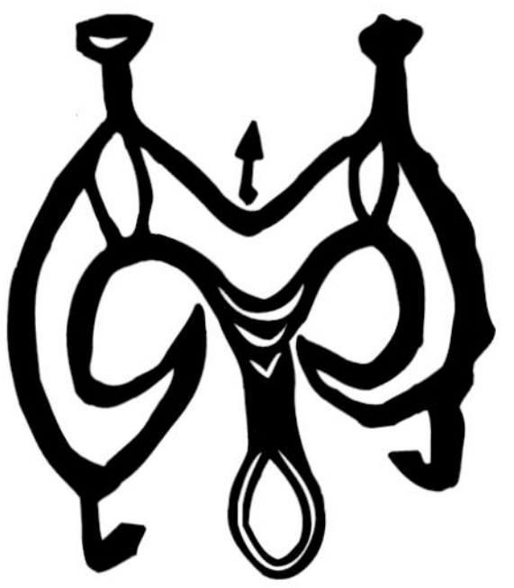

Figure 5.1 Flying fox (*tar*) motif from a Northwest Asmat style region shield. The motif here, on a shield carved after World War II, is a rather literal representation. For the entire shield, see Plate 7.14, page 80.

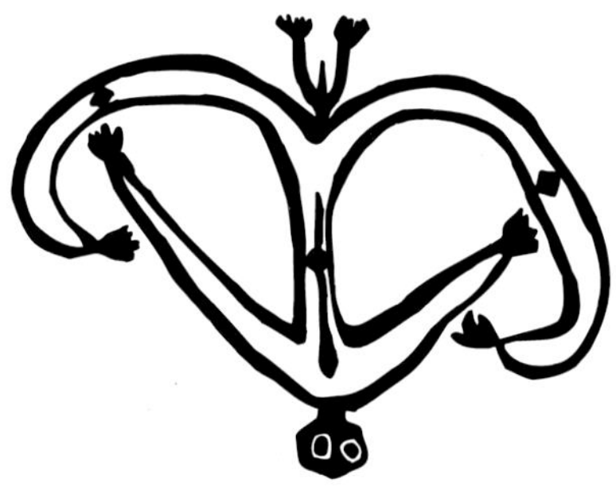

Figure 5.2 Flying fox (*tar*) motif from a Northwest Asmat style region shield. This, the dominant motif on the shield, is an interesting combination of flying fox and human characteristics. For the entire shield, see Plate 7.3, page 73.

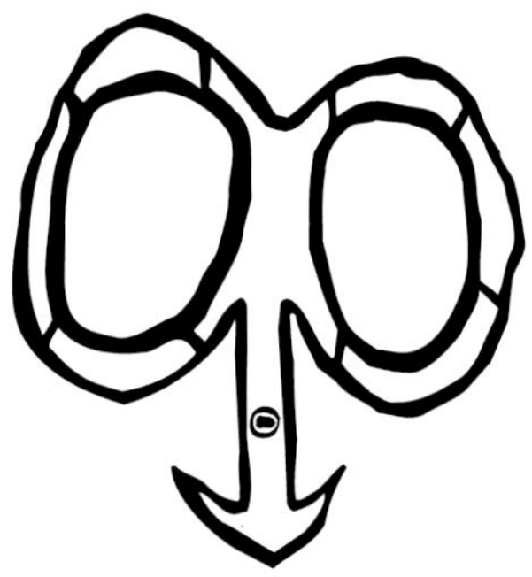

Figure 5.3 Flying fox (*tar*) motif from a Northwest Asmat style region shield. This is a highly abstracted representation. The wings have become mere circles, and the head a simple, arrow-like point. For the entire shield, see Plate 7.12, page 79.

Motifs on Asmat shields

The motifs on Asmat shields refer to the surrounding reality. They can reflect natural phenomena such as lightning or waves on the river, plant, animal or human shapes, or even objects such as nose ornaments. Animal figures occupy a dominant position, especially on shields from the Northwest Asmat region. Stylized hornbills, cockatoos, cuscus, crocodiles, snakes, butterflies and centipedes all appear on Asmat carvings.

Among the animal figures the flying fox occupies a dominant position. The flying fox, a large fruit bat, is associated with the aggressive and successful head-hunter. The tree is often taken as a metaphor for a human being, and its fruit, in turn, as the tree's "head." Thus fruit-eating animals, particularly large, dramatic ones like the flying fox, are important head-hunting symbols. (See also Chapter 1, page 15.)

In shield motifs, the animals are often not presented in full. They are often limited to a synecdoche, such as the tail of a cuscus. On Northwest Asmat shields, the animal motifs are often quite recognizable, particularly the above-mentioned flying fox (see Figure 5.1 at left), but there are representations of this motif, called *tar* in Northwest Asmat dialect, that display greater or lesser degrees of hybridity and abstraction (Figures 5.2 and 5.3).

On Central Asmat shields, more or less abstract motifs dominate. These motifs, almost always mirror-image pairs, are often symbolic representations of the human figure, or of the *bipanew,* the shell nose ornament that is an important head-hunting symbol (see Figure 5.5 opposite). Occasionally, recognizable human figures occur (Figure 5.9, page 60).

Although we have a general knowledge of the forms and genres of motifs occurring on Asmat shields, it is often difficult to interpret a specific motif with certainty. Of all the shields in this publication, only those collected by Adrian A. Gerbrands are accompanied by documentation as to the meaning of the motifs. We have the least information for the early shields, which often didn't even come with specific information as to where they were made, let alone who made them and the meaning of their motifs.

Thus, the majority of the interpretations of motifs offered throughout this book are not based on first-hand information but gathered while collecting other shields well after the Second World War. Gerbrands, in part based on

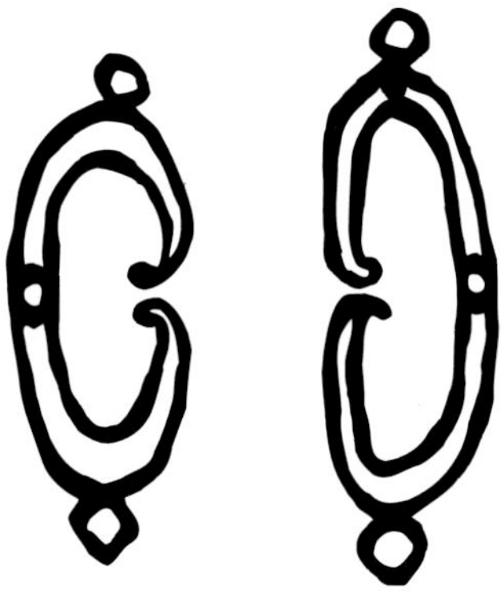

Figure 5.4 A pair of *bipanew* motifs from an old Northwest Asmat style region shield. The *bipanew* is a nose ornament made out of shell, and an important head-hunting symbol. Note the difference in cut between this motif and the more recently carved, Central Asmat version at right. For the entire shield, see Plate 7.2, page 72.

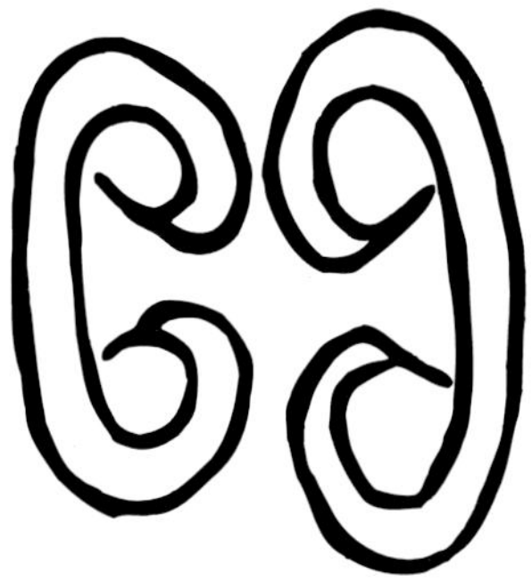

Figure 5.5 A pair of *bipanew* motifs from a Central Asmat style region shield. (Compare with version at left.) For the entire shield, see Plate 7.24, page 86.

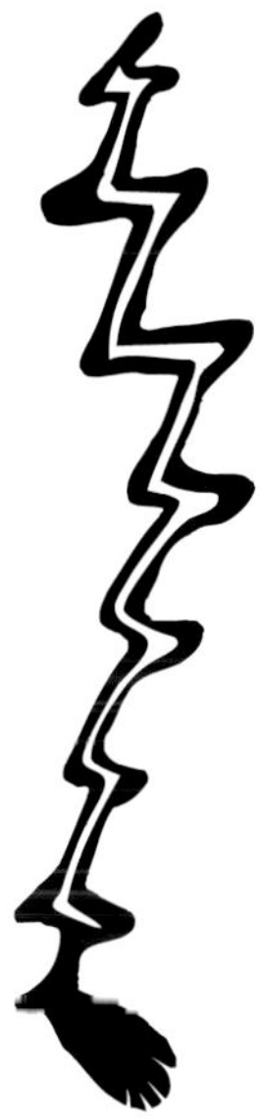

Figure 5.6 "Foam on the river" motif from an old Northwest Asmat style region shield. This zigzag may represent waves, or white water on the river. For the entire shield, see Plate 7.4, page 73.

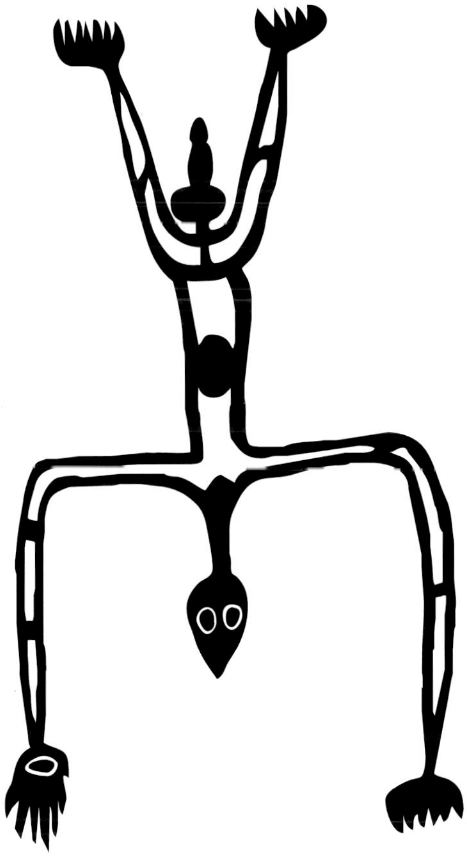

Figure 5.7 Hybrid motif from Northwest Asmat style region shield. This interesting motif, which dominates the shield on which it is carved, has both flying fox (*tar*) and human characteristics. Compare the flying fox motifs opposite, and the human motifs on page 60. For the entire shield, see Plate 7.6, page 75.

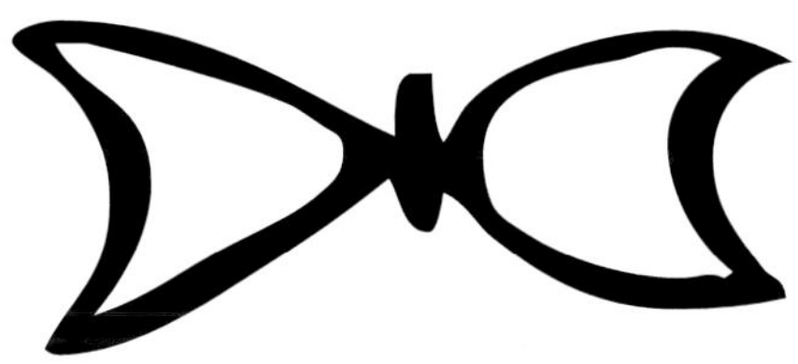

Figure 5.8 Nose ornament motif from a Northwest Asmat style region shield. This hour-glass–shaped motif represents a common nose ornament made of a pig's bone (*maka*). Like the *bipanew* shown above, this is a head-hunter's ornament. For the entire shield, see Plate 7.9, page 77.

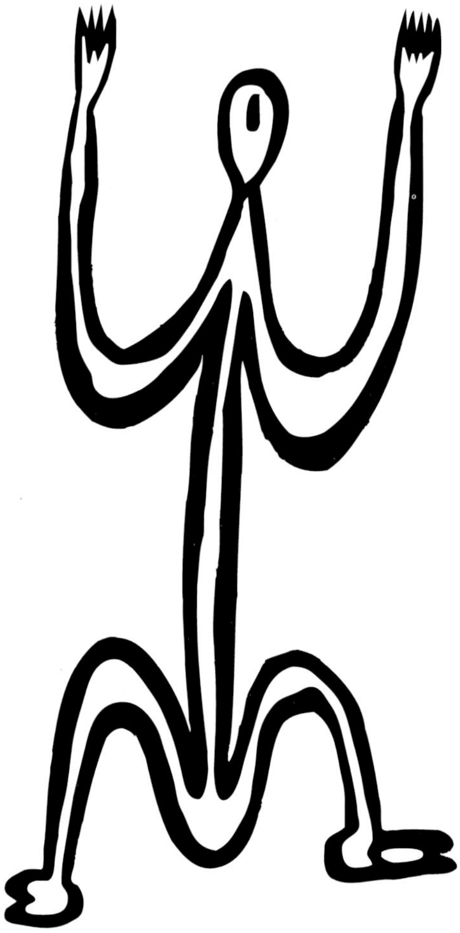

Figure 5.9 A large human figure motif from a Central Asmat style region shield. A human figure represented in this position is thought by Adrian A. Gerbrands (1967:30–34) to be composed of two praying mantis motifs in profile. The praying mantis is an important head-hunting symbol. For a praying mantis motif from the same shield, see Figure 5.10 at right. For entire shield, see Plate 7.41, page 99.

Figure 5.10 A praying mantis motif (*wenet*) from a Central Asmat style region shield. This is a detail from the same shield dominated by the motif in Figure 5.9 above. Note how two of these praying mantids, mirrored back to back, would be equivalent to the human figure above. The praying mantis is an important head-hunting symbol because of the female's habit of eating the male's head during mating. For the entire shield, see Plate 7.41, page 99.

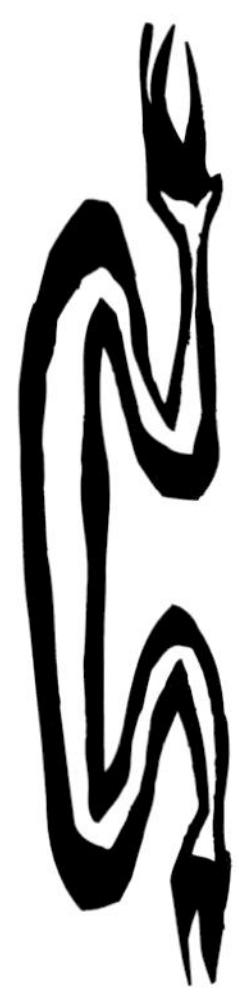

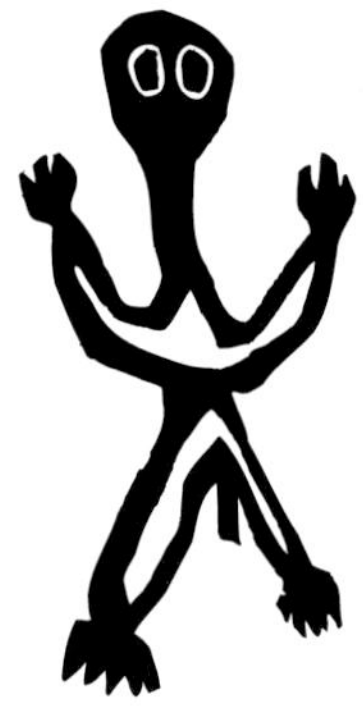

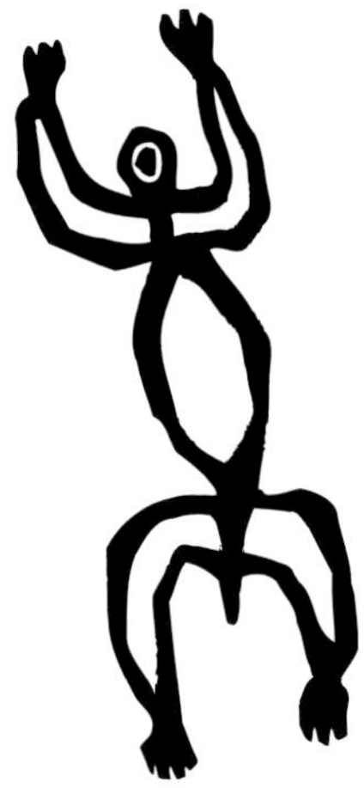

Figure 5.11 (left) and **Figure 5.12** Two small human figure motifs from the same old Northwest Asmat style region shield as Figure 5.13 below. For the entire shield, see Plate 7.3, page 73.

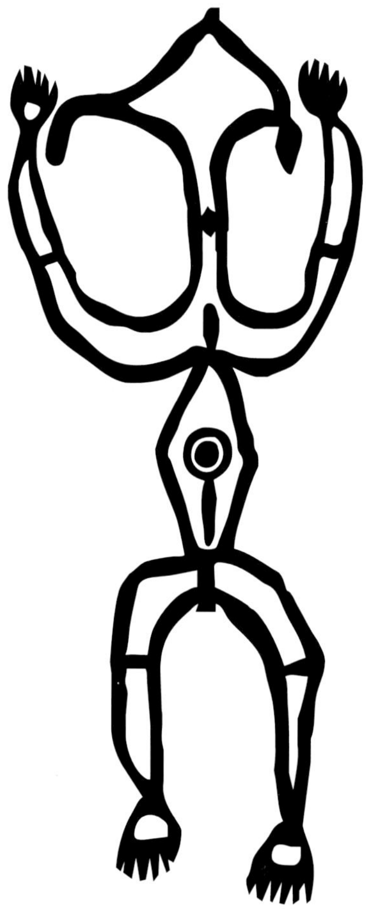

Figure 5.13 The dominant human figure motif from an old Northwest Asmat style region shield. This is a rather fanciful rendering, with perhaps some animal characteristics blended in, especially the flying fox (*tar*). For the entire shield, see Plate 7.3, page 73.

Michael Rockefeller's data (Gerbrands 1967b) and Tobias Schneebaum have done the most work in this area (Schneebaum 1985:176–190 and 1990:38–39).

The lack of data is not the only caveat one must bear in mind when trying to analyze motifs, however. Very similar motifs are variously interpreted in different villages and by different artists. Moreover, the Asmat do not make the same kind of distinctions as we might be tempted to make between different motifs.

For example, the distinctive S-shaped motif often found on Central Asmat shields has been interpreted by different informants in different ways: 1) The line along which the belly of a head-hunting victim was cut open (navel to hip, and from there, under the ribs to the sternum, ending at the nipple); 2) An imaginary line at the human belly enclosing the viscera; 3) *eu-wow* (*eu* means crocodile; *wow* means woodcarving).

The first two of these definitions work on what at first seem to be different registers—an actual S-shaped cut (equivalent, by the way, to the western forensic surgeon's "lazy S"), or a metaphorical enclosing line. These are probably effectively the same for the Asmat. The third definition (Gerbrands 1961) is a little less clear. Presumably the belly of a head-hunting victim is linked to the belly of a crocodile, or the method of efficiently slicing open either of these bellies is the same. Given the strong Asmat identification with animals, and the range of abstraction and metaphor in Asmat motifs, it is likely that the Asmat would see no important distinctions between any of these three explanations.

These caveats should not leave the impression that all interpretations are fabrications. One can reliably distinguish many of the most common, and presumably most important, motifs. The flying fox, for example, can be identified on many old shields, even at high levels of abstraction.

The figures accompanying this text illustrate a number of important motifs. Figures 5.1 through 5.3 should the Northwest style region's flying fox (*tar*) motif, ranging from a quite recognizable form to a highly abstracted one. Figures 5.4 and 5.5 show mirror-image pairs of the shell nose-piece motif (*bipanew*), contrasting Northwest Asmat and Central Asmat styles of representation. Figures 5.6 and 5.8 show, respectively, the "foam on the river" motif and the pig bone nose-piece (*maka*). Figure 5.7 shows a very distinct, hybrid flying fox and human figure. Figures 5.9 through 5.13 show a variety of human figure motifs.

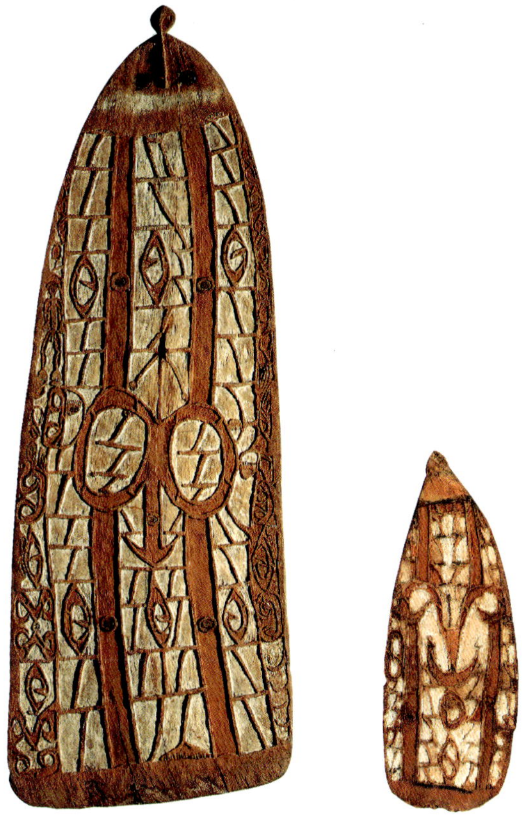

Plate 5.6 A large and a very small shield, both from the Northwest Style Region, and both displaying an interesting regional style. Both the large shield at left (RMV 1854-441, Photograph: Isaäc C. Brussee) and the small shield at right (RMV 1854-446, Photograph: Ben Grishaaver) were collected circa 1913 in the region of the Unir River by De Maatschappij ter Bevordering van het Natuurkundig Onderzoek der Nederlandsche Koloniën.

The large shield stands 195 centimeters and the small shield just 79 centimeters, making it the smallest shield known (not including the recent miniature shields that have been made for the tourist trade).

Seven shields of this type, characterized by two long vertical stripes, have been collected. The central motif, rendered in a highly abstract form on the larger shield, may be either a flying fox (*tar*) or a human figure. It has been suggested that the small shield was made in memory of a deceased child. (See also Plate 7.12 for a larger photograph, and more discussion of the larger of these two shields.)

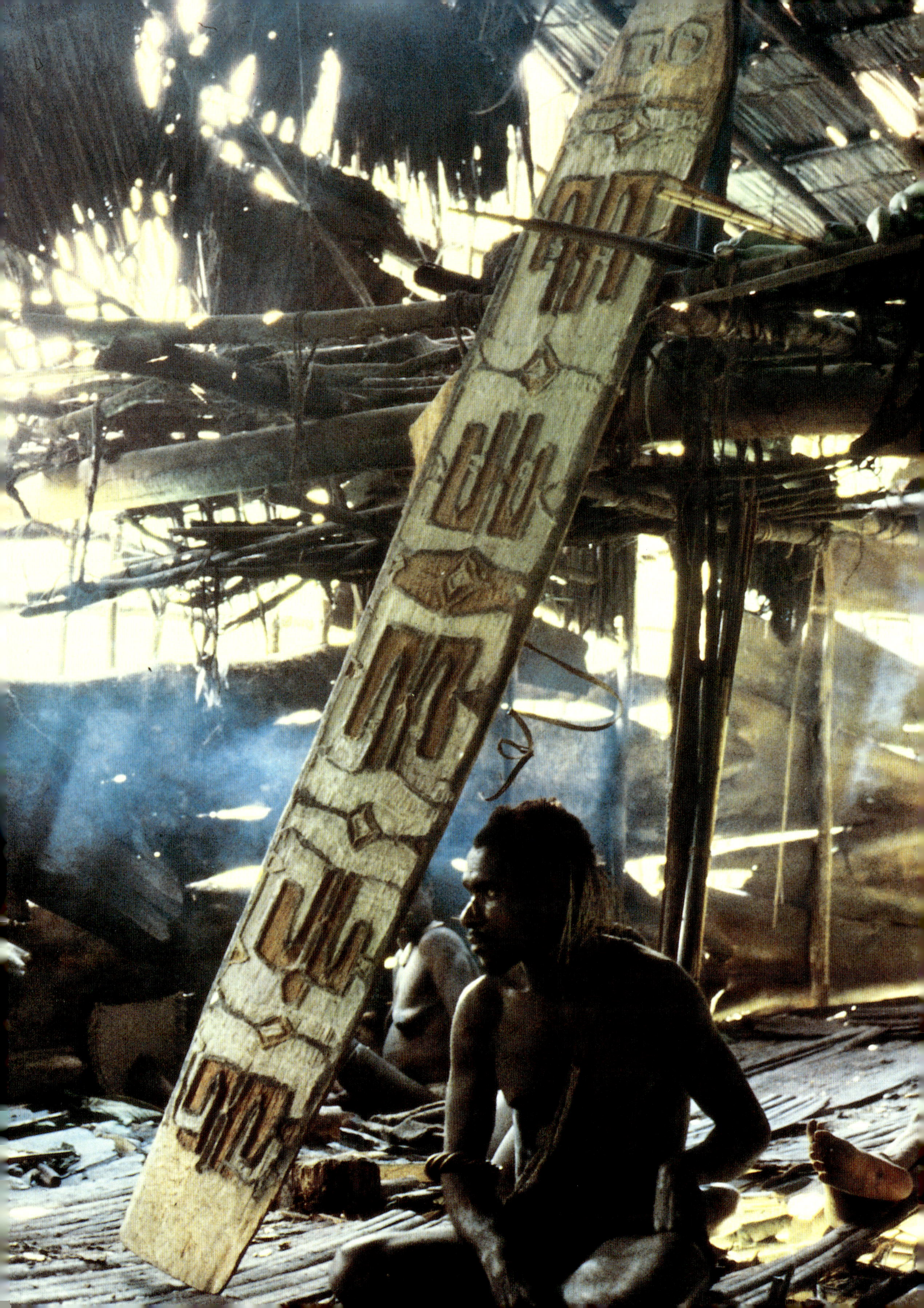

CHAPTER 6

Brazza: The Art of the Northeast

Gunter and Ursula Konrad

The Bras people live Northeast of the Asmat in the southern foothills between the river courses of the Balim/Friendship, the Brazza, the Kolff, the Modera, the Steenboom and the Eilanden(See maps pgs. 16-17). Until just two decades ago, the Bras lived a semi-nomadic existence, and were uninfluenced by modern culture.

Today, through the efforts of the Protestant missionaries working in the area and by order of the Indonesian government, the Bras have been moved from their forest home to more permanent, and easier to govern villages near the rivers.

The Indonesian government now formally refers to the Bras and other groups living in the nearby foothills as "Patipi," a word taken from the name of a government official.

Until the move to mandated riverside villages, the Bras lived in tall tree houses (see Plate 6.2, page 64). Such houses were common throughout the Asmat area, particularly in the foothills, before the arrival of the Europeans in the region. Social life here was marked by permanent and intensive warfare, and the tree houses were a defensive measure.

The Bras were an important trade link between the highlands and the coast, and despite the almost constant warfare, trade and intermarriage continued. The Bras supplied stone axes and tobacco to their southern neighbors, and traded palm wood for bows, bark for string, and rattan to the highlands people. After World War II, with the arrival of the Europeans in the coastal area and the introduction of steel axes, the trade stopped, and the Bras became isolated.

Life in the Brazza

In 1971, the Brazza expedition of the Völkerkundemuseum in Heidelberg, including ourselves and accompanied by the missionaries A. van der Wouw, M.S.C. and E. Zachman, O.F.M., reached the Brazza River. To our surprise we met a hitherto unknown people with a "stone age" culture.

During our first stay in the Brazza River area, we found not a single object of western technology: no steel knives, axes, tins, textiles or artificial ornaments. (Note: elsewhere in the region, even far inland, one can find items such as the little spoons from the 1959 Gaisseau Expedition across Dutch New Guinea.)

The tree stumps in the overgrown gardens we saw in 1971 looked like worn-out shaving brushes—the work of stone axes. We learned that various types of stone cutting tools were used to fell trees and cut out the branches that threatened to overgrow the gardens.

In one common type of stone axe, the head was fitted into a club-like handle of bamboo root. Also common were adzes, in which a thinner, sharper stone was lashed to an angled handle with rattan. These tools were also used by the Dani, Yali, Mek and Ok of the highlands.

The stones for these two instruments were produced in two fundamentally different procedures. Axe stones are shaped by soft tapping of the stone, and have a smooth finish. The cutting edge is rounded in profile. Adze stones, about 30 centimeters long, are formed by chipping. The cutting edge is noticeably sharper, and triangular in profile. Both stone tools were made by the Bras themselves, though most of the adze stones were traded from the mountain people.

The Bras traditionally lived in big clan-houses that stood 8 to 15 meters high on stilts or rooted trees that had been topped. The houses were divided by a wall into two halves: one occupied by the women, the other by men. Men and women entered the house through separate doors. A break in the dividing wall allowed members of the two sexes to talk to each other, or slip food across. Judging from the number of fireplaces we saw, from eight to twenty families lived together in such houses. In addition to the single, large tree house, a Bras settlement also consisted of three to eight small, ground-level houses.

Unlike the downstream Asmat, the Bras supplement their staple sago with gardens in which they grow sweet potatoes, manioc, taro, bananas, cucumbers and corn. They also grow tobacco. These garden plots can be some distance from the main clan house, and if this is the case, a kind of rough garden house, either a tree house or at near ground level, is built. These are inhabited as long as the gardens are yielding.

The Bras make dug-out canoes, but in keeping with the swifter, narrower rivers this far inland, these are much shorter than the long dug-outs used by the coastal Asmat.

Plate 6.1 Korowai man with a shield in a tree house. Tajan Village, 1979. The Korowai are the eastern neighbors of the Bras. Photograph: Tobias Schneebaum.

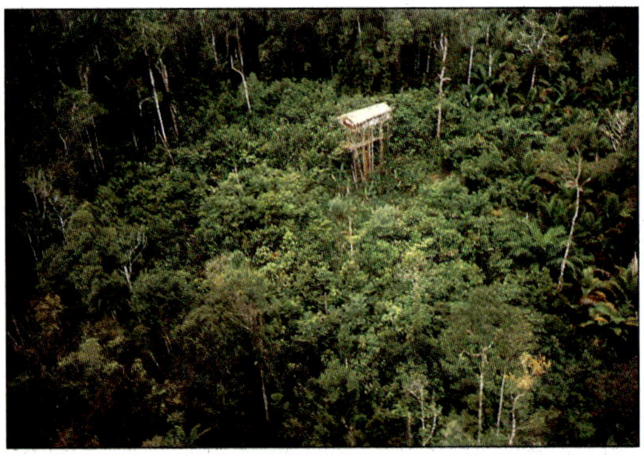

GUNTER KONRAD

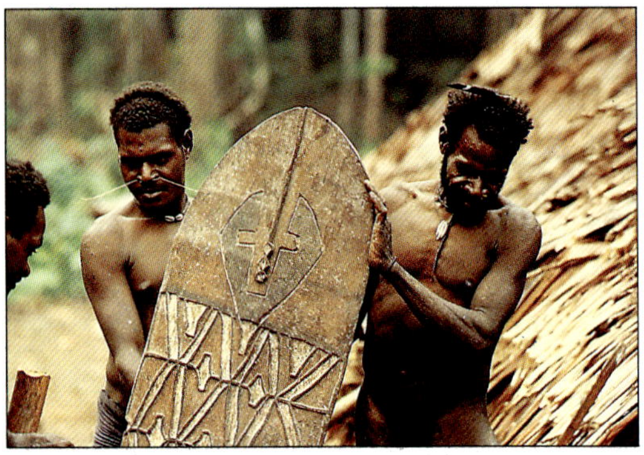

GUNTER KONRAD

Plate 6.2 (above, top) An aerial view of a semi-permanent Bras tree house. Brazza River area, Northeast Asmat. This is a garden house, providing a place to live while the garden is tended and harvested. The Bras now live in more or less permanent quarters along the rivers, but still use the tree houses when they are tending their gardens. 1990.

Plate 6.3 (above, bottom) Bras men with a shield. Modera River, Northeast Asmat. 1982.

Plate 6.4 (opposite) Chopping off a buttress root from a mangrove tree. The resulting plank will be used to make a shield. Basim village, Casuarina Coast, Central Asmat. 1979.

The Brazza shields

The Bras are known only for shields. They create no sculptures or monumental carvings. The front of a Brazza shield is divided into a "head," the ornamented "body" and a plain "foot." The head of a Brazza shield often has a well-defined face, which gives the shields a distinctly menacing appearance. Combined with the aggressive motifs, the shields almost seem to be laughing maliciously. It is not implausible that such a sight would make an enemy insecure.

Brazza shields tend to be large, more than two meters high and with a width of 60–70 centimeters. They are worked to a thickness of just half a centimeter to a centimeter, and thus are still easily carried. The front surface is scraped smooth with clamshells; the back displays the rough marks left by the adze.

Most Bras have a general aptitude for craft work, but like the Asmat, there are some who are particularly talented at woodcarving art. These men are called upon to make the shields. The esteem with which such a man is held is equivalent to that of a storyteller, a war leader, a singer or traditional healer.

Until the very recent introduction of steel tools, cassowary bone chisels were used to cut the reliefs. The depth of relief may vary from a few millimeters to one centimeter. The depth and sharpness of relief is determined by the patience and skill of the carver, and the grain and density of the wood.

Shields of hardwood are preferred for their strength, although carving them is much more difficult. Because hardwood is so dense, and the shield so large, the plank must be worked very thin so it can be easily handled. During times of war, softwood is used to allow an increase in production. Softwood shields sometimes show a clearer and deeper relief, but they are quite easily damaged. To prevent theft, shields are often hidden in the river, and softwood shields quickly become waterlogged and heavy under these conditions. (Astonishingly, the water does not harm the colors much.) Because of these disadvantages, the Bras regard them of minor value.

Like the downstream Asmat, the color palette includes white, red, and black. The Bras achieve an intensive red by mixing the bark of a special mangrove tree with burned shell powder. This is then added to burned, ocherous mud to yield a deep, blood-red pigment. The shell lime used for the white pigment is occasionally extended by

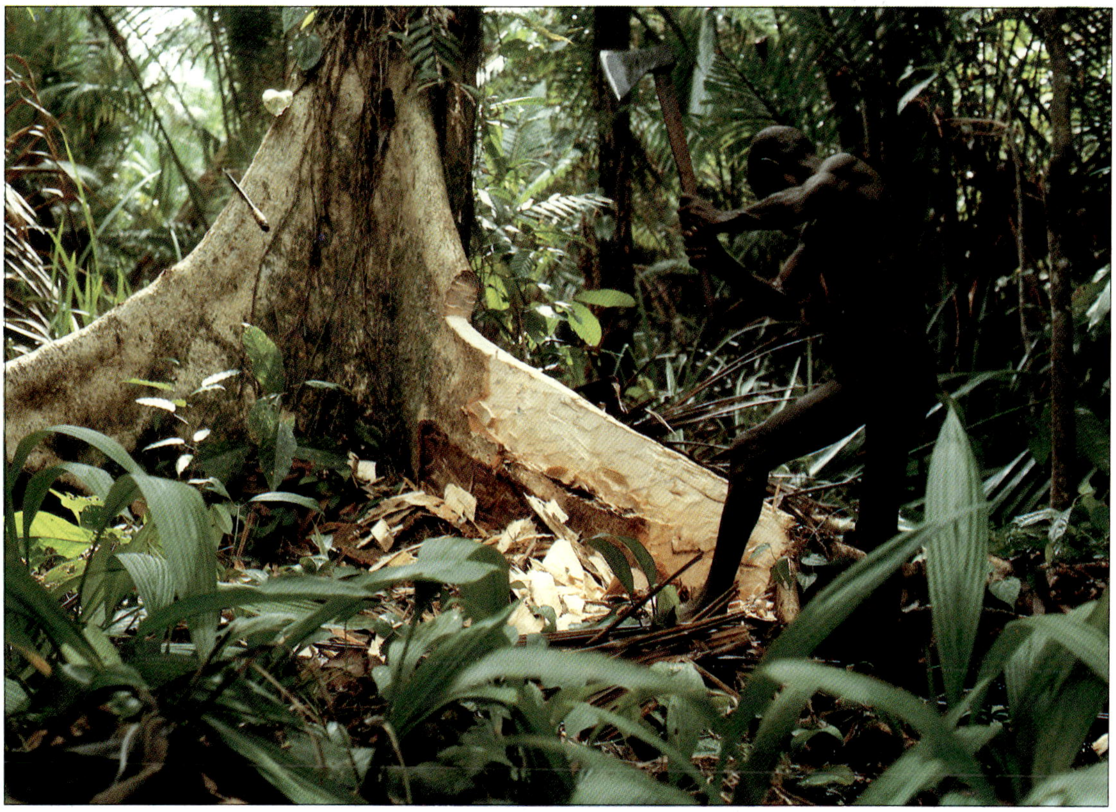

mixing it with white kaolinite clay, as shells are a sometimes scarce trade object in the region. The Bras also use sago sap to make their colors less prone to wearing off.

Shields and warfare

Like those of the downstream Asmat, Brazza shields are given the name of a beloved ancestor. This ancestor's spirit inhabits the shield. Thus, when he carries the shield, the warrior has his ancestor's strength in addition to his own. The ancestral spirit not only protects the warrior's body against spears and arrows, but can also defend it with cunning and deception. The latter in particular was a highly respected stratagem in Bras warfare. Direct maneuvers in warfare are considered stupid and risky. This is why the shields function both defensively and offensively.

When an opponent sees a Bras shield, he finds himself confronted by two enemies. He becomes irritated and panicky. Should he turn his attention to the psychological menace of the grimacing shield, or to the physical dangers of the spear or arrows?

The fear and confusion the shield's inspire explains why they are hung outside the houses to guard against their entrance by a hostile neighbor. It also explains why they are sometimes stolen, if an enemy is brave enough to do so.

In battle, the shields are usually carried by warriors armed with spears. They are less convenient for bowmen, and when carried, must be put on the ground and leaned against the man's shoulder when he is shooting. The large shields would seem to offer a good target for the clouds of arrows which are released during an attack. (In 1971–1973, fighting was very common in the area.) However, surprisingly few incidences of spear or arrow hits are found on the shields.

If any damage does occur, the shield is carefully repaired. Using a bone awl, perforations are made around the edge of the defect, and a chunk of wood is carefully tied with rattan to fill the gap. A warrior often keeps his shield for a lifetime. Sometimes the shield is inherited, although it is unknown whether in any cases the shield is split and used to cover the body of the deceased, as is often the case with the coastal Asmat.

Among the Bras, shields for children are also known. These are 50–60 centimeters high, and are in every detail a miniature of the full-sized shields.

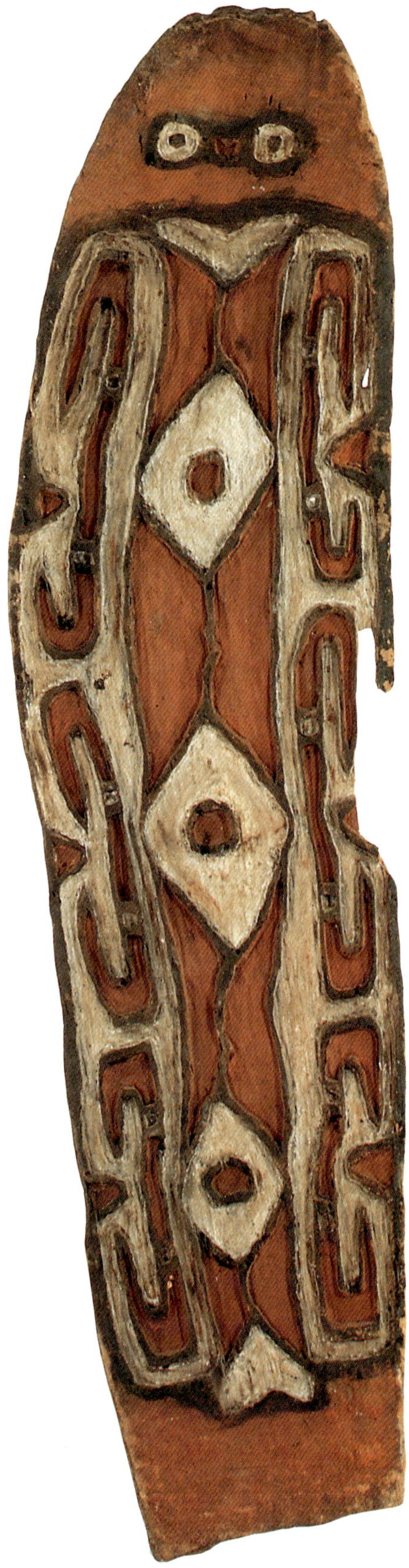

Plate 6.5 (left) Shield. Tami village, Bras people, Brazza River, Northeast Asmat. Wood, lime, red ocher, charcoal. 166.5 cm. Collected in 1971 by Gunter and Ursula Konrad. From the Konrad Collection, Völkerkundemuseum der Josefine und Eduard von Portheim Stiftung für Wissenschaft und Kunst, Heidelberg. KCS036. Photograph: Ursula Konrad.

The white diamond shapes, each with a red circle in the middle are the so-called "navel"motifs. The C-shaped motifs at the sides represent the shell nose ornament. This motif is rarely rendered on Brazza River shields, in contrast to Northwest and Central Asmat.

Plate 6.6 (opposite, left) Shield. Sepana village, Bras people, Brazza River, Northeast Asmat. Wood, lime, red ocher, charcoal. 207 cm. Collected in 1975 by Gunter and Ursula Konrad. From the Konrad Collection, Völkerkundemuseum der Josefine und Eduard von Portheim Stiftung für Wissenschaft und Kunst, Heidelberg. KCS043. Photograph: Ursula Konrad.

The curvilinear motifs, covering almost the entire body of the shield, represent fish intestines.

Plate 6.7 (opposite, right) Shield. Bras people, Brazza River, Northeast Asmat. (Village unknown.) Wood, lime, red ocher, charcoal. 178.5 cm. Collected in 1971 by Gunter and Ursula Konrad. From the Konrad Collection, Völkerkundemuseum der Josefine und Eduard von Portheim Stiftung für Wissenschaft und Kunst, Heidelberg. KCS034. Photograph: Ursula Konrad.

The motifs indicate the hands of ancestral spirits. These designs serve to protect the carrier of the shield while simultaneously threatening the enemy.

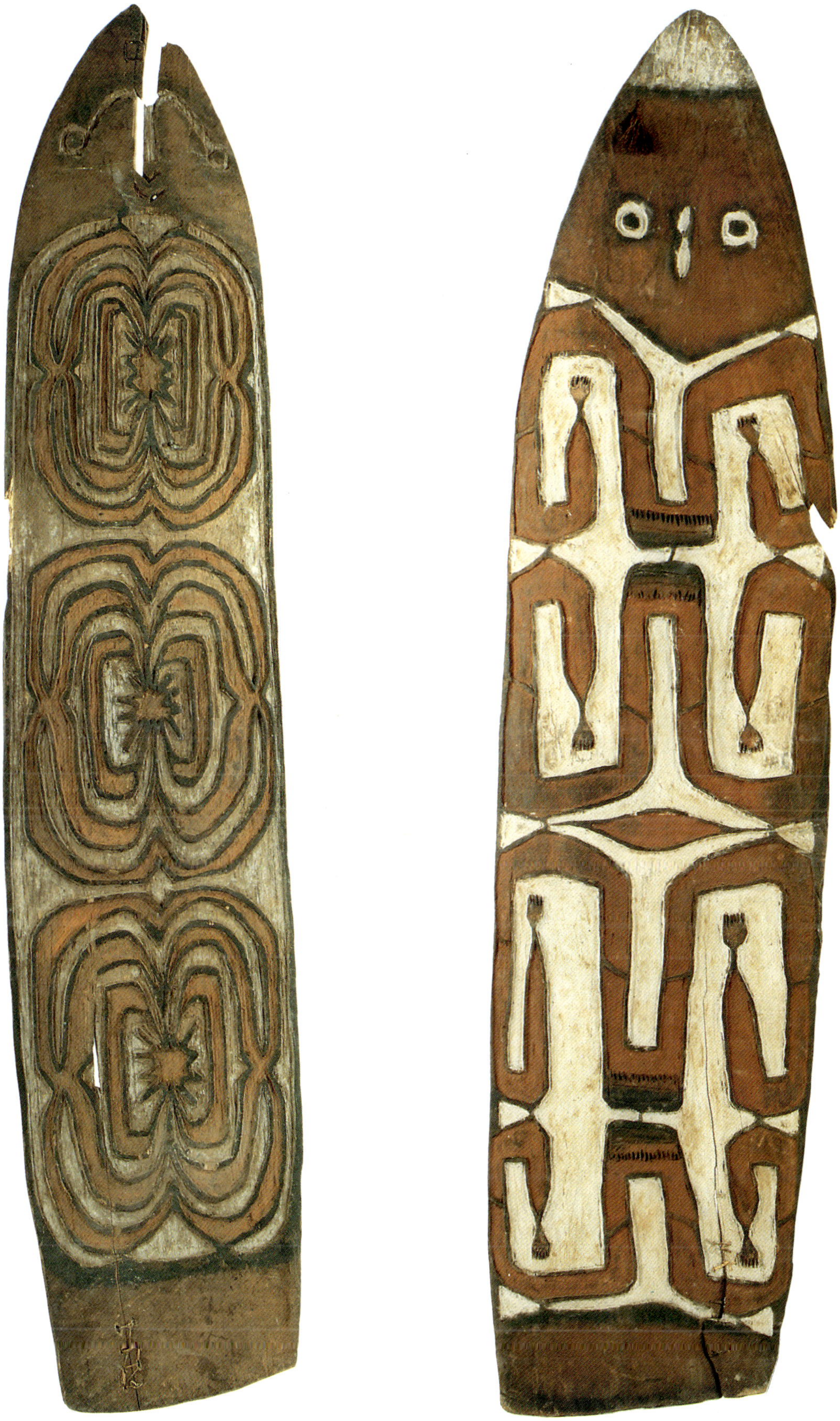

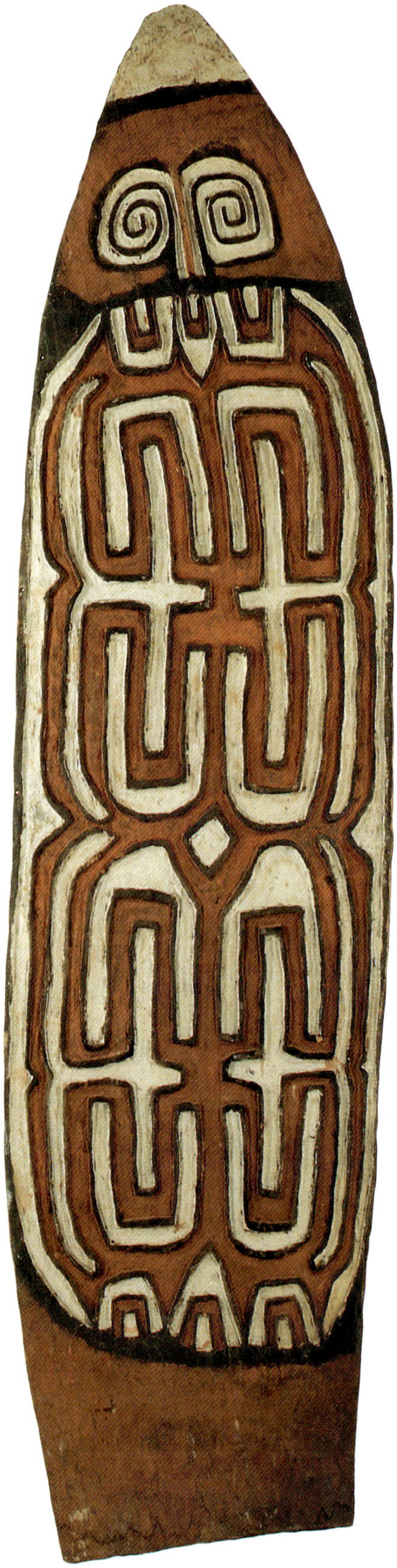

Plate 6.8 (right) Shield. Made by Bota, and owned by Bimaue. Bras village, Bras people, Brazza River, Northeast Asmat. Wood, lime, red ocher, charcoal. 206 cm. Collected in 1971 by Gunter and Ursula Konrad. From the Konrad Collection, Völkerkundemuseum der Josefine und Eduard von Portheim Stiftung für Wissenschaft und Kunst, Heidelberg. KCS035. Photograph: Ursula Konrad.

In this shield, the spiral-shaped eyes are joined with the nose.

Plate 6.9 (opposite, left) Shield. Batusun village, Bras people, Brazza River, Northeast Asmat. Wood, lime, red ocher, charcoal. 203 cm. Collected in 1971 by Gunter and Ursula Konrad. From the Konrad Collection, Völkerkundemuseum der Josefine und Eduard von Portheim Stiftung für Wissenschaft und Kunst, Heidelberg. KCS040. Photograph: Ursula Konrad.

The curvilinear motif underneath the "head" of the shield represents the intestines of a fish. The remaining motifs are representations of the eddy currents in the river.

Plate 6.10 (opposite, right) Shield. Jenak village, Bras people, Brazza River, Northeast Asmat. Wood, lime, red ocher, charcoal. 190.5 cm. Collected in 1975 by Gunter and Ursula Konrad. From the Konrad Collection, Völkerkundemuseum der Josefine und Eduard von Portheim Stiftung für Wissenschaft und Kunst, Heidelberg. KCS081. Photograph: Ursula Konrad.

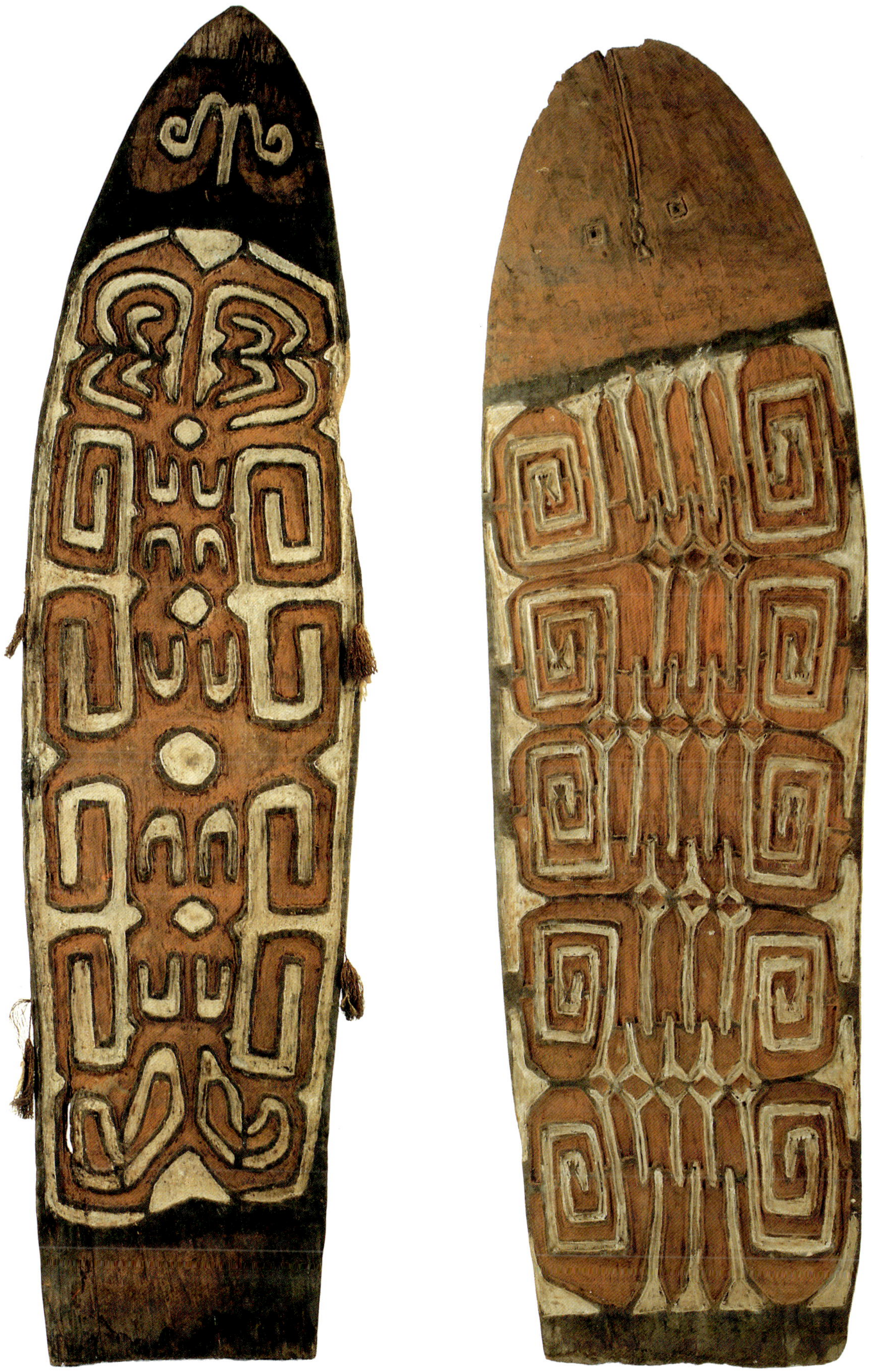

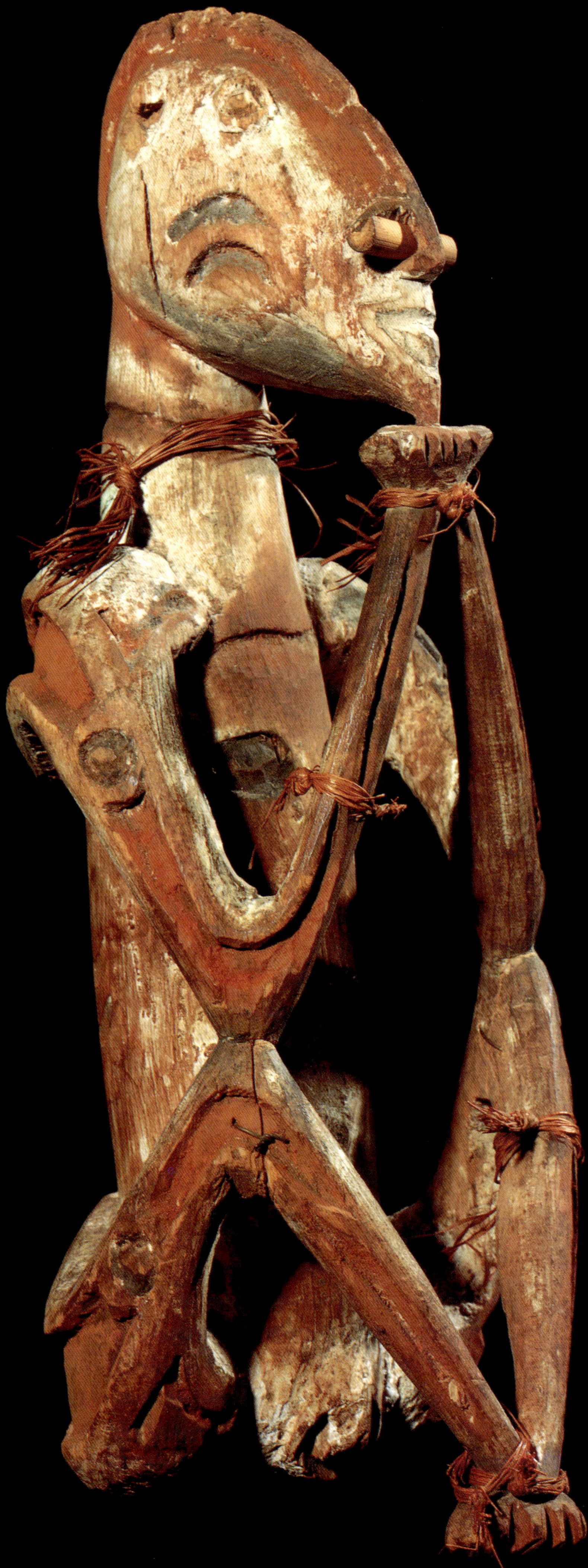

CHAPTER 7

Catalog of Woodcarvings

Dirk A.M. Smidt

In such a densely forested land, it comes as no surprise that wood is the most important material for construction of all kind, including artistic expression. Houses, canoes and paddles, spears, bows and arrows, and small objects like bowls and containers are all fashioned out of wood. And many of these received some form of decoration: the prows of canoes, the posts of the *jeu* houses, bowls, and paddle handles and blades.

But the most important carvings had a purpose that went far beyond the utilitarian. The great monumental sculptures, such as the *bisj* poles and the *wuramon* or soul canoes, shields, and figure carvings were all materializations of ancestor spirits. They were named after deceased ancestors, and were thus animated by the relatives' spirits. In a culture where no death was accidental, and all required avenging in a continuous cycle of warfare, it was the woodcarvings that became the important representations—and receptacles—of the power of ancestral spirits.

Part I: Shields

Asmat shields (*jamasj*) served a very practical function in warfare, protecting their owner from the spears and arrows of his enemy. But it was not just the thickness of wood that offered this protection. The symbols carved on the shield's surface radiated power, the power of the ancestors, which invigorated the shield's owner and struck fear in his enemies. In battle, a shield was more important than a spear or bow and arrows, even as an offensive weapon. A warrior would rather go into battle without his spear, than without his shield.

Both shields and figures are named after dead relatives. A single shield, although given only one name, can at the same time refer to more than one dead relative. The shield's namesake is often depicted in the form of a human figure at the top of the shield, at least in the Central Asmat style region. Other more abstract motifs, carved in deep relief on the front of the shield, sometimes refer to other ancestors with which the namesake of the shield had a relationship. (See, for example, Plate 8.9 on page 126.)

The magical power of shields gave the carrier exceptional power and courage, adding to the man's own strength the considerable strength of the ancestor after whom the shield is named. At times, particularly during the feasting leading up to raids, the relationship between a man and his shield is such that it is as if the ancestor had literally crawled into the warrior's skin.

It thus comes as no surprise that in warfare, moving shields terrified the enemy. Certain motifs in particular could literally paralyze a victim with fright. In this condition, he dropped his weapons and could easily be taken captive.

Shields were not just used in battle. In the case of a sudden, unexpected death, for example when a woman died in childbirth, the men ran with their shields to the riverbank to scare off the evil spirits responsible.

Asmat shields were traditionally made for a *jamasj pokmbu* or shield feast, which initiated a head-hunting expedition. The expedition sought to avenge the deaths of those after whom the shields were named. At the climax of this feast, the shields were placed in a long row in front of the men's house. Everyone had to leave the riverbanks and the river. The woodcarvers then pointed the shields East, towards the river and Safan, the realm of the ancestors.

The woodcarvers then took the shields to their new owners (who had commissioned the carvings) and returned the shields to the *jeu* loaded with gifts of food. The shields were leaned against the wall, and the food placed in piles. Then everybody—carvers and owners alike—gorged themselves on food, and danced all night to the music of drums. By morning, the men had worked themselves up to a fever pitch, and set off on their bloody expedition. (Konrad, Konrad and Schneebaum, 1991:43-48.)

Because of their symbolic and emotional value, shields were precious. In the Central Asmat region, when the maker of the shield or one of his relatives died, the small sculpture at the top was cut off. When the owner passed away, relatives sometimes made a crack in the shield. The owner's son, or another male relative, inherited the shield in this condition. Often the shield was broken up and laid on top of the corpse, which was then rolled into mats.

Plate 7.1 Statue of a woman. Pomatsj or Unir River (formerly Northwest and Lorentz respectively), Northwest Asmat. Wood, lime, red ocher, charcoal, sago leaf fiber, bamboo. 40.5 cm. Collected in 1908 or 1913 by A.J. Gooszen. Donated by Gooszen in 1919. RMV 1971-985. Photograph by Isaäc C. Brussee. (See also Plate 7.30.)

In the Northwestern Asmat region, a shield was seldom broken or split when the owner died. Here shields were passed down undamaged from father to son. In a special ceremony, the shield was solemnly handed over by the village war leader, with the exhortation that the son should fight just as bravely as did his father. The bystanders wept, and the son consoled them: "You don't have to cry. I will replace my father and fight like him." (Konrad, Konrad and Schneebaum 1981:47.)

A. Group of Shields I

Northwest Asmat
Collected: 1907–1908 or 1913
Note: If not otherwise noted, the provenance of a given piece has been determined by the collector.

The shields in this group (Plates 7.2–7.7) belong to the earliest collection of Asmat shields, obtained through A.J. Gooszen, leader of the South New Guinea detachment that carried out the first military exploration of the Asmat region.

Gooszen and his men collected in the Asmat region twice: in 1907–1908 and in 1913. He sent the collected material to the museum in parts, in 1911, 1912 and 1914. These shields were sent to the Leiden museum in 1914; because of the date they were dispatched, it is assumed they were collected in 1913, but this is not certain. Gooszen donated the shields to the museum in 1919.

One Asmat shield belonging to this group is considered to be the oldest of its kind (Plate 7.2). Being a very fine expression of art, it was included in the book *Topstukken uit het Rijksmuseum voor Volkenkunde/Masterpieces from the National Museum of Ethnology* (1987). It seems to have been carved with traditional tools. Despite the early date of collection, the other shields in this group appear to have been made with metal tools.

When Gooszen's shields reached the museum, they were unfortunately often covered with a layer of lacquer, as at the time this was thought to protect the wood. The lacquer dulled the original dry pigment, and this and their age make these shields appear less bright than more recently collected examples.

The Group I shields exhibit typical Northwest Asmat style characteristics: 1) a more or less oval to a triangular shape, with a face at the top and sometimes an extension; 2) the entire face of the shield is filled with motifs. Northwest shields are generally of modest size, and the height of these varies from 120 centimeters to 161 centimeters.

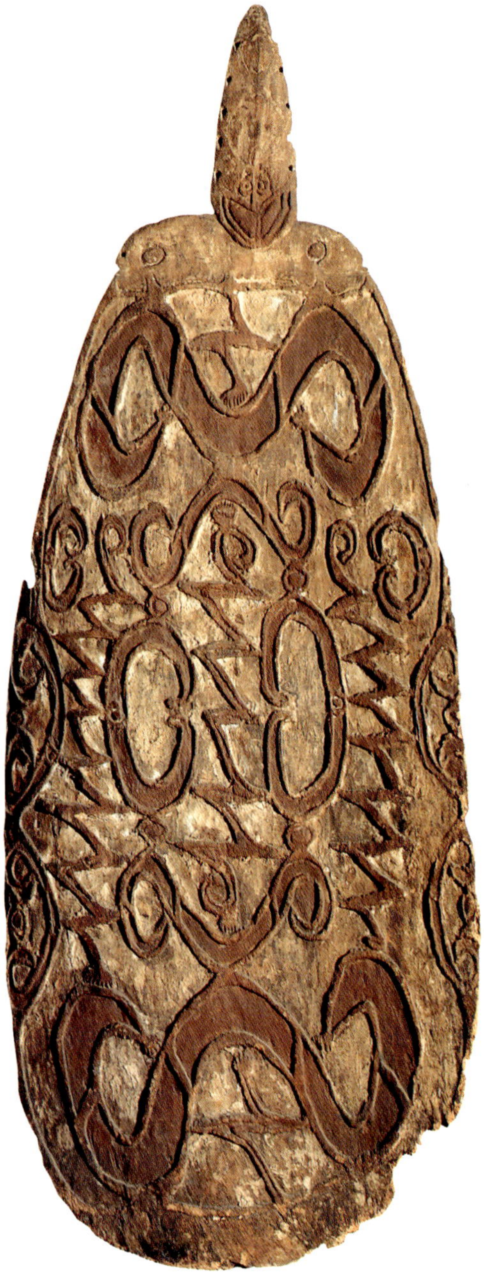

Plate 7.2 Shield. Either Unir or Pomatsj River (formerly Lorentz and Northwest respectively), Northwest Asmat. Wood, lime, red ocher, charcoal. 156 cm. Collected in 1908 or 1913 by A.J. Gooszen. Donated by Gooszen in 1919. RMV 1971-976. Photograph: Isaäc C. Brussee.

This shield, presumably dating from the 19th century, is the oldest shield in the museum's collection. It is probably the oldest Asmat shield in the world. The dominant motifs, at the top and the bottom, are the flying fox (*tar*), a motif associated with male ancestors. The C-shaped motifs represent a shell nose ornament (*bipanew*), which is a head-hunter's symbol.

Exhibited: "The Art of the Pacific Islands," National Gallery of Art, Washington, D.C. 1979, Cat. 21.7. (See: Gathercole, Kaeppler, and Newton 1979:292)

Illustrated: Kooijman 1956, Fig. 16; Smidt 1987c, Plate 116.

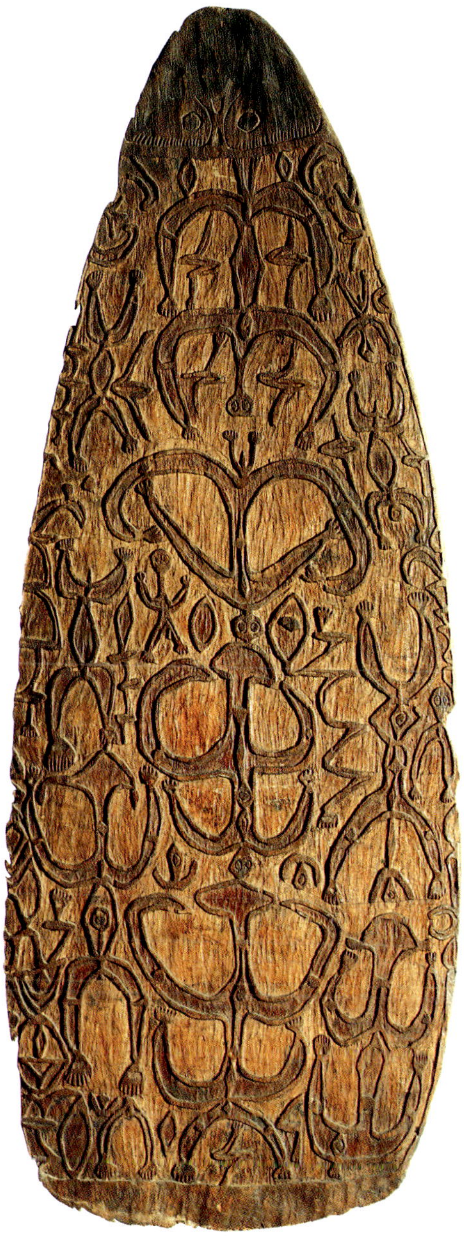

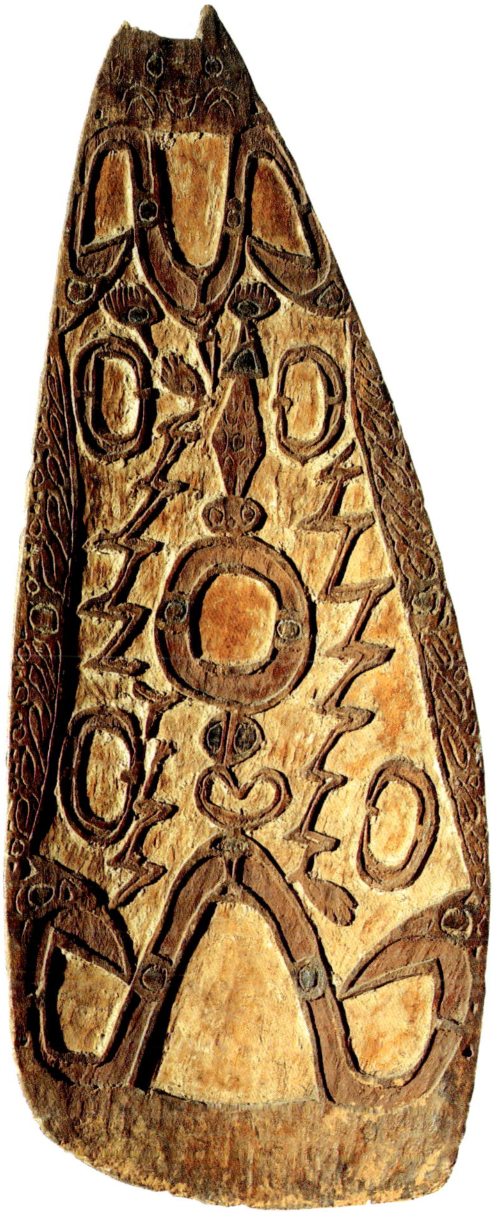

Plate 7.3 Shield. Pomatsj River (formerly Northwest), Northwest Asmat. Wood, lime, red ocher, charcoal. A layer of lacquer was applied after acquisition. 120 cm. Collected in 1908 or 1913 by A.J. Gooszen. Donated by Gooszen in 1919. RMV 1971-978a. Photograph: Isaäc C. Brussee.

The central, repeated motif in this shield seems to be a combination of a flying fox (*tar*) and human figure. The motifs along the rim are presumably human figures.

Plate 7.4 Shield. Pomatsj River (formerly Northwest), Northwest Asmat. Wood, lime, red ocher, charcoal. A layer of lacquer was applied after acquisition. 120 cm. Collected in 1908 or 1913 by A.J. Gooszen. Donated by Gooszen in 1919. RMV 1971-979d. Photograph: Isaäc C. Brussee.

Like the other Gooszen shields, this shield was collected without documentation on the meaning of the motifs. The large curvilinear shapes at the top and the bottom ends are possibly a stylized rendering of the flying fox (*tar*), a symbol for male ancestor or head-hunter. The upper shape could also be the arms, and the lower shape the legs, of a human figure represented by the entire shield. The C-shape, rendered four times, may be the shell nose ornament (*bipanew*), a head-hunter's symbol. The zigzag lines may be "lightning" or "foam on the river" motifs. (Schneebaum 1985:186, 190).

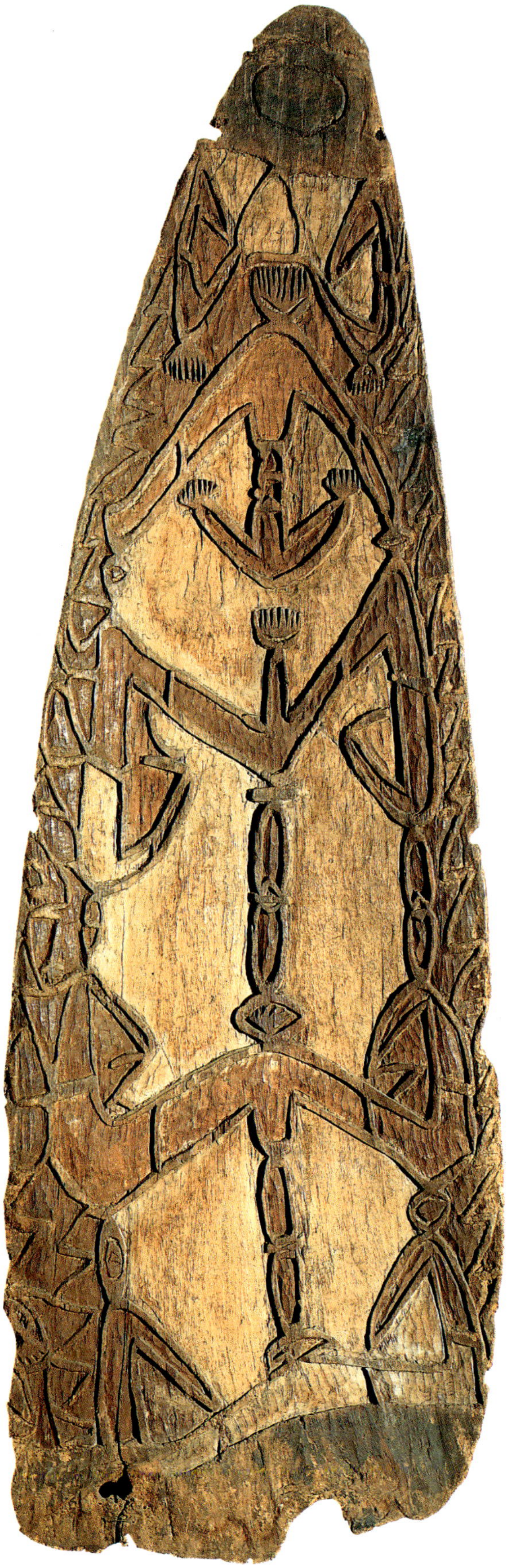

Plate 7.5 (left) Shield. Unir River (formerly Lorentz), Northwest Asmat. Wood, lime, red ocher, charcoal. A layer of lacquer was applied after acquisition. 161 cm. Collected in 1908 or 1913 by A.J. Gooszen. Donated by Gooszen in 1919. RMV 1971-977. Photograph: Isaäc C. Brussee.

The central row of dominant motifs are flying fox (*tar*) figures.

Plate 7.6 (opposite, left) Shield. Northeast River, Northwest Asmat. Wood, lime, red ocher, charcoal. 112 cm. Collected in 1908 or 1913 by A.J. Gooszen. Donated by Gooszen in 1919. RMV 1971-974f. Photograph: Isaäc C. Brussee.

The large, central motif appears to represent a flying fox (*tar*) with human characteristics. The legs are shaped as wings. The more or less similar figure at the top of the shield, depicted upside down, has human legs with male genitalia clearly visible. This rendering of a human-like flying fox is unique.

Illustrated: Kooijman 1955, Pl. 23; 1961, Pl. 22; circa 1984, Fig. 29.

Plate 7.7 (opposite, right) Shield. Northeast River, Northwest Asmat. Wood, lime, red ocher, charcoal. A layer of lacquer was applied after acquisition. 137 cm. Collected in 1908 or 1913 by A.J. Gooszen. Donated by Gooszen in 1919. RMV 1971-974d. Photograph: Isaäc C. Brussee.

The central motif is a flying fox (*tar*) with outspread wings, a head-hunting symbol.

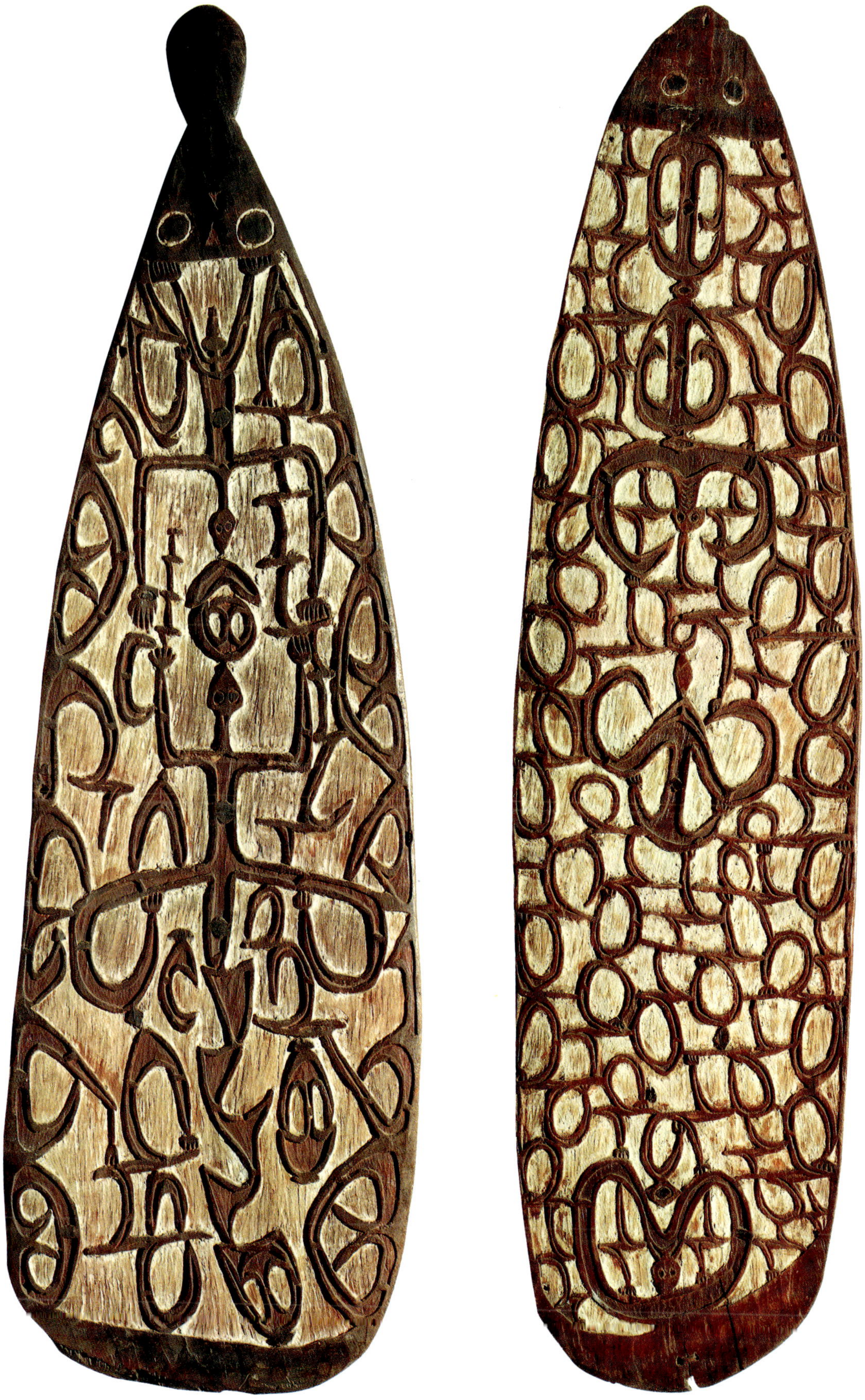

B. Group of shields II
Northwest Asmat
Collected: 1953

Three of the four shields in this group (Plates 7.8–7.11) were collected by the business man C.C. Verhey van Wijk, and one by the civil servant J.J. Spijker, at that time Resident of South New Guinea.

These shields not only were collected at a considerably later date than those of Group I, they are also less old and almost certainly made with metal tools. The motifs are carved deeper, and the contours are more distinct. Not having been lacquered, the colors are still bright.

Although less old than those of Group I, these are rare shields, and their high artistic quality is immediately apparent. The motifs are often animal figures, particularly the flying fox and certain birds. The shields in this group also display the C-shaped shell nose ornament (*bipanew*) motif, a headhunting symbol. On several shields the dominant motifs are rendered in a quite dramatic style and scale.

Like the shields in Group I, these show the typical style characteristics of the Northwest Asmat region. Compared to Group I, they also appear to have a number of special characteristics: 1) a small extension at the top of the shield, (in three cases this takes the shape of a small animal head), and 2) a frame or border filled with small, identical motifs.

Like the shields in Group I and Northwest Asmat shields generally, these shields are rather small, ranging from 130 centimeters to 142 centimeters in height.

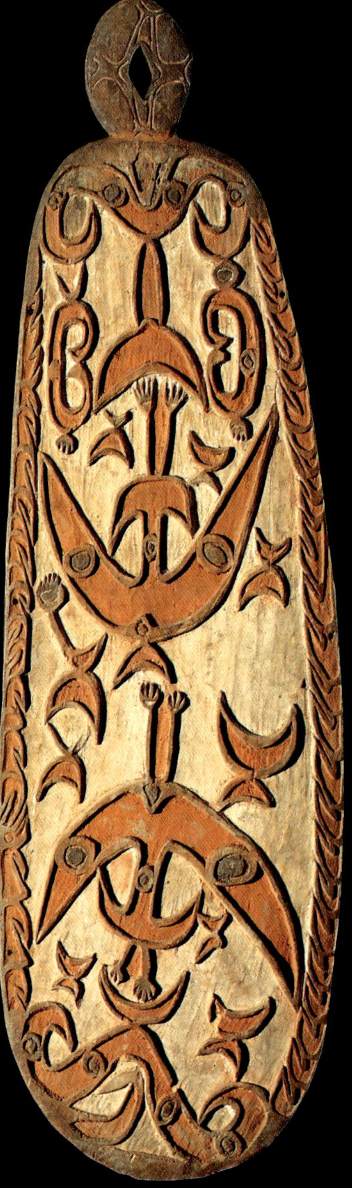

Plate 7.8 Shield. Komor village, Unir River (formerly Lorentz), Northwest Asmat. Wood, lime, red ocher, charcoal. 142 cm. Collected in 1953 by C.C. Verhey van Wijk. RMV 3070-255. Photograph: Isaäc C. Brussee.

On the back of this shield the collector has written: "Amor Jö Jemanmarapis." "Amor" is Komor, a village on the Unir River; Jö is an older spelling of *jeu* or men's house. Hence this shield came from Jeu Jemanmarapis in Komor village.

The large motifs in the center depict bird figures. The two vertical C-shaped motifs in the top part represent the shell nose ornament (*bipanew*), a headhunting symbol.

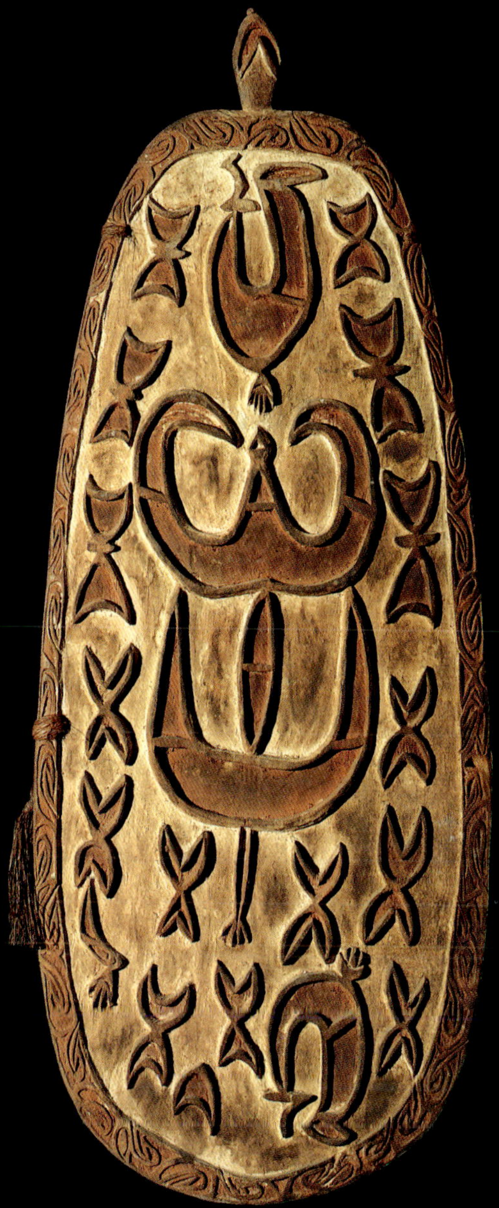

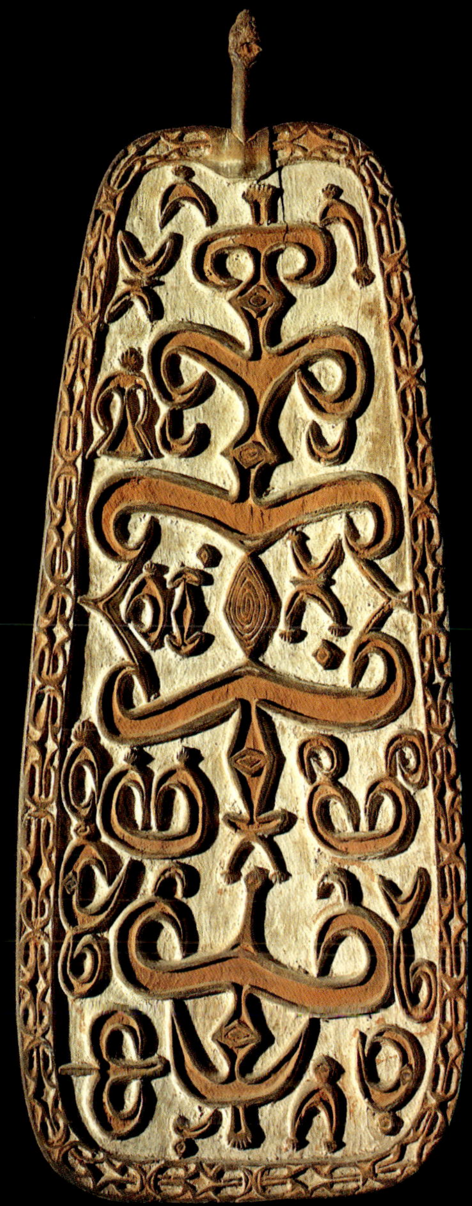

Plate 7.9 Shield. Collected in the vicinity of Sawa-Erma on the Pomatsj River (formerly Northwest), Northwest Asmat. Wood, lime, red ocher, charcoal. 139 cm. Collected in 1953 by C.C. Verhey van Wijk. RMV 3070-253. Photograph: Isaäc C. Brussee.
On the back of this shield the collector has written: "K. Potsi Jö Amominan Voepamok." This doubtless refers to the name of the *jeu* (spelled "jö") where the shield was obtained. On the front is written: "Fatsjep Basep."

The central motif is a flying fox (*tar*). The hourglass shape is a nose ornament of pig bone (*maka*), a symbol of the successful head-hunter. The rather abstract animal head protruding from the top of the shield is possibly a tortoise.

Plate 7.10 Shield. Sawa-Erma, Pomatsj River (formerly Northwest), Northwest Asmat. Wood, lime, red ocher, charcoal. 134 cm. Collected in 1953 by C.C. Verhey van Wijk. RMV 3070-248. Photograph: Isaäc C. Brussee.

The dominant motifs are flying fox figures (*tar*).

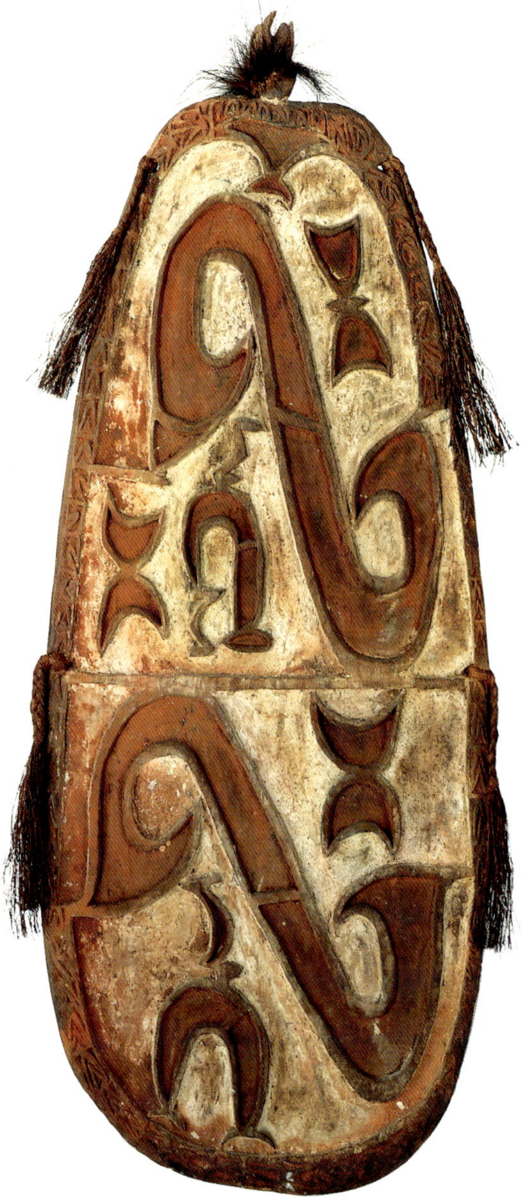

Plate 7.11 (Above) Shield. Presumably Komor village, on the Unir River (formerly Lorentz) or Sawa-Erma, on the Pomatsj River (formerly Northwest), Northwest Asmat. Wood, lime, red ocher, charcoal. 130 cm. Collected in 1953 by C.C. Verhey van Wijk. RMV 3070-234. Photograph: Ben Grishaaver.

On the back of this shield the collector has written: "K. Poto Jö Amominan Waout." The item was thus acquired at Jeu Amominan Waout. The large S-shaped motifs symbolize the human figure.

C. Group of shields III

Northwest Asmat

Collected: circa 1913, 1953–1959 and 1970

Of the six shields in this group (Plates 7.12–7.17), four were collected in the 1950s, three by the civil servant J.J. Spijker and one by the governmental physician W.M. Visser.

These four display the typical characteristics of shields from the Northwest Asmat region. They differ from the Group I and Group II shields, however, in the large rounded "head" or stingray motif at the top, and in their greater than average size for Northwest shields, in this case ranging from 167 centimeters to 192 centimeters.

Included in this group is a fifth shield (Plate 7.12) that was collected around 1913 through the Society for the Promotion of Natural History Research in the Dutch Colonies (Maatschappij ter Bevordering van het Natuurkundig Onderzoek der Nederlandsche Koloniën). Due to the recorded origin "Northwest Asmat" and the shield's large size it has been included in this group. However, this shield is an example of a unique style group within Northwest Asmat art. Most striking is the way it is divided into vertical strokes across almost the entire height of the shield.

Also quite unusual is the shield represented in Plate 7.17, with a very striking, wavy design the artist has called a cassowary quill motif. The design seems to be unique to Manep village. This piece was collected in 1970 by Jac. Hoogerbrugge.

Plate 7.12 (Opposite, left) Shield. Unir River (formerly Lorentz), Northwest Asmat. Wood, lime, red ocher, charcoal. 192 cm. Collected c. 1913 by the Maatschappij ter Bevordering van het Natuurkundig Onderzoek der Nederlandsche Koloniën. RMV 1854-446. Photograph: Isaäc C. Brussee.

The two vertical bars which run across almost the total length of this remarkable shield probably represent the raised arms and the legs of a human figure. Small circular shapes positioned in these straight bars could then be taken to represent elbow and knee joints. The distinctive, stylized motif in the center—two large circles and the arrow—could represent testicles and a penis, or it could be a variation on the flying fox (*tar*) in which the wings have been reduced to circles. An interesting small human figure has been carved into the rim on the left of the shield.

Illustrated: Fischer 1923, Taf. XXI, Fig. 823.

Plate 7.13 (Opposite, right) Shield. Jipajer village, Unir River (formerly Lorentz), Northwest Asmat. Wood, lime, red ocher, charcoal. 167 cm. Collected in 1954 by J.J. Spijker. RMV 3070-494. Photograph: Isaäc C. Brussee.

The two large, pretzel-like, motifs are flying fox (*tar*) figures. The round head at the top is the stingray (*puru*).

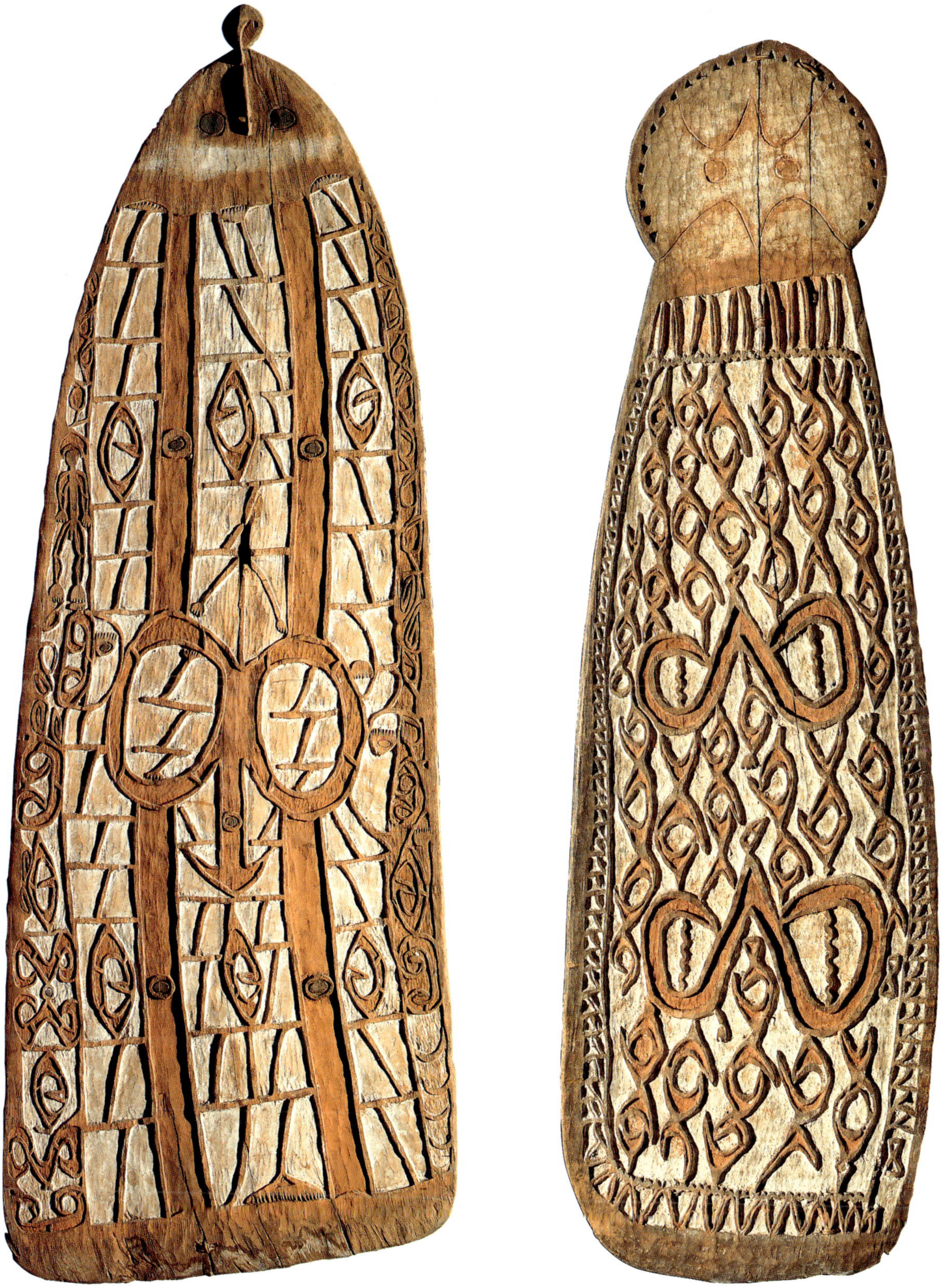

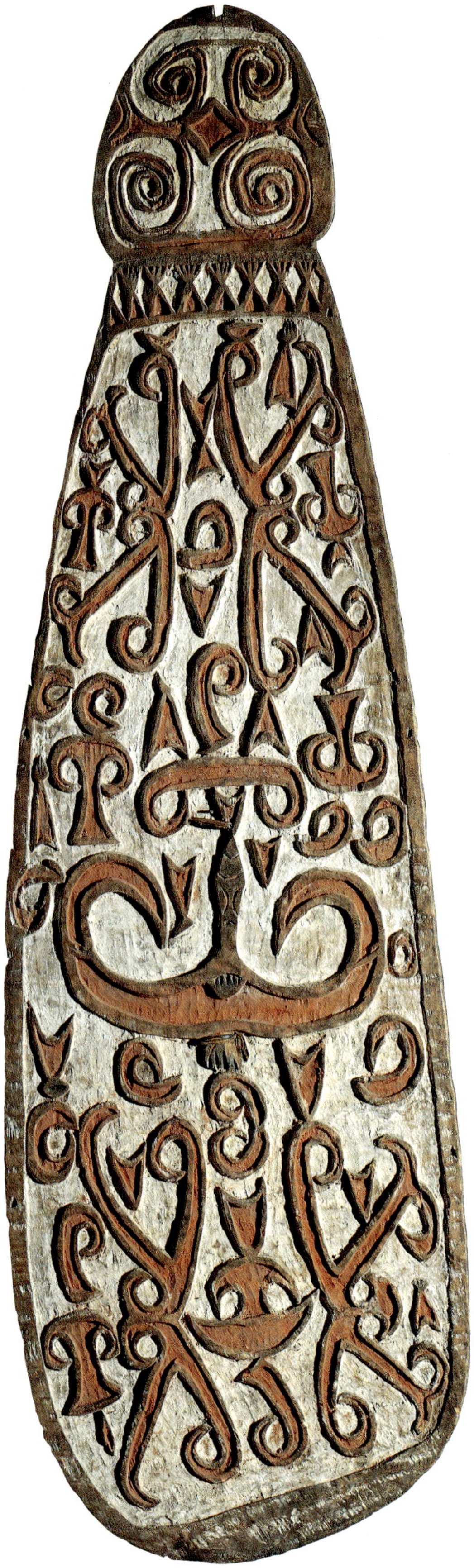

Plate 7.14 (left) Shield. Bu village, upper River Pomatsj (formerly River Northwest), Northwest Asmat. Wood, lime, red ocher, charcoal. 170 cm. Collected c. 1954 during a tour of duty by the Resident at the time J.J. Spijker. RMV 3530-9. Photograph: Isaäc C. Brussee.

The dominant motif (a little below the center) presumably represents a flying fox (*tar*).

Exhibited: "Melanesien, Schwarze Inseln der Südsee" (Eine Ausstellung des Rautenstrauch-Joest-Museums für Völkerkunde der Stadt Köln), Kunsthalle, Köln 1971, Cat. 295. (See: Stöhr 1971:135).

Plate 7.15 (opposite, left) Shield. Owus village, Central Asmat. Wood, lime, red ocher, charcoal. 192 cm. Collected in 1953 by J.J. Spijker. RMV 3070-247. Photograph: Ben Grishaaver.

Although collected in the Central Asmat area, this shield stylistically is associated with the Northwest Asmat area. The three dominant motifs represent flying foxes (*tar*).

Illustrated: Gerbrands 1990, pl. 12, p. 68.

Plate 7.16 (opposite, right) Shield. Navarpi village, Northwest Asmat. Wood, lime, red ocher, charcoal. 184 cm. Collected c. 1959. RMV B 116-2.

The larger motifs on this shield represent flying fox figures. The round head at the top is the stingray (*puru*). Photograph: Ben Grishaaver.

Exhibited: "Papoea-kunst in het Rijksmuseum/ Papuan Art in the Rijksmuseum," Rijksmuseum, Amsterdam 1966. (See: Kooijman 1966:95)

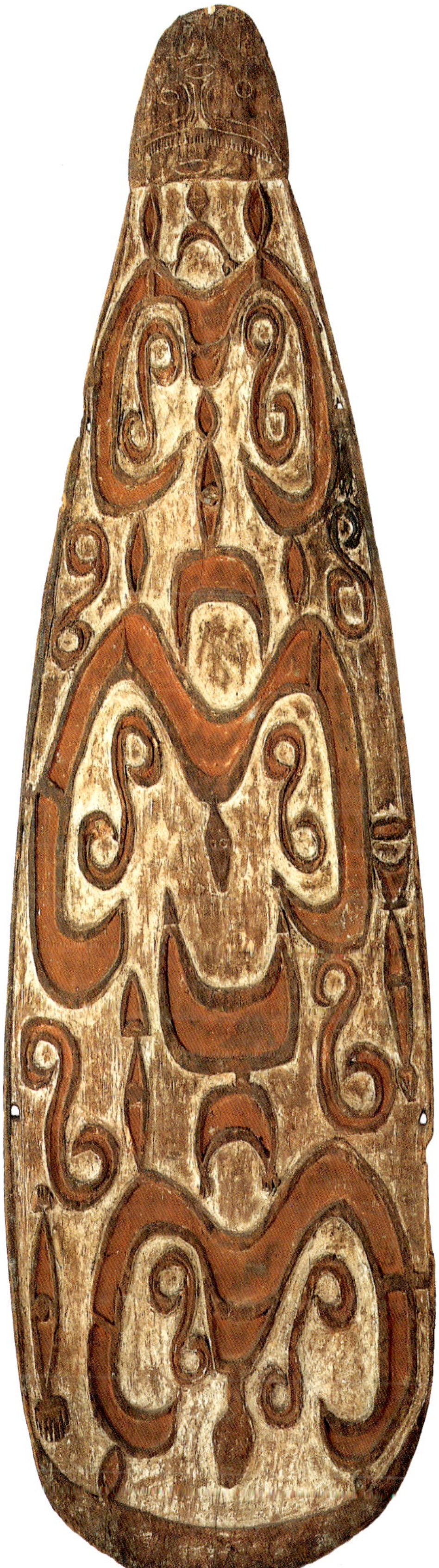

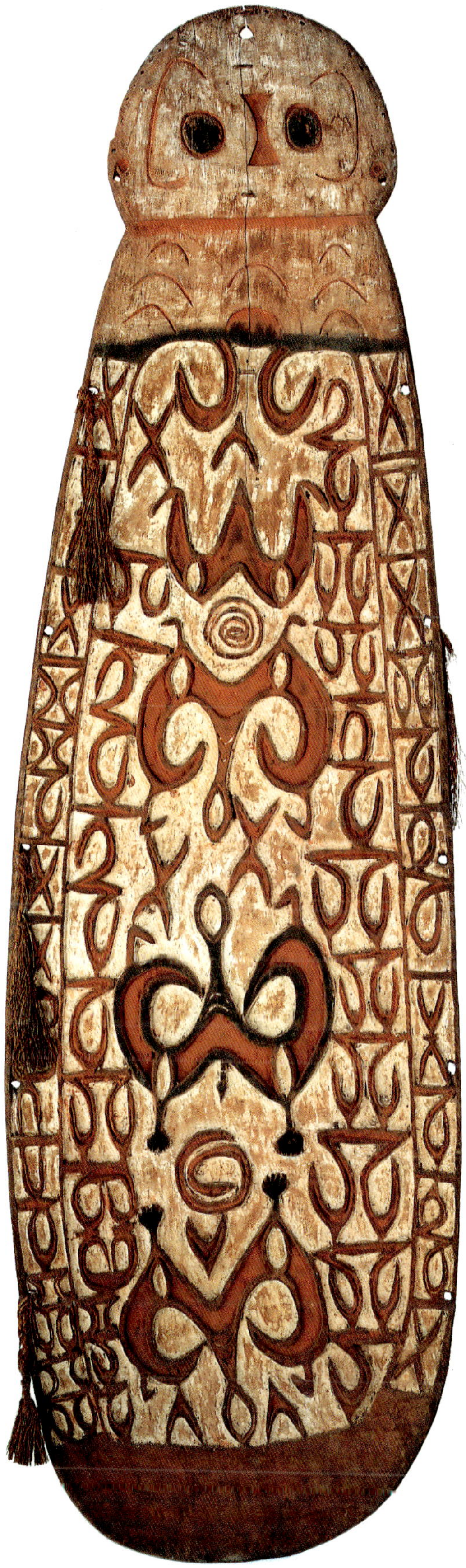

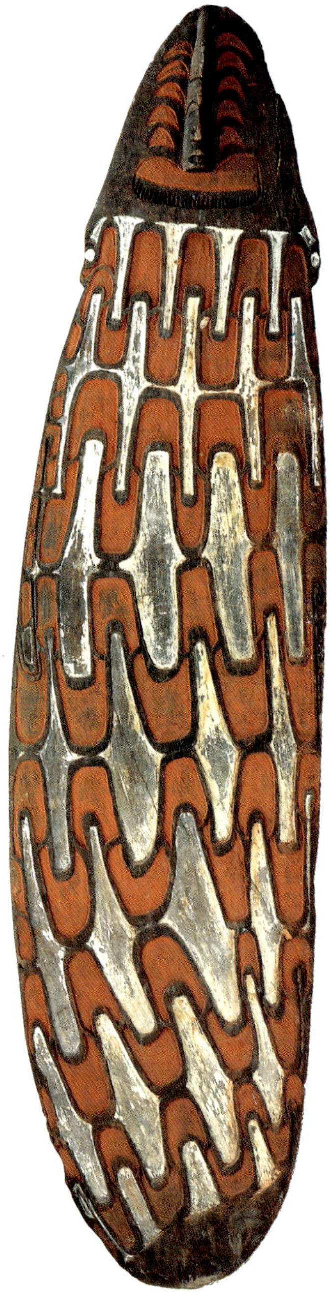

Plate 7.17 Shield. Carved by Ndaji. Manep village, Upper Unir River (formerly Lorentz) and Utumbuwe River area, Northwest Asmat. Wood, lime, red ocher, charcoal. Collected in 1970 by Jac. Hoogerbrugge. 182 cm. RMV 4455-1. Photograph: Ben Grishaaver.

Ndaji, a carver from the nomadic village of Manep, calls the unusual flowing pattern on this shield "pifa." The collector, Jac. Hoogerbrugge, has commented: "*Pifa* is daily used as the word for cassowary feather quill. It is not clear to me how the wave pattern on this shield could be called *pifa*. It is my impression that this ornament is typical for Manep and environs because I have not come across it anywhere else." (Personal communication from J. Hoogerbrugge to Dr. S. Kooijman, d.d. 24.9.1970).

D. Group of shields IV

Central Asmat
Collected: 1953 and 1961

Of the seven shields in this group (Plates 7.18–7.24) five were collected in the years 1953–1954: three by the civil servant J.J. Spijker, one by the governmental physician W.M. Visser, and one by a Chinese crocodile hunter whose name was not recorded. One shield was collected by Adrian A. Gerbrands in 1961 during his research on the individuality of woodcarvers in the village of Amanamkai.

Four shields show the typical style characteristics of the Central Asmat region (Plates 7.21, 7.22, 7.23, 7.24). These are, briefly: long and rectangular with a thin extension at the top and large, abstract motifs that are "mirrored" along a vertical axis.

Three of the shields shown here are somewhat anomalous. Plate 7.18 has a somewhat unusual shape, with a pointed top. The very striking shield in Plate 7.19 looks almost Citak. Plate 7.20, a shield that originates from a Central Asmat village near the imaginary border with the Northwest Asmat region, displays characteristics of both the Northwest and Central style regions. The height of these shields varies from 166 centimeters to 194 centimeters.

Plate 7.18 (opposite, left) Shield. Jufri village, Lower Unir River (formerly Lorentz), on the border region between Northwest Asmat and Central Asmat. Wood, lime, red ocher, charcoal. 188 cm. On the left side a traditional repair has been carried out with rattan stitches. Collected in 1954 by J.J. Spijker. RMV 3070-500. Photograph by Ben Grishaaver.

Plate 7.19 (opposite, right) Shield. Owus village, near the mouth of the Siretsj River, Central Asmat. Wood, lime, red ocher, charcoal, sago leaf fiber. A crack at the top end was repaired in traditional fashion with rattan. 205 cm. Collected in 1953 by J.J. Spijker. RMV 3070-250. Photograph: Ben Grishaaver.

This extraordinary shield with its strongly flowing pattern appears to stand apart. It was collected in Owus village, but this should not be taken as its place of origin. Like other Central Asmat shields, the motifs on this piece are rendered in broad strokes. However, the designs of most Central Asmat shields are "controlled," even rigid in some cases, and the motifs are presented as separate, interlocking units, quite unlike the shield shown here. In fact, the energetic design of this shield, as well as its overall shape, are somewhat reminiscent of Citak shields (see pages 87–89).

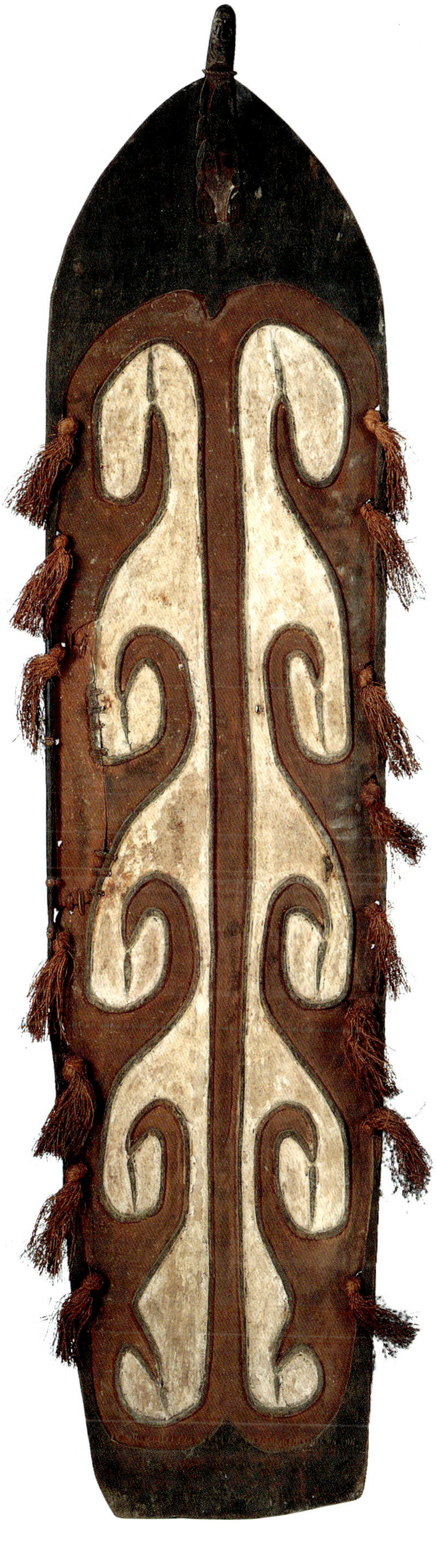

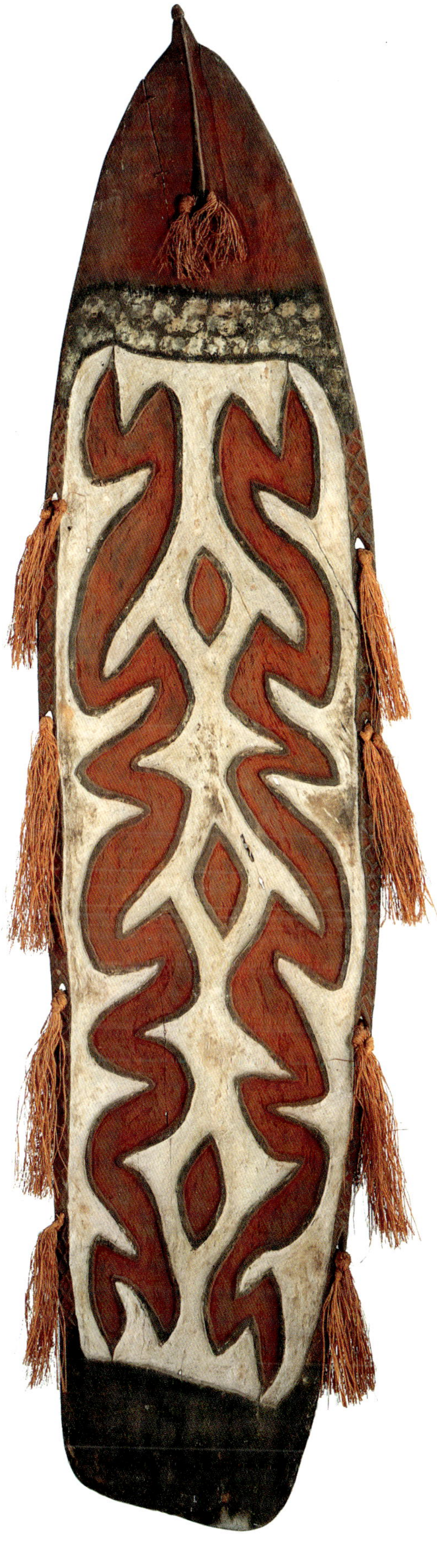

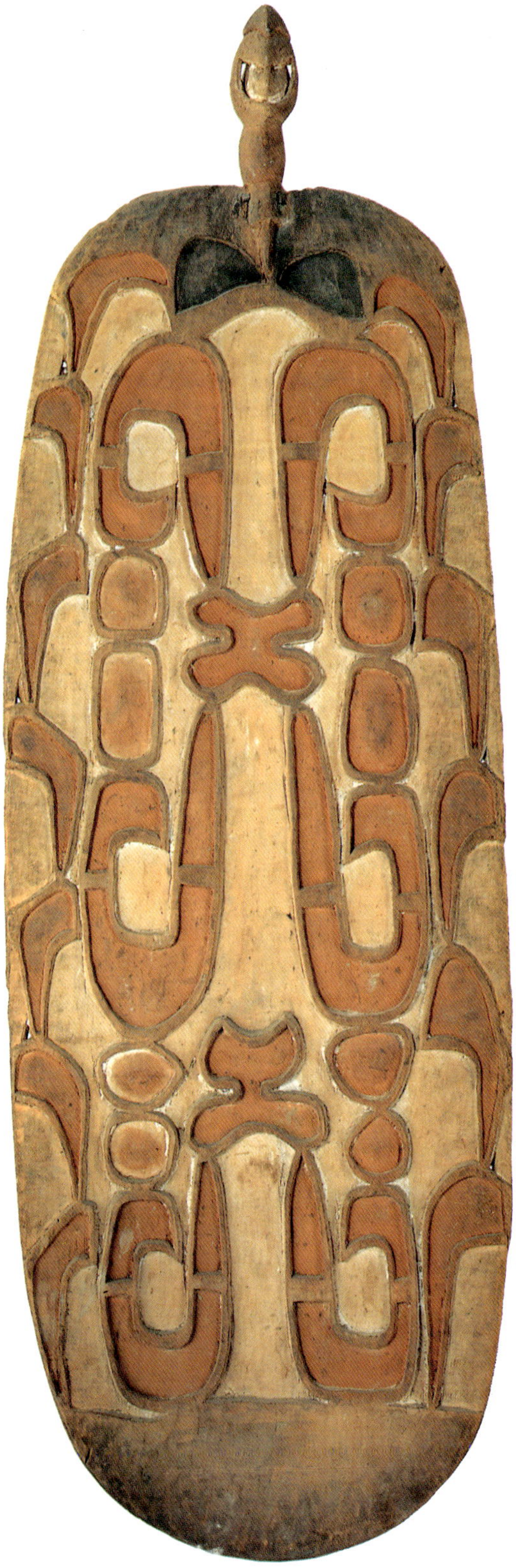

Plate 7.20 (left) Shield. Presumably vicinity Betjew village, Central Asmat. Wood, lime, red ocher, charcoal. 184 cm. Collected c. 1953 by an unknown crocodile hunter. RMV 3070-79. Photograph: Ben Grishaaver.

This shield stands midway between the style of the Central Asmat region and that of the Northwest Asmat region: the large motifs remind one of those of a typical Central Asmat shield; the further filling of the plane with smaller motifs, on the other hand, is a typical characteristic of Northwest shields.

Plate 7.21 (opposite, left) Shield. Basim village, Fajit river, Casuarina Coast, Central Asmat. Wood, lime, red ocher, charcoal, sago leaf fiber. 166 cm. Collected in 1961 by Adrian A. Gerbrands in Amanamkai village. RMV 3790-515. Photograph: Ben Grishaaver.

This characteristic Casuarina coast shield from Basim was acquired in Amanamkai, about 30 kilometers north of Basim. It was presumably taken from the people of Basim.

The lower half of the shield shows two mirror-image pairs of S-shaped motifs called *eu wow* (*eu* means crocodile; *wow* means woodcarving). The S-shape refers to a line along which the belly of a crocodile—or the belly of a head-hunting victim—was cut open. This line encloses, as it were, the soft parts of the abdomen.

Plate 7.22 (opposite, right) Shield. Casuarina Coast, Central Asmat. Wood, lime, red ocher, charcoal, sago leaf fiber. 181.5 cm. Collected c. 1958. RMV B 109-3. Photograph: Ben Grishaaver.

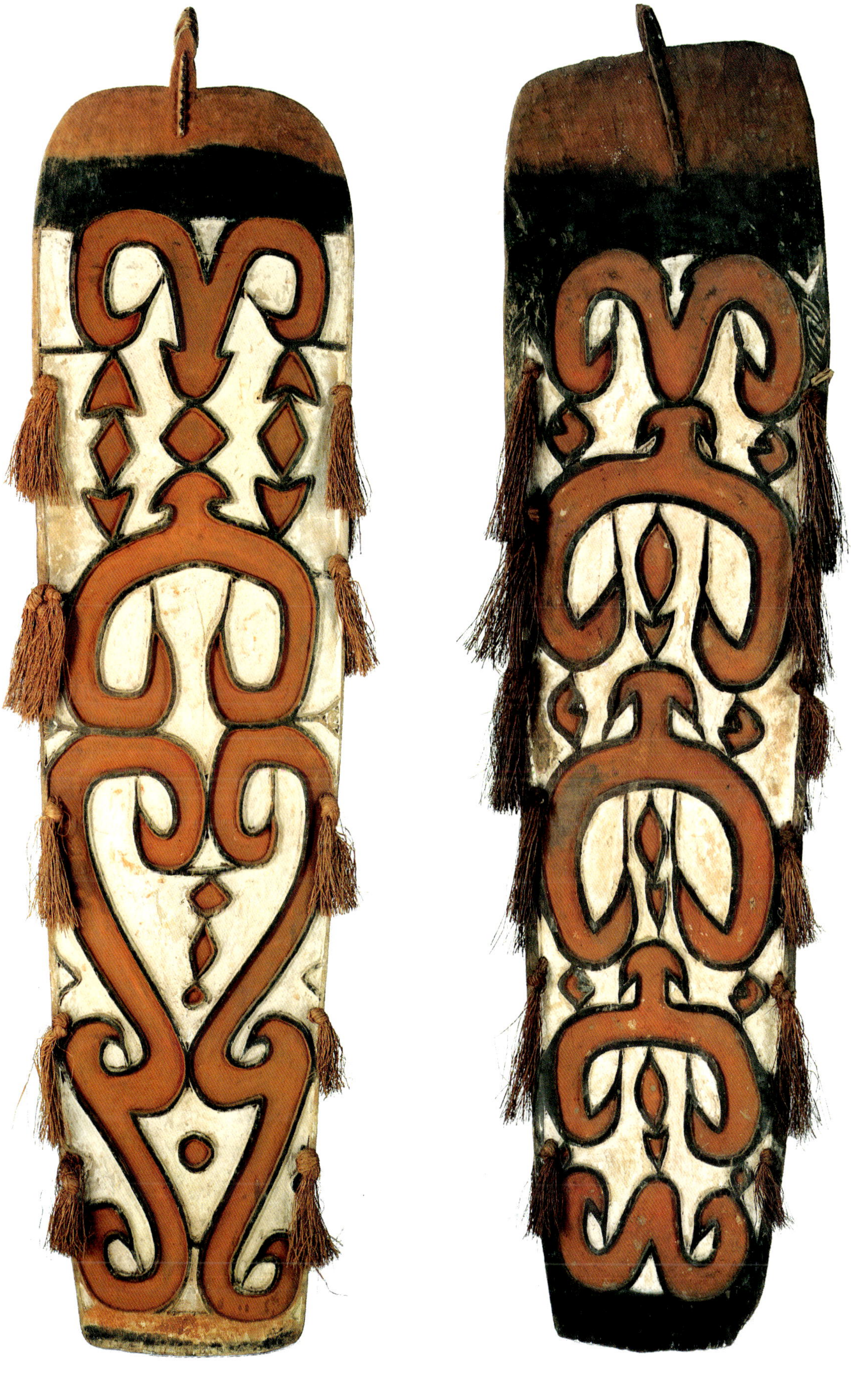

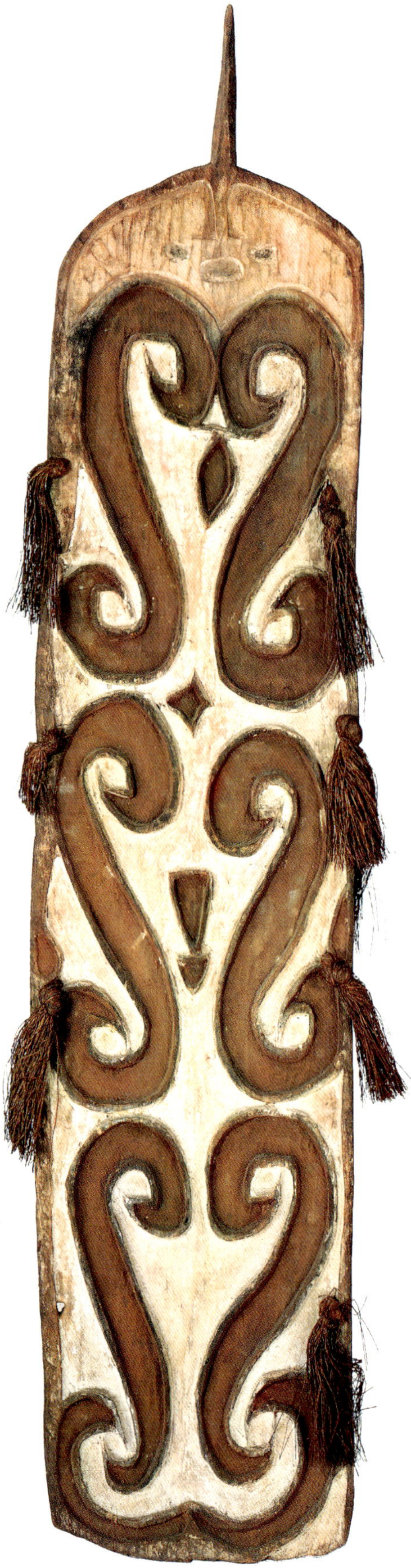

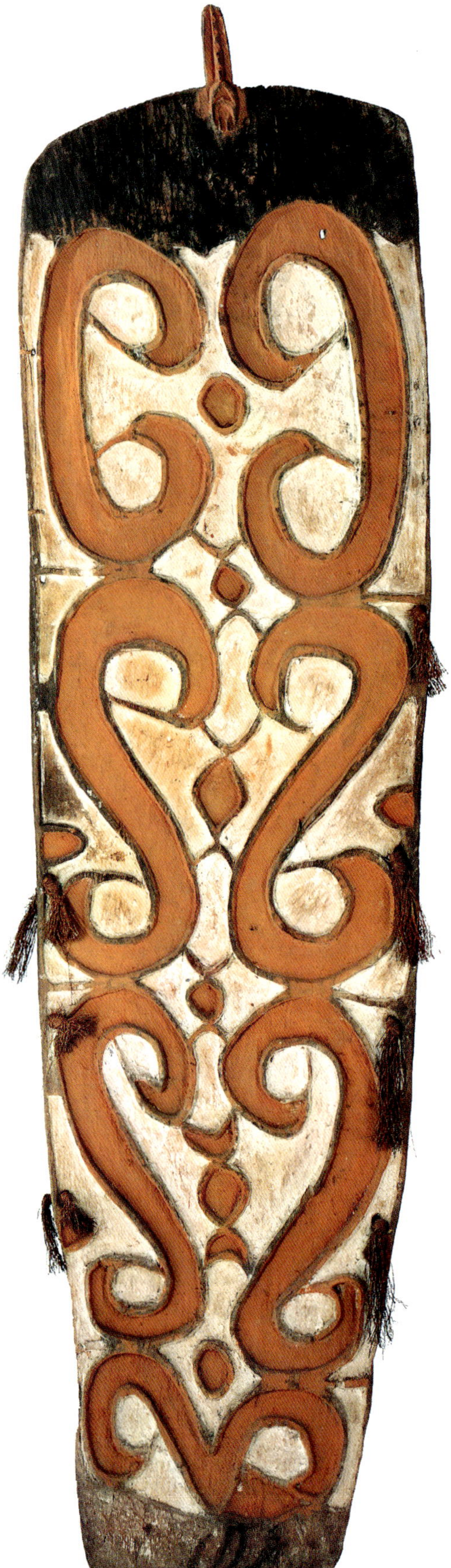

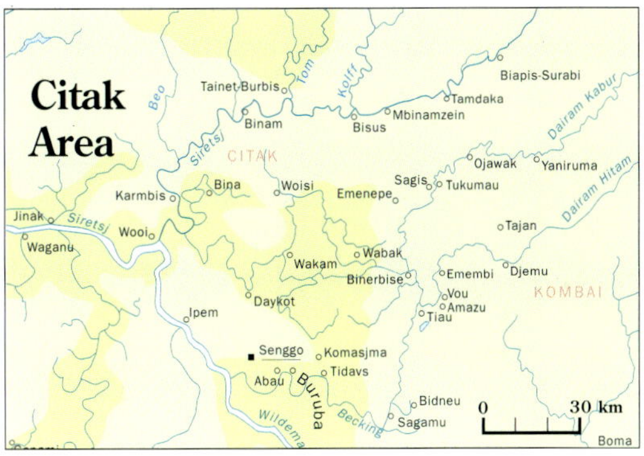

Figure 7.1 (above) Map of the Citak region

Plate 7.23 (opposite, left) Shield. Kaimo village, Siretsj River (formerly Eilanden). Wood, lime, ocher, charcoal. 187cm. Collected by J.J. Spijker in 1953. RMV 3070-252. Photograph: Ben Grishaaver.

Each of the three pairs of reversed, S-shaped motifs represents an ancestor. The S-shaped motif itself is the line along which the body of a head-hunted enemy was cut open—the navel to the hip-bone, and then back, beneath the ribs, to the sternum and finally ending at the nipple.

Illustrated: Gerbrands 1990, fig. 12, p. 67.

Plate 7.24 (opposite, right) Shield. Casuarina Coast, Central Asmat. Wood, lime, red ocher, charcoal, sago leaf fiber. 194 cm. Collected c.1958. RMV B109-2. Photograph: Ben Grishaaver.

Both of the C-shaped motifs at the top represent the shell nose ornament (*bipanew*), a status and a head-hunting symbol. Each mirror pair of S-shaped motifs represents an ancestor.

E. Group of Shields V

Citak

Collected: circa 1954

The area of the Citak—pronounced "Chee' täk," and sometimes spelled according to the old convention, "Tjitak"—is located east of the Central Asmat area (See map at left). It includes the Lower Wildeman, the Upper Siretsj and the Becking Rivers. The latter splits off in two upstream arms: the Dairam Kabur and the Dairam Hitam.

Because of the relative isolation of the area, Citak shields were first collected at a much later date than shields from Northwest and Central Asmat, and in lesser numbers. The major collections of Citak shields are in museums in the Netherlands, and in the Konrad Collection at the Museum of Ethnology of the Portheim Foundation in Heidelberg, the latter having been collected in the last few decades.

Although many Citak shields are great works of art, showing an inimitable sense of graphic design, the same culture has not produced any sculptural work, in contrast to the Asmat of the Northwest and Central regions.

"As Kooijman (1956) has tentatively suggested in regard to the heavy, leaf-shaped shields of the Awyu area (Digul River), the absence of recognizable elements of the human body (which do occur on shields in the Central Asmat area) may relate to the fact that the makers of these 'abstract' shields had no sculptural tradition (Citak and Awyu human figures are unknown), and therefore no frame of reference enabling them to include human figures or components, such as arms and legs, in their repertoire of shield motifs." (Smidt 1990:334, after Kooijman 1956).

Citak shields with recognizable human elements (even with a full-standing human figure) do occur however, although the ones with geometrical, "abstract" designs are much more typical. Some of the shields with anthropomorphic elements may reflect a comparatively recent stylistic innovation.

Typical characteristics of Citak shields are: 1) an overall "bullet" shape; 2) great height, averaging almost two meters; and 3) thinness, which makes them light and easy to maneuver with in the bush. The depth of carving is not as great as it is on Central Asmat shields. The frequent interruption of the overall pattern by small white blocks or "bridges" is another stylistic trait of Citak shields. (See also Chapter 5.)

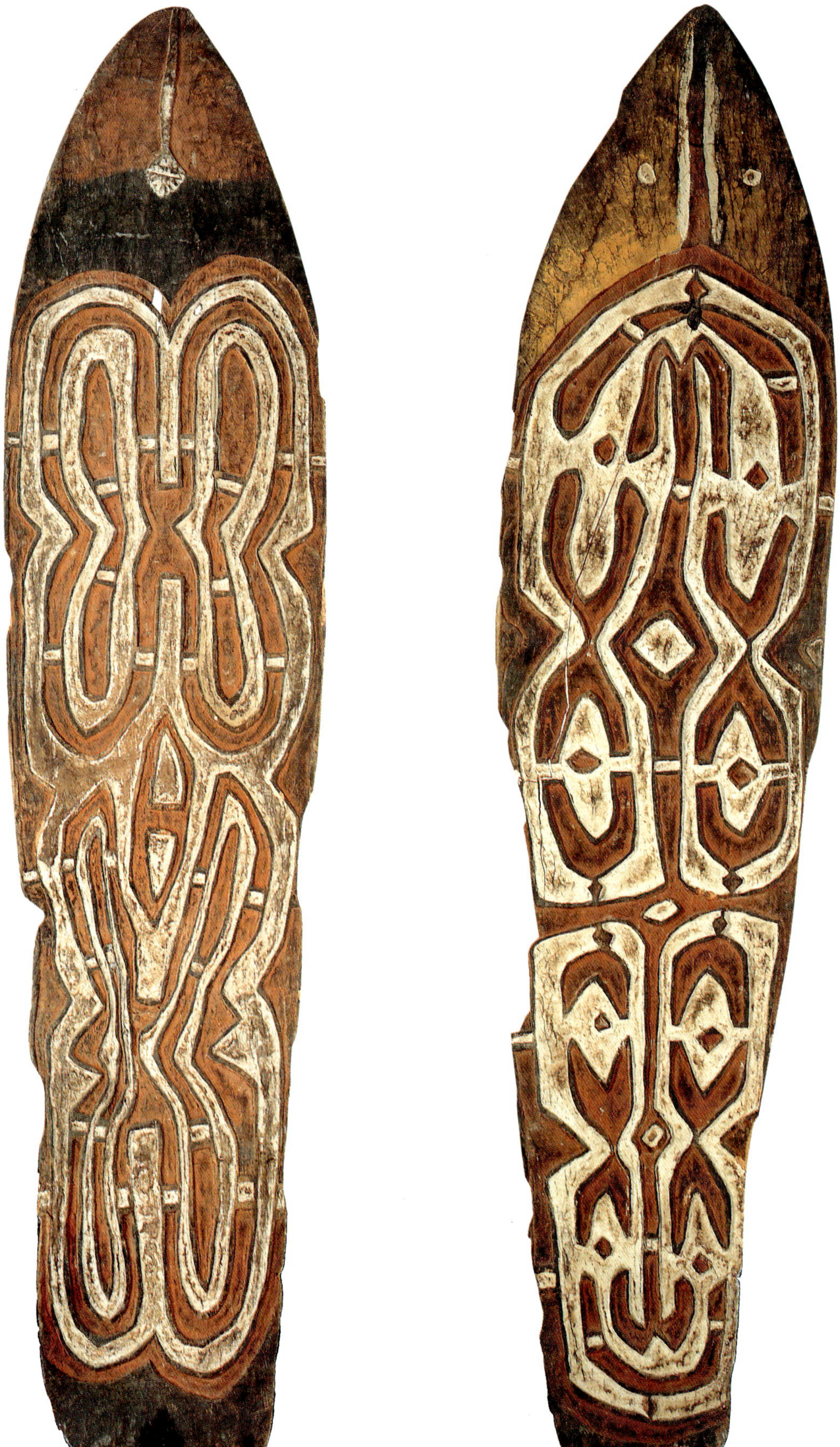

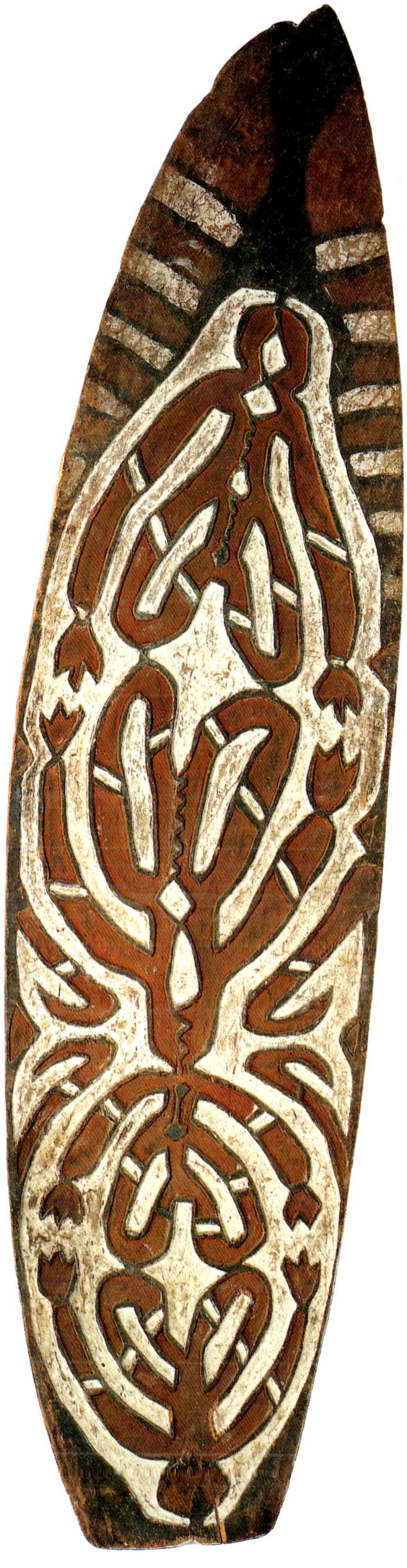

Plate 7.25 (opposite, left) Shield. Koremeku village, Wildeman River, Citak. Wood, lime, red ocher, charcoal. Some damage along the edges. 198.5 cm. Collected c. 1954 by J.J. Spijker. RMV 3530-7. Photograph: Ben Grishaaver.

The pattern on this shield consists chiefly of two "double eight" figures, each of which appears as a self contained unit. The lower part of this shield is rather corrugated.

Plate 7.26 (opoposite right) Shield. Woméni village, Suwa River, Citak. Wood, lime, red and yellow ocher, charcoal. Damaged along the edges. 195 cm. Collected c. 1954 by J.J. Spijker. RMV 3530-3. Photograph: Ben Grishaaver.

The meaning of the motifs on this shield is not known. They seem vaguely anthropomorphic, in which case the diamond shape that occurs a few times along the vertical axis might be interpreted as the navel.

Plate 7.27 (right) Shield. Woméni village, Suwa River, Citak. Wood, chalk, red ochre, charcoal. 191.5 cm. Collected c. 1954 by J. J. Spijker. RMV 3530-1. Photograph: Ben Grishaaver.

The ornamentation on this shield is unusual as it shows more readily recognizable anthropomorphic elements than most other Citak shields do. By and large Citak shields are characterized by a surface decoration of geometrical, abstract, motifs. The scene on this shield appears to represent two mirror-image pairs of anthropomorphic half-figures. The upper half of the lower pair seems to include a penis carved in relief.

II. Figure sculptures

By A.F.M. Tigges

Few references to the use of ancestor figures with the Asmat are found in specialist literature. It is well known that keeping alive the memory of the ancestors completely dominates the spiritual life of the Asmat. Every crafted object—a shield, an oar or even something small like a decorated neck pouch—carries an ancestor's name. In the days before head-hunting ended, one of the chief goals of this was to constantly prick the warrior's memory: This death must be avenged. *Bisj* poles and the dominant motifs on shields are known to serve this function, too. Gerard A. Zegwaard considers it quite likely that the free-standing ancestor figures served the same function. (Zegwaard, personal communication, 1983.)

Professor Adrian A. Gerbrands notes that for a carver to identify a specific statue as one of his ancestors implies that that ancestor has yet to be avenged. This is quite a responsibility, which is why he found owners of statues sometimes reluctant to state the name of the statues.

Gerbrands and René S. Wassing suggested that figures such as those illustrated below played a role in the *jeu pokmbu,* the consecration feast for a new *jeu* or men's house. In this celebration the myth of Fumeripitsj, the Asmat creator, is symbolically re-enacted.

Fumeripitsj created the first humans by animating carvings. The knees and elbows of the carvings were linked, and they could not stand until Fumeripitsj had beat a drum. As Gerbrands has noted, the Asmat come into the world and leave the world in the elbows-to-knees position, so it seems logical that this position should be associated with creation.

It is not clear if the figures were used only once or during more than one feast. Wassing stated he had seen such figures rolled up in mats and kept in the men's house. The late Irianese anthropologist Arnold Ap and Tobias Schneebaum suggest that the carvings are temporary, and provide fertility to the sago fields:

"[M]any carvings, particularly ancestral figures, were made for ceremonial occasions, after which they were broken up and placed within the fields of sago in the swamps so that the spirits therein might nourish and protect the trees." (Schneebaum 1983:13.)

Note: These comments are based on research conducted by A.F.M. Tigges in 1983, published in Tigges 1985b.

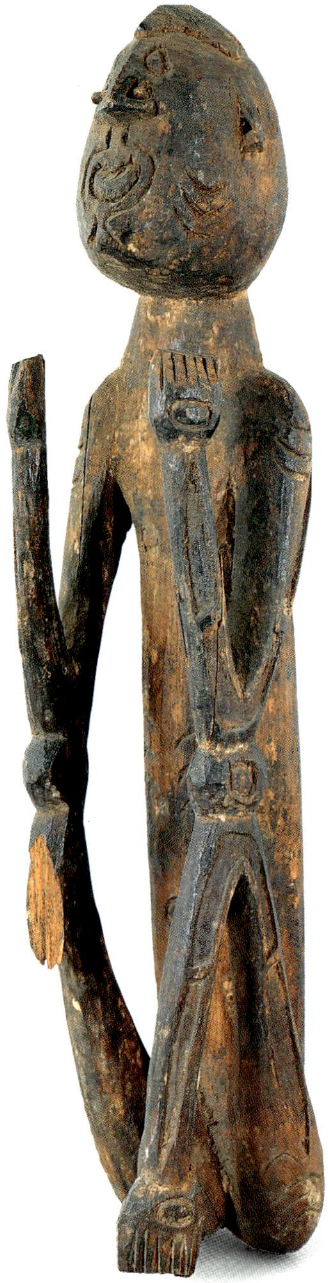

Plate 7.28 Statue of a man. Pomatsj River (formerly Northwest), Northwest Asmat. Wood. Presumably this sculpture was originally colored with lime, red ocher and charcoal. A layer of lacquer was applied after acquisition, giving the figure a dirty brown color. 63.5 cm. Collected in 1908 or 1913 by A.J. Gooszen. Donated by Gooszen in 1919. RMV 1971-986. Photograph: Ben Grishaaver.

The characteristic squatting position with the arms held high comes from the Asmat myth of creation. The first people were wooden statues, with their elbows and knees connected. The creator Fumeripitsj animated them, after which they stood up. The position of the statue is also reminiscent of the praying mantis, an important head-hunting symbol.

A. Group of Figures I
Northwest Asmat
Collected: 1907–1954

All statues collected before World War II in the collection of the National Museum of Ethnology originate from the Northwest Asmat region. Central Asmat statues were obtained only in the 1950s and 1960s. There is no satisfactory explanation for this discrepancy. Both men and women are depicted in these statues, and women form the majority: 15 of the 25 pre-war statues in the museum's collection are of women.

The five Asmat statues acquired through A.J. Gooszen in 1907–1908 or 1913 belong to the oldest and earliest collected Asmat statues. Four are illustrated here (for the other, see page 139). Three of the "Gooszen statues" depict women; two depict men. Four display the distinctive elbow to knee position, associated with the creation myth of Fumeripitsj. Because of its exceptional esthetic qualities, the sculpture shown in Plate 7.30 was selected for inclusion in *Topstukken uit het Rijksmuseum voor Volkenkunde / Masterpieces from the National Museum of Ethnology* (1987). The statue in Plate 7.34 is unique in the entire scope of Asmat art, and was selected for the exhibition "The Art of the Pacific Islands" at The National Gallery of Art in Washington D.C. in 1979.

Two exceptional statues of women (Plates 7.31 and 7.32) were collected in 1937 by R.R. van Ravenswaay Claasen, while as Chief of Police he traveled together with the civil servant Felix Maturbongs through the Asmat region in search of a place to establish a government post. One of these statues (Plate 7.32) is one of the few Northwest Asmat statues with additional ornamentation in still good condition.

A unique statue of a woman (Plate 7.33), striking among other things because of its large size (more than two meters high) was acquired by the museum in 1940. Nothing is known about the donator, Mr. Sjoers, or about the conditions and date of collecting.

Statues *in coitu* are a rarity in Asmat woodcarving art. They are not found in the earliest collections. A near life-size example (Plates 8.1 and 8.20), collected in 1961 by Adrian A. Gerbrands, is unique. Smaller ones, made in the sixties and seventies to sell, are known from the Central Asmat region (see Kooijman and Hoogerbrugge 1976, Figures 64 and 81). The statue *in coitu* (Plate 7.35) included in the following series is, as far as is known, the only example from an earlier date.

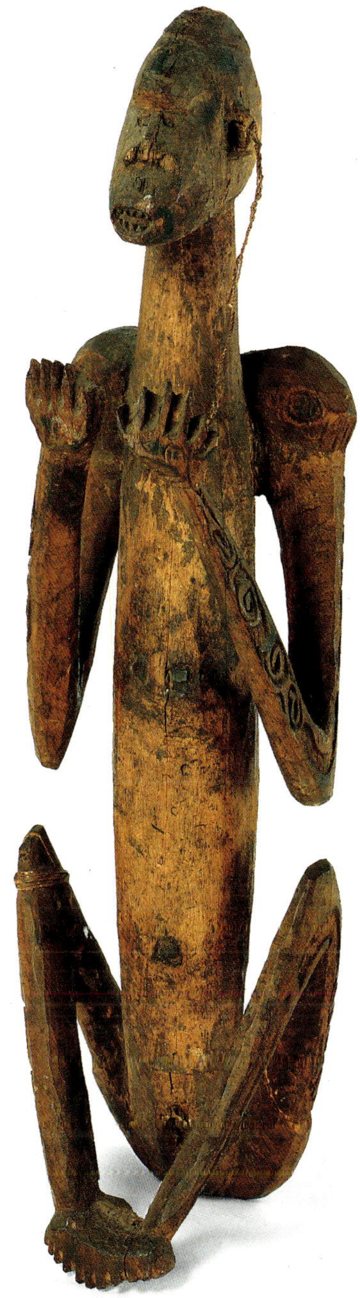

Plate 7.29 Statue of a woman. Unir River (formerly River Lorentz), Northwest Asmat. Wood, sago leaf fiber, rattan. The original colors—presumably from lime, red ocher and charcoal—have faded over time. 102 cm. Collected in 1908 or 1913 by A.J. Gooszen. Donated by Gooszen in 1919. On display in the National Museum of Ethnology's branch in Breda since 1970. RMV 1971-982. Photograph: Ben Grishaaver.

This female figure belongs to the earliest collected and oldest Asmat figures known to exist. The right knee is split and repaired using a rattan bandage. The outside of the arms and legs is ornamented with relief carving that strongly resembles the motifs found on the shields from the same area. See the comments under Plate 7. 28 for the significance of the squatting position.

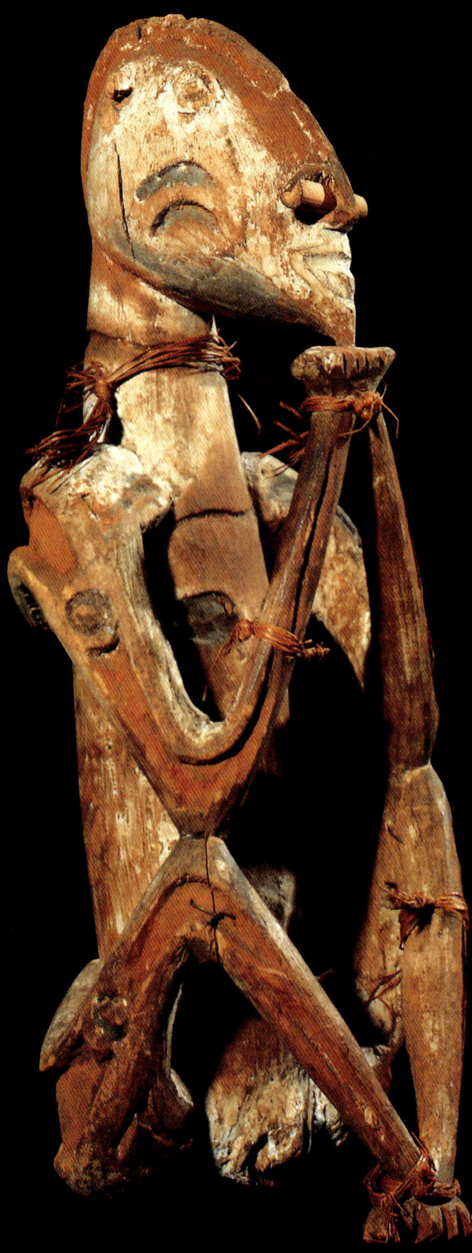

Plate 7.30 (left) Statue of a woman. Pomatsj or Unir River (formerly Northwest and Lorentz respectively), Northwest Asmat. Wood, lime, red ocher, charcoal, sago leaf fiber, bamboo. 40.5 cm. Collected in 1908 or 1913 by A.J. Gooszen. Donated by Gooszen in 1919. RMV 1971-985. Photograph: Isaäc C. Brussee.

This statue is one of the few old Asmat sculptures still existing. Singular are the small size and the shape of the head. The insect-like head, together with the position of the arms and legs, raised associations with the praying mantis, an important head-hunting symbol, and the *ambirak*, a non-human, malicious female creature from Asmat mythology. As a stooped figure the *ambirak* is carved in some soulships or *wuramon* (See also three canoe prows, Plates 7.57, 7.60, and 7.63).

The elbows to knees position is also reminiscent of the Fumeripitsj creation myth. The first people were carved of wood, with elbows and knees attached, and by playing a drum, Fumeripitsj separated their limbs and brought the statues to life. They stood up and started dancing. Today, during the consecration of new *jeu* houses, men initially dance with their elbows against their knees.

Illustrated: Fraser 1962, pl. 101; Gerbrands 1950, fig. 12; Hoogerbrugge (ed.) 1977, fig. 125; Kooijman 1959a, fig. 18; Schlocker 1965, fig. 14; Smidt 1987a, pl. 115.

Plate 7.31 (opposite, left) Statue of a woman. Unir River (formerly Lorentz), Northwest Asmat. Wood, lime, red ocher, charcoal, *Coix* seeds, cassowary quill and feathers. 130 cm. Collected c. 1937, presumably during a tour of duty, by R.R. van Ravenswaay Claasen. RMV 2412-2. Photograph: Ben Grishaaver.

The position of the lower arms and their unusual extensions give this statue a unique quality. The shape is strongly suggestive of a sago pounder, which is used to break up the woody pith of the sago tree prior to washing out the starch.

Illustrated: Kooijman 1961, pl. 19.

Plate 7.32 (opposite, right) Statue of a woman. Reiger River, a tributary of the Unir (formerly Lorentz), Northwest Asmat. Wood, lime, red ocher, charcoal, sago leaf fiber, *Coix* seeds, feathers. 104 cm. Collected c. 1937 during a tour of duty by R.R. van Ravenswaay Claasen. RMV 2412-3. Photograph: Isaäc C. Brussee.

The fiber skirt and the ornamentation of cassowary feathers and *Coix* seeds on this remarkable statue match the traditional attire of an Asmat woman.

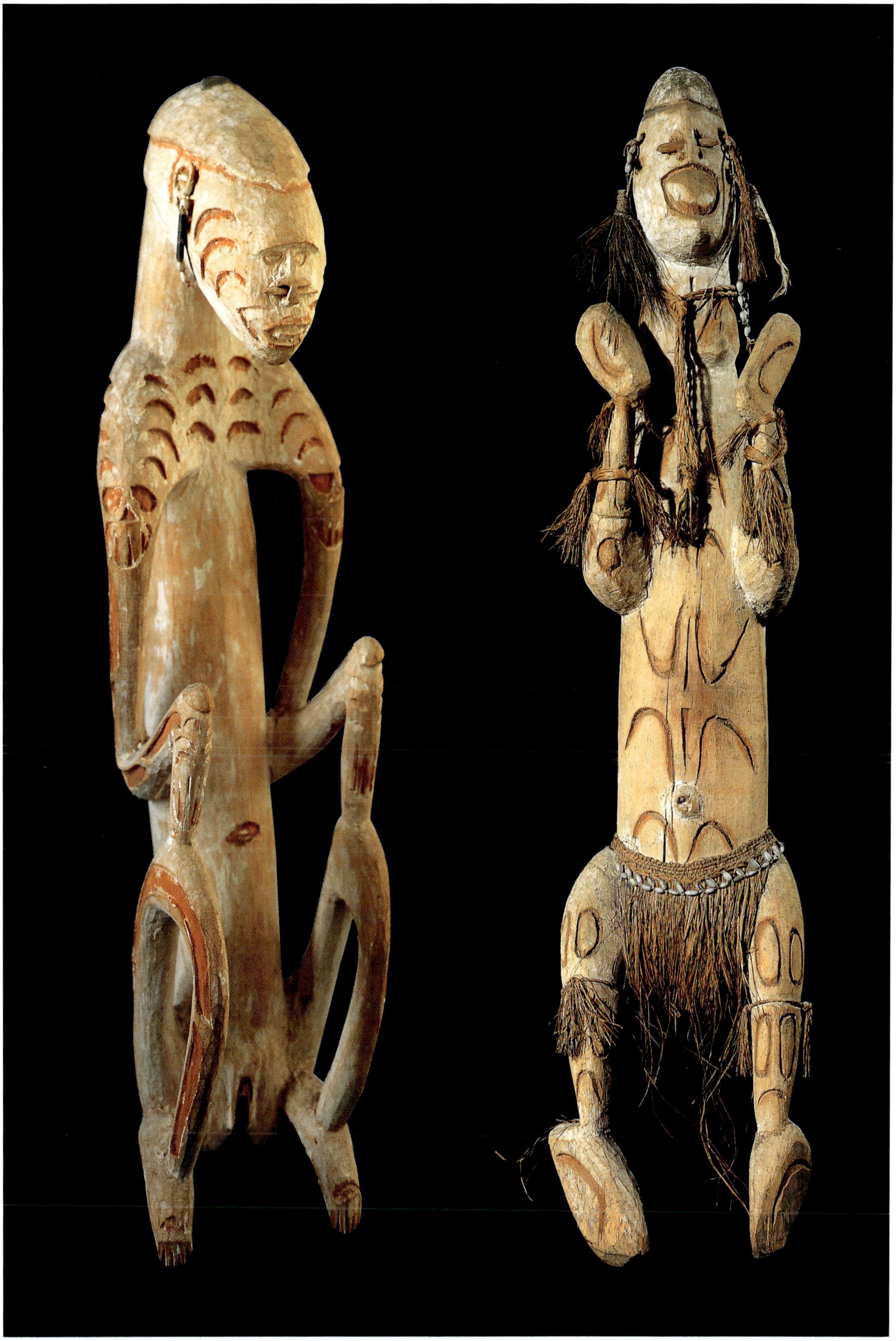

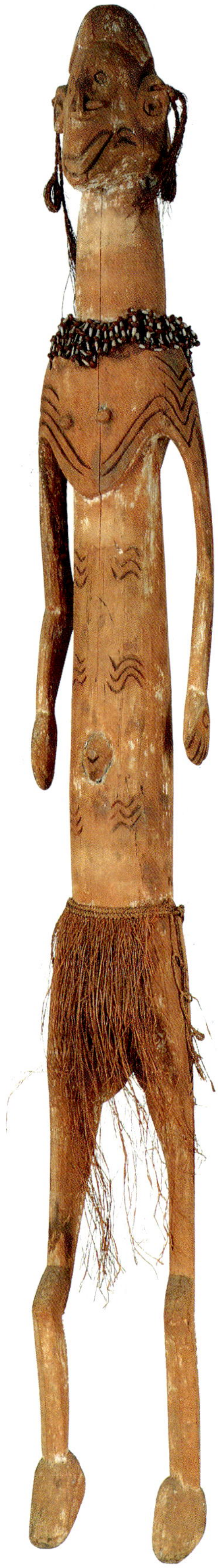

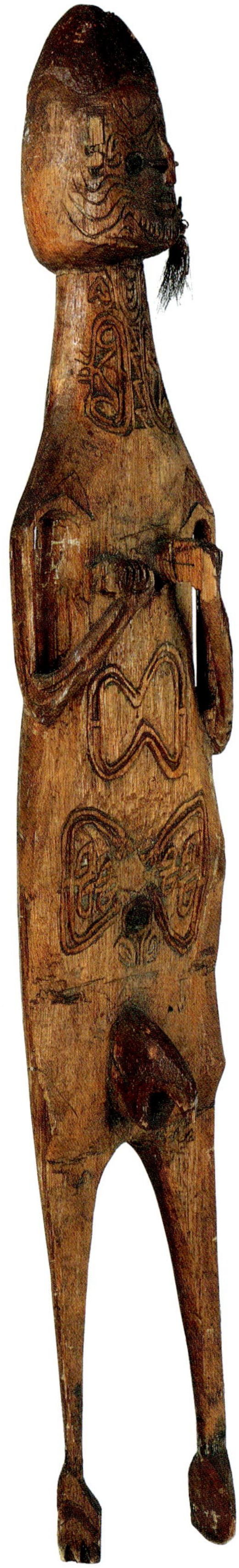

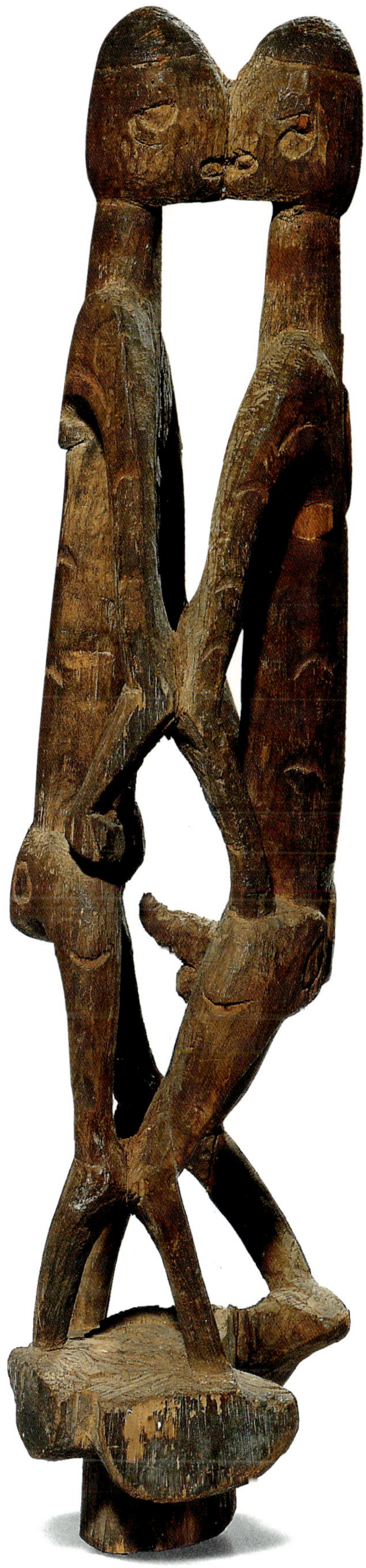

Plate 7.33 (opposite, left) Statue of a woman. Presumably mid Unir River (formerly Lorentz) or Utumbuwe River, border region of Northwest Asmat and Central Asmat. Wood, red ocher, lime, *Coix* and *Abrus* seeds, sago leaf fiber. Date of collecting unknown. Acquired by the museum in 1940. Donated by Mr Sjoers. RMV 2445-32. Photograph. Ben Grishaaver.

Unfortunately there are no data on the collecting of this unique statue. The statue's size is exceptional. It wears a string of *Coix* and *Abrus* seeds around its long neck. Around the hips is a skirt of sago leaf fiber. The loose strands were presumably originally pulled up in the fashion of an Asmat woman's skirt.

Plate 7.34 (right) Unir River (formerly Lorentz), Northwest Asmat. Wood, lime, red ocher, charcoal, *Coix* seeds, feathers, sago leaf fiber. 128 cm. Collected in 1908 or 1913 by J.A. Gooszen. Donated by Gooszen in 1919. RMV 1971-981. Photograph by Ben Grishaaver.

This statue, one of the few old Asmat statues remaining, was collected during the first military expedition of Southwest New Guinea. As is the case with most pieces collected at an early date, there is no documentation on the village of provenance, the maker, or the function and meaning of the motifs. The motifs on the neck and torso are similar to ornaments carved in shields. Such ornamentation on figures is most unusual, however.

Exhibited: "The Art of the Pacific Islands," National Gallery of Art, Washington (D.C.) 1979, Cat. 21.5 (zie: Gathercole, Peter, Adrienne L. Kaeppler en Douglas Newton 1979:290-291).

Illustrated: Hoogerbrugge and Kooijman 1976, fig. 9.

Plate 7.35 (right) Statue of a couple *in coitu*. Exact origin unknown. Wood, lime, red ocher, charcoal. 60 cm. Acquired by the museum in 1953. Donated by Mr and Mrs Marcus-van den Nieuwenhuizen. RMV 3070-288. Photograph: Isaäc C. Brussee.

Though one need not wonder what this statue depicts, its meaning in the context of the Asmat culture is almost unknown. Today, such statues are made to sell, but an older piece such as this one is rare. A unique characteristic of this statue is that both heads are connected in an apparently passionate kiss.

Exhibited: "De jaargetijden van de mens," Rijksmuseum voor Volkenkunde, Leiden 1987. (Zie Smidt 1987a).

Illustrated: Rawson 1973, fig. 204; Smidt 1987a, fig. 7, p. 21.

B. Group of Figures II
Abstract and animal figures
Northwest Asmat
Collected 1951–1954

Two figures (Plates 7.36 and 7.37) showing an unusual, almost abstract design were collected in 1951 by M. Paliama, at the time head of the local government of the Mimika region. According to Father Gerard A. Zegwaard, who accompanied Paliama, they traveled to the Unir and Pomatsj Rivers (then the Lorentz and Northwest respectively) in Northwest Asmat and via the Por to the Utumbuwe, in the border region between Northwest and Central Asmat. The statues combine human and animal features, in one case a human and a praying mantis (Plate 7.37), in the other a human and a bird (Plate 7.36).

Although often included as elements in a larger carving, separate animal figures are rare in Asmat woodcarving. The bird figure (Plate 7.38) and the tortoise figure (Plate 7.40) are therefore exceptional. Both objects were acquired circa 1953 through the physician W. van Dijk outside the Asmat region. The function of these carvings is unknown.

Finally, this group of sculptures includes a small cup (Plate 7.40) with a human head as a sculptural element.

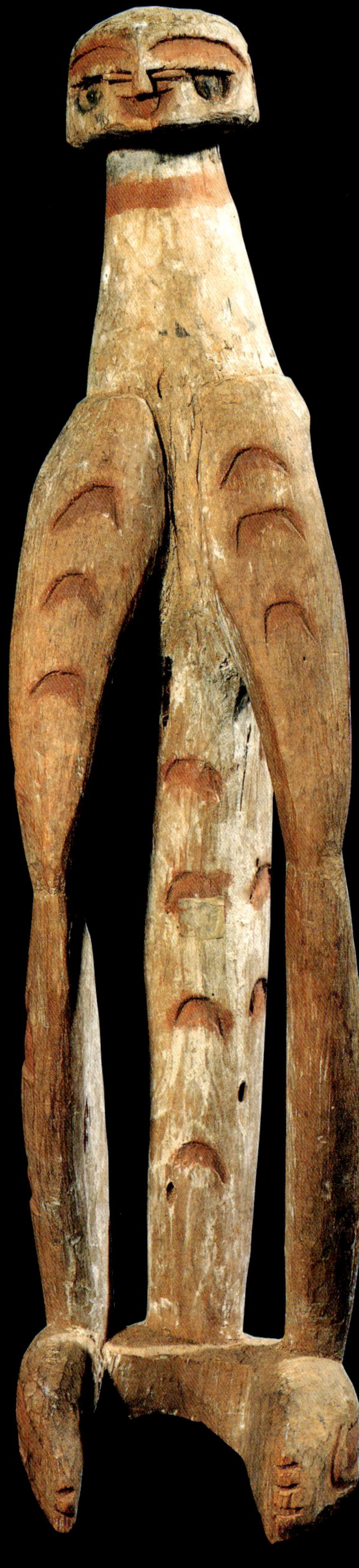

Plate 7.36 (right) Abstract figure. Presumably River Pomatsj (formerly River Northwest), or the River Unir (formerly River Lorentz) Northwest Asmat. Wood, lime, red ocher, charcoal. 63 cm. Collected in 1951 by Mr. Paliama, then head of the regional Mimika government. RMV 3070-8. Photograph: Isaäc C. Brussee.

This atypical statue appears midway between a bird and a human figure. Other than Plate 7.37, no similar examples are known.

Illustrated: Kooijman c. 1955, fig. 22b.

Plate 7.37 (opposite, left) Abstract figure. Presumably Pomatsj River (formerly Northwest), or the River Unir (formerly River Lorentz), Northwest Asmat. Wood, lime, red ocher, charcoal. 65 cm. Collected in 1951 by Mr. Paliama, then head of the regional Mimika government. RMV 3070-9. Photograph: Isaäc C. Brussee.

Illustrated: Kooijman 1956, fig. 4.

Plate 7.38 (opposite, right) Bird figure. Precise origin unknown. Wood, lime, red ocher, charcoal. 63 cm. Collected c. 1954. RMV 3154-3. Photograph by Isaäc C. Brussee.

The function of this object is undocumented.

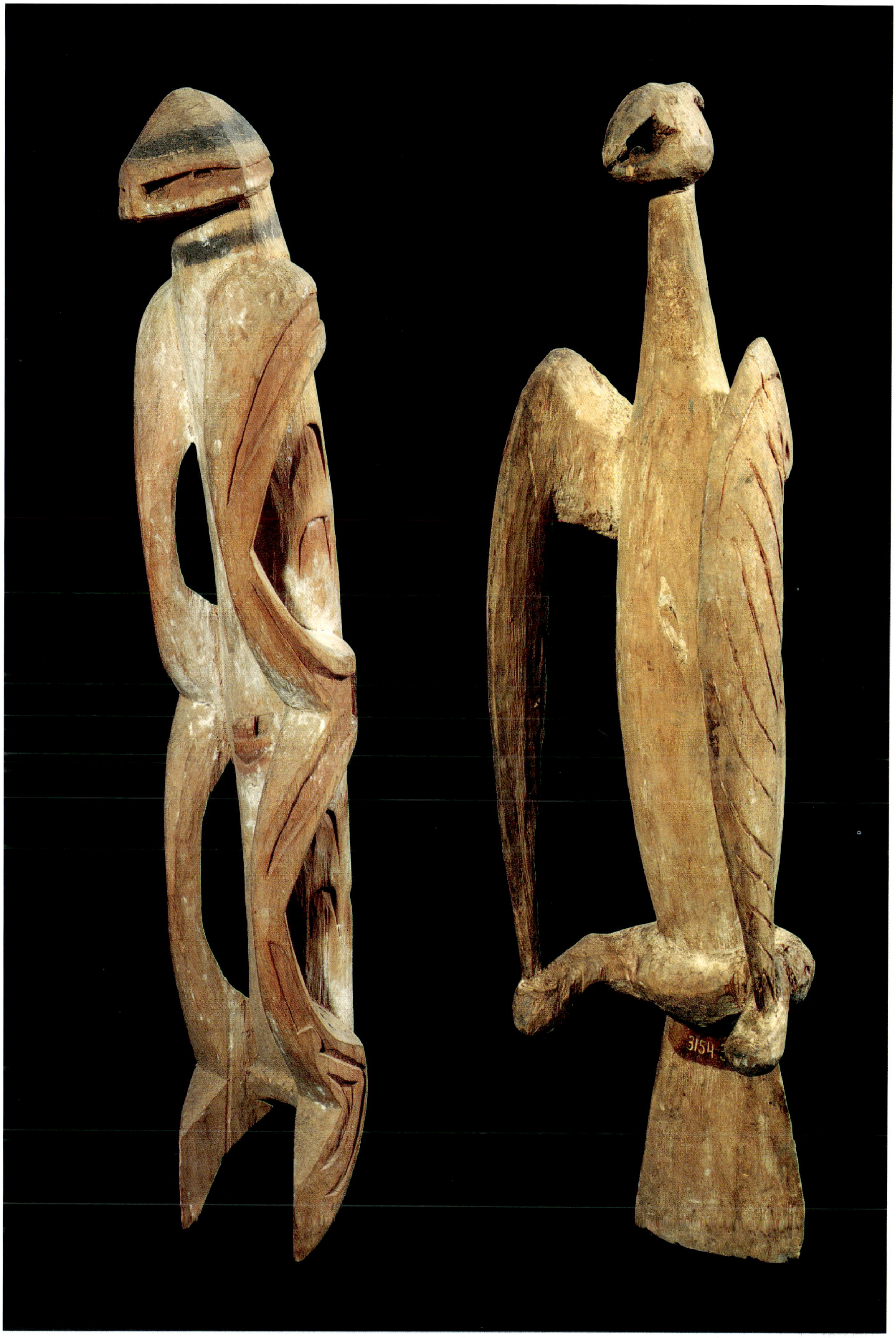

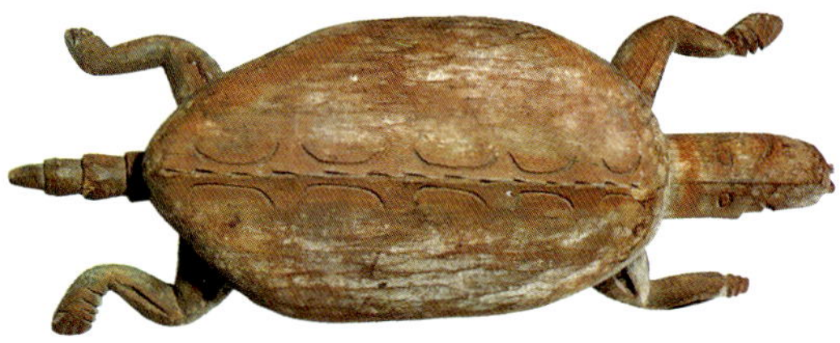

Plate 7.39 Tortoise figure. Presumably Northwest Asmat. Wood, lime, red ocher, charcoal. 68 cm. Collected c.1954. RMV 3154-1. Photograph: Isaäc C. Brussee.

The tortoise (*mbu*) is a fertility symbol because of the many eggs this animal lays. A figure of a tortoise is a central element of the long *wuramon* or soulships that function in an initiation ritual. *Wuramon* are made only in the Northwest Asmat region. In some villages boys receive scarifications on the chest during the initiation as they lay across the tortoise figure of the soul dug out. As a separate object the tortoise figure is a rarity.

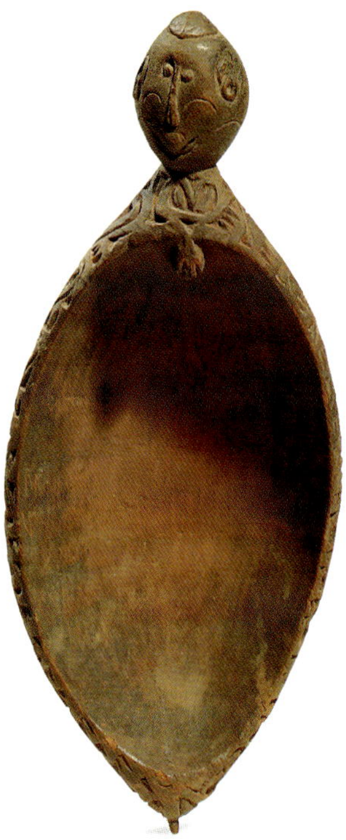

Plate 7.40 Small cup. Sawa village, Northwest Asmat. Wood, red ocher, charcoal. 42 cm. Collected in 1953 by C.C. Verhey van Wijk. Place of origin determined by Gerard A. Zegwaard. RMV 3070-288. Photograph: Isaäc C. Brussee.

Presumably used as a small paint cup.

C. Human Figure as a Motif

Northwest and Central Asmat
Collected: 1913 and 1953-1954

The human figure (Plates 7.41–7.44) is an important motif in the Asmat woodcarving art. Humans are depicted, for instance, in detached figure sculptures, on elements of *bisj*, on shields, and on cups.

Human figure sculptures fall into roughly two types: 1) standing upright, with straight legs and arms, the latter either hanging free along side the body or resting on the hips; 2) squatting, with raised arms. In this latter case, the knees are often connected to the elbows and the hands come together under the chin.

The series of "objects" depicted here explore the second motif, with the distinctive Asmat elbows-to-knees position.

A figure sculpture (Plate 7.42) serves as a starting point. This can then be compared to the representation of the human figure on two shields, and in the shape of a cup.

As represented on shields, the human figure ranges from clearly recognizable (Plate 7.41) to almost completely abstract (Plate 7.44). On the latter shield the human figure is reduced to stylized arms and legs. It is still recognizable, however, particularly when one compares the image on this shield (from Central Asmat) to the other objects in the series.

Like the figure, which comes from the Northwest Asmat style region, the abstract shield shows upright ridges across the arms and legs (so-called "small bridge pieces." This similarity can perhaps be explained by the fact that the shield, though classed as Central Asmat, was collected in a village not far from the imaginary border between Northwest and Central Asmat.

The stylized human figures on the first shield (Plate 7.41) shows a striking resemblance to the cup (Plate 7.43). This similarity is not a coincidence: both were collected in the same village by J.J. Spijker, Resident of South New Guinea at the time, during a tour of duty through the Asmat region November 21–27, 1953. He also collected the second shield (Plate 7.44), this time during a course of duty in February–March 1954. These three objects hail from Central Asmat.

The figure sculpture hails from Northwest Asmat. Although donated to the museum by the Vereeniging Maloeka (Moluccas Association) in Ambon, it was presumably collected by A.J. Gooszen, in 1908 or 1913.

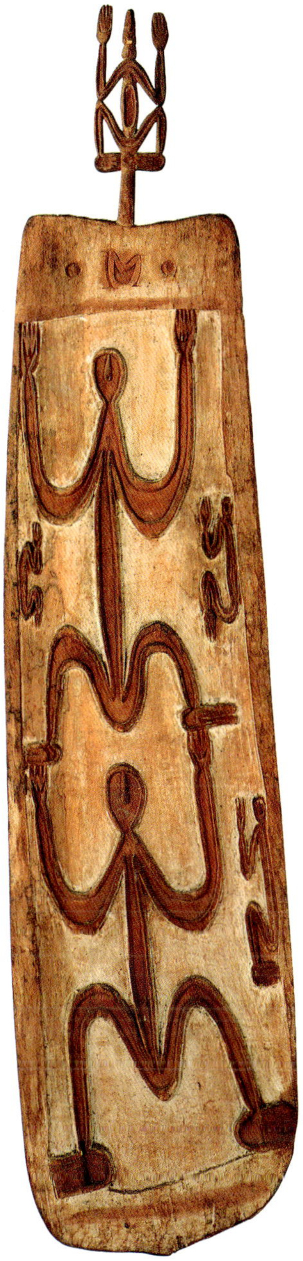

Plate 7.41 Shield. Kaimo village, Siretsj River (formerly Eilanden), Central Asmat. Wood, lime, red ocher, and charcoal. 157 cm. Collected by J.J. Spijker in 1953. RMV 3070-245. Photograph: Ben Grishaaver.

The human figures represented in the shield show similarities with the shapes of sago cups and paint cups (Plate 7.43). The smaller motifs represent praying mantis figures. The human figures on this shield are composed of two praying mantis motifs (rendered in profile) placed back to back. (See the small motifs on the edge of the shield.) The similarity between man and the praying mantis, a head-hunting symbol, is evoked.

Exhibited: "Melanesien, Schwarze Inseln der Südsee" (Eine Ausstellung des Rautenstrauch-Joest-Museums für Völkerkunde der Stadt Köln), Kunsthalle Köln 1971-1972, Cat. 296. (Zie Stöhr 1971:135)

Illustrated: Kooijman 1956, fig. 13.

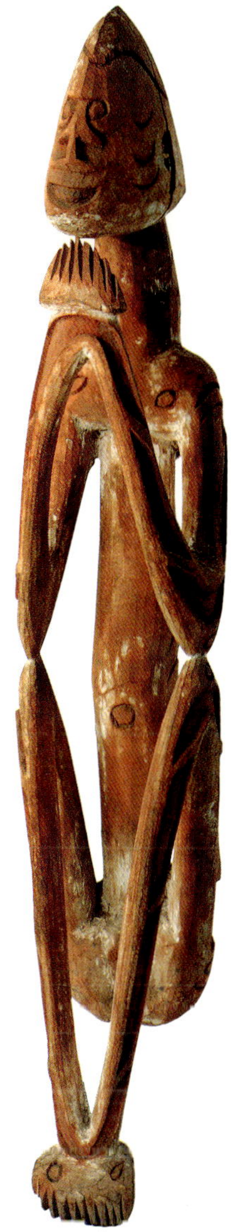

Plate 7.42 Statue of a man. Upper Unir River (formerly Lorentz), Northwest Asmat. Wood, lime, red ocher, charcoal, *Coix* seeds, sago leaf fiber. 111 cm. Presumably collected c. 1908 by A.J. Gooszen. Acquired by the museum in 1939. Donated by the Vereeniging Maloeka (Moluccas Association). RMV 2468-36. Photograph: Ben Grishaaver.

Jac. Hoogerbrugge has surmised that this figure may have been collected by A.J. Gooszen (see Tigges 1985:105). His assumption is plausible. There is a connection between Gooszen and the Moluccas: on June 11, 1907 (a few weeks prior to the beginning of the military exploration of South New Guinea under his leadership) Gooszen was transferred to the garrison's battalion of Amboina and Ternate. On February 13, 1912 he was even appointed to be Military Commander of Amboina and Ternate (Lamme 1987:151). It is likely that there has been some contact between him and the Vereeniging Maloeka, which was headquartered in Ambon.

The penis of this figure has disappeared, presumably chopped off for puritanical reasons.

Illustrated: Kooijman c. 1955, fig. 22a; 1956, fig. 3; Bodrogi 1981 (vol. 1), pl. 85.

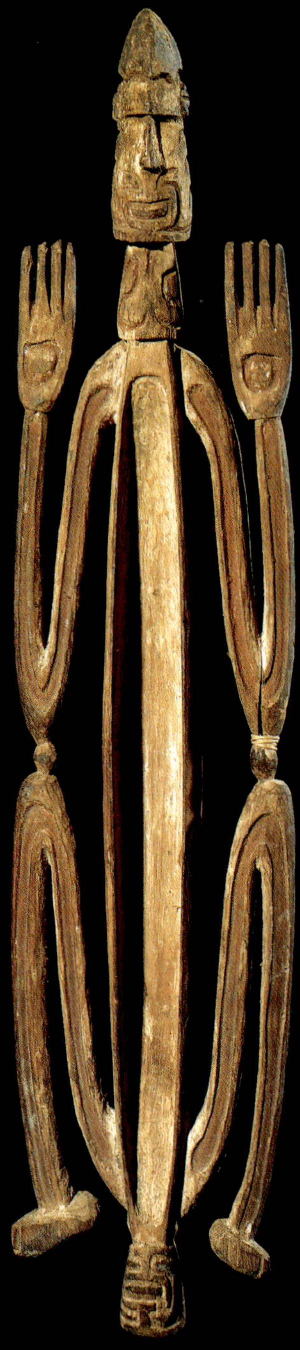

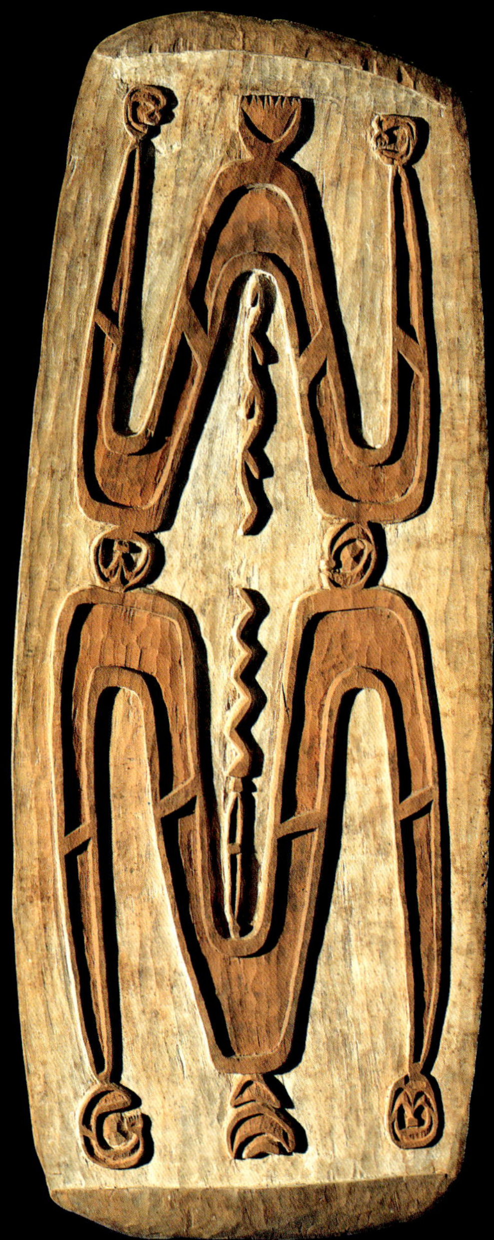

Plate 7.43 Cup in the shape of a person. Kaimo village, Siretsj River (formerly Eilanden), Central Asmat. Wood, lime, red ocher, charcoal. 77 cm. Collected in 1953 during a tour of duty by the former Resident J.J. Spijker. RMV 3070-275. Photograph: Isaäc C. Brussee.

The function of this type of object is not certain. Possibly it was a ceremonial bowl in which to serve sago grubs.

Plate 7.44 Shield. Vicinity Betjew village, border region between Northwest and Central Asmat. Wood, lime, red ocher, charcoal. 137 cm. Collected in 1953 by J.J. Spijker. RMV 3070-501. Photograph: Isaäc C. Brussee.

The ornamentation carved in this exceptional shield represents a human figure abstracted to a pair of (raised) arms and (squatting) legs. A characteristic detail are the slanting ridges or cross-lines in the arms and legs. These can also be seen in the arms and legs of three-dimensional figures (see Plate 7.42).

Illustrated: Kooijman 1956, fig. 21.

III. Monumental carvings

The Asmat are renowned for their monumental carvings, particularly such large creations as the *bisj* ancestor poles, and the *wuramon* soul canoes. But these carvings have limited regional distribution, and none can any longer be considered common. In the past, the ceremonies in which these carvings featured often directly led to head-hunting raids.

Bisj

In the past, *bisj* were made as a visible sign of the commitment by the living to avenge the death of their relatives. The poles are made from mangrove trees, cut so that one of the broad buttress roots is still attached. This is to serve as the open-work pennant or *tsjemen*—literally "penis"—of the pole. The *tsjemen* is decorated with head-hunting symbols. The poles themselves display likenesses of the ancestors.

The process of cutting and transporting the tree for the *bisj* is analogous to the killing and transporting of an enemy. (See Chapter 1.) Upon its arrival in the village it is welcomed by the women with the same ritual as was used for the reception of the corpse of a slain enemy. The poles are made by master carvers near the *jeu*. Before being erected, the names of those dead relatives or ancestors represented are made public. In the past, a head-hunting raid took place after the ceremony to actually avenge the dead represented in the poles.

There are two different ways of displaying the *bisj*: in Central Asmat they are displayed vertically, their pointed ends stuck in the ground. On the Casuarina Coast they are mounted in a slanting position, supported by scaffolding. In both areas, after the *bisj* ceremony the poles were traditionally taken to the sago swamps and left to rot; the souls of the deceased thus released would then promote the growth of the sago.

Wuramon

Wuramon or "soulships" resemble dug-out canoes in their general shape, but they have no bottom. Figures—spirit passengers—are carved in a row. A tortoise (*mbu*) is always placed in the center of the *wuramon*. There appear to be two general types: one contains mainly human figures, the other the bird-like *ambirak*, a dangerous type of female spirit being that lives in rivers and streams. The carved figures take the names of those who have recently died.

Wuramon are carved only in Northwest Asmat. Like *bisj*, *wuramon* are used in a ceremony in front of the *jeu* to promise vengeance for the souls of the dead. However, they also have an important function in initiation ceremonies. (See Plate 1.10, page 23, for a detail of a *wuramon*.)

Omu

Omu are perhaps the rarest of the large carvings. They are known only from a few villages in Northwest Asmat. Unfortunately, almost nothing is known of them, including what the word means. Some *omu* were found in feast houses deep in the jungle. At a ceremony, men dance with the *omu*, which are decorated with certain leaves, in the *jeu*. After the dance the *omu* are tied along the roof beam of the house. (Gerbrands 1967b: 296 and Schneebaum 1985: 104–105.)

Crocodile poles

Crocodile poles are restricted to the southern part of the Casuarina coast. In a way they are the equivalent of the *bisj* poles of Central Asmat and the *wuramon* of Northwest Asmat. Like *bisj* and *wuramon*, they were used to carry off the souls of the dead. They seem to have been limited to commemorating people who had been killed by crocodiles, however. Crocodiles are now quite scarce in the Asmat region.

Basu suangkus

The words "basu suangkus" literally mean: "show the heads," that is, make visible the heads of those men who have been killed in battle (Konrad, Konrad and Schneebaum 1981: 109). *Basu suangkus* are restricted to the middle and upper course of the Siretsj River, Central Asmat. They are quite rare; it is not surprising that only a few museums have examples in their collections.

They are displayed in a ceremony which, in the past, culminated in a head-hunting raid to avenge those depicted. Today, the feasting ends with a wild pig hunt.

Basu suangkus consist of heavy logs which have a human head or even a complete human figure carved at either end, while the central cylindrical section is undecorated. Two of such carvings together with two smaller undecorated logs form a unit. The square in the middle receives a basket of sago grubs, an Asmat delicacy. For the *basu suangkus* feast held in Jaosakor in 1979, an estimated 3,000 sago palms were felled to yield enough of the grubs. (Konrad, Konrad, and Schneebaum 1981: 109).

A. Group of Bisj
Central Asmat
Collected: 1954, 1961

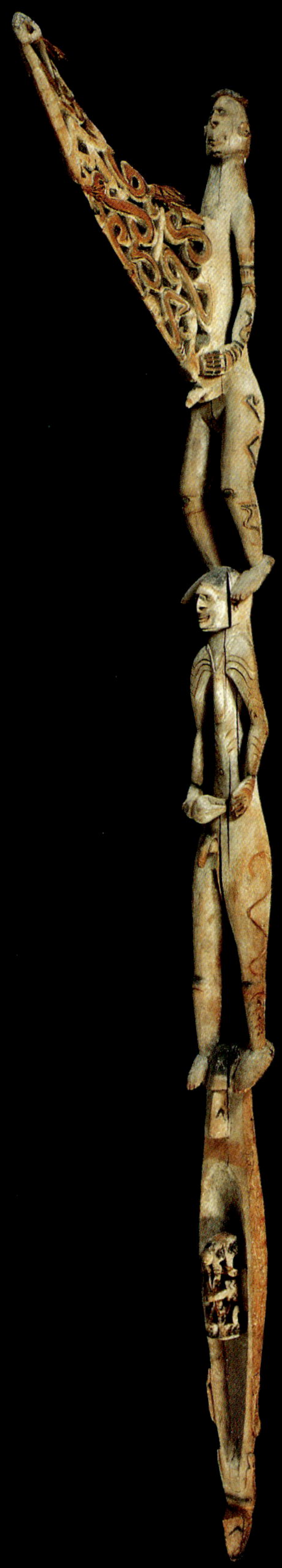

Plate 7.45 (right) *Bisj*. Carved by Chief Bifarq. Otsjanep village, Ewta River, Casuarina Coast. Wood, lime, red ocher, charcoal, sago fiber. 535 cm. Collected in 1961 by Michael Clark Rockefeller. Donated to the museum in 1962 by Mary C. and Nelson A. Rockefeller, from the estate of their son Michael. RMV 4104-2. Photograph: Ben Grishaaver.

This *bisj*, made by Chief Bifarq of of Jeu Kayer, consists of two male figures standing on top of each other. The lower figure holds a carved *Syrinx* sp. shell above its genitals. Such a shell, which may be also be worn in real life by important men, has the same symbolic value as the skull of an enemy (compare to *bisj* RMV 4104-1 opposite.)

The lowest part of the *bisj* is formed by a model canoe which contains two sitting figures facing each other, a rare feature. This may indicate that the *bisj* could be seen as a metaphorical canoe to carry the souls of the dead to the realm of the dead.

Illustrated: Smidt 1970: figs. 3b, 5, 6b and 6c for details of the pole, photographs of the maker, and a man wearing a *Syrinx* shell above his genitals.

Plate 7.46 (opposite, left) *Bisj*. Amborep village, Siretsj River (formerly Eilanden), Central Asmat. Wood, lime, red ocher, charcoal. 525 cm. Collected in 1954. RMV 3242-1. Photograph: Ben Grishaaver.

This *bisj*, together with RMV 3242-2 (see Plate 1.12, page 25) was made for a death ceremony that took place in the village of Amborep around 1954.

This *bisj* consists of (from top to bottom): a male figure with its penis carved above the openwork pennant, another male figure, and a small female figure sitting opposite the male figure, and finally a third male figure.

At the pointed tip of the *tsjemen* the head of a hornbill is carved—the notches on top of the upper beak, the incisions in the inner edges of the beak, and the tongue are clearly visible. Most of the other motifs in this pennant are S-shaped. An unusual aspect of this *tsjemen* is that an area at its base, approximately 20 centimeters wide was carved in relief rather than as openwork.

Plate 7.47 (opposite, right) *Bisj*. Carved by Chief Mbatumos. Otsjanep village, Ewta River, Casuarina Coast. Wood, lime, red ocher, charcoal, sago leaf fiber. 576 cm. Collected in 1961 by Michael Clark Rockefeller. Donated to the museum in 1962 by Mary C. and Nelson A. Rockefeller from the estate of their son Michael. RMV 4104-1. Photograph: Ben Grishaaver.

This *bisj*, made by Chief Mbatumos of the ceremonial house of Kayer, consists of two male figures standing on top of each other. The lower male figure holds a carved human head above its genitals, perhaps in reference to the male initiation ceremony, during which the young men hold the skull of a slain enemy thusly.

Illustrated: See Smidt 1970: figs. 3a, 6a and 8a for a photograph of the maker and several details.

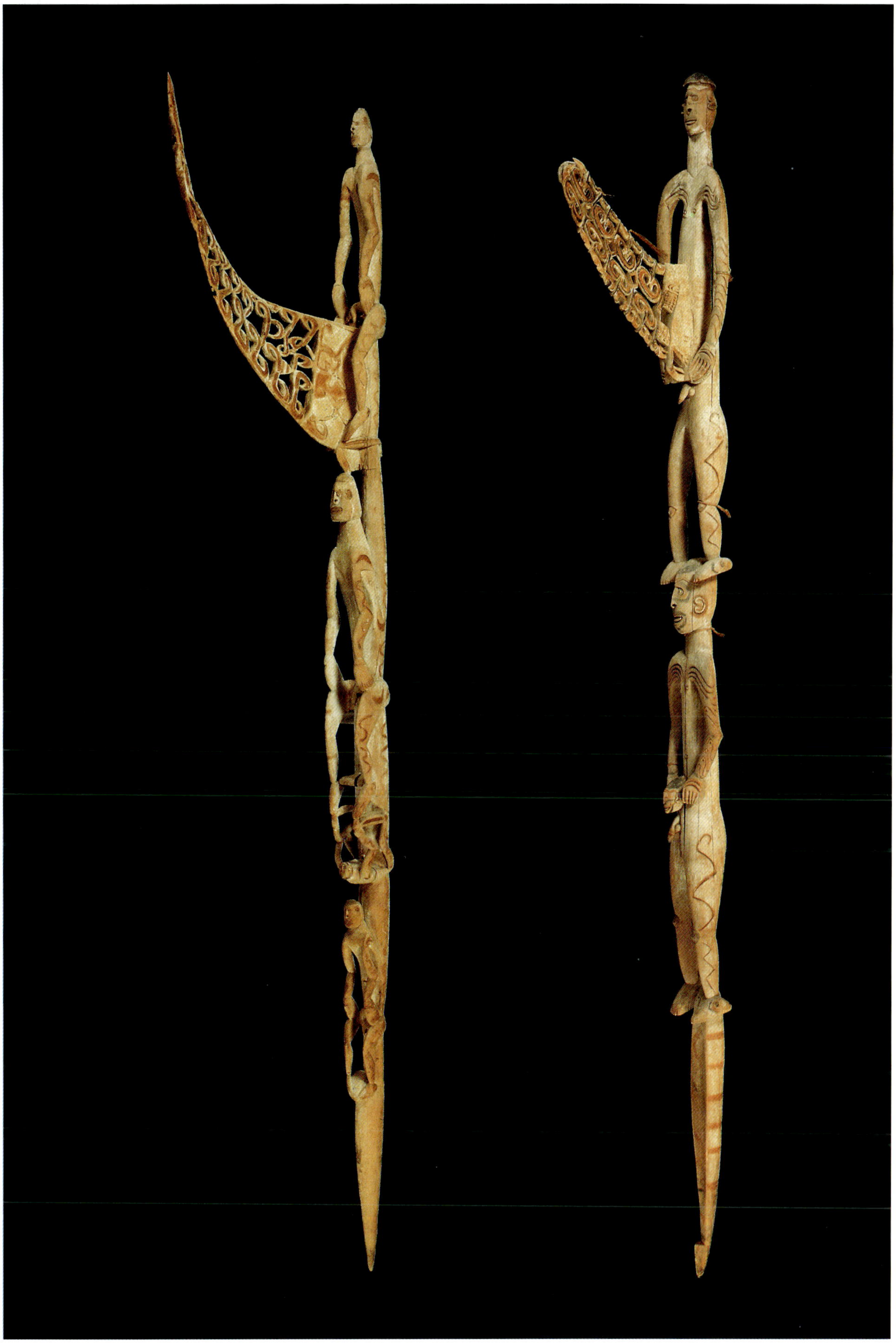

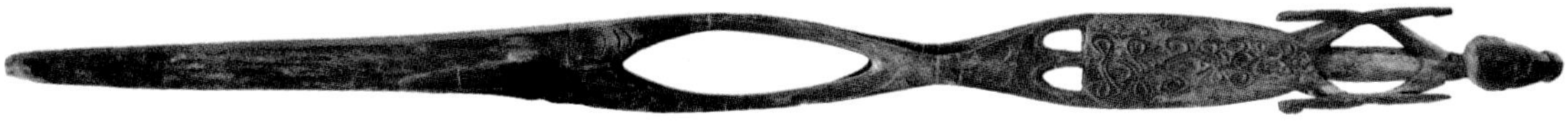

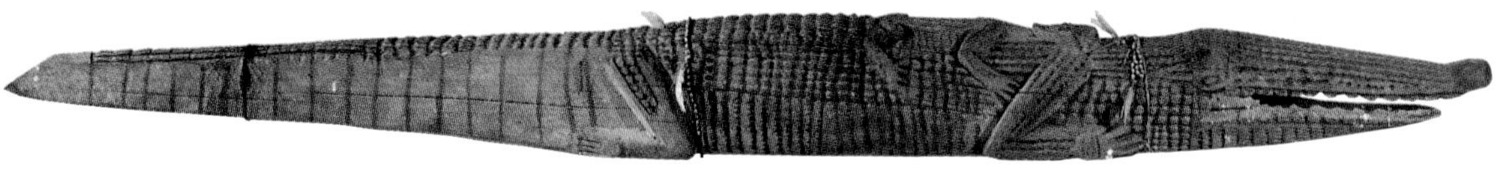

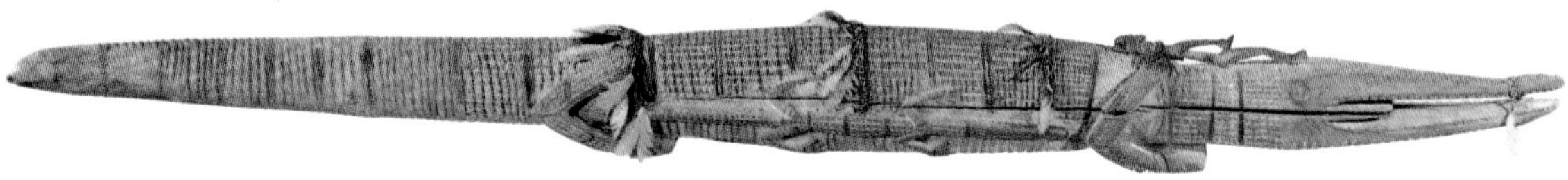

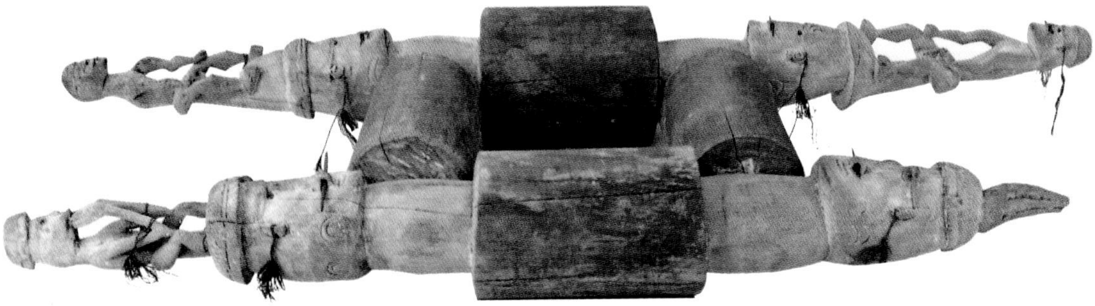

B. Other Large Carvings

Northwest and Central Asmat

Collected: 1970–1980

Plate 7.48 (top) *Omu*. Pupis village, Northwest Asmat. circa 3 meters. Collected by Gunter and Ursula Konrad. In the Konrad Collection at the Museum of Ethnology of the Josefine and Eduard von Portheim Foundation (Völkerkundemuseum der Josfine und Eduard von Portheim Siftung) in Heidelberg. A027. Photograph: Ursula Konrad.

Almost nothing is known of the meaning of *omu*.

Plate 7.49 (second from top) Crocodile. Santambor village, Casuarina Coast. 351 cm. Collected by Gunter and Ursula Konrad. In the Konrad Collection at the Museum of Ethnology of the Josefine and Eduard von Portheim Foundation (Völkerkundemuseum der Josfine und Eduard von Portheim Siftung) in Heidelberg. A025. Photograph: Ursula Konrad.

This carving and the one depicted in Plate 7.50 were made for a feast in 1978. Human figures have been carved on the bodies of both crocodiles. They are decorated with bands of sago frond, and tassels.

Plate 7.50 (third from top) Crocodile. Santambor village, Casuarina Coast. 274 cm. Collected by Gunter and Ursula Konrad. In the Konrad Collection at the Museum of Ethnology of the Josefine and Eduard von Portheim Foundation (Völkerkundemuseum der Josfine und Eduard von Portheim Siftung) in Heidelberg. A026. Photograph: Ursula Konrad.

See comments above for Plate 7.49.

Plate 7.51 (bottom) *Basu suangkus*. Awok village, Central Asmat. 334 cm. Collected by Gunter and Ursula Konrad. In the Konrad Collection at the Museum of Ethnology of the Josefine and Eduard von Portheim Foundation (Völkerkundemuseum der Josfine und Eduard von Portheim Siftung) in Heidelberg. A021.1–4. Photograph: Ursula Konrad.

The *basu suangkus* features in a vengeance feast, in which the people depicted in the heads were subsequently revenged. In fact, the men are said to have not been able to eat the sago grubs until they came back with the requisite heads. The *basu suangkus* is a collective effort, and each end of the logs is worked by a different carver. This particular carving was used in a feast in Awok in 1979. (Konrad, Konrad and Schneebaum 1981.)

IV. Drums
Northwest and Central Asmat
Collected: 1908 or 1913, 1953, 1954, 1953–1962

The Asmat drum is loaded with symbolism. The creator Fumeripitsjs built a *jeu,* made several woodcarvings, and animated them by beating a drum. Drums are still beaten to act out this story at the inauguration of a *jeu,* and at other ceremonial occasions. The grips are usually decorated with head-hunting symbols.

Drums are often kept for a very long time. When not in use, they are stored on a rack above the fireplaces where they stay dry, and where the smoke keeps away the insects. Years of exposure to this soot gives old drums a rich, black color.

The process of making a drum was recorded in the unique documentary film *Matjemos* by Adrian Gerbrands (1963). It is difficult and delicate work, although it is almost made to look easy by a capable woodcarver like Matjemos.

A short log for a drum is laboriously hollowed out using water and a stick of hard wood, and later fire. The outside is shaped with a long chisel into an hour-glass form, retaining a large ridge for the grip. Then the grip, usually the most decorative part of the drum, is shaped.

When the carving is finished, a piece of lizard skin is stretched over one of the openings, cemented in place with a mixture of shell lime and blood, and strengthened with a cane ring.

To minimize unwanted vibrations a few knobs of beeswax are pressed on the tympanum. In the humid tropics, a drum skin loses its tension rapidly, and every few minutes the player must stop and retune. He does this by holding the lizard skin head over the fire, which dries and tightens it.

The pitch of the drum is determined by its length and diameter. The drums of Central Asmat are taller than those of Northwest Asmat, reaching a height of 125 centimeters.

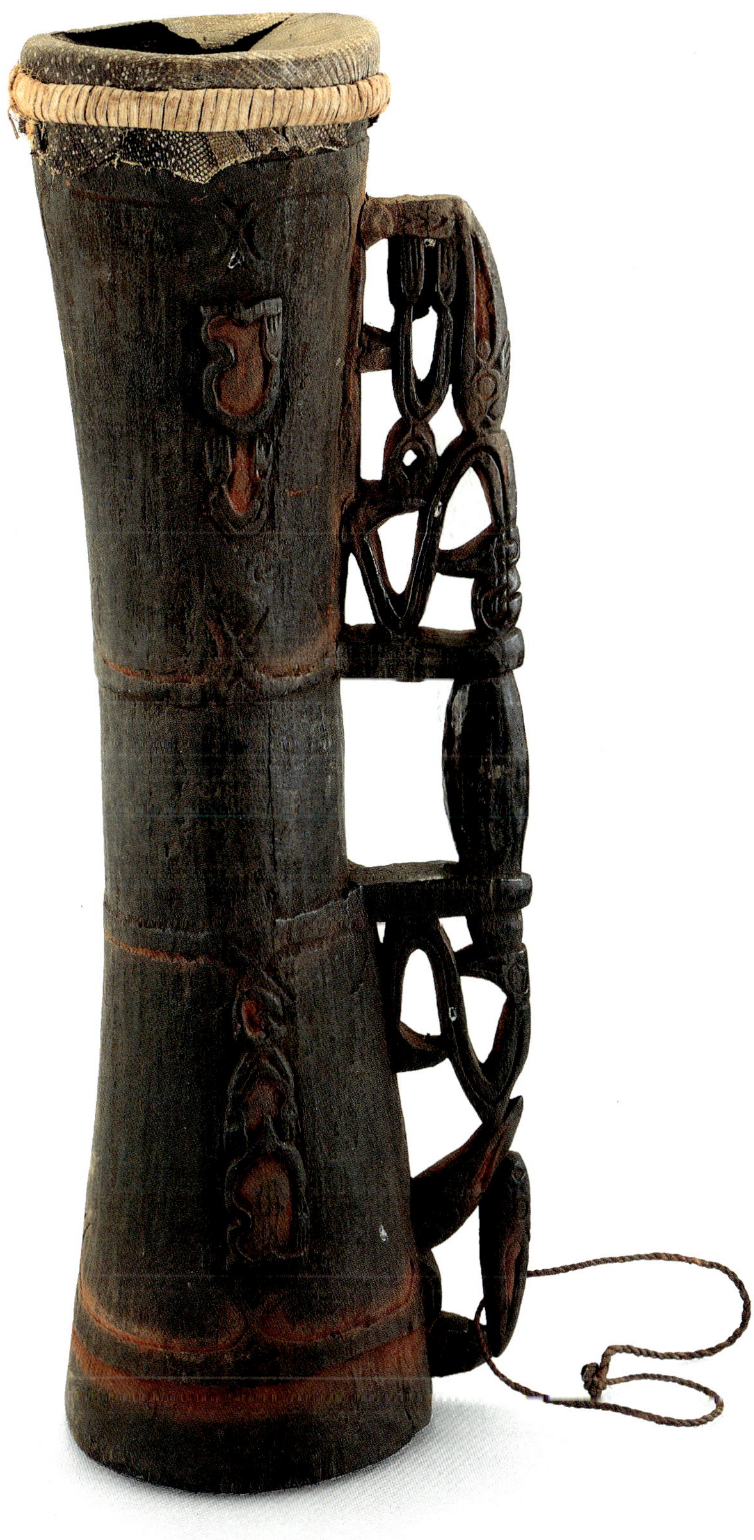

Plate 7.52 Drum. Casuarina Coast, Central Asmat. Exact provenance unknown. Wood, red ocher, lizard skin, rattan. Patina from use. 65.5 cm. Collected c. 1958 by W. M. Visser. RMV B 109-14. Photograph: Ben Grishaaver.

Stylized hornbill beaks are rendered at the top and bottom of the openwork ridge that serves as the grip. The upper motif clearly shows the characteristic parallel notches that represent the distinctive casque on the bird's beak. On the body of the drum, motifs are carved in relief, some of which may represent the fingers and hand, or elbows, of a spirit (see Gerbrands 1967b:219, fig. D), while others are stylized human figures.

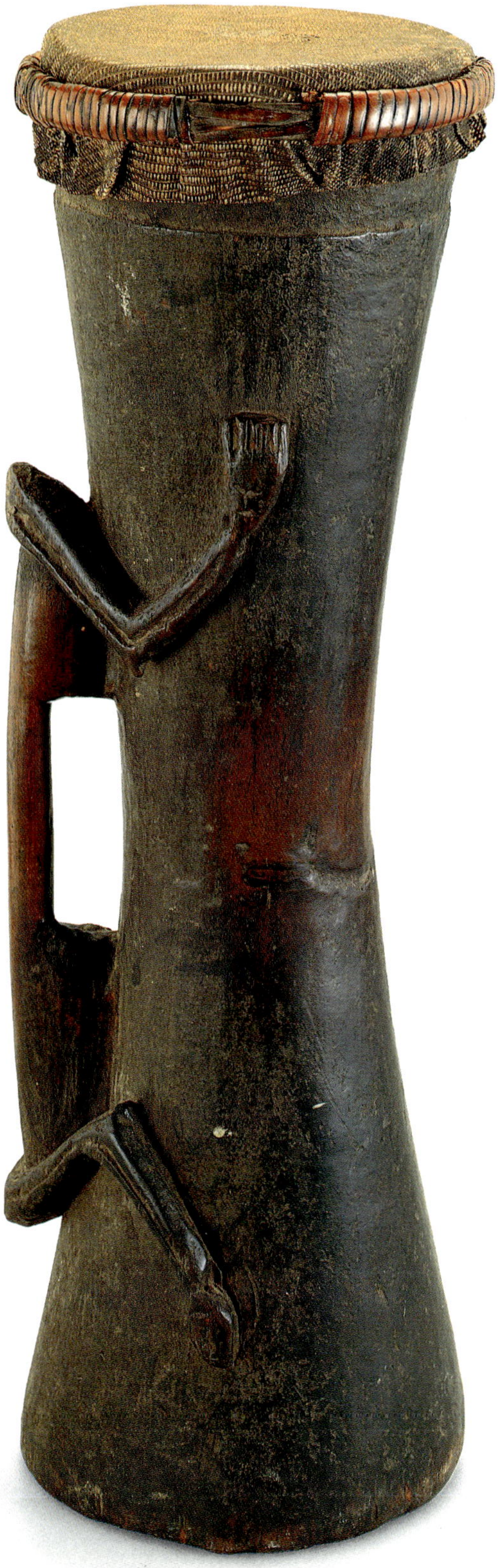

Plate 7.53 (left) Drum. Northwest Asmat, exact provenance unknown. Wood, lizard skin, rattan. Patina from use. 67 cm. Collected sometime between 1953 and 1962 by J. van Bodegom. Donated in 1979 by Mrs. van Bodegom. RMV 5029-1. Photograph: Ben Grishaaver.

This old drum shows a stylized representation of the praying mantis carved in and around the grip. The rendering of the insect is restricted here to basic lines (compare to the drum made by Matjemos, illustrated on page 51, which shows greater detail in the execution of the praying mantis). The detail in the hands make this head-hunting symbol rather anthropomorphic.

Plate 7.54 (opposite, left) Drum. Atsj village, lower Betsj River, Central Asmat. Wood, lizard skin, rattan. Patina from use. Damaged at bottom rim. 75 cm. Collected in 1953 by J.J. Spijker. RMV 3070-290. Photograph: Ben Grishaaver.

This magnificent drum shows considerable age. At the bottom of the grip is carved an upside down human head, with open mouth and visible tongue. The upper and lower parts of the hourglass-shaped drum body is finely carved with intricate patterns.

Plate 7.55 (opposite, right) Drum. Atsj village, lower Betsj River, Central Asmat. Wood. Patina from use. The lizard skin drum membrane is missing. 77 cm. Collected in 1953 by J.J. Spijker. RMV 3070-471. Photograph: Ben Grishaaver.

This is a well carved, old drum.

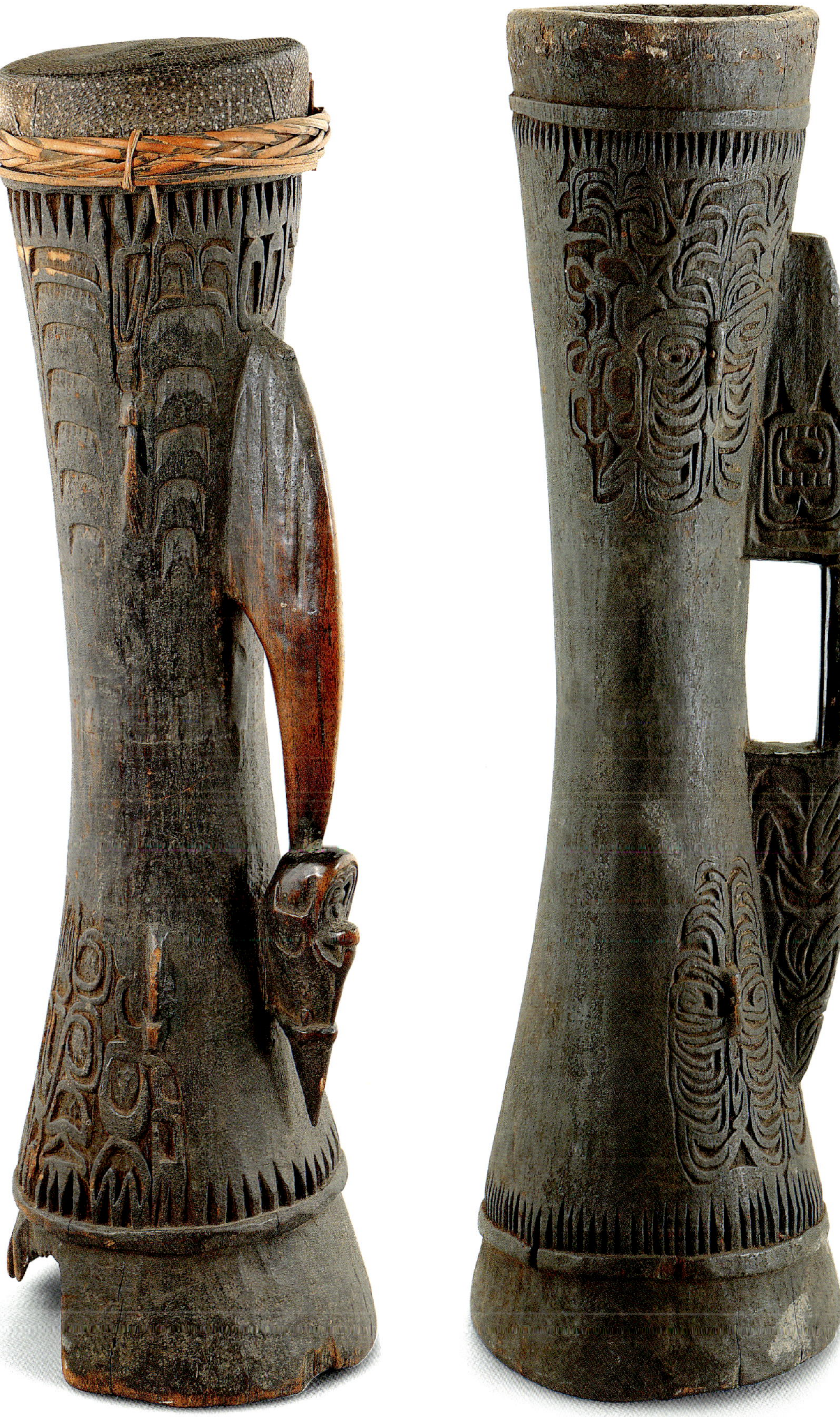

Plate 7.56 (below) Drum. Pomatsj River (formerly Northwest), Northwest Asmat. Wood, lizard skin, rattan. Patina from use. A layer of lacquer was applied after acquisition. 63 cm. Collected in 1908 or 1913 by A.J. Gooszen. Donated by Gooszen in 1919. RMV 1971-994. Photograph: Ben Grishaaver.

This drum, collected during the first military exploration of Southwest New Guinea, must be one of the oldest Asmat drums in existence. Judging from the deep black color (from storage over the fire), wear, and fine patina on this drum, it must have been of considerable age at the time of collection. This drum was probably carved in the 19th century. With no firm field data, the meaning of the strongly carved motifs of the grip must remain hypothetical. They may be interpreted as *was,* or cuscus tails. (Compare: Schneebaum 1985, page 126).

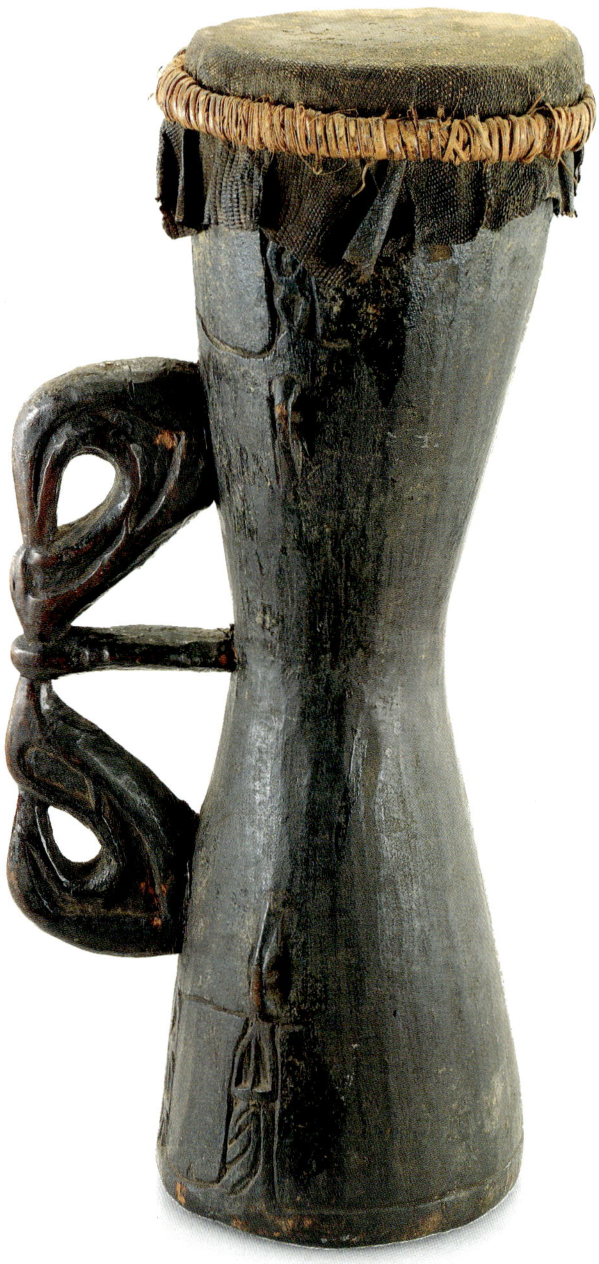

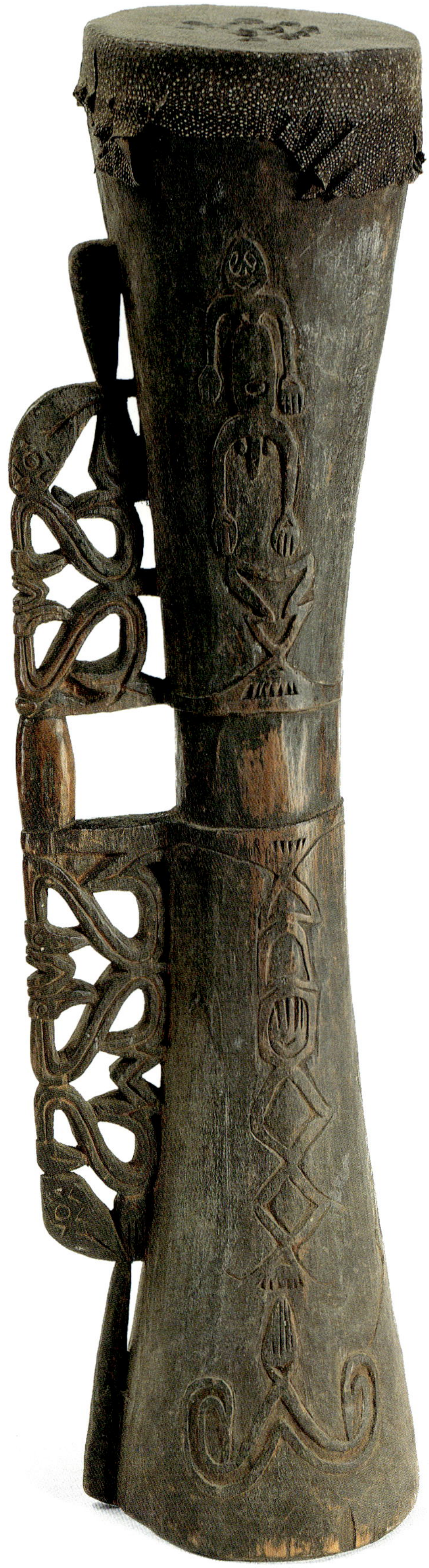

Plate 7.57 (opposite, right) Drum. Casuarina Coast, Central Asmat. Exact provenance unknown. Wood, lizard skin. Patina from use. 104 cm. Collected by W.M. Visser. RMV B186-2. Photograph: Ben Grishaaver.

Large drums such as this example are typical of carvers from the Casuarina Coast, the southernmost part of the Asmat lands. The openwork carved ridge in which the grip is embedded shows a combination of S-shaped figures and stylized bird beaks. A human figure is the most eye-catching of the motifs carved on the body of the drum.

Plate 7.58 (below) Drum. Northwest Asmat. Exact provenance unknown. Wood, lime, red ocher, lizard skin, rattan, sago leaf fiber. 65 cm. Collected in 1954 by J.J. Spijker. RMV 3070-541. Photograph: Ben Grishaaver.

In the openwork carving of the grip, two stylized bird's heads, rendered beak to beak, can be discerned. At the meeting of their beaks is a small human head.

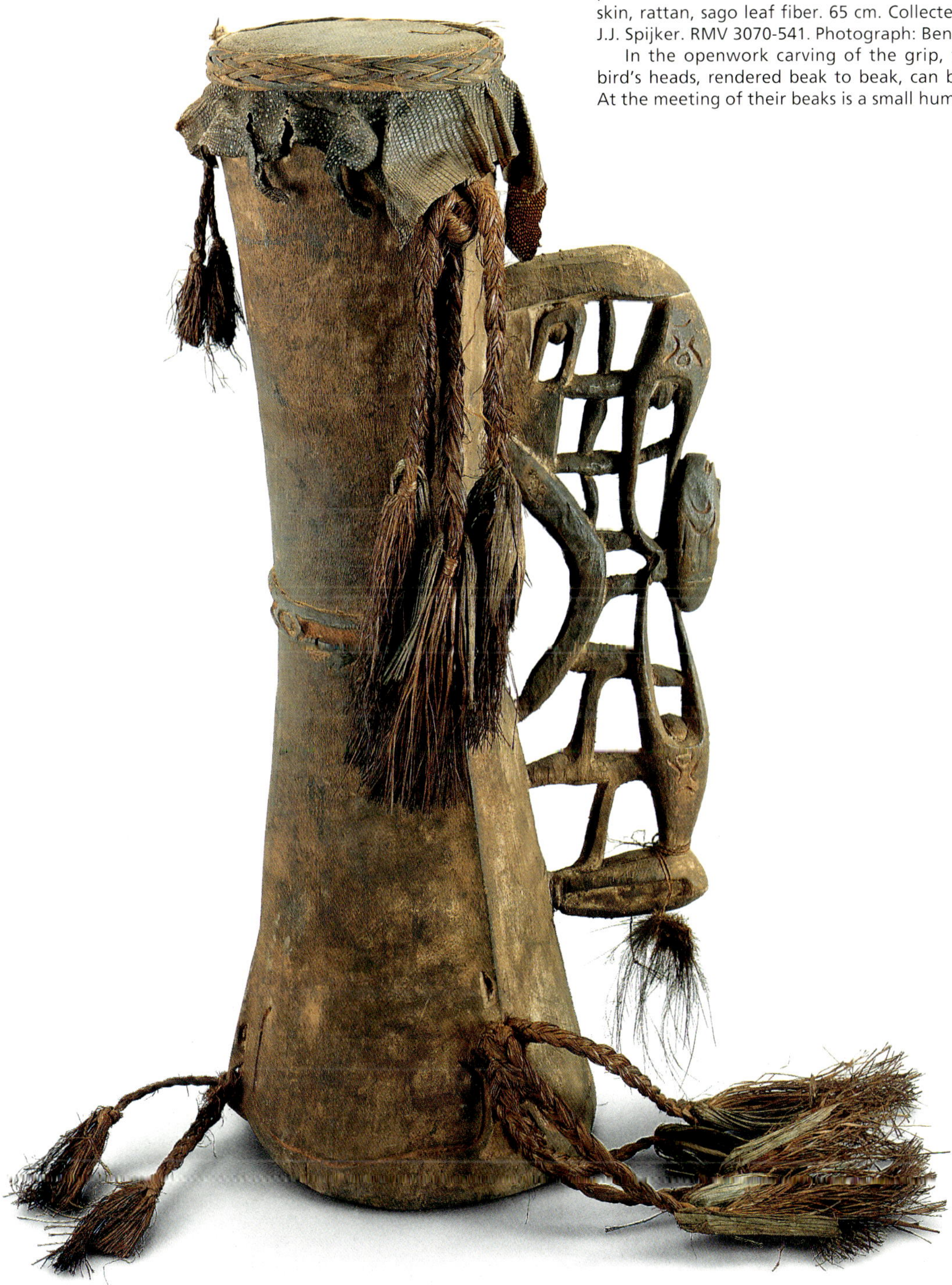

V. Canoe Prows
Northwest and Central Asmat
Collected: 1953, 1961, 1970

The most striking feature of ceremonial and (in the past) war canoes—aside from their great length—are the large and elaborately carved prow heads (*tsji tsjemen*) they display. Like the openwork part of the *bisj*, these are the *tsjemen*, or "penis" of the canoe (*tsji*).

In all but a few cases, entire canoes were considered much too large to ship overseas, so collectors took just the decorated prows of the canoes. There are also reports that prow heads may on occasion be carved separately, and attached to the prows. Far more commonly, however, the prow is of a unit with the canoe.

Ancestor figures, animals such as the praying mantis, the hornbill and even the cassowary are carved in the *tsji tsjemen* in a recognizable manner. Various other small head-hunting symbols often occur in the prow heads.

These motifs, at the head of the canoe, create a sense of unity between the men paddling the canoe and their ancestors, whose spirits protect them. Prow heads of ceremonial canoes, like all important woodcarvings, are made by specialists or master carvers.

Plate 7.59 Canoe prow. Sawa village, Pomatsj River (formerly Northwest), Northwest Asmat. Wood, lime, red ocher, charcoal, sago leaf fiber. 78 cm. Collected in 1953 by C.C. Verhey van Wijk. RMV 3070-465. Photograph by Ben Grishaaver.

This exceptional prow consists of a single *ambirak* figure bent over a human head. The *ambirak* is a dangerous mythological animal. (Provenance and interpretation of the carving provided by Gerard A. Zegwaard.)

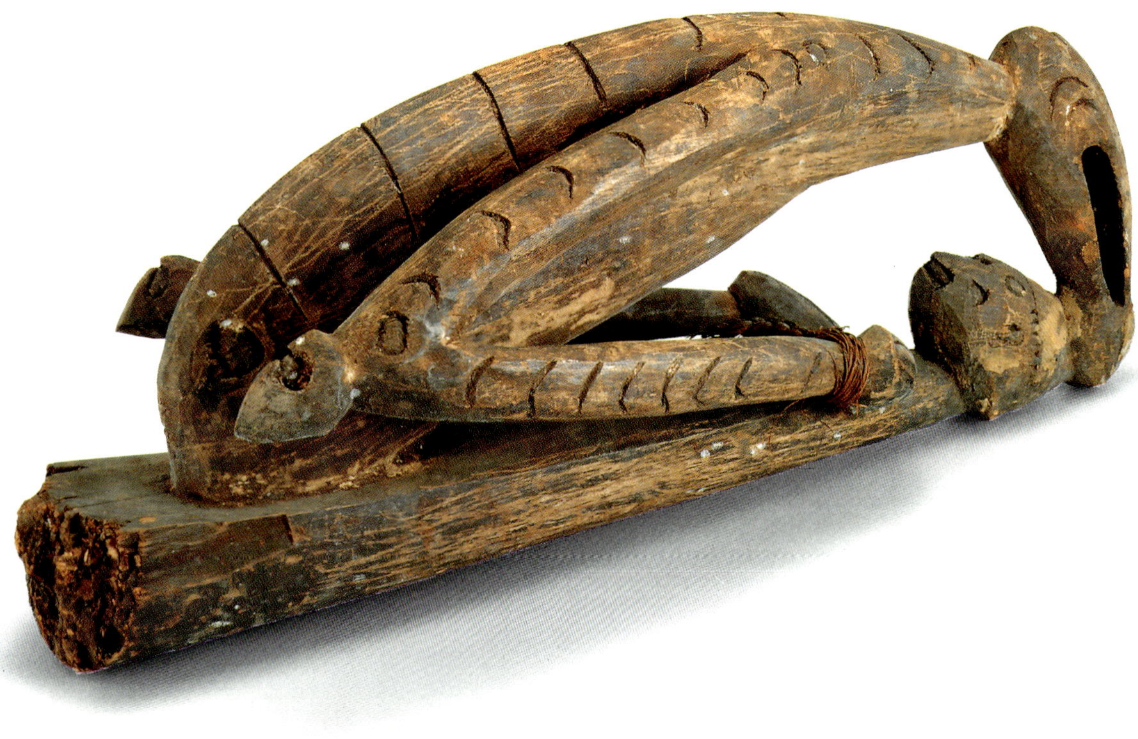

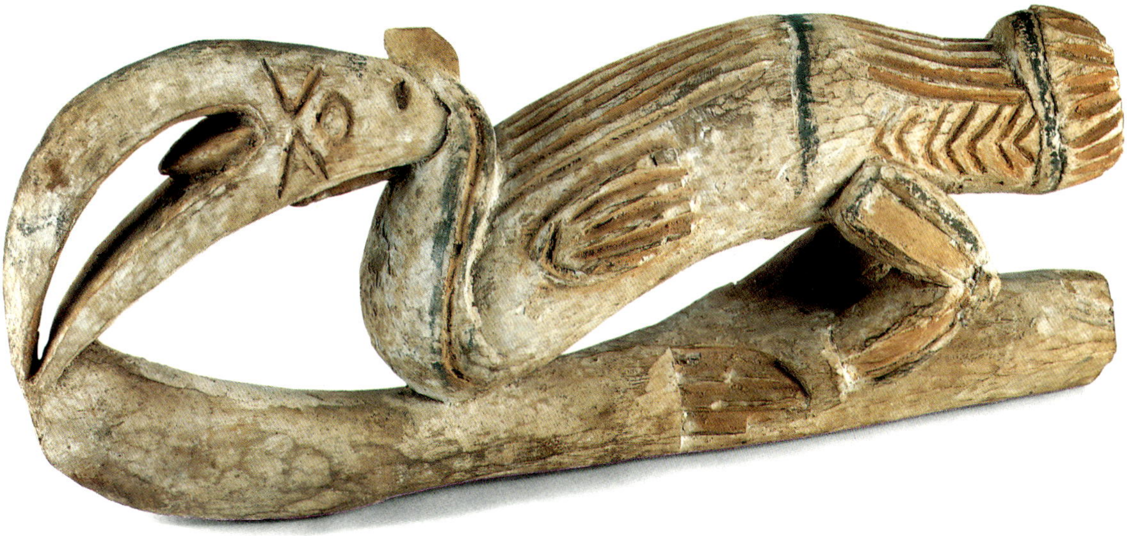

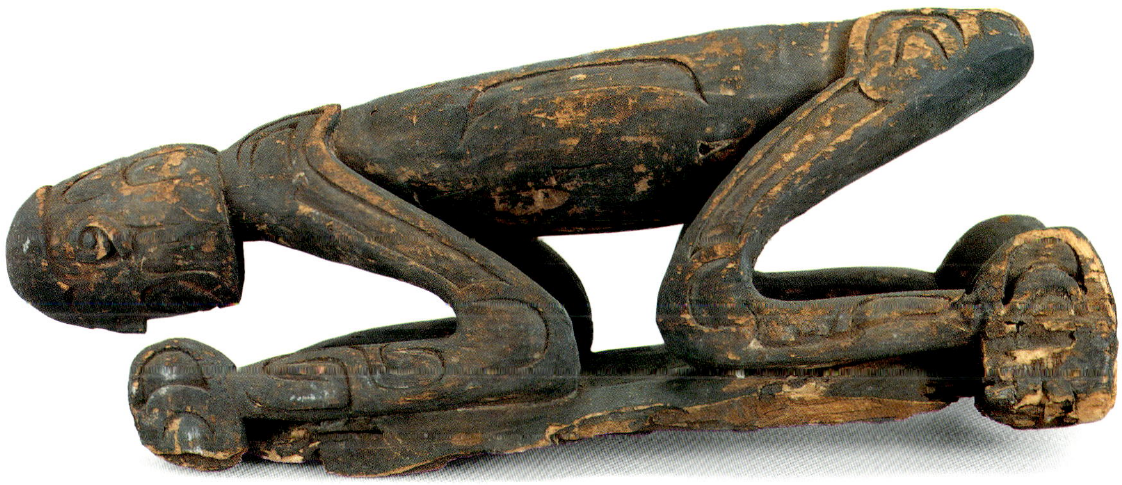

Plate 7.60 (above, top) Canoe prow. Carved by Pos. Naneh (also spelled Naneu) village, Fajit river, upstream from Basim, Casuarina Coast. Wood, lime, red ocher, charcoal. 73.5 cm. Collected in 1970 by Jac. Hoogerbrugge. RMV 4455-2. Photograph: Ben Grishaaver.

This prow is more recent than any of the others shown here. According to Pos, the maker, this carving represents a cassowary (*piru*). Compare to Plate 7.62, which although considerably older and with stylistic characteristics of its own, has comparable elements, such as the blunt "tail," and short parallel stripes apparently representing wings. Jac. Hoogerbrugge considers prows with a cassowary carving to be rare, as he has only seen six or seven such prows, and only in the southern Asmat area.

Plate 7.61 (above, bottom) Canoe prow. Carved by Bapmes. Amanamkai village, As river, Central Asmat. Wood. There are no traces of pigment left, and the item is blackened with soot, because it was stored above a fireplace. 80 cm. Collected in 1961 by A.A. Gerbrands. RMV 3790-34. Photograph by Ben Grishaaver.

Adrian Gerbrands called this extraordinary prow, "one of the best pieces of Amanamkai sculpture I have ever seen" (Gerbrands 1967a: 52). Made by Bapmes, it represents a praying mantis (*wènèt*) with the head of an ancestor, *kawé kusj* (*kawé* means "ancestor," *kusj* means "head" or "skull"), or an ancestor in the shape of a praying mantis. Thus Bapmes calls this prow *wènèt kawé.* The head has a mouth with strongly drawn out corners. This stylistic characteristic tends to appear on older pieces. On the cheeks, and behind the ears, scarifications (*jürfepin*) are visible. (Interpretation by A.A. Gerbrands; see also Gerbrands 1967a:41–52 on Bapmes and some of his other work.)

Plate 7.62 (below, top) Canoe prow. Presumably Northwest Asmat, but exact provenance unknown. Wood, lime, red ocher, sago leaf fiber. 83 cm. Collected in 1953 by C.C. Verhey van Wijk. RMV 3070-298. Photograph: Ben Grishaaver.

This delicately carved prow consists of three main elements: a figure with strongly curved back, possibly the malevolent *ambirak* (see also Plates 7.57 and 7.63); a seated human figure with long, bent arms (reminiscent of the pincers of the praying mantis); and a small squatting human figure.

Plate 7.63 (below, bottom) Canoe prow. Area of Sawa village, Pomatsj River (formerly Northwest), Northwest Asmat. Wood, lime, no traces of other pigments. 112 cm. Collected in 1953 by J.J. Spijker. RMV 3070-520. Photograph by Ben Grishaaver.

This prow is unique for its strongly carved abstract, curvilinear motifs. At the tip end two bird beaks can be discerned.

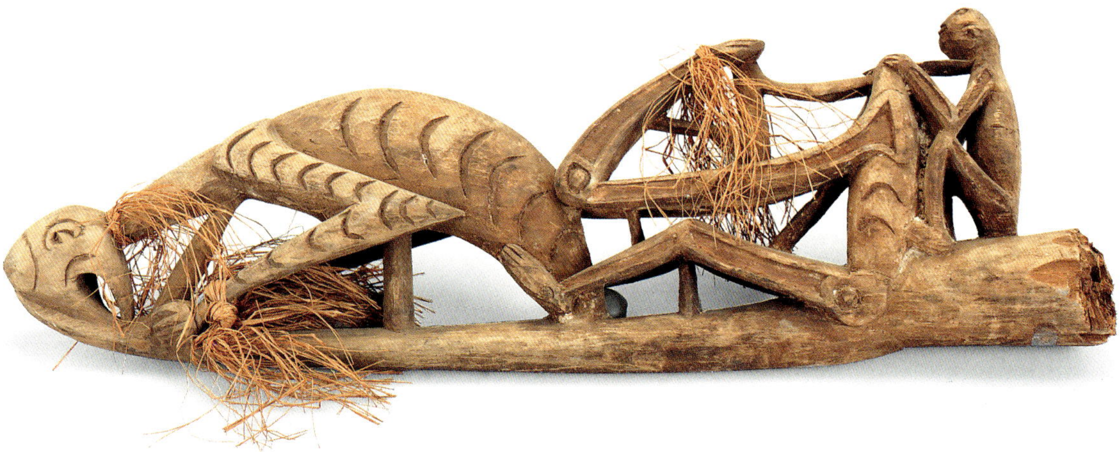

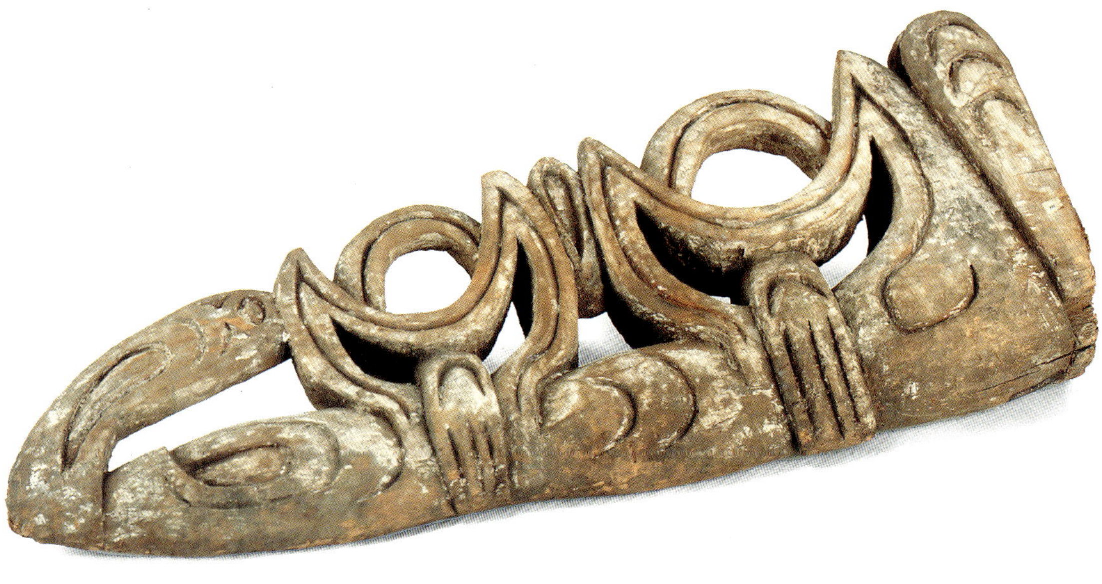

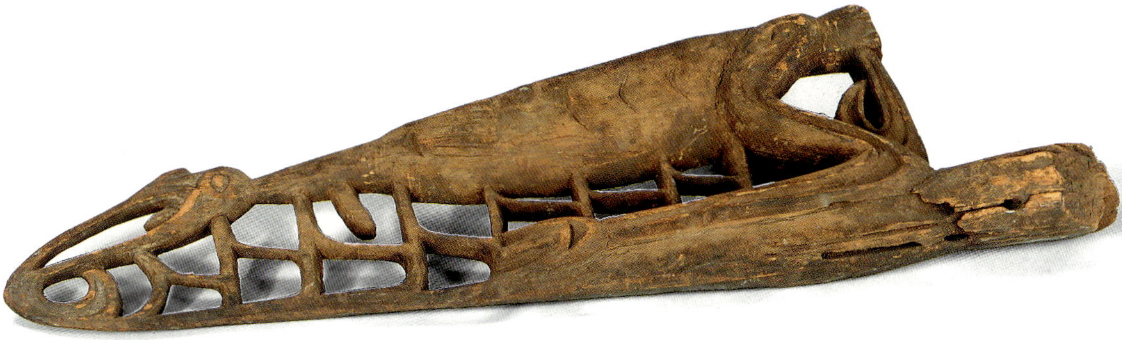

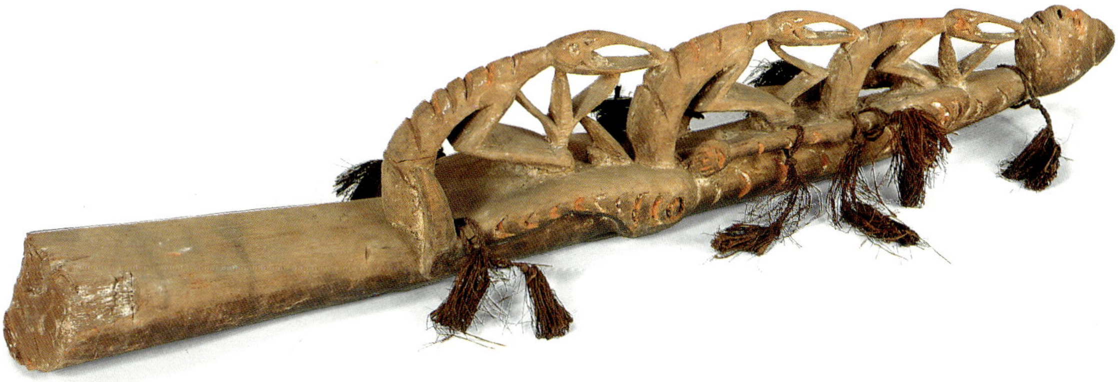

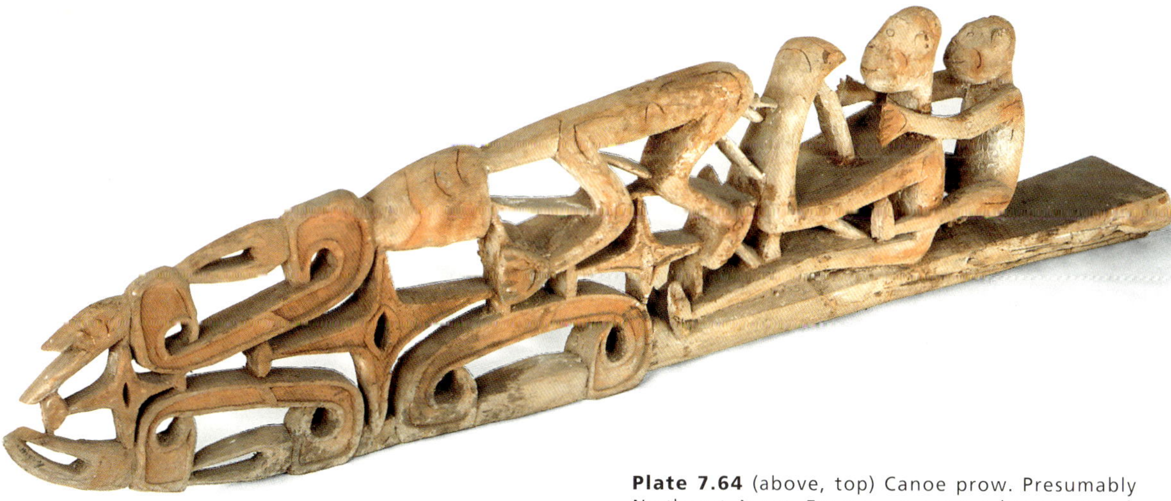

Plate 7.66 (above, bottom) Canoe prow. Presumably Northwest Asmat. Exact provenance unknown. Wood, lime, red ocher, charcoal. 183 cm. Collected in 1953 by C.C. Verhey van Wijk. RMV 3070-503. Photograph: Ben Grishaaver.

This large canoe prow consists of two sitting human figures (a small and a larger one (suggesting a mother with a child on her back). The central element in the openwork part is a human figure bent over in knee-elbow position (suggesting the praying mantis). The three C-shaped motifs may be the shell nose ornament *bipanew*. Other recognizable elements are two star-shaped motifs in the middle and several bird beaks.

Plate 7.64 (above, top) Canoe prow. Presumably Northwest Asmat. Exact provenance unknown. Wood, no traces of color left. 110 cm. Collected in 1953 by C.C. Verhey van Wijk. RMV 3070-519. Photograph by Ben Grishaaver.

This prow consists of a bird figure. The long legs, the wattle pointing downwards from the neck, and the casque on the upper part of the beak suggest the cassowary, the largest native land animal in New Guinea.

Plate 7.65 (above, middle) Canoe prow. Presumably Northwest Asmat. Exact provenance unknown. Wood, lime, red ocher, sago leaf fiber. 109 cm. Collected in 1953 by C.C. Verhey van Wijk. RMV 3070-299. Photograph by Ben Grishaaver.

This prow consists of a lying male figure and three birdlike figures possibly representing *ambirak*, malevolent mythological animals (compare with Plate 7.57).

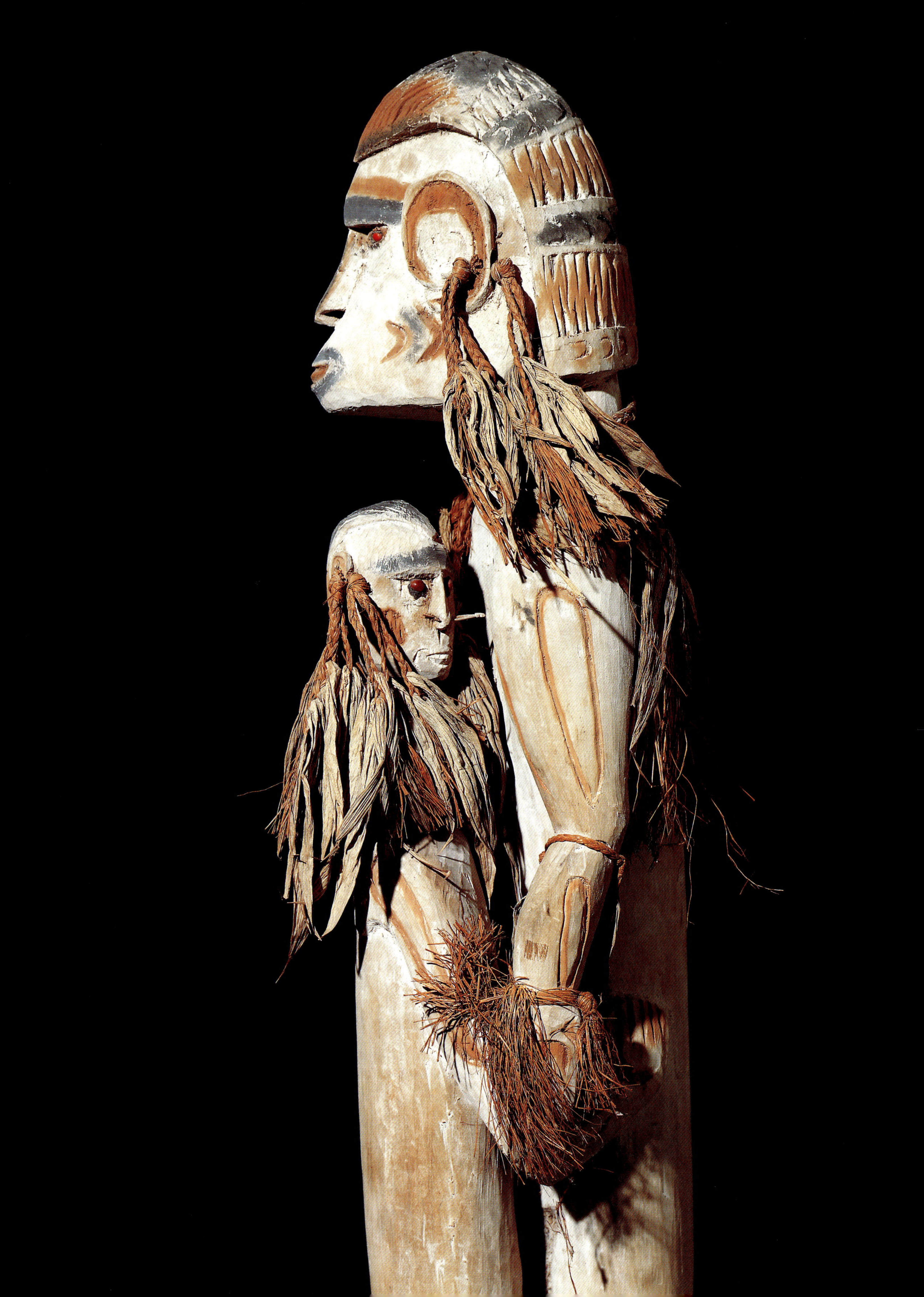

CHAPTER 8

Atjametsj: Unique Collection of Statues and Shields

Adrian A. Gerbrands

At three o'clock in the afternoon of Wednesday June 28, 1961 three dugouts set off from the village of Amanamkai, on the Awor, a small tributary in the lower course of the As River (see Figure 8.1, map, page 116).

Amanamkai, with 700 inhabitants, was then one of the larger villages in the Asmat region. The village consisted of three quarters, each organized around a large, rectangular *jeu* or ceremonial house. The *jeu* stood with their facades parallel to the Awor, the small river that flowed right through the village, forming, as it were, its main street. Along the rear wall of each of the three *jeu* was a row of some twenty fireplaces, one for each family group. Inside two of the *jeu,* near each fireplace, an exquisitely carved *bisj* or ancestor pole had been placed. Those *bisj* were tangible proof of the talents of the twenty or so renowned woodcarvers, or *wowipitsj*, who lived in Amanamkai.

The houses in this village were strung out in a row along the river. In the middle were the temporary homes of two cultural anthropologists: myself, then associated with the Leiden museum, and David B. Eyde, then a student of anthropology at Yale University. The two of us had used Amanamkai as a base for our fieldwork since the end of 1960.

On June 24, three guests had arrived at Amanamkai: Michael C. Rockefeller, son of Nelson A. Rockefeller, then governor of New York; Michael's friend Samuel Putnam, who had recently taken up medicine at Harvard University, and René S. Wassing, who came along as a representative of the Dutch Bureau of Native Affairs at Hollandia (now Jayapura).

During the four days of their stay, Eyde and I had organized some cultural entertainments for our guests, including a large exhibition of dugout canoes on the As River, and a mock initiation dance for a new *jeu.* To conclude their visit to the area, we were going to accompany our guests on a expedition of several days to a number of villages on the Casuarina Coast.

That proved easier promised than done. To begin with, I had nearly exhausted my wits and patience trying to persuade the owners of three dugouts—necessary to carry the four large (and clumsy) white men—to make their boats available. Once this was accomplished, finding the necessary oarsmen, at least six for each dugout, presented even more difficulties. This despite my promise of a very generous fee (by the standards then prevailing) of a whole stick of tobacco for each rowing day, plus a lengthy piece of fishing line and hook on our return to Amanamkai.

When the dugouts finally departed, it was with just sixteen oarsmen, rather than the eighteen that were, considering the load, necessary. Rockefeller and I sat in the first boat, in the second sat Wassing and the Asmat interpreter Simon, and finally in the last dugout, Putnam with the largest part of the baggage. David Eyde was not able to accompany us because finding a fourth boat and oarsmen was under the circumstances out of the question.

It turned out later that the reason for this unusual reluctance on the part of the men of Amanamkai was that they knew of the hostile relationship between Omadesep and Otsjanep villages, both of which were on our itinerary, and they feared getting caught up in difficulties. My prestige—and the bonus on return—had in the end enticed sixteen rowers to take the risk.

Down the river

Three o'clock in the afternoon seemed a strange time to leave. In just three or four hours, after a brief tropical dusk, night would fall. And finding one's way through the swamp-forest at night is a difficult business. However, that night would be a full moon, and in the tropics, a full moon can cast almost as much light as the sun. Finding our way would not be a problem, and we would be able to avoid hazards like fallen trees or heavy branches overhanging the river.

More important even than this, however, was that at three o'clock the strong, slow tidal current was with us, heading towards the Arafura Sea. Particularly as we were short two oarsmen, traveling with the current was essential. It would allow the heavily laden dugouts to move down the Awor River, then down the As River, and finally to the Betsj. From there, our plan was to reach the more inland villages on the Casuarina Coast:

Plate 8.1 Detail from a statue of Auwenembes, holding his wife Ndambutsj. This carving was made by Ndafor of Atjametsj village, and is part of a unique collection of shields and sculptures collected by Adrian A. Gerbrands for the Leiden museum in 1961. RMV 3790-518. Photograph: Isaäc C. Brussee. For more on this sculpture see Plate 8.20, page 131.

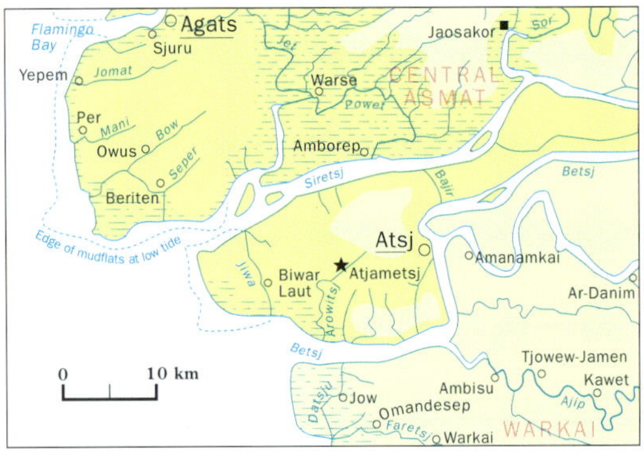

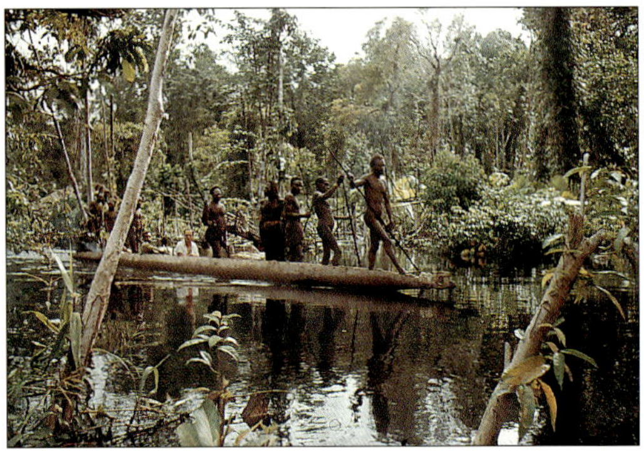

DAVID B. EYDE

Jow, Omadesep, Warkai and Otsjanep, the latter, at the time, being our ultimate destination.

As everywhere in the Asmat region, the villages in this region are situated on the banks of the large rivers or their tributaries. Because there are no roads or paths in the swamps, travel is entirely by water routes.

Villages sometimes build simple accommodations on high poles near the mouth of "their" rivers, as a place for the groups of fishing women, together with their children and the men who accompany them for protection, to overnight. When hostilities between villages occur, these riverside bivouacs are also used as watch posts. The villages of Jow and Omadesep each had such watch posts, which also served as a guesthouse for passing travelers. The bivouac at Jow, located on the Betsj River, was the first one the dugouts passed after leaving Amanamkai.

The journey had so far passed without difficulty. The strong tidal current had taken the three boats and their heavy loads downstream at quite a high speed, and the trip had taxed the oarsmen little. Rowing in an upright position in the Asmat manner, our oarsmen urged the boats along with smooth, almost lazy strokes of their paddles.

It was already seven o'clock in the evening; the sun had set an hour ago in a blaze of red-orange, and entered Safan, the realm of the ancestors. The moon had appeared, startlingly large, and shot quickly above the treetops, grinning coldly. By seven, the moon stood high in the sky, where it should be. Its silver light shone down on the small group of dugouts gliding silently through the forest. Now and then the river splashed softly against the thin sides of the canoes. We were captives of the moonlight. No words were spoken, except for a single, barely audible fragment of a word from the lookout, when it was necessary to avoid a water-logged trunk or an overhanging branch.

On to Omadesep

As the journey had been satisfactory so far, and rowing in the cool of the radiant moon night went well, we decided to continue to the next house for temporary visitors, which belonged to Omadesep. This was about two hours further along the coast, where the Faretsj River empties into the sea. For a moment the oarsmen objected, afraid of the swell on the sea to which the dugouts, with their low sides, were unequal. The sea, however, was calm and there was no wind. Although the tide now receded, it remained high

Figure 8.1 (above, top) Map of the Atjametsj area.

Plate 8.2 (above, bottom) A dugout traveling through the swamp woods at high tide. Adrian A. Gerbrands is seated in the center. The vicinity of Amanamkai village, Cental Asmat, 1961.

Plate 8.3 (Opposite) Adrian Gerbrands writes: "Atjametsj turned out to be a small, rather poor village with just one *jeu*...." This modest appearance, however, proved deceptive. The single *jeu* contained an impressive group of shields and statues. Atjametsj village, Central Asmat, 1961.

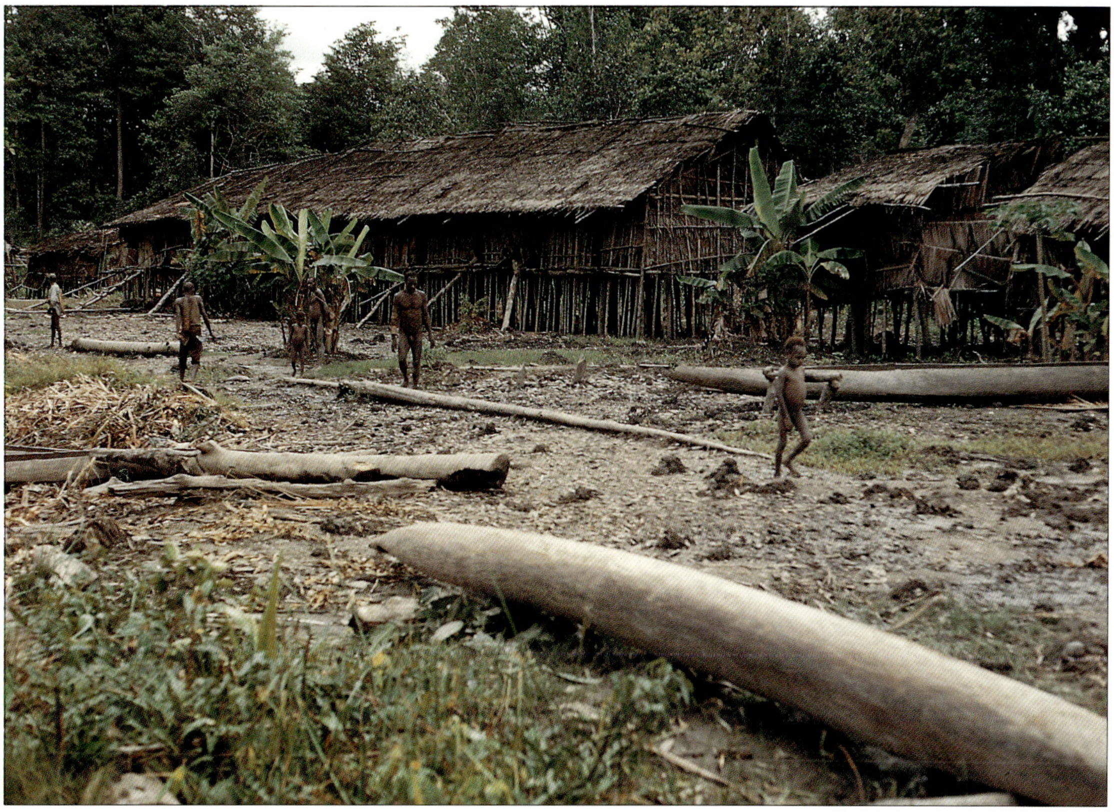

ADRIAN A. GERBRANDS

enough to continue the journey traveling right along the coast. The dugouts are round-bottomed, and without keels, and their draft is very shallow. Thus they can pass through the shallows protected by the coastal mangroves. Enormous swarms of a species of starlings flew around the boats, filling the air with their excited chirping, and the heavy rustling of thousands of wings. Thanks to the full moon, which still stood in the sky, the three boats reached the Omadesep's bivouac at around nine o'clock in the evening.

That house was in an extremely bad condition. The floors consisted only of thin logs, sometimes spaced more than a hand's width apart. There were some remnants of bark which must at one point have served to cover the shelter's floor, and fortunately this was sufficient to serve as a sleeping accommodation.

We continued our journey to Omadesep the next morning. The people of Omadesep at once started to eagerly offer us all kinds of woodcarvings in exchange for tobacco, knives, fishing line and fish hooks. The majority of the items presented were of a very mediocre quality, carved quickly for exchange with some white man visiting their village.

The village also had four nice large *bisj*, ancestor poles left over from a recent feast. They were much too long and heavy to load onto the three dugouts, and we still had quite a journey yet to undertake. But Rockefeller purchased them for his father's museum, the Museum of Primitive Art in New York[1] with the stipulation that the village men were to deliver them to the administrative capital of Agats. Later, with the same stipulation, six beautiful *bisj*—and one or two war shields—were purchased in the village of Otsjanep.[2]

As it would take several days to arrange the large dugouts required to transport these carvings, we decided to go on ahead in the direction of Agats. We set a day to meet the boats from Otsjanep in Jow village's temporary house at the mouth of the Betsj River. From there, we would

1. Michael Rockefeller's Asmat collection is now housed in the Rockefeller Wing of the Metropolitan Museum of Art in New York.

2. Two of these six *bisj* were donated by Mary C. and Nelson A. Rockefeller to the Leiden museum in 1962. These are illustrated in Plate 7.45, page 102, and Plate 7.47, page 103.

continue our journey to Agats together. The people of Otsjanep were afraid to travel north of the Betsj without the white men along for protection.

On the appointed day we arrived at Jow's bivouac. After two days, the men from Otsjanep had still not arrived. Our Amanamkai oarsmen suggested that the men from Otsjanep had been afraid to travel past the village of Omadesep with their *bisj* and war shields. Given the state of relations between the two villages, there was a reasonable chance that the jealous Omadesep would ransack them or take a heavy toll.

Tired of waiting, we decided to pay a visit to the nearby villages of Biwar Laut and Atjametsj, just across the wide mouth of the Betsj (see map page 116), before heading back to Amanamkai. In Biwar Laut Rockefeller purchased a pair of paddles with very long, beautifully carved shafts. But that was all we found at this small, "boring" village. We thus decided to immediately row on to Atjametsj, three hours upstream, on the upper course of the Arowitsj River, a small creek that runs into the wide mouth of the Betsj.

The carvings of Atjametsj

Atjametsj turned out to be a small, rather poor village with just one *jeu*. According to the men from Amanamkai, Jeu Atjametsj had originally been part of the large and powerful village of Atsj, situated further upstream at a bend in the Betsj River. After a quarrel, the people of this *jeu* had fled to the current site. Hidden in the swamp forest on the remote upper course of the Arowitsj River, the villagers were relatively safe from retaliation or predatory raids from Atsj.

Given this modest setting, it thus came as quite a surprise when, inside the *jeu,* we found seven large ancestor statues and seven war shields. The shields were placed along the wall of the *jeu* towards the river; the statues seemed to be placed at random through the entire *jeu*. Each statue was tied to a palisade of thick branches which reached through the rather unsound floor of the jeu to the muddy ground below.

Along the rear wall of the *jeu* was the usual long row of fireplaces. In Atjametsj there were 19 fireplaces in all, representing 18 family groups. The central fireplace or *mboijir* stood in the middle, with nine family fireplaces on each side. By Asmat standards at the time, this was quite a large *jeu*. Later we learned that the allocation of statues was not as random as it first seemed. The woodcarvings were placed opposite or near the fireplaces of the family groups with which they were associated (see Figure 8.2, page 121).

Michael Rockefeller was tempted to acquire this collection of woodcarvings for the museum in New York. However, our three dugouts were already overloaded, and crossing the choppy mouth of the Betsj River was risky enough as it was. Therefore, it had to be enough to take detailed photographs of everything *in situ,* and to try to collect as much information on the pieces as possible. The latter did not prove to be a simple matter, as the people of Atjametsj were extremely reluctant to answer our questions.

Our informants gave vague answers when asked about the character of the feast for which the statues and shields were made. On one occasion they spoke briefly about a *jamasj mbui*, a shield feast; on another occasion they spoke of a *wash mbui*, a statue feast. Eventually we came to understand that the statues had served an essential role in a kind of elaborate shield feast.

The feast of the statues

The reason they acted in such a reserved manner regarding the character of the feast never became clear. Presumably the terms *jamasj mbui* and *wash mbui* were sufficient for the people of Atjametsj and Amanamkai, so that further explanation was unnecessary. I suppose it is something like the term "carnival." A general term, but sufficiently clear to a European.

This feast for which the statues and shields were made had no doubt required weeks, if not months of preparation. The people of Atjametsj could not say exactly when it had taken place, although it was presumably several months ago. It should be kept in mind that the Asmat do not have a calendar at their disposal. Within their culture and in a land without important seasons, they really do not need one. The time of day is given in general terms only by referring to the sun's position in the sky. To indicate long spells of time the Asmat refer either to periods of full and new moon, to rainy and dry seasons, or to spring tide and neap tide.

The statues and shields are materializations of

Plate 8.4 Large twin statue of Auwenembes holding his wife Ndambutsj in front of him. Made by Ndafor for his paternal grandfather Magawut. Ndambutsj is Magawut's sister. Atjametsj village, Central Asmat, 1961. (See also: Plate 8.1, page 114, a detail of the statue; Plate 8.19, page 131, a photograph of the carver; and Plate 8.20, page 131, a color photograph of the sculpture.) Photograph: Adrian A. Gerbrands.

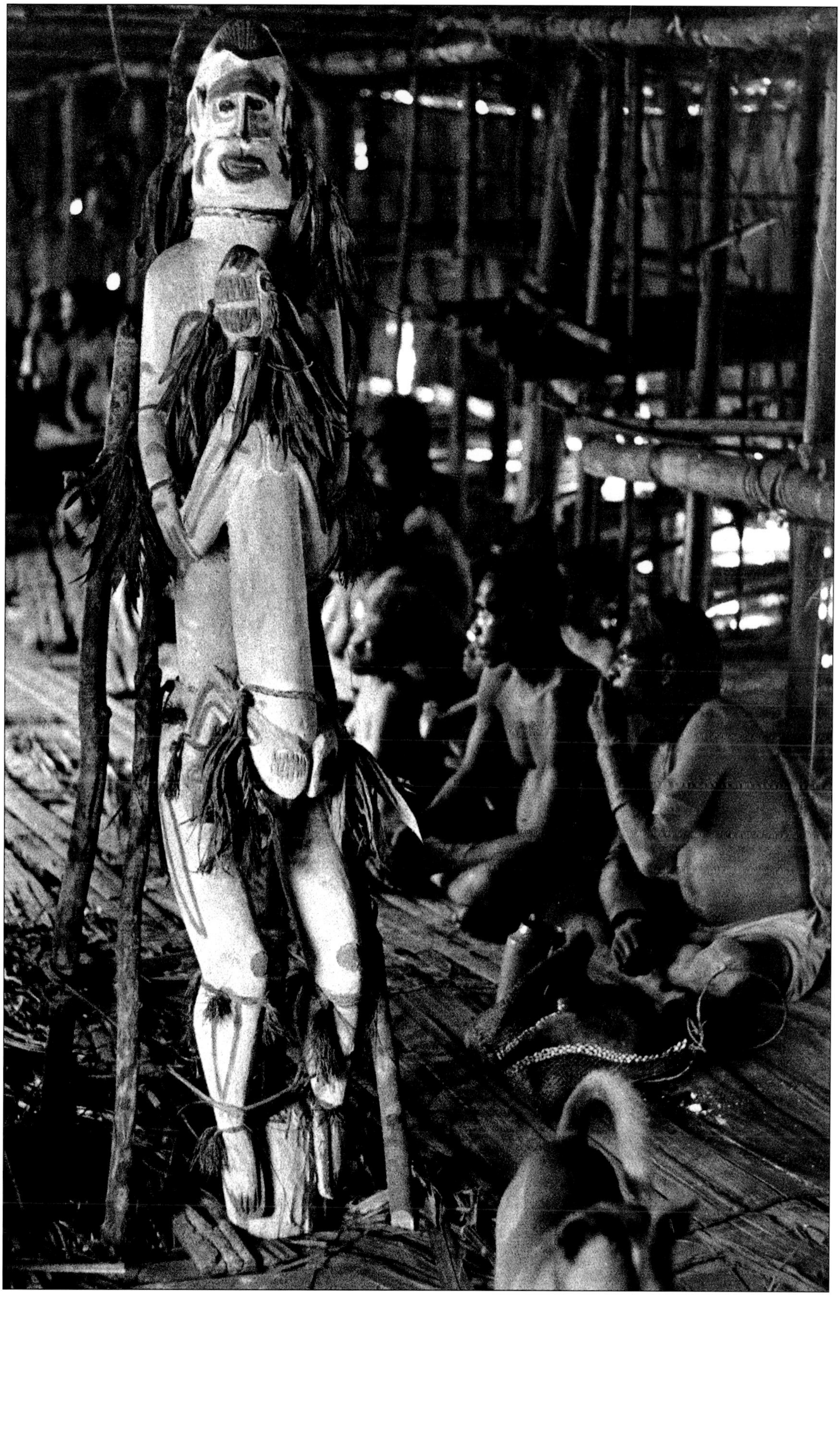

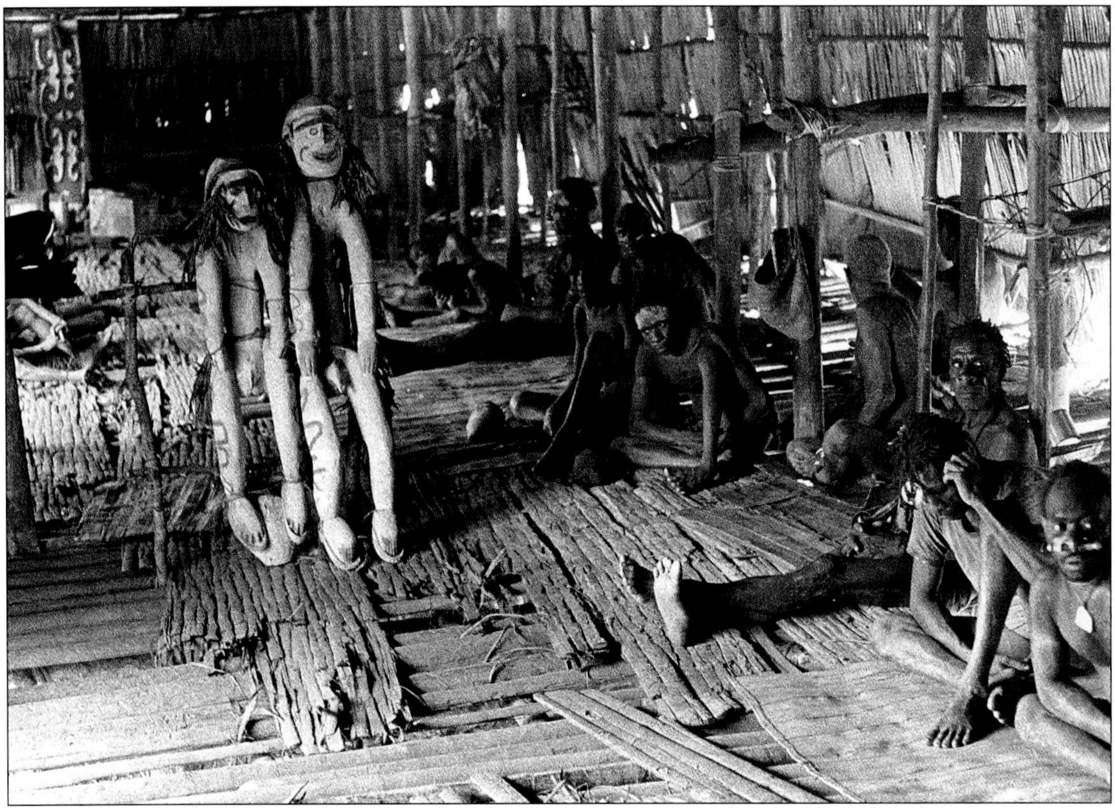

specific ancestors. Extensive negotiations between the various family groups are necessary before an accord is reached on which ancestors will be depicted. In these negotiations relative prestige and rivalry between the families, and even between individuals, often play an important part. The choice of an ancestor is not only an honor for the group of his or her next of kin, it also obliges the group to present an adequate banquet to the guests. This requires large amount of sago, and especially, very large quantities of sago grubs, the larvae of the Capricorn beetle. To breed these grubs, great numbers of sago palms must be felled, punched full of holes, and left in the sago grounds for 30 to 40 days.

Binding commitments must be made with those members of the community who are known to be skilled woodcarvers. Typically one turns to carvers who are members of his own family group, because these are the easiest to pressure to make the required statues and shields.

Night after night, sacred songs are recited by those who know these songs well, accompanied by the few men known as good drummers too. During the feast itself, the men dance in the *jeu* night after night.

All in all, preparing and ultimately holding such a feast is no mean feat. The structures of power in an Asmat *jeu* are rather vague, resting on seniority, on family reputation, and last—but not least—on personal authority. Except for seniority, these are shifting categories, and under such conditions it is clear proof of their organizing abilities when the leaders succeed in holding the feast at the more or less appointed time.

It did not prove difficult to find out the names of the ancestors associated with the statues and shields—there was no difference of opinion about this. In the few cases that two ancestors were depicted in one and the same woodcarving, it was apparently a married couple. The motifs on the shields also depicted ancestors, sometimes of generations ago. The exact family relationship

Plate 8.5 Interior of the *jeu,* looking downstream from the central fireplace, with two sculptures and a shield visible. The statue on the left (RMV 3790-516) was made by Fupie, and represents his grandfather Ndomepon. The statue on the right (RMV 3790-517) was made by Safanminim, and represents his father. Atjametsj village, Central Asmat, 1961. (See also: Plates 8.25 and 8.26, page 134; Plates 8.27 and 8.28, page 135.)

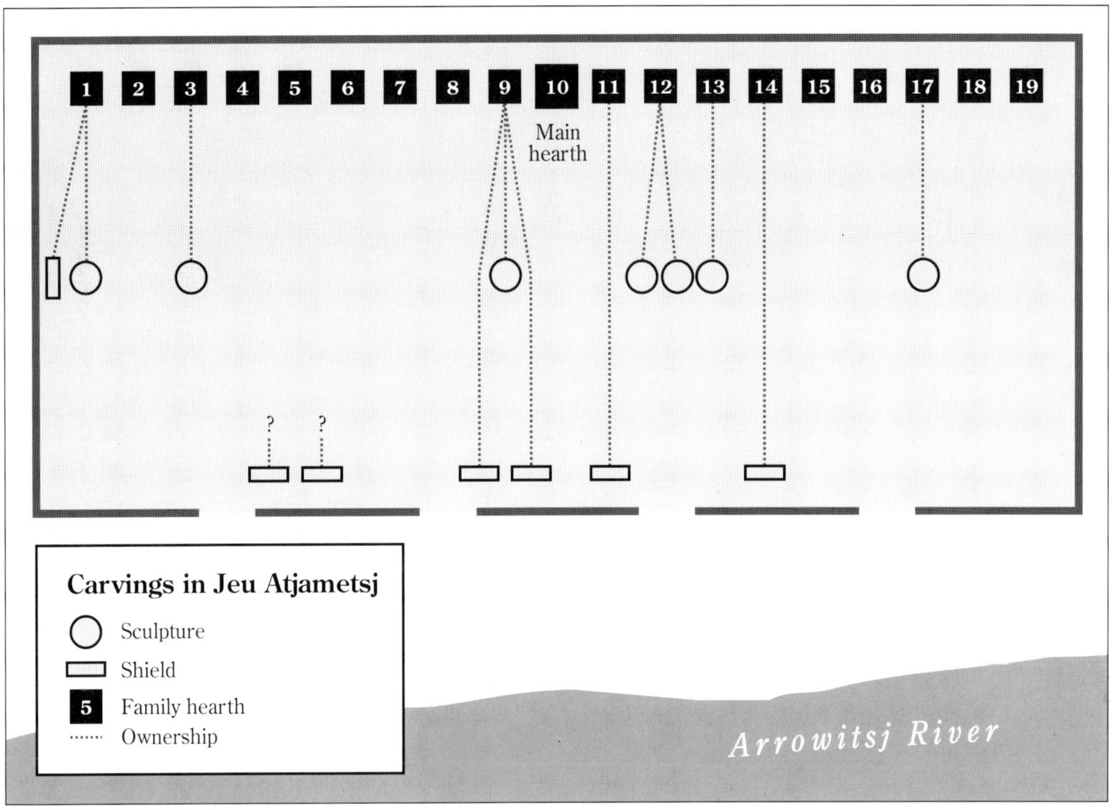

between the depicted ancestors and the person who presented himself as the owner of the statue or shield was not always quite clear. This in part owed to the difficulties of interpretation presented by Asmat family terms.

Owners and *wowipitsj*

Another uncertainty at first were the names of those who had carved the various statues and shields. The reason for this was that although the Asmat appreciate the role of the woodcarver, and this gives him status, in the context of the work of art, he is subordinate in position to the commissioner. To the Asmat, the owner of a woodcarving is more important than the carver.

The myths and stories of origin recited during the feast shape the essence of the relationship between a human being and his ancestors, and it is the relationship between the owner and his ancestors that is given tangible shape in the statue or shield. Thus the woodcarver is indeed essential, but still of secondary importance.

Initially, the people of Atjametsj were completely unable to grasp why I continually asked for the maker's names. Only later did they understand that I aimed at getting to know the various woodcarvers. By then they had probably heard from the oarsmen who had come along that in Amanamkai that I was particularly interested in learning about the *wowipitsj*.

I never stopped taking their photographs. I gave them tobacco, knives, fishing lines and fishing hooks in exchange for woodcarvings. Sometimes, I even gave them a real axe for an ancestor image, or indeed even more for an old shield. Since I was not willing to exchange every piece and accepted only well carved and highly finished pieces, only the better woodcarvers, the acknowledged *wowipitsj* from the village, stood a chance of getting a piece of tobacco or one of the other much sought after items. This indeed strained the traditional relationships of power within the village.

Generally speaking, a woodcarving was traditionally commissioned by a family head. There was really no question of payment in the western sense. The woodcarver simply did what the head

Figure 8.2 Floor plan of Jeu Atjametsj with the locations of statues and shields as found on July 4, 1961. Adapted from a sketch by Adrian A. Gerbrands.

of the family told him to do. However, when I negotiated for a carving, I did so directly with the individual woodcarvers. This was, in a sense, going behind the back of the head of the family. Further, I did not "pay," as was good practice among the Asmat, the head of the family who had commissioned the carving, but the woodcarver himself. According to traditional Asmat thinking on these matters, the woodcarver had no rights, or only a small part of the rights, to an individual carving.

Obtaining the carvings

In the early morning of the following day, July 4, three dugouts set off for Agats, loaded with everything Rockefeller and his companions had collected during the past days. Much to Rockefeller's disappointment, the Atjametsj collection had to be left behind. There was absolutely no room for it in the boats.

Later, Rockefeller, Putnam and Wassing left Agats on a governmental patrol boat back to Merauke. Simon, the Asmat interpreter, and I returned together with the oarsmen in the three dug-outs to Amanamkai, and settled with the owners of the boats and their oarsmen.

Prior to the start of the boat trip I had agreed with Rockefeller that the latter was in principle to acquire each offered object for the Museum of Primitive Art, bearing in mind that I, when in my opinion a piece of extremely high quality was offered, was to have priority to trade for the piece to the benefit of the National Museum of Ethnology in Leiden.

In Atjametsj this was indeed the case. The collection of statues, as found in the *jeu,* formed a unique set. First, because the pieces made up the complete collection of statues prepared for a single feast. Second, because the documentation was excellent. I had discovered the names of those who gave the feast, and the ancestors for whom the feast was given. It was also known which woodcarvers had made which pieces. Photographs were taken of the pieces were taken as they stood in the *jeu,* and later it was possible to photograph most of the woodcarvers. Finally, the entire collection was of a very fine quality.

Obtaining the sculptures

All in all, this seemed to me more than enough reason to acquire the collection as a whole for the Leiden museum. Because of a lack of cargo space in the boats, I had had to leave the collection behind in Atjametsj on July 4. Immediately after returning from Agats, I organized a number of boats together with David Eyde and Simon to acquire the carvings. Finding the necessary oarsmen this time was no problem at all. If the tide is right, the journey from Amanamkai and back can be completed in one day.

In Atjametsj, the owners were quite willing to part with the collection in exchange for seven 3.5-pound steel axe heads (one for each of the statues), seven 2.5-pound axe heads (one for each shield), and five chopping knives, two smaller knives, and thirty slices of tobacco. Delivery to Amanamkai was included in the bargain, and payment was to be made upon receipt. Converted to the prices then valid in the Asmat region, the axes, knives and tobacco in this transaction represented a substantial payment (circa Hfl. 255). For this amount, the collection had traveled to Amanamkai. A long, complex and certainly not inexpensive road had to be followed before the carvings were to reach the Leiden museum.

It was not clear why the men of Atjametsj had kept the collection in the *jeu* that long after the feast had ended. Perhaps they hoped that the carvings—as they had heard took place in other villages—could be exchanged for goods with government officers, missionaries, or perhaps even a passing tourist. In principle, however, there was not much chance of this because Atjametsj was very isolated, nestled deep in the forest.

The strategy had, however, succeeded now! In the euphoria of the successful transaction, and this time without a doubt in connection with information as to my research provided by the rowers from Amanamkai, nearly all the woodcarvers served as the oarsmen who accompanied the statues to Amanamkai. I was able to take their photographs one by one, a process to which they happily submitted.

On arrival at Amanamkai, the statues in particular aroused general admiration. Mbatai, a *jeu* leader in Amanamkai and the same man who had adopted me as his son, spontaneously cried, "Akat! Akat!" the Asmat exclamation for something considered beautiful. He complemented me on this new acquisition.

Until I was able to arrange transport to Agats, and from there to Leiden, the collection was kept in my house in Amanamakai. For days on end, there was a hustle and bustle caused by the village men who came to look at and admire the collection. Matjemos, one of the best woodcarvers in Amanamkai, returned a number of times to study the statues.

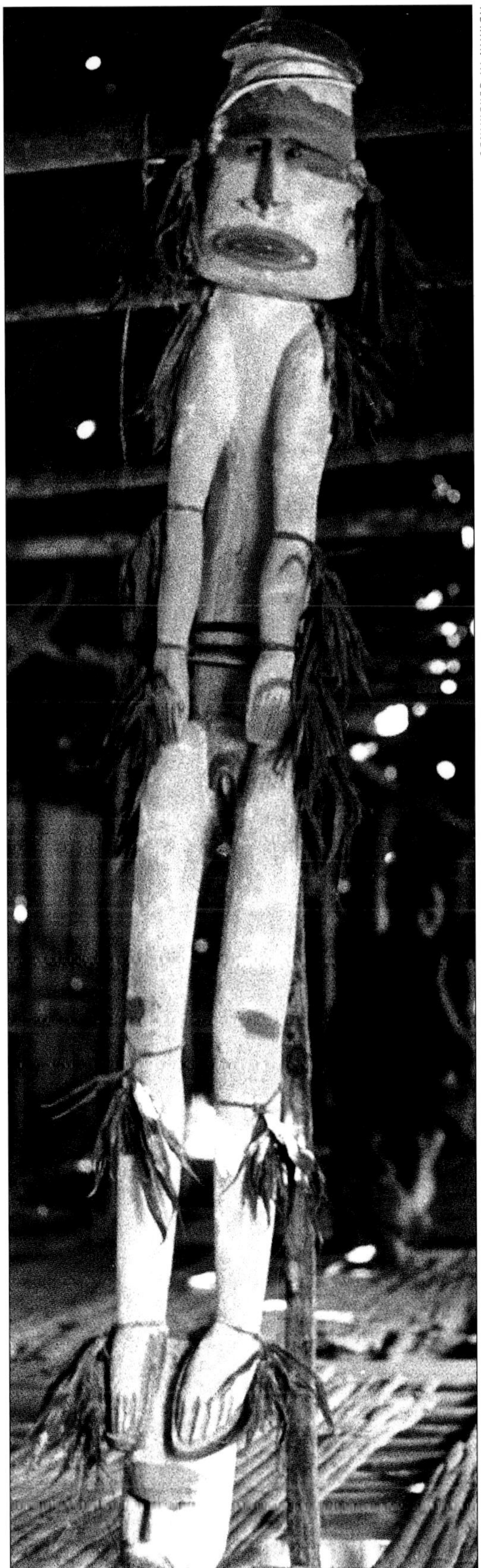

When I asked him which statue he liked the most ("Akat awut?"), he pointed without any hesitation to the large twin statue of a man holding his wife in front of his chest (Plate 8.20, page 131). He had more trouble with the worst statue, but after some hesitation, he chose the large statue of a woman standing on her husband's skull (Plate 8.24, page 133). Assatji, head of Jeu Amman, also immediately chose the twin statue of man and wife as the best, but he did not point out the "worst," presumably because he did not understand the question. Further questioning was of no use, because the other interviewees, over and over, gave the same answer they had heard Matjemos and Assatji give. This, they assumed, was the answer I wanted to hear.

Matjemos was clearly very impressed by the twin statue. After looking at the statue for a number of days, he told me was also going to make such a statue. However, nothing came of this plan—at least during the remainder of my sojourn at Amanamkai. On August 9, 1961 I left Agats for Merauke, and then to the Netherlands.

Rockefeller returned with Wassing at the end of September for a long journey through the entire Asmat region. During this time, they acquired an Asmat collection for the Museum of Primitive Art in New York. To transport his finds, Rockefeller had rigged up a catamaran from two large dug-outs, and equipped it with an outboard motor. Towards the end of their expedition, on November 18, 1961, the unwieldy boat capsized in the tidal bore at the broad mouth of the Betsj River. Rockefeller tried to swim to the coast, but was lost. Wassing, clinging to the capsized boat was later picked up by government patrol boats.

Rockefeller's Asmat collection is now kept in a wing named after him in the Metropolitan Museum in New York. Using the partly saved journal and photographs of his trip, I later edited Rockefeller's journal and published the collection for the Museum of Primitive Art in *The Asmat of New Guinea: The Journal of Michael Clark Rockefeller*, New York, 1967.

Plate 8.6 (left) The large statue of Mbin (RMV 3790-521), standing on her husband Wumbeitsjasem's skull. Mbin was an elder sister of Ndopor, the maker and owner of the statue. Atjametsj village, Central Asmat, 1961. (See also: Plate 8.24, page 133, for a color photograph of the sculpture.)

Plate 8.7 (overleaf, page 124) Interior of the *jeu*, from the central fireplace looking upstream, with four of the seven ancestor statues. Atjametsj village, Central Asmat, 1961. Photograph: Adrian A. Gerbrands.

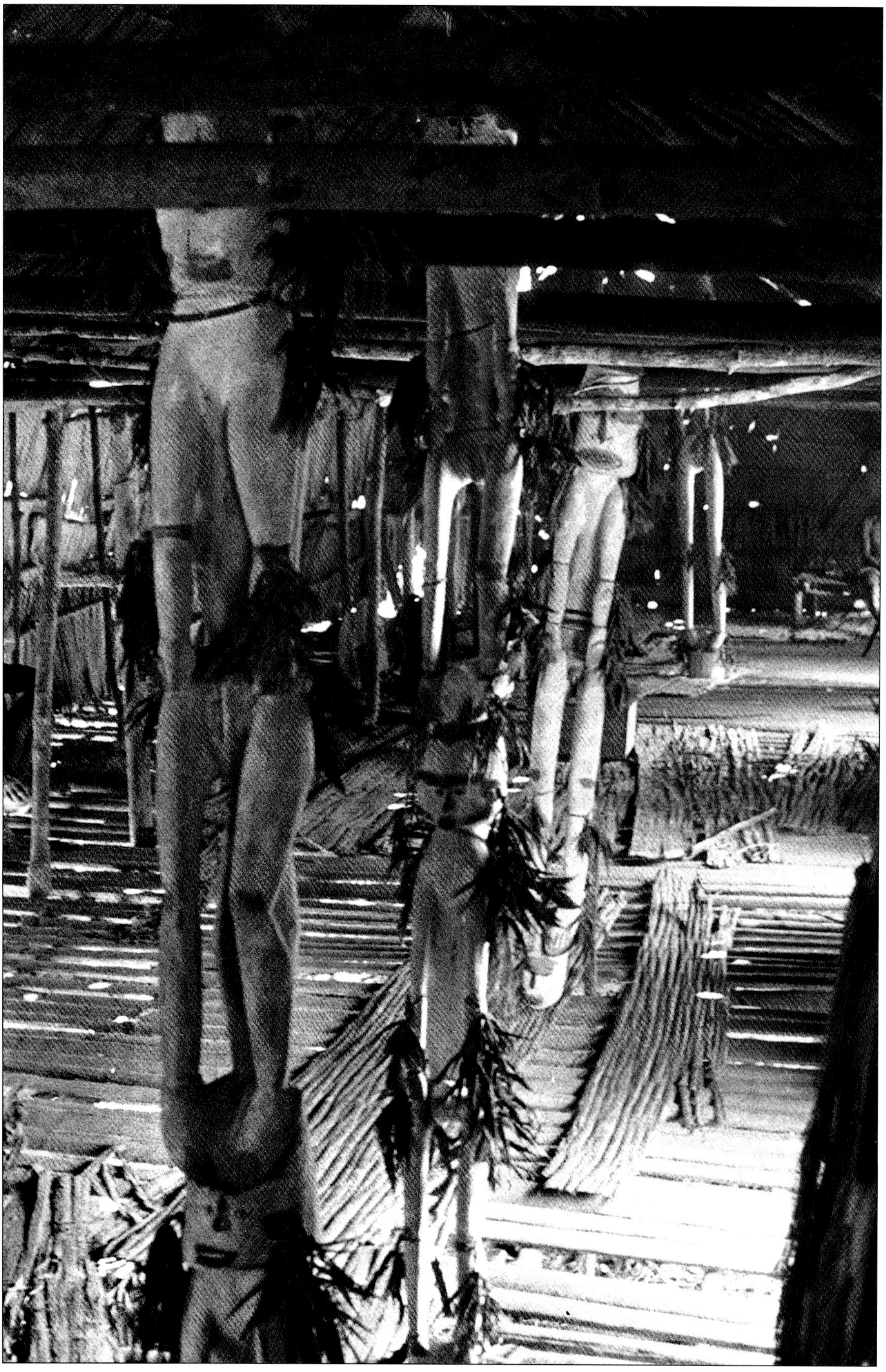

I. The Atjametsj collection
Central Asmat
Collected: 1961

The Atjametsj collection consists of a unique group of seven statues and seven shields (Plates 8.8–8.28). They were found in 1961 in the *jeu* of the village of Atjametsj by Adrian A. Gerbrands and Michael C. Rockefeller. The statues stood in the middle of the men's house, on the open part of the fireplaces, and were supported by wooden scaffolding. The shields leaned against the walls.

The woodcarvings were made for a feast for the dead. Gerbrands was able to find out who each piece commemorates as well as who carved each. Since they had already served their purpose at the time of the collectors' arrival, Gerbrands was able to acquire them for the museum. The Leiden museum received the items in 1961.

A. Shields

The seven shields (Plates 8.8–8.16) generally display the style characteristics of the Central Asmat Style Region (see also: Group of Shields IV, page 82). These shields differ from the norm, however, in that the abstract motifs are mirrored on both the horizontal and vertical axes.

A very striking aspect of the Atjametsj shields is the extension each of them has at the top. Most Central Asmat shields have a small point at the top, but few have such elaborate sculptures as, for example, the shield in Plate 8.11. Three of the shields measure more than two meters. In the whole group, the height varies from 167 centimeters to 217 centimeters.

All the shields are decorated with small tassels of sago leaf fiber, and most shields are inlaid with some bright red *Abrus* seeds at the top.

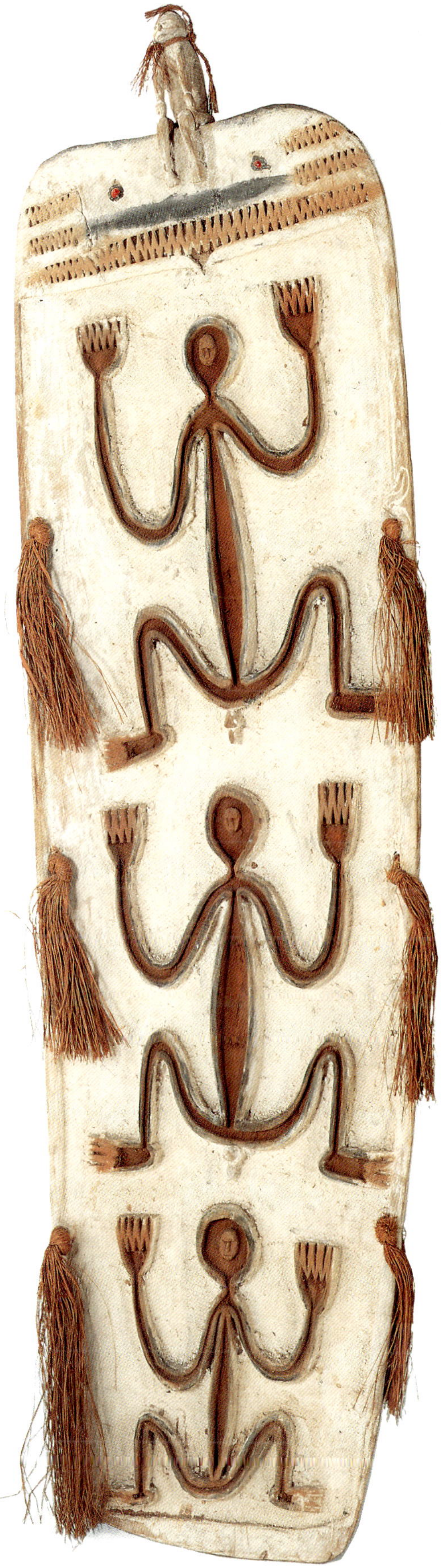

Plate 8.8 Shield. Made by Tjokotsj. Atjametsj village, Central Asmat. Wood, lime, red ocher, charcoal, sago leaf fiber, *Abrus* seeds. 167 cm. Collected in 1961 by Adrian A. Gerbrands. RMV 3790-525. Photograph: Ben Grishaaver.

The small human figure at the top represents Twerawiutsj, an elder sister of the maker, Tjokotsj. The human figures in relief represent (from top to bottom): Ewomber, Tjoktosj's elder brother; Jiirtinaq, Tjokotsj's younger brother; and Jiwei, Tjokotsj's elder sister.

Exhibited: "De jaargetijden van de mens," Rijksmuseum voor Volkenkunde, Leiden 1987. (See Smidt 1987b:79, pl. 2) Note: All the pieces in the Atjametsj collection were exhibited in this show.

Illustrated: Rockefeller 1967, p.168; Hoogerbrugge en Kooijman 1976, fig. 7; Gerbrands 1990, fig. 11, p. 66.

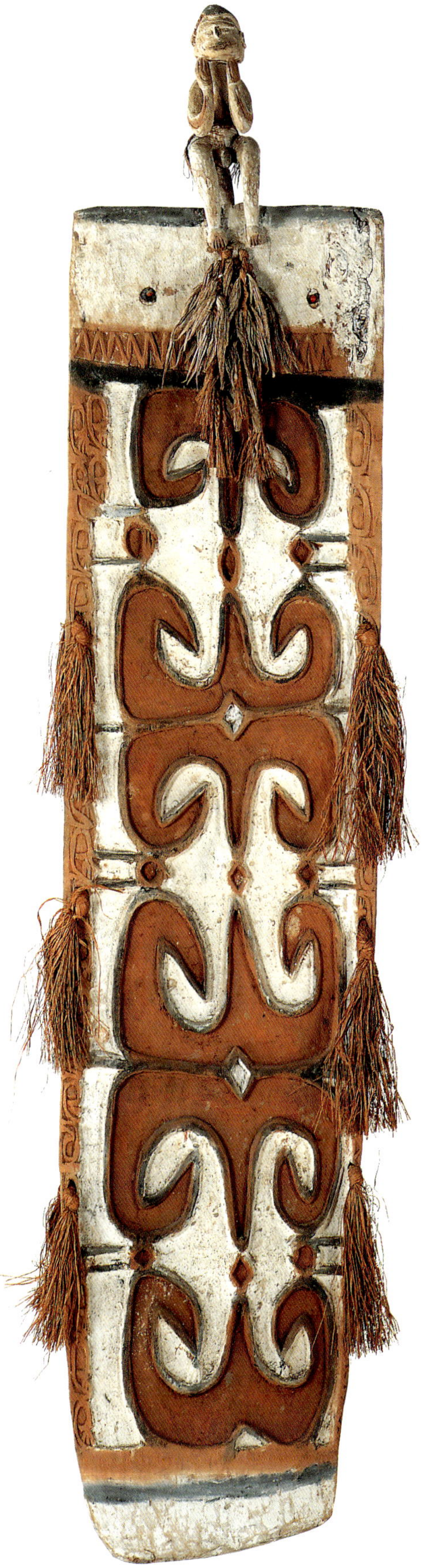

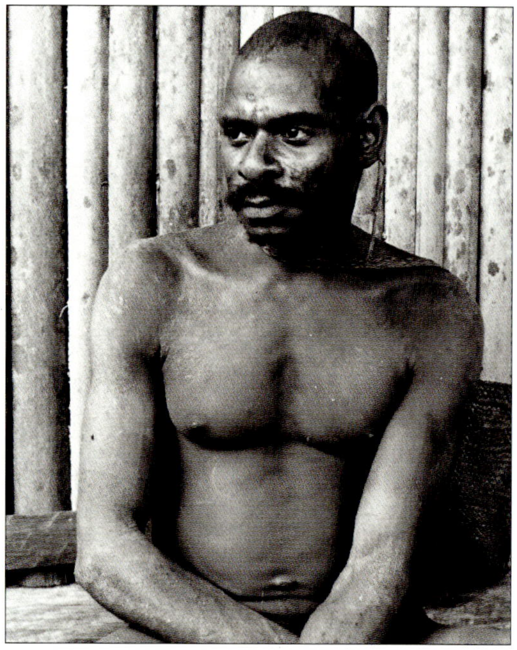

ADRIAN A. GERBRANDS

Plate 8.9 (left) Shield. Made by Papies. Atjametsj village, Central Asmat. Wood, lime, red ocher, charcoal, sago leaf fiber, *Abrus* seeds. 217 cm. Collected in 1961 by Adrian A. Gerbrands. RMV 3790-527. Photograph: Ben Grishaaver.

The figure at the top represents Sinimpitsj, the father of Papies, the maker. The motifs in relief represent stylised ancestor figures.

Illustrated: Gerbrands 1990, pl. 14, p. 70.

Plate 8.10 (top) Portrait of the carver Papies.

Plate 8.11 (opposite, left) Shield. Made by Jokor. Atjametsj village, Central Asmat. Wood, lime, red ocher, charcoal, sago leaf fiber, *Abrus* seeds. 207 cm. Collected in 1961 by Adrian A. Gerbrands. RMV 3790-528. Photograph: Ben Grishaaver.

The figure on top, and the motifs in relief, depict ancestors. It is not sure if each of the three pairs of reversed hooks refer to an ancestor, or if each double hook does so separately.

Plate 8.12 (opposite, right) Shield. Made by Jopar. Atjametsj village, Central Asmat. Wood, lime, red ocher, charcoal, sago leaf fiber. 217 cm. Collected in 1961 by Adrian A. Gerbrands. RMV 3790-529. Photograph: Ben Grishaaver.

The figure on top represents Ammon, a younger brother of the owner. The two mirror-image pairs of curled motifs form a stylized representation of the owner's mother and his younger sister.

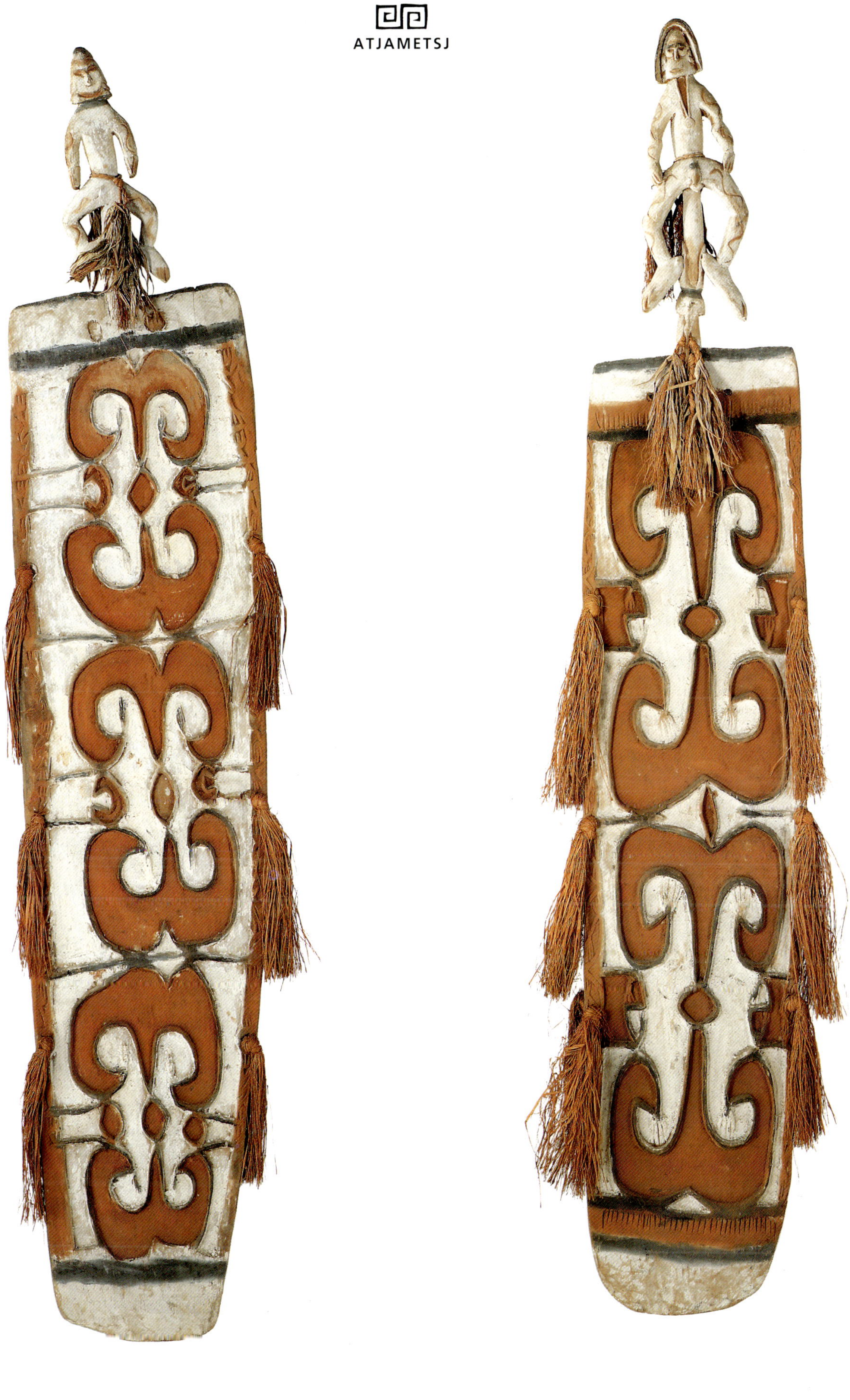

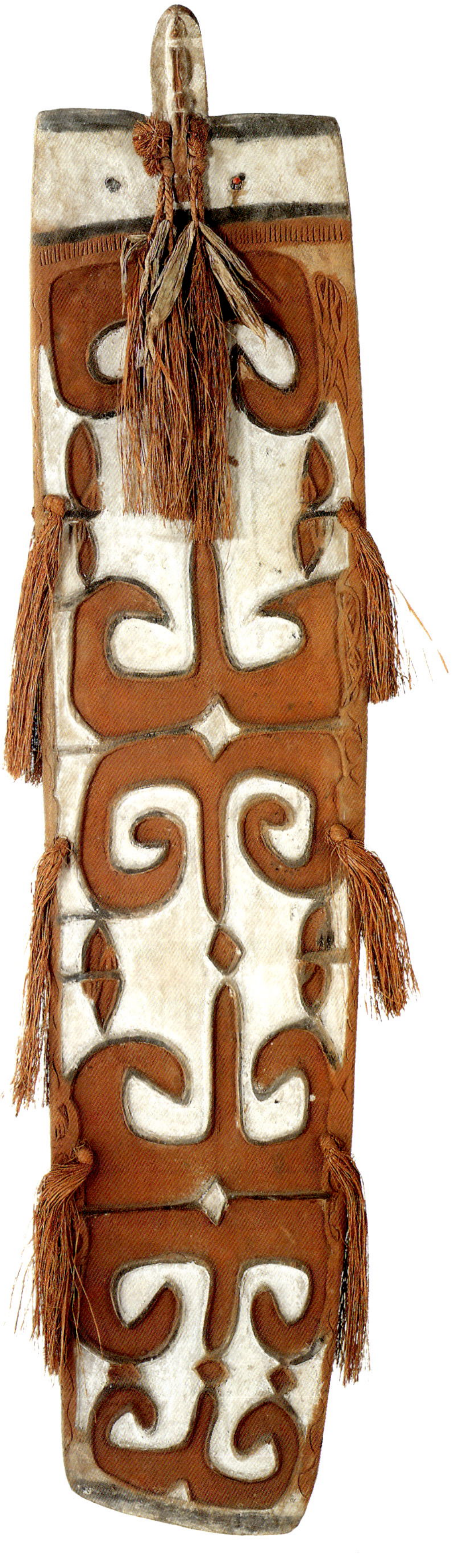

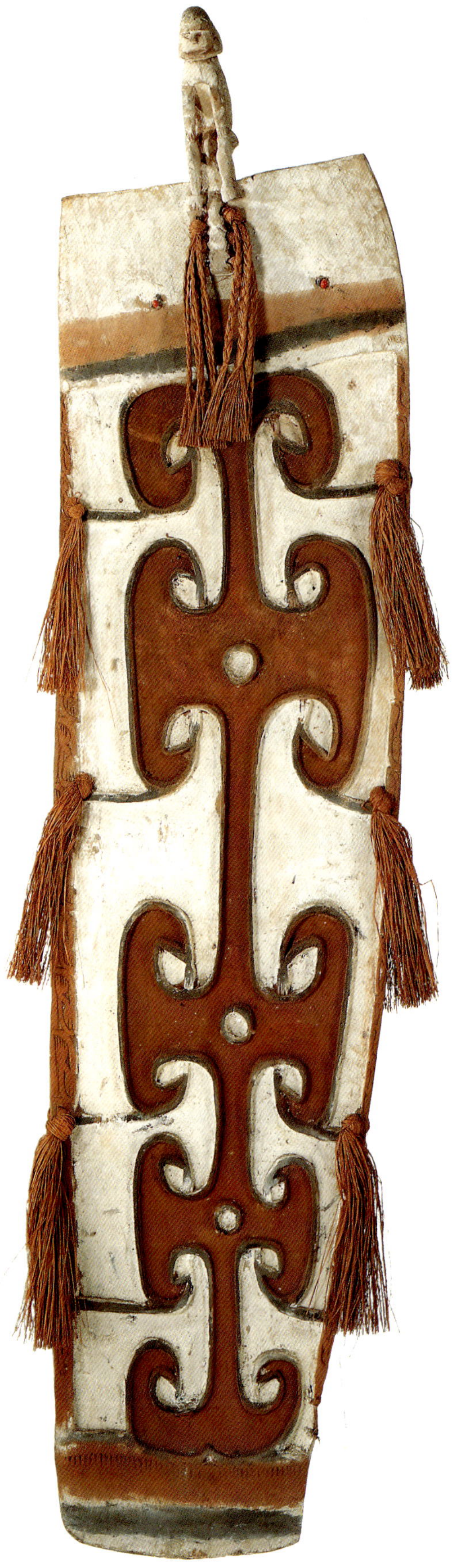

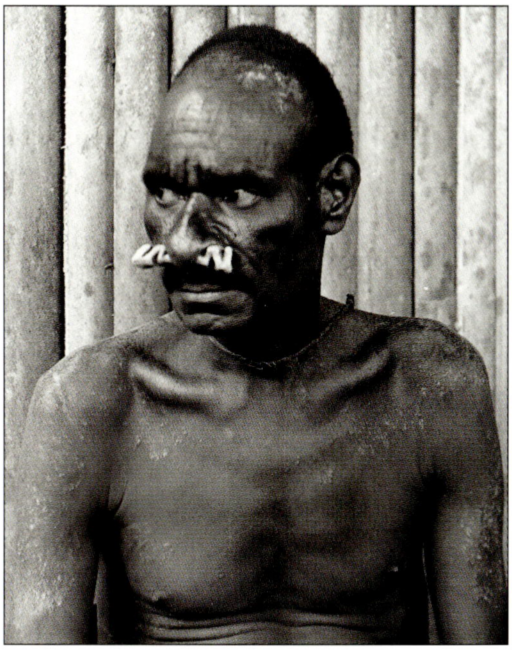

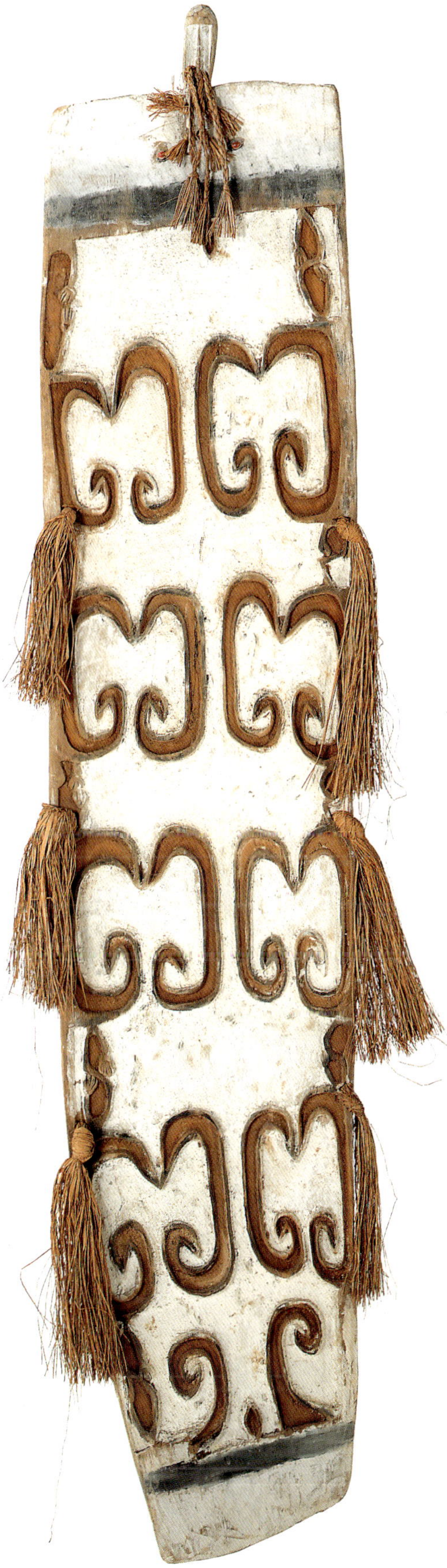

Plate 8.13 (opposite, left) Shield. Made by Jout. Atjametsj village, Central Asmat. Wood, lime, red ocher, charcoal, sago leaf fiber. 190 cm. Collected in 1961 by Adrian A. Gerbrands. RMV 3790-526. Photograph: Ben Grishaaver.

The small figure at the top represents Jopitsj, grandfather of Jout, the maker. The three mirror-image pairs of curled motifs form a stylized representation of three additional ancestors.

Plate 8.14 (opposite, right) Shield. Made by Kokoripitsj. Atjametsj village, Central Asmat. Wood, lime, red ocher, charcoal, sago leaf fiber. 194 cm. Collected in 1961 by Adrian A. Gerbrands. RMV 3790-523. Photograph: Ben Grishaaver.

The small figure on the top represents Kokoripitsj's father Tjimenjeki. The motifs in relief represent three stylized ancestor figures. The circles may represent navels.

Plate 8.15 (above) Portrait of the carver Junum.

Plate 8.16 (right) Shield. Made by Junum. Atjametsj village, Central Asmat. Wood, lime, red ocher, charcoal, sago leaf fiber. 174 cm. Collected in 1961 by Adrian A. Gerbrands. RMV 3790-524. Photograph: Ben Grishaaver.

The small stylized figure at the top represents Dauwur, the maker Junum's mother. The C-shaped motif occurring several times in the mirrored pairs represents the nose ornament (*bipanew*) made of shell, a status and head-hunting symbol.

Illustrated: Rockefeller 1967, p. 168.

Part II: Figure Sculptures

These statues (Plates 8.18–8.28) represent deceased relatives of the makers. The relatives memorialized in the sculptures can be in the same generation as the carver, or a generation or two back. Several statues here show a combination of two figures, which is very rare. Figures standing on top of each other, although common on *bisj*, do not occur in separate sculptures. Other than those in this collection, no old Asmat statues are known to have such a design.

The statue of a man holding his wife, presumably *in coitu* (Plate 8.20) is very unusual. Although a few small statues *in coitu* are known (see Plate 7.25, page 95), the near life-size dimensions of this statue, and the very distinctive design by the carver Ndafor, make this statue unique.

Several statues are noteworthy for thier large size. Three statues are more than two meters high; the largest measures 255 cm. No other old Asmat statues in collection exceed 130 centimeters.

The Atjametsj statues are decorated with leaves and bits of sago leaf fiber. The eyes of a number of statues are inlaid with bright red *Abrus* seeds.

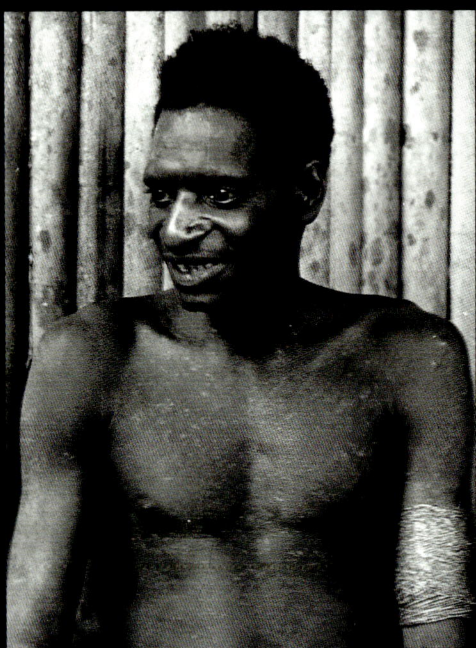

ADRIAN A. GERBRANDS

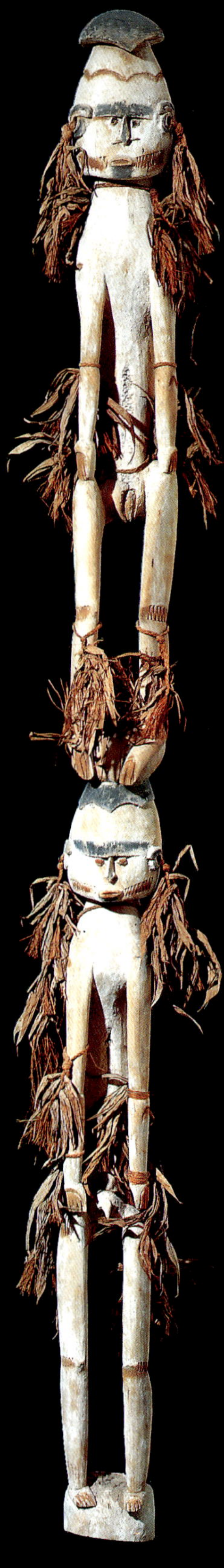

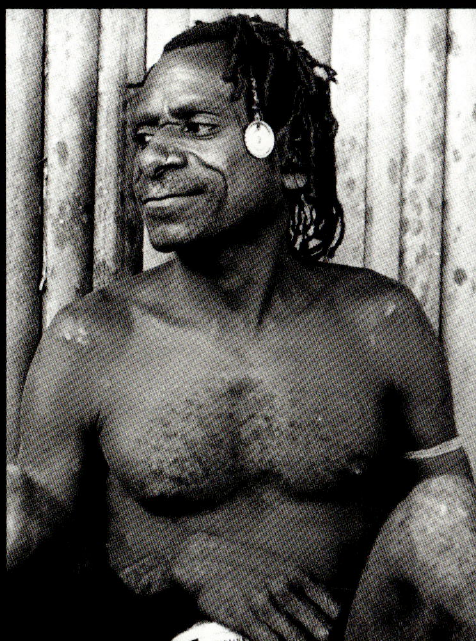

ADRIAN A. GERBRANDS

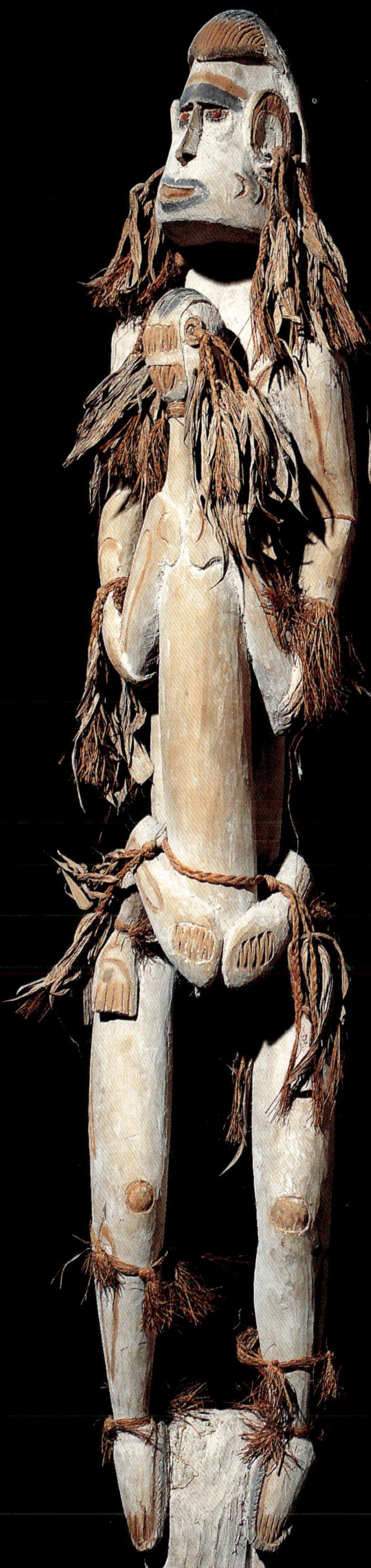

Plate 8.17 (opposite, left) Portrait of the carver Pasei.

Plate 8.18 (opposite, right) Statue of a woman standing on a man. Made by Pasei. Atjametsj village, Central Asmat. Wood, lime, red ocher, leaves. 241 cm. Collected in 1961 by Adrian A. Gerbrands. RMV 3790-520. Photograph: Isaäc C. Brussee.

The woman represents Jewer, standing on her spouse Tamban, respectively the grandmother and grandfather of the maker, Pasei.

Illustrated: Rockefeller 1967, p. 162.

Plate 8.19 (above) Portrait of the carver Ndafor.

Plate 8.20 (right) Statue of a man and a woman. Made by Ndafor. Atjametsj village, Central Asmat. Wood, lime, red ocher, leaves, sago leaf fiber, *Abrus* seeds. 183 cm. Collected in 1961 by Adrian A. Gerbrands. RMV 3790-518. Photograph: Isaäc C. Brussee.

The male figure represents Auwenembes holding his spouse Ndambutsj close (possibly *in coitu*). Made by Ndafor, Ndambutsj's second cousin. (See also: Plate 8.1, a detail of the carving; Plate 8.4, photograph of the carving *in situ*.)

Illustrated: Rockefeller 1967, pp. 164–165; Heermann 1977, omslag; Smidt 1987b, pl. 1, p. 78.

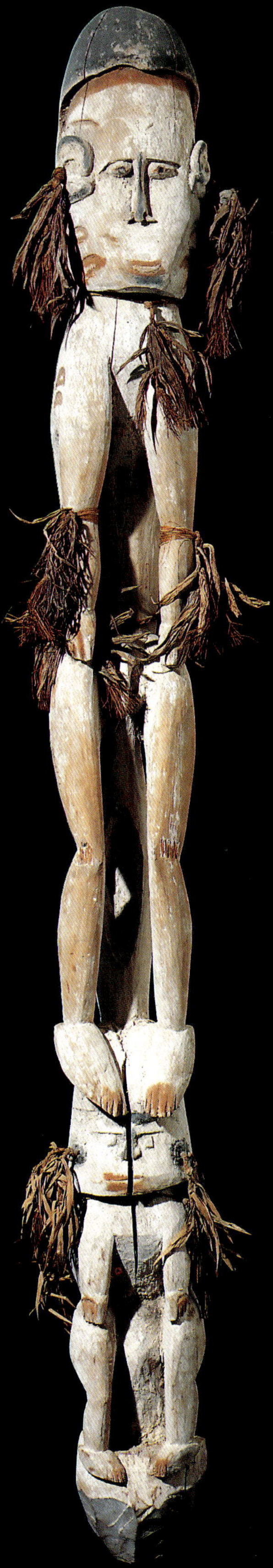

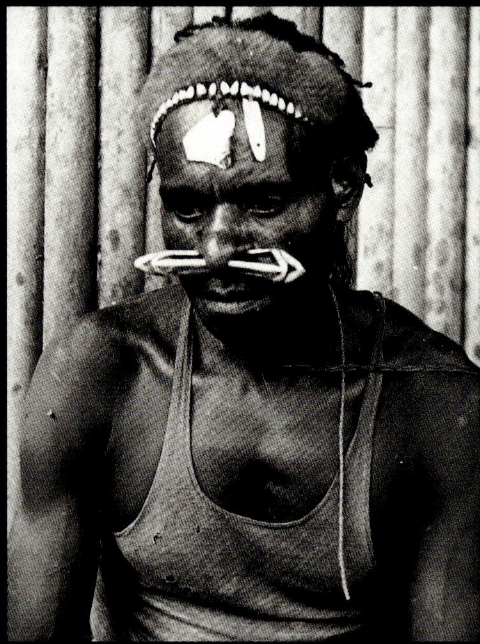

ADRIAN A GERBRANDS

Plate 8.21 (left) Statue of a man standing on a woman. Made by Juwisiri. Atjametsj village, Central Asmat. Wood, lime, red ocher, charcoal, leaves, sago leaf fiber. 226 cm. Collected in 1961 by Adrian A. Gerbrands. RMV 3790-519. Photograph: Isaäc C. Brussee.

Made by Juwisiri. The large figure represents Pirematsj, standing on his wife Kokai, respectively the father and mother of the maker.

Illustrated: Rockefeller 1967, p. 162, 168.

Plate 8.22 (above) Portrait of the carver Juwisiri.

Plate 8.23 (opposite, left) Statue of a man. Made by Mbiwir. Atjametsj village, Central Asmat. Wood, lime, red ocher, charcoal, leaves. 225 cm. Collected in 1961 by Adrian A. Gerbrands. RMV 3790-522. Photograph: Isaäc C. Brussee.

The figure represents Ambojit, the maker's elder brother.

Illustrated: Rockefeller 1967, p. 161, 163.

Plate 8.24 (opposite, right) Statue of a woman standing on a skull. Made by Ndopor. Atjametsj village, Central Asmat. Wood, lime, red ocher, charcoal, leaves. 181 cm. Collected in 1961 by Adrian A. Gerbrands. RMV 3790-521. Photograph: Isaäc C. Brussee.

The figure represents Mbin, an elder sister of the maker, Ndopor, standing on the skull of her husband Wumbeitjasem. (See also Plate 8.6, page 123, for a photograph of the sculpture *in situ*.)

Illustrated: Rockefeller 1967, p. 162 (onder); Smidt 1987b, fig. 4, p.77.

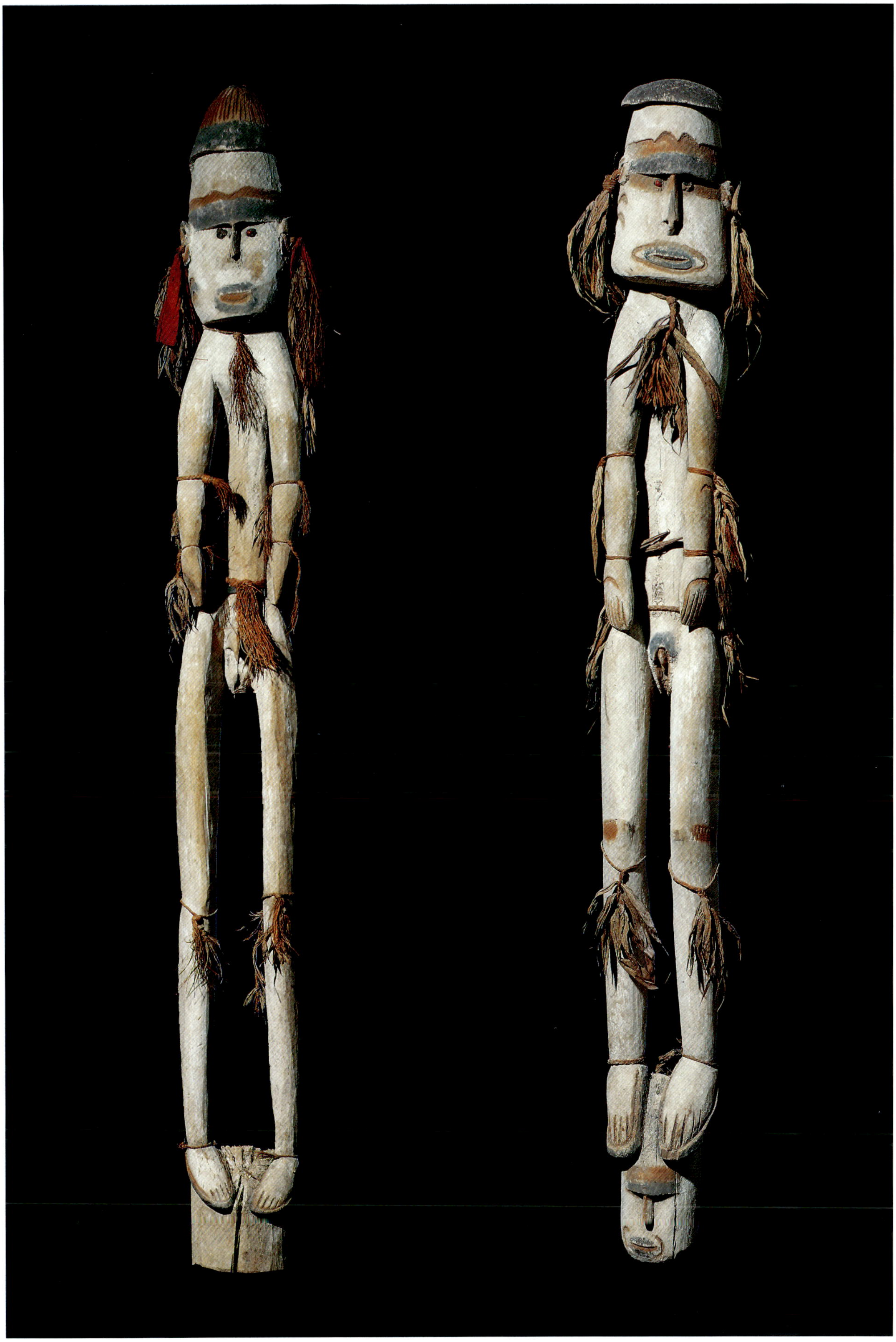

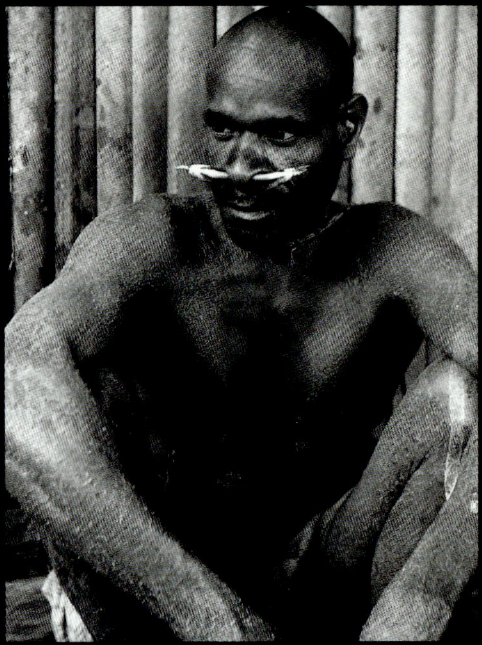

ADRIAN A. GERBRANDS

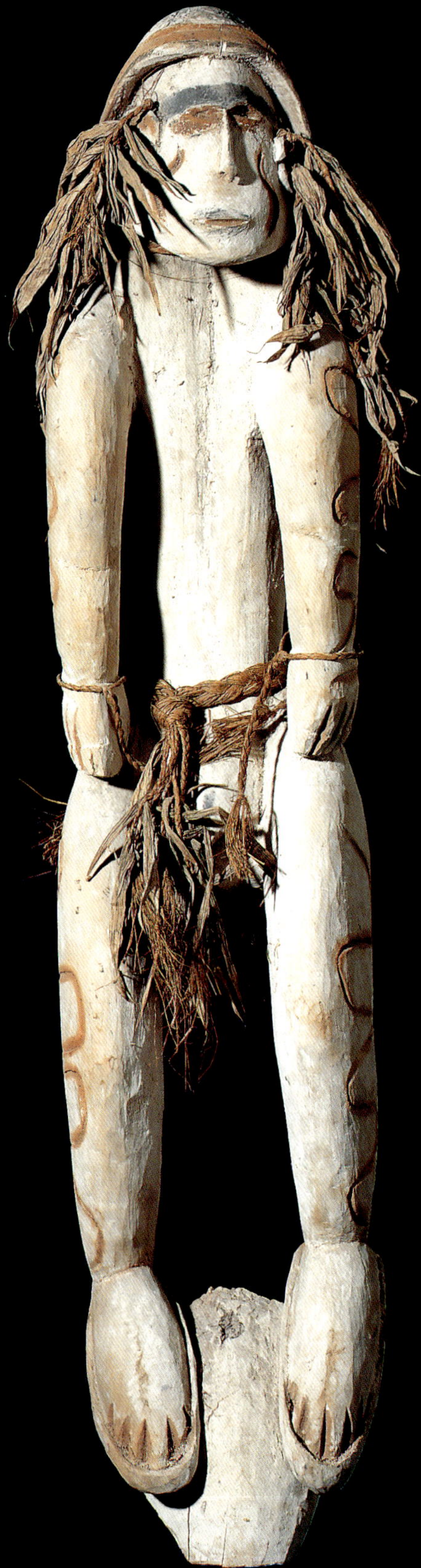

Plate 8.25 Portrait of the carver Fupie.

Plate 8.26 Statue of a man. Made by Fupie. Atjametsj village, Central Asmat. Wood, lime, red ocher, leaves, sago leaf fiber. 122 cm. Collected in 1961 by Adrian A. Gerbrands. RMV 3790-516. Photograph: Isaäc C. Brussee.

The figure represents Ndompon, the maker's grandfather (on his father's side). This statue stood next to the one depicted in Plate 8.28 in the *jeu*. (See also Plate 8.5, page 120, for a photograph of this sculpture *in situ*.)

Illustrated: Rockefeller 1967, pp. 159, 164, 166-167; Smidt 1987b, fig. 3, p. 77.

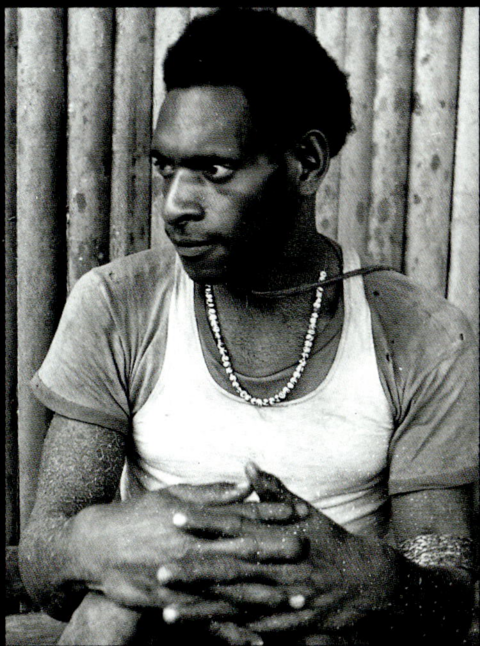

ADRIAN A. GERBRANDS

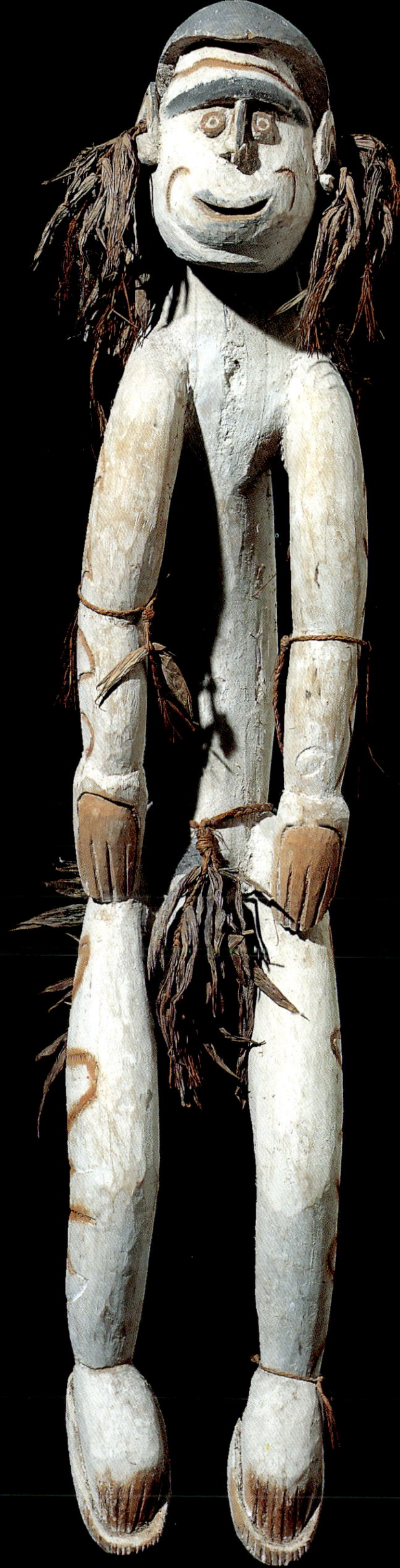

Plate 8.27 Portrait of the carver Safanminim.

Plate 8.28 Statue of a man. Made by Safanminim. Atjametsj village, Central Asmat. Wood, lime, red ocher, leaves, sago leaf fiber. 137 cm. Collected in 1961 by Adrian A. Gerbrands. RMV 3790-517. Photograph: Isaäc C. Brussee.

The figure represents Kandei, the grandfather (on his father's side) of the maker, Safanminim. This statue stood next the one depicte in Plate 8.26 in the *jeu*. (See also Plate 8.5 for a photograph of this sculpture *in situ*.)

Illustrated: Rockefeller 1967, pp. 159, 164, 166-167; Smidt 1987b, fig. 3, p. 77.

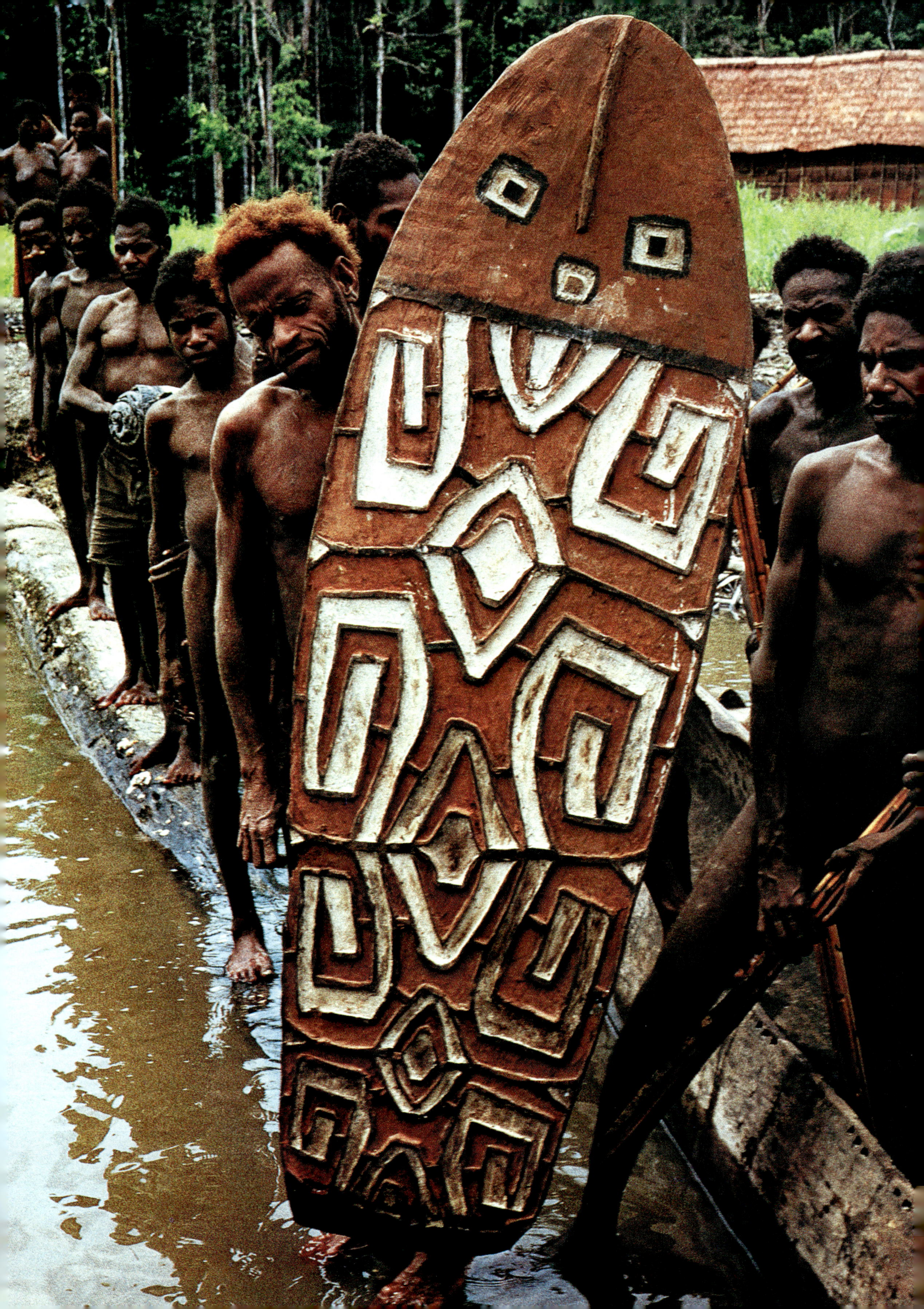

CHAPTER 9

Collection: Military, Explorers and Anthropologists

Adriaan Lamme with Dirk A.M. Smidt

The Asmat collection of the National Museum of Ethnology at Leiden includes 3,500 objects.[1] The history of this collection, which began in 1837, can be divided into four main stages: from von Siebold to Gooszen (1837–1907); the Gooszen Collection (1907–1913); "the Kooijman shipment, Merauke" (1953–1954); and the Gerbrands Collection (1960–1961).

I. From von Siebold to Gooszen 1837–1908

The National Museum of Ethnology in Leiden's Asmat collection—and the collection of the museum as a whole—originated with a collection of Japanese and other ethnographic objects acquired by Dr.Ph. F. von Siebold. Von Siebold, who worked as a physician at the Dutch trading station at Deshima from 1823 to 1830, collected the Japanese objects personally; the others he obtained through a third party.

Von Siebold's ultimate desire was to found a museum. He opened his collection to the public in 1837, and King William bought it for the state in 1838. The doctor's collection was combined with the ethnographic part of the collections of the Royal Cabinet of Rarities (Koninklijk Kabinet van Zeldzaamheden) in 1883.

At the time it was opened to the public, the Von Siebold Collection included numerous objects from Oceania, including Samoa, Tonga, Tahiti and New Zealand. There were about 100 objects from New Guinea.[2] Fourteen of these have been identified as from Mimika, west of the Asmat. The provenance of some 30 objects is simply stated: "Southwest New Guinea." Presumably, several of these come from the Asmat.

Museum records do not list von Siebold's source for these objects, but they were probably collected either by Kolff in 1826, or by Salomon Müller during the 1828 Triton Expedition. This latter expedition charted the west and southwest coast of New Guinea.

Before the 20th century, contacts with the Asmat were fleeting at best, and these oldest objects, presumably dating from 1826 or 1828, are simple ethnographica: a few spears, and some fiber bracelets and skirts. The remainder of the 19th century presented essentially the same picture: limited collecting of a few common objects, with no shields or sculptures at all.[3]

The 20th century did not begin much better. The 1904–1905 expedition of the Royal Netherlands Geographical Society (Koninklijk Nederlandsch Aardrijkskundig Genootschap), during which Flamingo Bay (then still called East Bay) was "discovered," resulted in only a handful of objects (series 1549)—including, however, the first shield. (See Plate 9.2, page 138.) Four years later, in 1909, five shields (series 1698) were acquired from the Government of the Dutch East Indies. These were probably collected in 1907 during the H.A. Lorentz expedition to South New Guinea for the Dutch East Indian Committee for Scientific Research (Indisch Comité voor Wetenschappelijke Onderzoekingen) at Batavia.

It is striking how few shields, and even fewer sculptures, are found in these early collections. For example, the collection put together by the Society for the Promotion of Natural History Research in the Dutch Colonies (Maatschappij ter Bevordering van het Natuurkundig Onderzoek in de Nederlandsche Koloniën) and acquired in 1913 totals 539 objects (series 1854), but does not include a single figure sculpture.

II. The Gooszen Collection

Collecting during military exploration[4]
1907–1913

"Reviewing everything was in fact a huge labor. It was not regarded as such by his contemporaries; they took it as a matter of course, as one also has accepted his huge but poorly documented collec-

Plate 9.1 A shield, carved by Tipo, Wowi village, Siretsj River. Citak, Eastern Asmat. 1969

1. Because some difficult to locate objects are included in the category "Southwest New Guinea, General," the exact number of Asmat objects can not be precisely determined.

2. There are 92 registration numbers. In the past the same number was sometimes allocated to more than one object (three arrows, for example) causing the actual number of objects to be higher than one would expect from the registration numbers.

3. This, for example, applies to the collections of C.B.H.C. Rosenberg and F.G. Beckmann, both members of the 1858 Etna Expedition.

4. This segment is based on Adriaan Lamme's research. His results are laid down in an unpublished report (Lamme 1987) from which the material for this chapter was drawn.

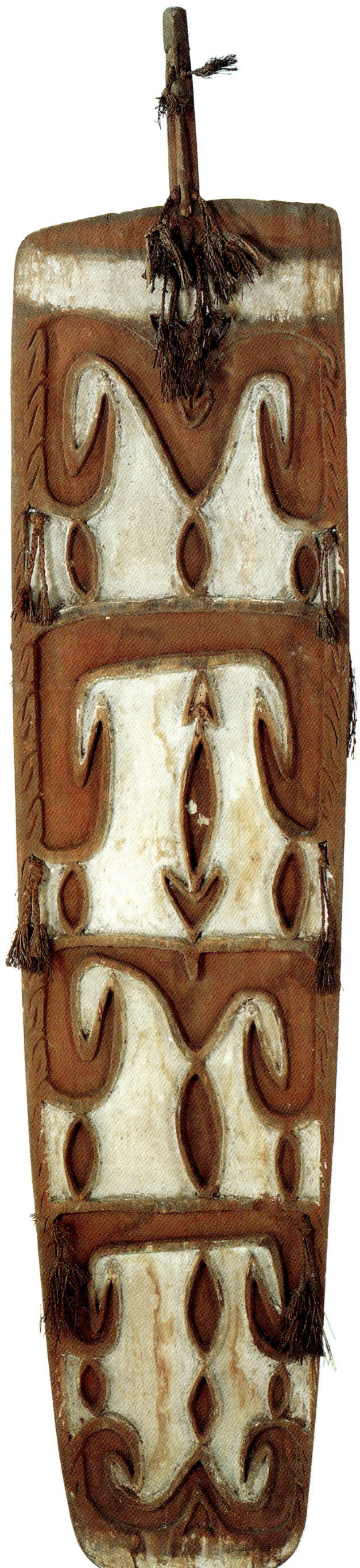

tion of ethnographica as more or less a matter of course, just as I once complained about an error in his map, sighing over his insufficient documentation."[5]

Military exploration: 1907–1908

The first large and representative Asmat collection, including more than one shield and sculpture, was assembled in the years 1907–1908 and 1913 by Antony Jan Gooszen, a captain[6] in the Dutch Indies Army who commanded the exploration detachment for South New Guinea. Gooszen was born the son of Protestant clergyman M.A. Gooszen in 1864 in Wilnis, in the province of Utrecht. He was 42 at the time of his assignment to South New Guinea. He accepted this task, he writes, with "pride and joy."

In 1907, only the coastline of southwestern New Guinea was known. The immense interior remained terra incognita, despite three centuries of western presence in the region. Governor-General J.B. van Heutsz decided to survey Dutch New Guinea by military detachment.

The few scientific expeditions undertaken until then, including Prof. Wichmann's expedition from February to August 1903, financed by the Society for the Promotion of Natural History Research in the Dutch Colonies (Maatschappij ter Bevordering van het Natuurkundig Onderzoek in de Nederlandsche Koloniën) and de Rochemont-Posthumus Meyjes's expedition in 1904–1905, financed by the Royal Netherlands Geographical Society (Koninklijk Nederlandsch Aardrijkskundig Genootschap), added little to Holland's knowledge of southern New Guinea. The same can be said of The H.A. Lorentz Expedition—also financed by the Society for the Promotion of Natural History Research—which was about to start in May 1907.

As a commander of the exploration detachment, Gooszen had to form a team at record speed, and subsequently explore and map an area of some 180,000 square kilometers. For this he was given two years. The assistant-resident Hellwig, in an official letter, described the goal of the exploration as follows:

"First one must attempt to compose a map of

---

5. The author is referring specifically to A.J. Gooszen's chartering of the South and Southwest coast of New Guinea during the first military exploration of the area in 1907–1908. (J. van Baal 1987:ii.)

6. He was promoted to Major in 1911, to Lieutenant-Colonel in 1914, and to full Colonel in 1917.

the country, not a topographical map, but a good atlas map. One must further strive at acquiring a survey of the country and people, that is to say of the condition of the soil, products, distribution of the population, etc. Furthermore the navigability of the rivers must be explored." (Gooszen 1909:18.)

Although the enterprise had a military character, it was determined beforehand that military force should be kept to a minimum:

"One reservation has to be made regarding that exploration. If contrary to expectation, penetrating into the interior should go with quite violent action, the exploration should then immediately come to an end, as otherwise one is led down a path the end of which can not even by approximation be determined." (Colijn, in: Departement van Oorlog in Nederlandsch Indië 1920:9.)

The commander, Captain Gooszen, and J.H. Daam, of the same rank and division, were charged with mapping, as well as support for the geological and ethnographic research. Second-class health officer B. Branderhorst was placed in charge of the medical service, and in charge of flora and ethnographical research. Mining engineer O.G. Heldring would carry out the geological research. Several naturalists from the zoological museum and the botanical gardens were on hand to collect zoologica and botanica. From may 1908 onwards, naturalist I.M. Dumas also rendered assistance. In all, the detachment included some 200 men.

It is apparent from a speech Gooszen delivered for the Dutch East Indian Military Society (Indische Krijgskundige Vereeniging) at Batavia one and a half years later, that the expedition had acquired numerous articles with which to exchange for art and ethnographic objects, such as beads, axes, *parangs*—the Malay machete—and knives. Gooszen added: "[S]everal firms have been asked to send all kinds of things that were cleaned up from the show-tables, to be used for exchanging and as gifts for the population." (Gooszen 1909:19-21.)

The first collecting: 1907–1908

The exploration detachment for South New Guinea departed from Surabaya, Java, on June 24, 1907 and disembarked at Merauke on June 11.

One can hardly discern from the Department of War's official "Report of the military exploration of Dutch Nieuw-Guinea 1907–1915" what adventures or people the explorers met on the

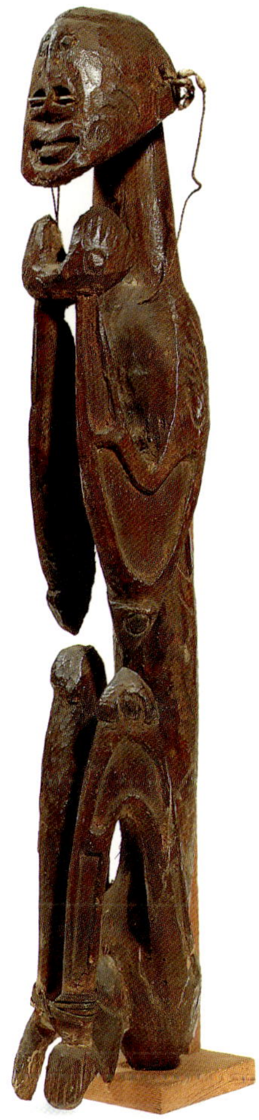

Plate 9.2 (opposite) Shield. Lower course of the Betsj River (formerly Kampoeng), Central Asmat. Wood, lime, red ocher, sago leaf fibre. 162 cm. Collected in 1904–5 during the Southwest New Guinea expedition of the Koninklijk Nederlandsch Aardrijkskundig Genootschap. RMV 1549-45. Photograph: Ben Grishaaver.

This is the earliest collected (but not the oldest) Asmat shield in the collection of the National Museum of Ethnology, Leiden. (For the oldest Asmat shield, see Plate 7.2, page 72.)

Exhibited: 70 jaar Asmat houtsnijkunst / 70 tahun seni pahat Asmat / 70 years of Asmat woodcarving (in het Volkenkundig Museum Justinus van Nassau, Breda), Rijksmuseum voor Volkenkunde, Afd. Breda, Breda 1976-1977, Cat. 5 (see: Hoogerbrugge en Kooijman 1976)

Illustrated: Rouffaer et al. 1908, pl. 10, fig. 190.

Plate 9.3 (above) Statue of a man. Pomatsj River (formerly Northwest), Northwest Asmat. Wood, sago leaf fiber, *Coix* seeds. A layer of lacquer was applied after acquisition, giving the figure a dirty brown color and causing the colors to become vague. Presumably, the original colors were originally provided by lime, red ocher, and charcoal. 58 cm. Collected in 1908 or 1913 by A.J. Gooszen. Donated by Gooszen in 1919. RMV 1971-986a. Photograph: Isaäc C. Brussee.

Like many of the old sculptures, this one shows the characteristic elbows to knees squatting position that recalls the Asmat creation by Fumeripitisj. (See page 91.)

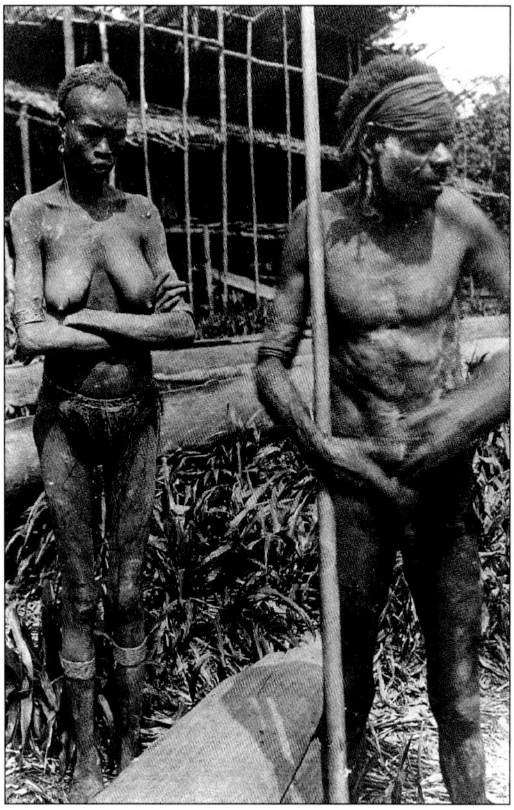
EXPLORATION DETACHEMENT FOR SOUTH NEW GUINEA

Plate 9.4 (above) Asmat woman and man. This comes from among the earliest known photographs of the Asmat, which were taken circa 1908 by the exploration detachment for South New Guinea.

Plate 9.5 (opposite) The staff of the exploration detachment. As marked, beginning at center: (1.) R.L.A. Hellwig, Assistant Resident; (2.) A.J. Gooszen, Captain of the Infantry, commander; (3.) J.H. Daam, Captain of the Infantry; (4.) O.G. Heldring, mine engineer, geologist; (5.) G.M.A. Elbers, Chief Navigating Officer of the Govt. Navy; (6.) I.M. Dumas, naturalist; (7.) B. Branderhorst, Health Officer 2nd Class. The three assistants were not identified. This photograph was most likely taken in mid-1908, on the South Coast of Dutch New Guinea.

South coast; the publication includes only a dull summary of the exploration trips.

Thankfully, however, historians have another source. On July 23, 1907 the *New Rotterdam Courant* (*Nieuwe Rotterdamsche Courant*) published the first installment of a series of essays titled: "The Exploration of New Guinea (Het exploreeren van New Guinea)." Fourteen of these essays were to be published, the last on June 8, 1908. They were all signed "Pionier," A. J. Gooszen's pen-name. The *Courant* of October 5, 1907 states:

"We [Captain Gooszen and assistant-resident Hellwig] have just returned from an interesting trip: we visited the Lorentz expedition,[7] which is now in the heart of New Guinea.[8] It was not easy to get there: the weather and the river current did not cooperate, but we reached our goal. First with the steamer from Merauke to the East Bay and up the Northern Utumbuwe River until the waterway became so difficult it did not allow further steaming. Along the riverbanks were timber trees, overgrown with lianas and creepers climbing from tree to tree....

"At long last a sign of life! From a tributary a few dugouts appear, canoes in fact in which some 10 to 12 standing rowers. Crying out noisily, they let us pass and then try to follow. A few strokes of red material thrown overboard give rise to a rowing competition whereby the winners eagerly pick up those pieces of cloth as a reward for the effort"

With regard to collecting objects, he states:

"The ethnographical haul was a small one. In the beginning some contact with the population was made while slowly steaming up the river, and in that way it was possible to exchange several ethnographica, but this stopped later. During the first days of May a flotilla of dugouts full of armed natives blocked the boats from going to a kampung. A gunshot fired over their heads made them howl, but not shrink; their attitude even turned menacing, so we refrained from further attempts to make contact and returned on board."

Later, in installment 14, in the June 14, 1908 *Courant*, about a journey along the North Utumbuwe River:

7. In April 1907 a scientific expedition was sent to the South of New Guinea led by H.A. Lorentz. The expedition's goal was scientific research of the area around the East Bay and the Utumbuwe Rivers emptying into it.

8. The *New Rotterdam Courant* texts were edited and modernized by Adriaan Lamme.

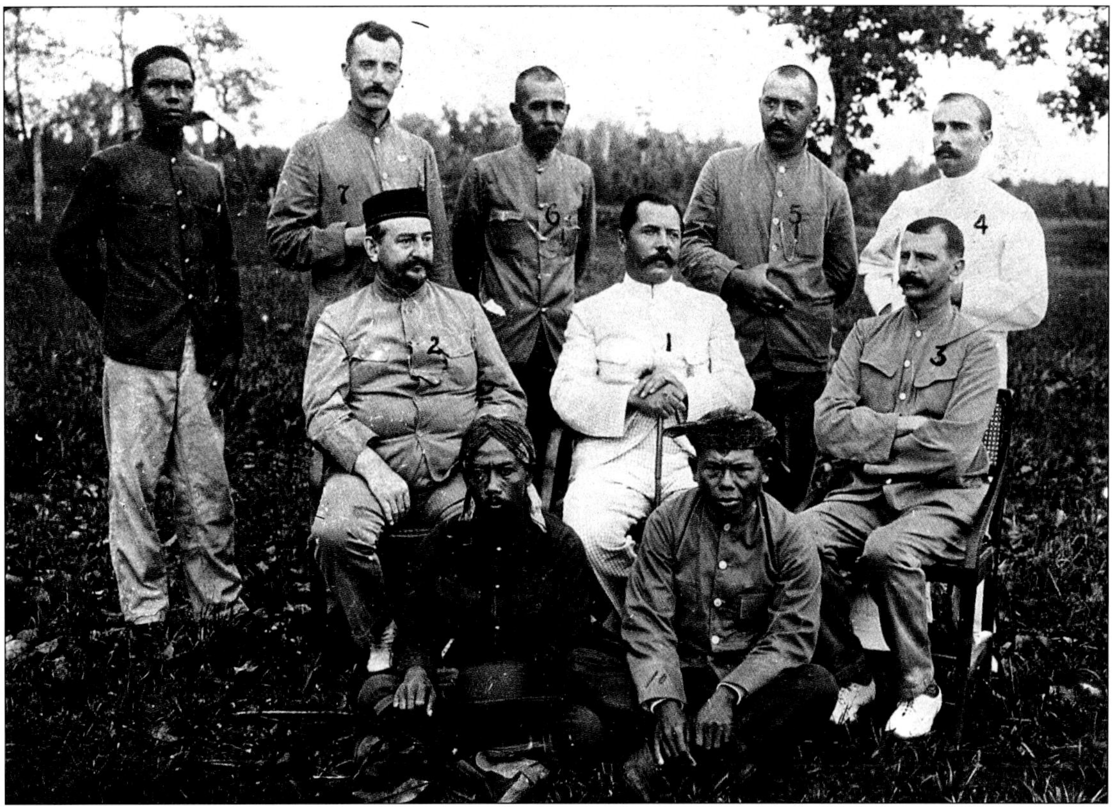

EXPLORATION-DETACHEMENT FOR SOUTH NEW GUINEA

"In the kampongs along the riverbanks the population was present. Many large and small dugouts set off; the oarsmen, standing in an upright position, cleaved the water rhythmically and tried to keep up with us. Women and children on the riverbank and all shouted, gabbled, sometimes howled like dogs...

"In this way we passed three kampongs and let the anchor fall a little past the last. Not much later the ship was approached by a number of dugouts...A few knives were hung over the stern on small ropes and trembling with nerves and excitement they approached the desired objects.... At long last a knife was grabbed and in exchange for this a bow or arrows tied to the rope. Where one sheep goes, more follow, and in this manner a number of ethnographica were exchanged. One of those men made the gesture of cutting off a neck, as if to ask if we were on a head-hunting expedition; our vehement negation seemed to reassure him and his friends."

Ill health: mid-1908 to 1912

The exploration wore heavily on the health of the detachment of explorers—beriberi and malaria were the order of the day. Even Gooszen had problems with "an indisposition" around April 21, 1908 forcing him, "to his own bitter regret," to ask the government for dispensation from the task assigned to him. In a letter to his father dated May 14, Pioneer, aboard the watch boat *Zwaluw,* writes: "In August the expeditions overland start again, ... but without me." (Journal of the Royal Netherlands Geographical Society [Tijdschrift van het Koninklijk Nederlands Aardrijkskundig Genootschap] 1909:152)

Captain Gooszen was immediately evacuated to Java, where, after recovering slightly, he gave a number of lectures. On these occasions he showed skeleton maps of the explored region, drawings of woodcarvings, dugouts and huts, and a collection of lantern-slides.

During a lecture for the *Indische Krijgskundige Vereeniging* at Batavia, Gooszen also presented a collection of ethnographica. He concluded his lecture with a plea for more interest in ethnography within the Dutch East Indies army.

On October 21, 1909 Gooszen was sent to Europe as "Captain of the General Staff of the Dutch East Indian Army (Generalen Staf van het Indische Leger)." Semi-officially he was considered to be on leave, so his health could improve.

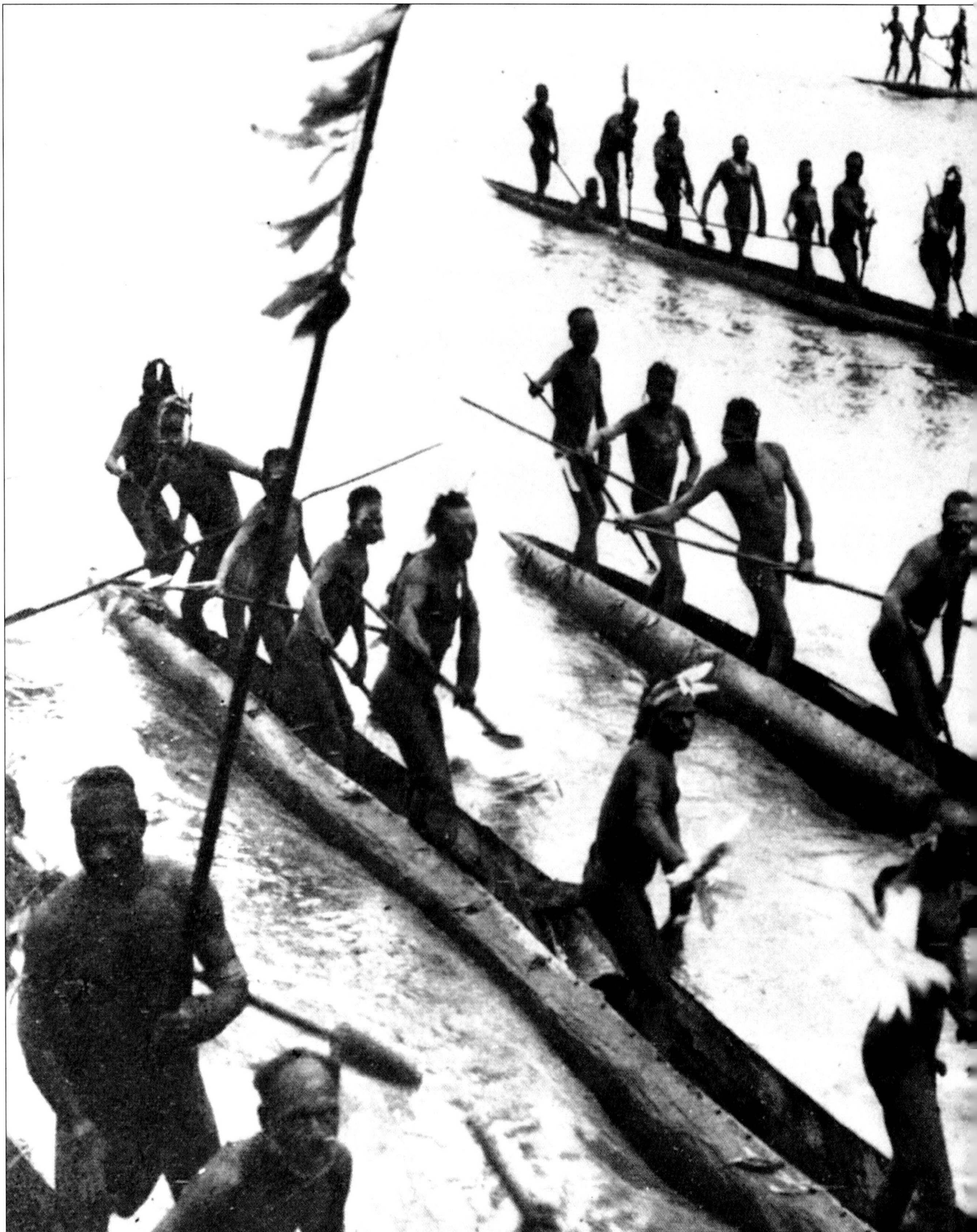

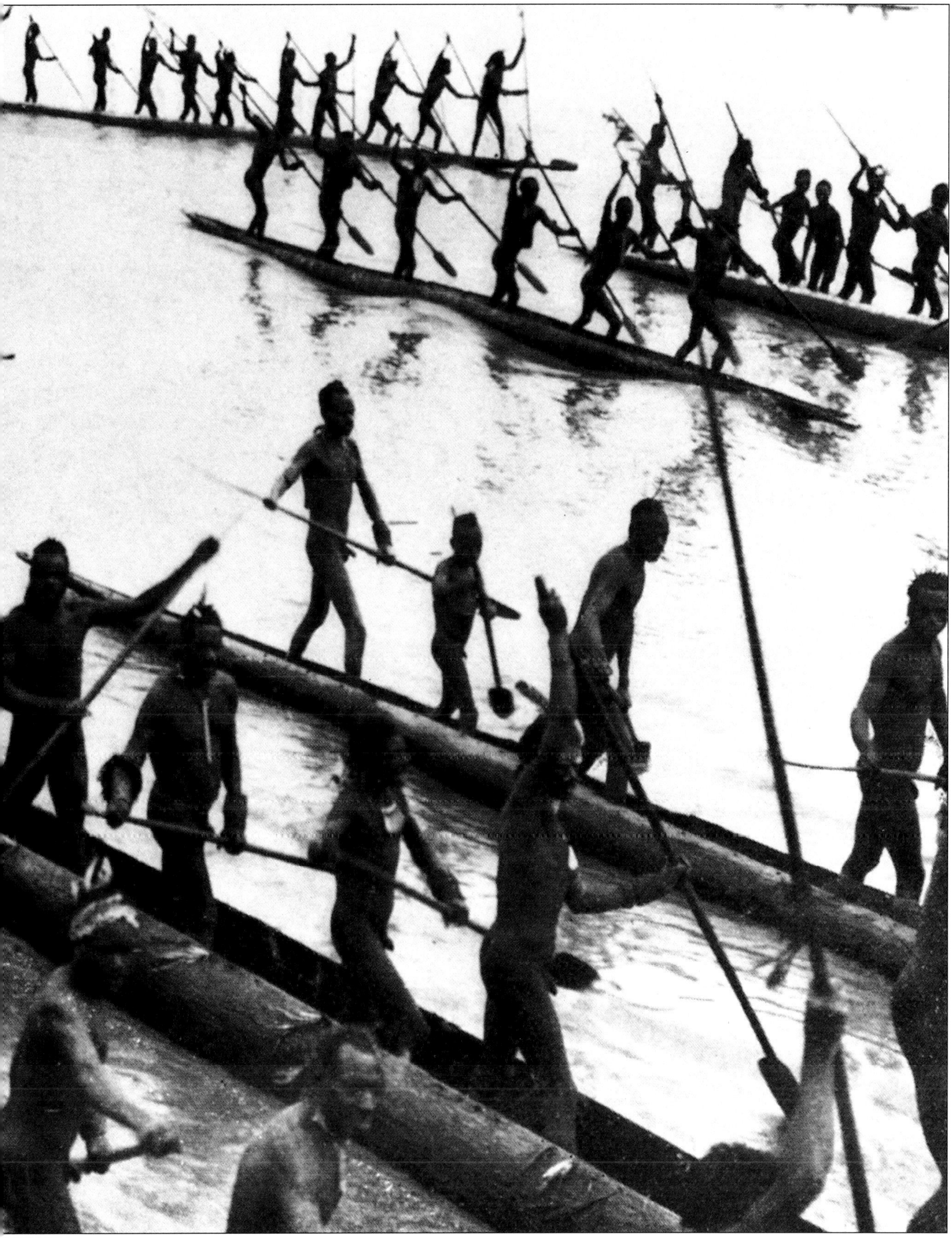

In the Netherlands Gooszen also lectured on his explorations in New Guinea, and in 1911 he donated a part of his collection to the Leiden museum (then called the Rijks Ethnographisch Museum). The Dutch government gazette reported, on August 23, 1911:

"[The] Rijks Ethnografisch Museum has received as a present from Mr. A.J. Gooszen, Major in the Dutch East Indies Army, on leave at the Hague, a collection of 50 objects from the South and Southwest coast of Dutch New Guinea, consisting of weapons, objects of daily use, ornaments and decorated skulls. A group of drawings concerning the ornamentation and the building of houses and a collection of photographs were added. These form a very valuable supplement to the collections from these parts, received as a gift during the final years of the Dutch New Guinea government. Inventoried as series 1779. Thanks of the Government were conferred to the donator." (*Nederlandsche Staatscourant* 1911, no. 197.)

On October 8, 1911 Gooszen, who had by this time been promoted to major, arrived together with his wife in the Dutch East Indies for the third time. He was now 46 years of age.

Last period of collecting: 1913

On February 13, 1912 Major Gooszen was appointed Military Commander of Amboina and Ternate in the Moluccas, and after June 1 was placed in supreme command of the military exploration of South, West and North New Guinea. He had direct control not only of the expedition, but also of processing and correlating the acquired data.

In this period Gooszen did very little collecting himself. He left this to his subordinates, not because he wanted less involvement with collecting ethnographica, but because his high position allowed him little time for fieldwork. During these final stages of exploration, he did personally lead an exploration to the so-called "Unknown River," later named the Northeast River.

Just as much of Gooszen's collecting during this period was second-hand, so were many of his publications. This is the case for "Exploring New Guinea," a series of articles he published in the *Courant* between March 19, 1913 and August 3, 1914. Again, he used the name "Pionier," but unlike the Pioneer of 1907–1908, who wrote lively accounts based on personal experience, the later Pionier simply rewrote the reports from the patrol commanders that landed on his desk.

His collecting activities continued unabated, however. In a letter to H.H. Juynboll, at that time director of the Leiden museum, he speaks of his growing collection as itself a "museum."

The end of military exploration

The exploration of South New Guinea was completed around November 1913; the two-year period anticipated in 1907 had been greatly exceeded. Gooszen, then 49, left with his family for Holland on July 14, 1914. On January 19, 1915 the military exploration of Dutch New Guinea (at that moment almost completed) came to an end. The cost of the operation came to more than 5.5 million guilders, of which almost half were personnel costs. A total of 140 soldiers died in the process, and many more had fallen ill or were wounded.

The military aspect of the exploration seems to have been limited. The "Advisor for Administrative Affairs of the Outer Possessions" (Adviseur van Bestuurszaken der Buitenbezittingen) even states "how much it was to be praised that unnecessary bloodshed was avoided." The government approved of the "moderate action" carried out by Gooszen and his men, and pointed out that sending military exploration detachments was "by no means aimed at the preparation for establishing our authority." (Department of War in the Dutch East Indies [Department van Oorlog in Nederlandsch Indie] 1920:79–81.)

The Gooszen collection

Gooszen sent collections of ethnographica to the Leiden museum four times:

1) In 1911, a collection of 50 objects from the South and Southwest coast of New Guinea, inventoried as series 1779.

2) In 1912, a collection of more than 500 ethnographical objects, mainly from southwest New Guinea, with some from the Kei islands. The carefully assembled collection includes numerous ornaments, weapons, objects for daily use, decorations of canoes, amulets and several large statues. Inventoried as series 1889.

3) In 1914, more than 375 objects.

4) Finally, also in 1914, the largest dispatch: 5,691 objects, of which no less than 4,603 from New Guinea (the rest from the Moluccas). This collection is inventoried as series 1971.

Gooszen collected a total of 6,616 objects for the museum. Of these, 933 are from the Asmat. This collection is not only very large but also quite representative. In it are all kinds of items

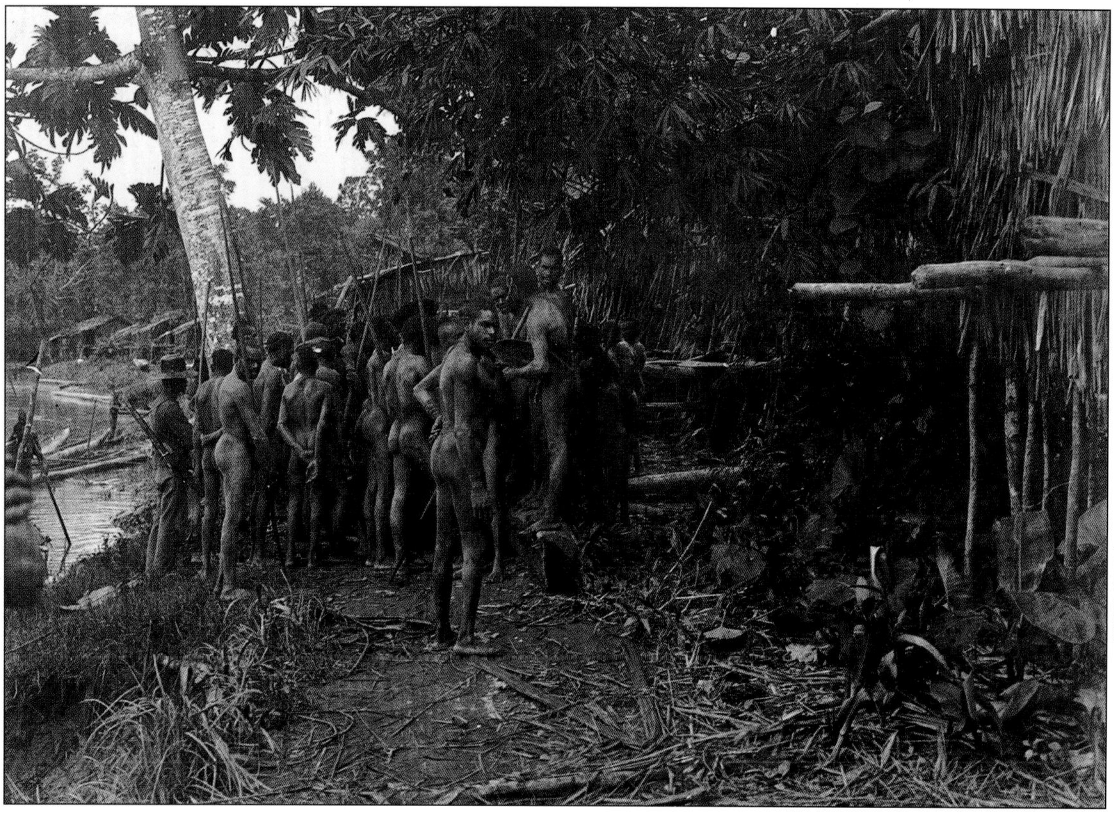

PHOTO ARCHIVE TROPENMUSEUM, KONINKLIJK INSTITUUT VOOR DE TROPEN, AMSTERDAM

meant for daily use, elements of decorations for the body and weapons, such as carrying-nets, tobacco pipes, lime tubes, fire-tongs, bone tools, sago beaters, sago cups, fishing nets, strings, girdles, bracelets, nose ornaments, skull caps, chest pendants, fibre skirts, small bags, axes, oars, spears, arrows and bows, as well as a good number of woodcarvings.

The most striking omissions are monumental woodcarvings, especially known from collections dating from after World War II, such as *bisj* and *wuramon*. Also striking is the absence of mask costumes. One can only speculate as to why these were left out. Perhaps Gooszen never saw such objects, or perhaps they were simply too large to bring along.

Gooszen's collection did include the kind of objects at the heart of this publication: shields and sculptures. At present the museum collection includes 6 sculptures collected by Gooszen, and 25 shields. This does not reflect the state of affairs at the time when the collection was received, however, as on a few occasions the museum has parted with a Gooszen piece in trade. Nor was everything he sent included in the museum's collection. As was Gooszen's intention, his collection was divided up by the Leiden museum, with duplicates sent to other museums.

According to museum archives, parts of Gooszen's donation were sent to the Museums of the Royal Military Academy (Koninklijke Militaire Academie) at Breda, the Chief Course (Hoofdcursus), Nature is Art's Teacher (Natura Artis Magistra), the Ethnographical Museum of the Zoological Society in Amsterdam (Ethnografisch Museum van het Zoölogisch Genootschap), and to the Museum voor Land- en Volkenkunde (now Museum voor Volkenkunde) in Rotterdam, among others.

Plate 9.6 (overleaf) Canoes on the Lorentz River ("Boote vom Lorentz-Fluss.") This photograph is thought to have been taken during the Lorentz Expeditions of 1907 or 1909. This is a very early photograph of the Asmat, presumably taken from the expedition's boat. (It appears in Fischer 1923:144, Tafel 26, Fig. 1.)

Plate 9.7 (above) Soldiers of the exploration-detachement collecting ethnographica, circa 1908. The Asmat are exchanging crafted objects for steel knives and axes, red cloth and other items. At left stands an inland fuselier carrying a carbine. The photograph was taken by the exploration-detachement for South New Guinea.

Everything Gooszen send to the museum was donated, although the final installment was sent only in 1919 after negotiations with the museum over a paid position at the museum. Gooszen asked for an appointment as a kind of "temporary supernumerary curator" to help catalog and dispose of his collection. Instead, he received a moderate fee for three month's work, and a medal of honor from the Queen, given to him in 1920 as "token of appreciation of his interest in public collections of science and art, shown by donation." (*Nederlandsche Staatscourant* 1920, no. 11.)

In hindsight, it seems that it might have benefited the museum to reward him in a more generous manner. One should not credit too highly the documentation Gooszen must have collected in the field, particularly given the kind of tense encounters that took place in the context of a military exploration. But there are passages in the museum archives which suggest that important information about the objects Gooszen collected may have been left in his head.

In mid-1920 Gooszen departed for the fourth and last time to the Dutch East Indies. On April 18, 1922, in Surakarta, Java, Colonel Antony Jan Gooszen passed away. He was 57 years old.

III. The "Kooijman shipment, Merauke"
Collecting by trade, government and mission
1953–1954

In 1953 the curator of the Leiden museum's Oceania Department, Dr. S. Kooijman, was in South New Guinea studying the Marind-anim, who live south of the Asmat. Because of contacts he made with the government, traders, missionaries and one or two fellow anthropologists, he was able to acquire ethnographical material at his station in Merauke. Through this happy circumstance, large collections of great scientific and esthetic value were gathered in a single year and sent through Kooijman to the museum. The entire "Kooijman shipment, Merauke"—series 3070—includes 526 objects, from the Merauke area to Mimika.

A rare series of Asmat shields, reproduced in this publication, bear witness to the special style and high esthetic quality of some of this material. These shields were collected by C. C. Verheij van Wijk, who had established himself in 1953 as director of the N.V. South New Guinea Import Export Company (IMEX) at Agats. At that time he was hunting crocodiles and trading crocodile skins. Verhey van Wijk did not restrict himself to collecting woodcarvings. Through him Kooijman acquired common utensils and body decorations.

The Verhey van Wijk Collection includes four mask costumes, one of which is reproduced here (see Plate 3.10, page 41) and sixteen shields, three of which are reproduced here (see Plate 7.8, page 76; Plate 7.9, page 77; and Plate 7.11, page 78). The shields Verheij van Wijk collected are particularly interesting, as they form a completely individual type. Despite the size of the collection, it does not include a single statue.

A collection of 85 objects assembled by then Resident J. J. Spijker during his tours of duty in the Asmat region form another important resource from this period. Of the fourteen shields he collected, six are included in this publication. (See Plate 7.10, page 77; Plate 7.13, page 79; Plate 7.14, page 80; Plate 7.15, page 81; Plate 7.41, page 99; and Plate 7.44, page 100.)

The documentation of the above-mentioned collections is limited, although Verheij van Wijk was sometimes inclined to note the name of the village, or even of the *jeu* on the back of the shields in chalk. Information on the meaning of the motifs, or the individual history of each shield is, however, completely lacking.

During this period, anthropologist J. Pouwer documented some Asmat items he had acquired incidentally while studying the Mimika. For esthetic reasons, none of these is included in this book. However, Pouwer served as an intermediate between Kooijman and Paliama, the head of the regional government of Mimika, to transfer an elaborate collection of Asmat objects Paliama had collected during a tour of duty in the area in 1951. In this material were two special abstract sculptures, included in this book. (See Plate 7.36, page 96 and Plate 7.37, page 97.)

Asmat material collected in September and October 1952 by F.R.J. Eibrink Jansen, at that time Controleur I, was also sent, via Pouwer, to Merauke. (See Plate 5.3, page 54.)

IV. The Gerbrands Collection
Collecting and anthropology
1960–1961

Next to the Gooszen Collection, the Gerbrands Collection constitutes the largest group of Asmat objects of the National Museum of Ethnology. It was assembled by anthropologist Adrian A. Gerbrands, at the time adjunct director of the Leiden museum, between December 1960 and August 1961. At the time Gerbrands was living in Amanamkai and researching Asmat woodcarving and the individuality of Asmat woodcarvers.

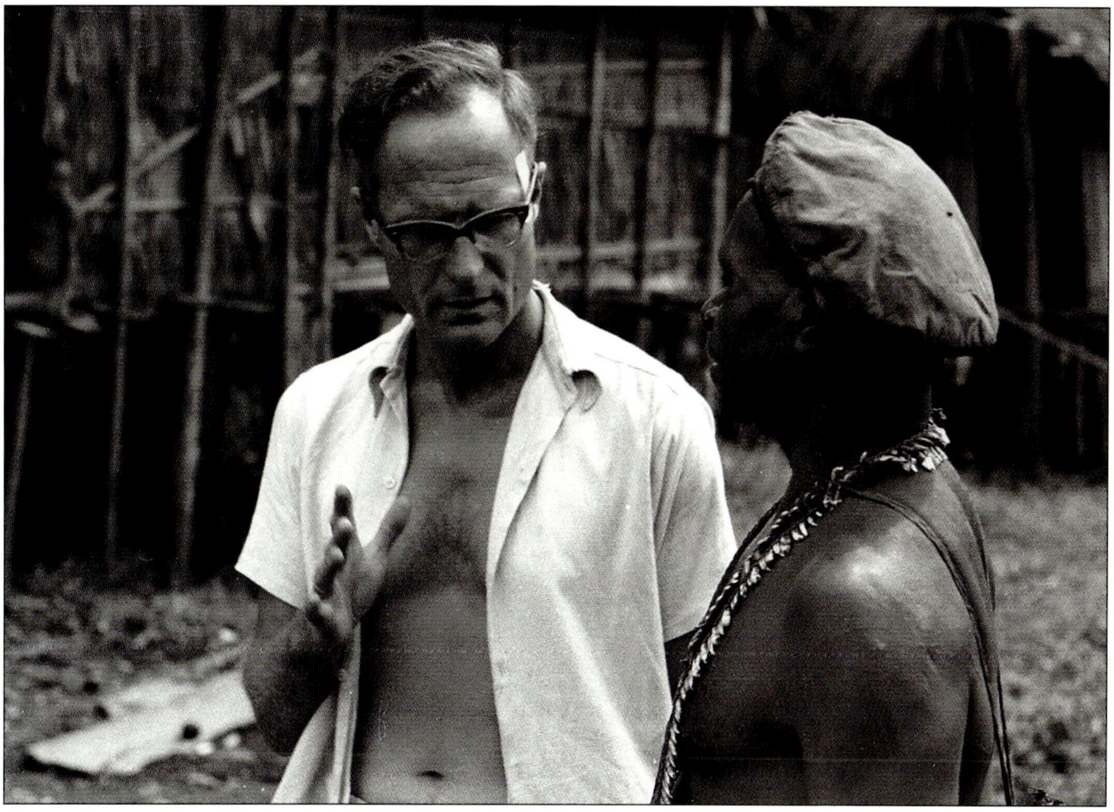

C. L. VOORHOEVE

The Gerbrands Collection totals 599 objects, and an additional 64 pen and ink drawings made at Gerbrands's invitation by Asmat woodcarvers. Despite that his research focused on the art of woodcarving and woodcarvers, Gerbrands did not restrict himself to shields or sculptures. In his collection we find all kinds of objects both for ceremonial and daily use: drums, mask costumes, canoe prows, paint cups, paddles, spears, bone daggers, shell and bone nose ornaments, stone adzes, chisels, sago beaters, bamboo horns, pipes, and even magic potions and decorative socks for And, of course, the collection contains a great variety of woodcarvings. A number of these were specially made on Gerbrands' request, to show the individuality of the woodcarvers. This group of carvings includes traditional statues made by artists such as Matjemos, Ndojokor and Bifartji, and such experiments as the "legs of a table" (Gerbrands 1967).

In addition to the contemporary carvings, Gerbrands also obtained a number of older pieces: drums, canoe prows, cups and spears. He also collected eight used, quite old shields. Old figure sculptures are absent, however.

The other skilled collectors who visited the area at the time of Gerbrands or more recently—especially Michael Rockefeller and Gunter and Ursula Konrad—were also able to obtain older shields, but no old statues. Perhaps shields have a higher emotional value than sculptures, and the sculptures just are not kept.

The objects in the Gerbrands Collection are by far the best documented of all the museum's Asmat materials. Gerbrands has included information about the motifs, the name of the maker and the owner and, particularly for the older pieces, the object's family history. Gerbrands took numerous photographs, now included in the photo archives of the museum, and some of these are reproduced in this book.

After the Gerbrands Collection, very few Asmat pieces have been acquired by the museum. In 1970 and 1977 the museum acquired some modern carvings through Jac. Hoogerbrugge. These objects were the result of the Asmat Art Project, a development project to encourage Asmat artists (see Chapter 10, page 149).

Plate 9.8 Adrian A. Gerbrands talking to Uastan, head of Jeu Awok, Anamankai village. Central Asmat, 1961.

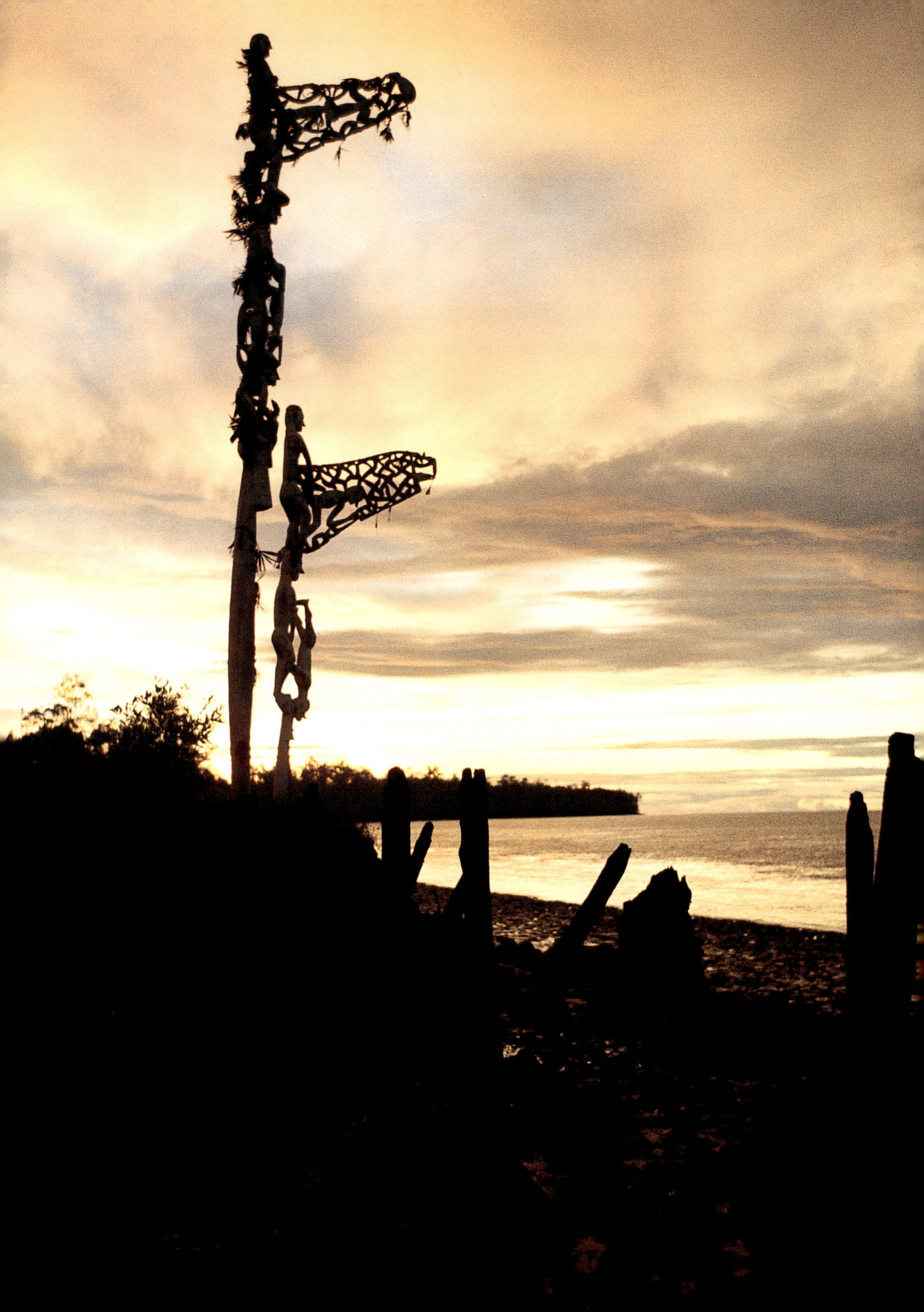

CHAPTER 10

Art Today: Woodcarving in Transition

Jac. Hoogerbrugge

The traditional style of Asmat woodcarving, as seen in the figure sculptures and shields collected in the first period of significant European contact, 1904–1913, remained unchanged during the subsequent four decades. This can be readily seen by comparing objects obtained during the post-war collecting boom, from 1953–1954, to those from the first decade of the 20th century.

This comes as no surprise because the Asmat region, with no prospect for economic development and decidedly hostile population, was after 1913 left to its own devices by the Dutch colonial administration. This neglect lasted until 1953, when the Dutch government and the Catholic mission each opened a permanent post on Flamingo Bay at a previously uninhabited location dubbed Agats—from the Asmat *akat,* for "good"—near the village of Sjuru.

The subsequent opening up of the area was carefully watched by European ethnographic museums, particularly in Holland. The Dutch museums were quick to send representatives to collect, on their behalf, as many "genuine" artifacts as possible. By "genuine," I mean items that were both traditional in design and had been used. This collecting boom caused great upheaval among the woodcarvers, who were suddenly confronted with a hitherto unknown demand from outside. Thus, they set out enthusiastically to produce new objects which, to their great dismay, they soon found out were not in demand. Because they were new, they lacked the patina of age sought by the museum representatives.

Fortunately a new demand developed around 1960. This came from the Dutch residents working in New Guinea who, because of the imminent transfer of sovereignty, began to leave the island. Eager to take pieces of authentic Asmat art home with them, these customers provided a welcome outlet for the growing group of Asmat woodcarvers. The residents were less critical, but at the same time more open-minded than the professional collectors. Additional opportunities to sell carvings arose in 1961, when Michael C. Rockefeller made two collecting expeditions through the Asmat area, and Adrian Gerbrands carried out his field study of the Asmat woodcarvers in Amanamkai.

Then, suddenly, it was all over. In 1963, a small Indonesian army and police force took charge of the region. Worried about the dangers of the unfamiliar Asmat "head-hunting culture," and in keeping with the charged military atmosphere that surrounded the transfer of sovereignty, the Indonesians took strict measures against dancing, drumming and carving, as such were deemed a prelude to head-hunting.

All carving, except for the making of a few practical items like canoes and paddles, came quickly to a halt. Not only were new carvings banned, but the government ordered many of the old carvings destroyed. This slump lasted until 1968, when the Indonesian government, in consultation with the United Nations, decided to again open up the Asmat area to outside contacts. A joint effort between the United Nations Department of Small-Scale Industries and the United Nations Development Program resulted in the Asmat Art Project (1968–1974).

The Asmat Art Project

The Asmat Art Project sought to re-encourage carving and other cultural activities among the Asmat. As a result, a more relaxed atmosphere developed and, occasionally at first, feasts were again held. The woodcarvers gradually regained their self-confidence and resumed their craft. They made objects for their own village, feasts and also, via the Asmat Art Project, for museums and collectors around the world (see brochure I.L.O. Geneva, 1969 and 1974)

Thus, around 1970, a real revival of Asmat woodcarving took place. Increasingly, younger men, who had attended village schools, took part in the carving. The Crosier Mission played an important role in this development. The Catholic missionaries, influenced by Vatican II, encouraged the Asmat to respect their indigenous traditions, and took pains to instill a similar respect into the area school teachers, who were usually of non-Asmat origins. In 1973, Bishop Alphonse A. Sowada, who had been working in the Asmat area since 1961, established the Asmat Museum of Culture and Progress (Museum Kebudayaan dan Kemajuan Asmat) in Agats. Here was an Asmat art museum for the Asmat themselves to use. The museum continues to keep high quality examples of woodcarving art, and to sponsoring carving

Plate 10.1 *Bisj* poles at sunset along the Central Asmat coast. Photograph by Gunter Konrad, circa mid-1970s.

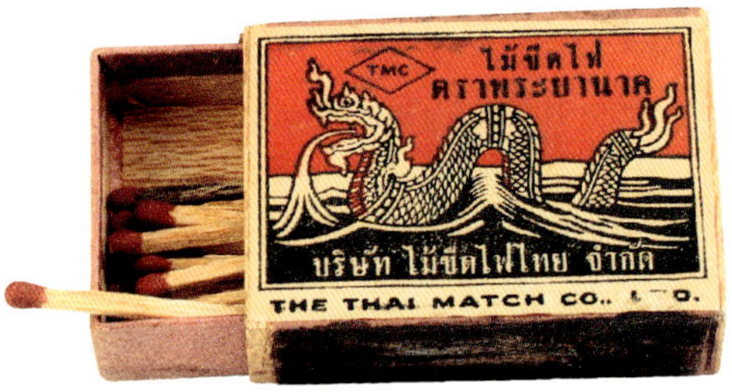

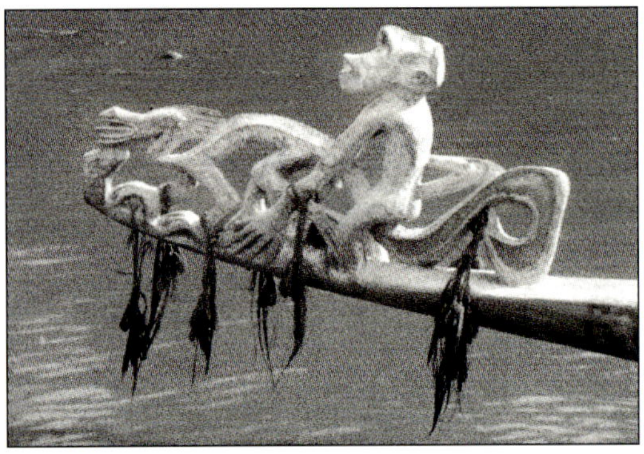

JAC. HOOGERBRUGGE

Plate 10.2 (above, top) Matchbox depicting a Chinese dragon, made in Thailand. This picture was copied by Ambek when he carved the canoe prow below. Photograph: Ben Grishaaver.

Plate 10.3 (above, bottom) This canoe prow, depicting a man riding a dragon, was taken by the carver, Chief Ambek, from the match box above. This dragon reminded Ambek of the mythical Asmat snake Jok. Biwar Laut village, Jiwe River, Central Asmat, 1972. A variation of this modern style, showing a man riding a pig, can be seen in Plate 10.6, page 153.

Plate 10.4 (opposite) Men lined up behind a canoe, displaying the shields they have for sale. Otsjanep village, Ewta River, Casuarina Coast. 1971.

contests and feasts.

Also, from 1972 on, small groups of tourists began visiting the region, first on board the m.v. *Lindblad Explorer,* and later, increasingly by small plane via the Ewer airfield. This had a stimulating effect. Feasts were staged and carvings put on display and sold directly to the foreign visitors. At this time Gunter and Ursula Konrad began their extensive collecting tours in the region, gathering the objects that would become the Konrad Collection at the Museum of Ethnology in Heidelberg.

In August 1984 a national Indonesian newspaper sponsored a huge exhibition of Asmat woodcarvings in Jakarta, and arranged for fifteen Asmat woodcarvers to demonstrate woodcarving techniques. In 1986 a number of prominent Jakartans, set up a special Asmat Foundation which aims at assisting the Asmat woodcarvers with the promotion of their work. The chief patron of this organization is Ibu Tien Suharto, wife of the current president of Indonesia. In 1987, the organization sponsored Asmat cultural festivals in a number of European cities, where Asmat woodcarvers and dancing groups displayed their skills. Similar events were staged in the United States in 1991.

Changes in Asmat woodcarving

From around 1954, in addition to producing traditional objects for local use, Asmat woodcarvers have also made objects for sale to outsiders. In the beginning these objects did not differ much from those the woodcarvers were used to making. Before long, however, new tastes, tools and materials led to adaptations and innovations, as can be seen in the collections brought together in the years from 1954–1962.

Characteristic of this new style Asmat art are the flat openwork carvings called *ajour*. These lacy carvings resemble the traditional decorative work that was done at the tops of long paddles. Seeing that visitors often bought a paddle just for the sake of the decorated top which, because of transportation problems, was usually unceremoniously sawed off, the woodcarvers reacted cleverly by making just the openwork top.

This innovation was supported by the Catholic missionary van Pey who, in 1960, started to supply the woodcarvers of the village of Atsj with scrap pieces of ironwood board, left-overs from the mission sawmill. The development spread to neighboring villages and, as a result of the competitive atmosphere, the *ajour* carvings

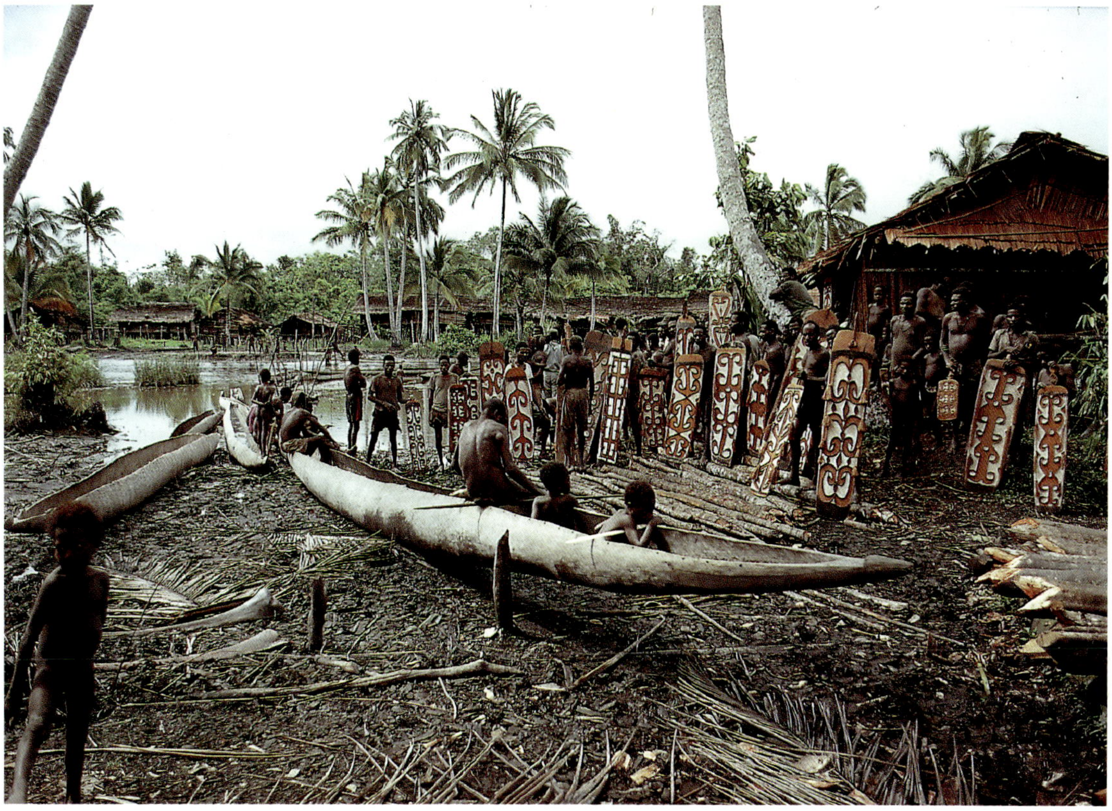

GUNTER KONRAD

became bigger, more intricate and sometimes extremely delicate.

Also new are the small-scale, freestanding human statues. These are much like the traditional ancestor figures, but greatly reduced in size. This type of carving was a reaction to collectors' preference for so-called "art objects," which to their minds meant it should depict a human figure, rather than mere "ethnic objects" such as drums, horns, bowls and the like. Traditional Asmat figures, however, were often much too large to easily carry.

As small-scale lumbering operations got underway during this period, lots of waste ironwood became available. This explains why in lumber villages—like Atsj—ironwood was increasingly used for carving. The use of hardwood was not in itself new. Paddles and spears, for example, had always been made from it. What was new, however, was the availability of the material to every individual who felt like making a carving.

In the past, carving was a communal affair. A group of carvers sat around making, for example, shields, for the "feast of the shields." This was not a continual affair, but happened irregularly, whenever the *jeu* leaders saw a need for it. With the availability of ironwood, and the new market for woodcarvings, an individual woodcarver could now make any piece he fancied, at any time—and sell it to a passing tourist.

The greater freedom in this situation is reflected in a greater range of style and quality in the carvings. While many of these new ironwood carvings are below par, some are real masterpieces. For example, see the "uchu" sculptures collected in 1961 by Michael Rockefeller in the village of Per, just a few miles from the government center at Agats.

Spirit of innovation

Typical of the spirit of the time are small sculptures depicting more than one human figure, on top or in front of each other, reminiscent of the constructions found in *bisj*. Also, the human figure is increasingly depicted "in action," for example holding an axe, spear or dagger, carrying a child, or holding in his hands a bird or snake, giving the impression that the ancestor figure has "come to life."

One worthwhile innovation took place in the village of Sawa-Erma, located on both sides of the wide Pomatsj River. Sawa-Erma (once two sepa-

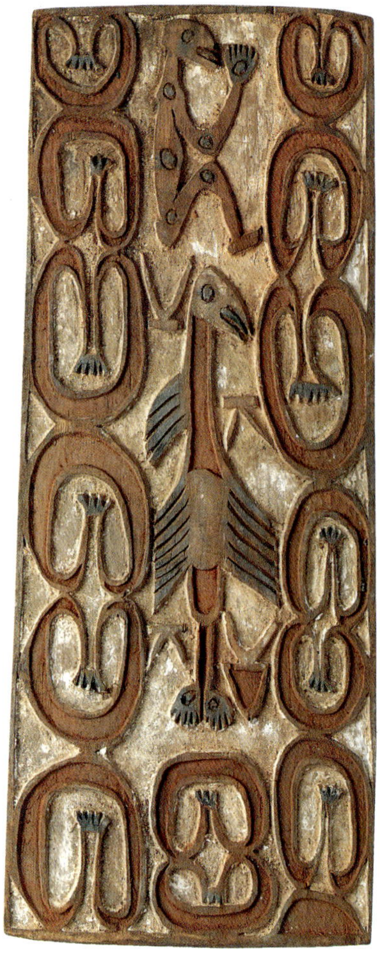

Plate 10.5 (above) Panel. Made by Vewab in 1970. Sawa-Erma village, Pomatsj River (formerly Northwest River), Northwest Asmat. Wood, lime, red ocher, charcoal. 59 cm. Collected by J. Hoogerbrugge. RMV 4928-18. Photograph: Ben Grishaaver.

Sawa-Erma is the only village in the Asmat area where panels such as this one are carved. Contrary to what one might assume, this piece was not commissioned by people from outside the village. The central bird figure is an Asmat version of Garuda, the mythological bird that serves as the national emblem of Indonesia. The repetitive motif at the sides and bottom, is called *anih.* It was interpreted by the maker of the panel as a *kaki seribu,* a sort of centipede.

Plate 10.6 (opposite) Contemporary sculpture of an ancestor figure riding on a mythological pig. Made by Amunsar in 1974. Biwar Laut, Jiwe River, Central Asmat. Wood, lime, red ocher. 88 cm. Collected by Jac. Hoogerbrugge. RMV 4928-12. Photograph: Ben Grishaaver.

This freestanding carving, made out of one piece of wood, is exceptional when compared to traditional Asmat woodcarvings or other recent carvings. Amunsar also incorporated this new theme (of a man riding a pig) into a canoe prow demonstrating "divergence from the traditional design" (see Hoogerbrugge and Kooijman 1976: fig. 57).

rate villages) is renowned for its wild new canoe festivals, and for the fine openwork prow heads of these canoes. Michael Rockefeller, for example, added a number of Sawa-Erma prow head to his collection in 1961.

Collecting canoe prows, however, means chopping them off from the canoes. This was a very unpopular thing to do, and it is not surprising to see that the woodcarvers later made prows separately. Thus a new type of openwork carving began to appear. In the beginning, these looked very much like a traditional prow. but since the utilitarian restrictions were gone, and competition was rampant, the innovation developed into sculptural form in its own right.

It is in this same village that I witnessed the birth of yet another new type of carving. One morning in 1969 I saw a group of six or seven men busy smoothing the shafts of their newly made paddles with clamshells. I saw that Ekam had just started to carve the relief ornamentation on the blade of his canoe paddle (see Plate 4.2, page 48). I watched him carefully, and made a series of sketches showing the manner in which Ekam laid down his design (see Figure 4.1, page 48).

Surprised by my interest, the other men sat down next to me and, joined by woodcarvers from other sections of the village, started to correct my drawings. Apparently not satisfied, Tokobeh, one of the best carvers in the village, went home and returned with a bamboo horn which he was in the process of decorating. He told me that I should also make drawings of these ornaments, which were more difficult to apply because of the round and slippery surface.

Impressed by Tokobeh's craftsmanship, I suggested that each of the good woodcarvers in the village make for me his own "drawing" carved on a flat piece of board or panel. These I promised to buy at my next visit. I had .expected these carvings to be interesting documentation. But when I collected then two months later, they proved to be highly attractive designs composed of the various ornaments usually occurring on shields, bamboo horns, and other carved items.

It was evident that the men thoroughly enjoyed making these panels. Some of them had fitted stylized drawings of human and animal figures into their compositions, so the result looked like a narrative "storyboard," rendering spirit scenes from old myths.

So, by chance, a new type of carving had come into existence.

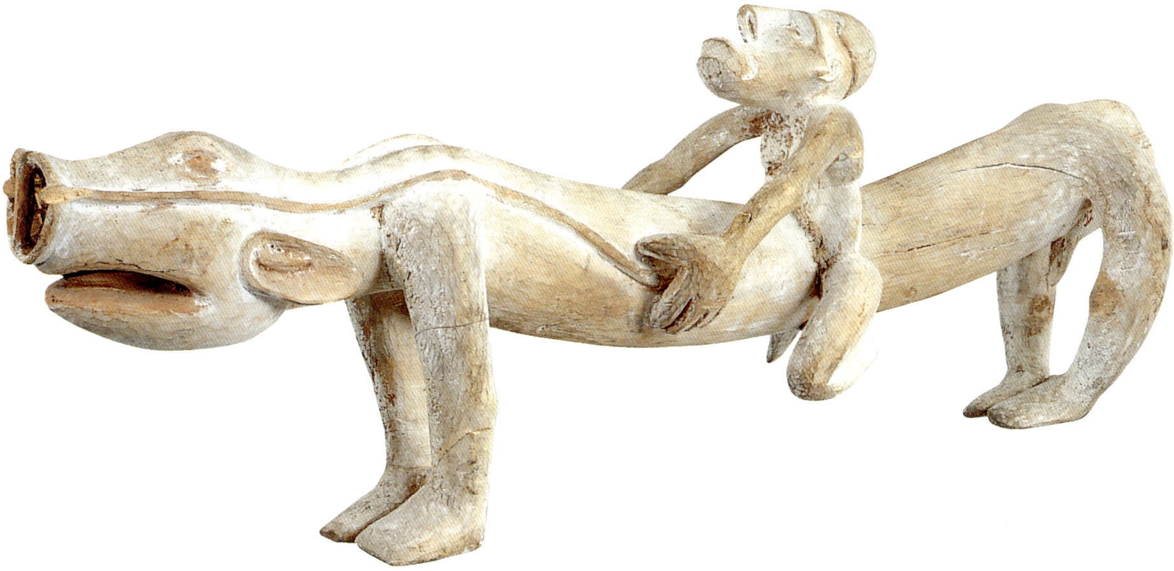

An Asmat dragon

The outside influences in the Asmat region also brought with them foreign motifs. In Biwar Laut, in 1972, chief Ambek took me by surprise when he visited me in a new canoe. The prow was completely different from any other I had seen in Asmat—a human figure riding a twisting snake! When I asked Ambek the origin of such a motif, he produced a matchbox, made in Thailand. (See Plates 10.2 and 10.3, for photographs of the canoe and matchbook.) Ambek had obtained the matches aboard a lumber ship, with the picture of Naga, the Hindu dragon-snake. Ambek had recognized in Naga the mighty Asmat snake Jok, the main character of a number of local myths. Because the foreign subject fit conveniently into his traditional range of ideas, Ambek probably succeeded in making of this foreign motif a real Asmat carving.

This idea seems to have spread, as a few months later, woodcarvers in the village of Omandesep came to Agats to sell a collection of carvings, among which I found a *bisj* with a Naga crawling up against the main human figure.

In 1970, the great woodcarver Biwartjawipitsj, also from Biwar Laut, came to visit me at the Agats Art Shop. He proudly showed me a 45-centimeter-high carving of a bird, with outstretched, openwork wings, a style unknown to Asmat art. It seemed that he had gotten the idea from a poster he had seen at the Government office in Agats. On the poster was the mythical eagle Garuda, the Indonesian national emblem. Biwartjawipitsj had never heard of Garuda, but he associated the poster with the mighty sea-eagle War, one of the main characters in the myths of the origins of the coastal Asmat.

I was delighted to see that Biwartjawipitsj, not understanding what kind of object Garuda was carrying in its claws (a ribbon with the national motto) had solved this problem in a spontaneous Asmat manner. His Garuda carried a very reasonable load—a fish!

These few examples illustrate the creative atmosphere of the seventies. The woodcarvers had managed to cope with the changes taking place around them by creating additional art forms, in keeping with traditional styles. In this way, I believe traditional Asmat art has been enriched by these contemporary expressions, without losing its characteristic features.

How the experiences gained by the woodcarvers who have recently journeyed to Jakarta, Europe and the United States may have influenced and affected their style remains to be seen. Since they had never before traveled in any vehicle other than a canoe, or gone any further than their own rivers and forest, the experience must have been overwhelming.

We look forward to future developments with great interest. Finally, despite the increased contact, the Asmat remain isolated. Wood continues to be the material of choice and necessity for daily utensils and ceremonial objects alike. Thus the prestige a good woodcarver still enjoys comes not just from his ability to sell his work, but because he is an expert needed by the community.

Bibliography

Amelsvoort, V.F.P.M. van
1964 *Culture, Stone Age and Modern Medicine. The Early Introduction of Integrated Rural Health in a Non-literate Society. A New Guinea Case Study in Medical Anthropology*. Assen.

Ap, Arnold C.
1974 Death and Mourning among the Keenok. *Asmat Papers* Part I, Research Report 5:57–73.

Baal, J. van
1987 Voorwoord. In: Adriaan Lamme, Van pioniers en koppensnellers. De militaire exploratie van de Zuidkust van Nieuw-Guinea, 1907–1908, pp. i–iii. Ms., Arnhem.
1989 Ontglipt verleden. Vol II. Franeker.

Bodrogi, Tibor (ed.)
1982 *Stammeskunst I. Australien, Ozeanien, Afrika*. Budapest. (First published in Hungarian, 1981.)

Bodrogi, Tibor, and Frank Tiesler
1982 Ozeanien. In: Tibor Bodrogi (ed.), *Stammeskunst I. Australien, Ozeanien, Afrika*, pp. 77–193. Budapest.

Boeren, Ad
1976 Schilden uit het Asmat-gebied en het stroomgebied der Wildeman-, Mappi- en Digoelrivieren. (Unpublished research report on Asmat shields in the collection of the Rijksmuseum voor Volkenkunde in Leiden.)
1985a Asmat motieven. Regels van combinatie en transformatie. In: Ad Boeren, Fransje Brinkgreve and Sandy Roels (eds.), *Teken van leven. Studies in Etnocommunicatie*, 171–186. ICA Publikatie 71. Leiden.
1985b Warshields from South Irian Jaya. Style Differences and Principles of Ornamentation. Ms., Leiden.

Buijse, J.A.
1989 Verslag van een onderzoek in het Museum Justinus van Nassau. 2 vols. Breda. (Unpublished report.)

Claerhout, Adriaan
1975 *Een voorouderpaal uit Yepem, Asmatgebied, Nieuw-Guinea*. Verhandelingen van het Etnografisch Museum van de Stad Antwerpen 2. Antwerpen. [Summaries in French, German and English.]

Corbin, George A.
1988 Art of the Asmat of Irian Jaya, Southwest Island New Guinea. In: George A. Corbin, *Native Arts of North America, Africa, and the South Pacific. An Introduction*, pp. 210–219. New York.

De Hoog, J. (see: Hoog, J. de)

Departement van Oorlog in Nederlandsch-Indië
1920 *Verslag van de militaire exploratie van Nederlandsch Nieuw-Guinee 1907–1915*.

Fischer, H.W.
1923a Ethnographica aus Süd- und Südwest-Neu-Guinea. *Nova Guinea* 7:37–145.
1923b Ethnographica von den Pesechem und aus Südwest-Neu-Guinea (Nachtrag). *Nova Guinea* 7:145–163.

Flam, Jack D.
1984 Matisse and the Fauves. In: William Rubin (ed.), *'Primitivism' in 20th Century Art. Affinity of the Tribal and the Modern*, vol 1. (2 vols.), pp. 211–239. New York.

Fraser, Douglas
1962 *Primitive Art*. Garden City, New York.

Fuhrmann, Ernst
1922 *Neu-Guinea* (In the series: Kulturen der Erde. Material zur Kultur- und Kunstgeschichte aller Völker, vol 14). Hagen i.W.

Gajdusek, D. Carlton
1990 Ethnographic Collecting and Ethnographic Studies in the Context of Medical Research Among the Asmat. In: Tobias Schneebaum, *Embodied Spirits: Ritual Carvings of the Asmat*. Salem, Massachusetts: Peabody Museum of Salem. 76–79.

Gastaut, H.
1972 *Le crâne. Objet de culte, objet d'art*. Marseille.

Gathercole, Peter, Adrienne L. Kaeppler, and Douglas Newton
1979 *The Art of the Pacific Islands*. Washington.

Gerbrands, Adrian A.
1951 Kunststijlen in West Nieuw-Guinea. *Indonesië* 4:251–283.
1961 Ongepubliceerde veldaantekeningen.
1962 Symbolism in the Art of Amanamkai, Asmat, South New Guinea. In: *The Wonder of Man's Ingenuity*. Mededelingen van het Rijksmuseum voor Volkenkunde, Leiden 15, pp. 37–41.
1963 *Matjemosh. A Woodcarver from the village of Amanamkai, Asmat Tribe on the Southwest Coast of New Guinea*. Utrecht. (*Cine-film*, 16 mm, colour, sound, duration: 27 minutes.)
1966 *De taal der dingen*. Den Haag.
1967a *Wow-Ipits. Eight Asmat Woodcarvers of New Guinea*. (Art in its context. Studies in Ethno-Aesthetics. Field Reports 3.) The Hague–Paris.
1967b [Editor] *The Asmat of New Guinea. The Journal of Michael Clark Rockefeller*. New York.
1968 De houtsnijders van de Asmat. In: Reader's Digest, *Rond de wereld- thuis. Met Het Beste op reis*, 342–351. Amsterdam.
1969 The Concept of Style in Non-Western Art. In: Daniel P. Biebuyck (ed.), *Tradition and Creativity in Tribal Art*, pp. 58–70. Berkeley and Los Angeles.
1979 The Art of Irian Jaya. A Survey. In: Sidney M. Mead (ed.), *Exploring the Visual Art of Oceania. Australia, Melanesia, Micronesia, and Polynesia*, pp. 111–129. Honolulu.
1990 Made by Man. Cultural Anthropological Reflections on the Theme of Ethnocommunication. In: Pieter ter Keurs and Dirk Smidt (eds.), *The Language of Things. Studies in Ethnocommunication*, Mededelingen van het Rijksmuseum voor Volkenkunde, Leiden 25, pp. 45–74. Leiden.

Gianinazzi, Claudio, and Christian Giordano (eds.)
1989 *Culture Extraeuropee. Collezione Serge e Graziella Brignoni / Extra–European Cultures. The Serge and Graziella Brignoni Collection.* Lugano.

Girard, Francoise
1970 Grand mât sculpté érigé pour la commémoration des victimes de la chasse aux têtes par les Asmat de la Nouvelle-Guinée indonésienne. *Objets et Mondes* 10(4):283–298.

Goes, H.D.A. van der, et al.
1862 Nieuw-Guinea, ethnographisch en natuurkundig onderzocht en beschreven in 1858 door een Nederlandsch Indische Commissie. Amsterdam.

Gooszen, Antony Jan [see Pionier]
1909a Land en volk van Zuid Nieuw Guinea. *Tijdschrift van het Koninklijk Nederlandsch Aardrijkskundig Genootschap* 26:798–800.
1909b Het Militaire Exploratie detachement voor Zuid-Nieuw-Guinea. *Orgaan der "Indische Krijgskundige Vereeniging"* 1908, 23.
1913a De Noordwest-rivier en de Bibis- of Van der Sande–rivier als toegangswegen tot het Oranje-gebergte. *Tijdschrift van het Koninklijk Nederlandsch Aardrijkskundig Genootschap* 30:525–532.
1913b Hoe Nederlandsch Nieuw-Guinea geëxploreerd werd en wordt. *Tijdschrift van het Koninklijk Nederlandsch Aardrijkskundig Genootschap* 30:638–651.

Harrer, Heinrich
1976 *Unter Papuas. Mensch und Kultur seit ihrer Steinzeit.* Innsbruck und Frankfurt.

Heermann, Ingrid
1977 *Melanesien. Mensch und Natur—Mythos und Kunst.* Stuttgart.

Hoog, J. de
1963 Enige beschouwingen over de kunst van de Casuarinenkust. *Kultuurpatronen* 5–6:7–39.

Hoogerbrugge, Jac.
1969 *Asmat Artists Present: A Collection of Primitive Art and Ethnographic Objects.* Geneve.
1973 An Evaluation of Present-day Asmat Woodcarving. *Irian. Bulletin of Irian Jaya Development* 2(1):24–35.
1974 *Asmat Artists Present: A Collection of Fascinating Asmat Arts and Crafts.* Geneve.
1977 [Ed.] *The Art of Woodcarving in Irian Jaya / Ukiran–ukiran kayu Irian Jaya.* Jayapura and Jakarta.

Hoogerbrugge, Jac. and Simon Kooijman
1976 *70 jaar Asmat houtsnijkunst/ 70 Years of Asmat Woodcarving.* Breda.

Kaufmann, Christian
1980 *Ozeanische Kunst. Meisterwerke aus dem Museum für Völkerkunde Basel.* Basel.

Koninklijk Nederlandsch Aardrijkskundig Genootschap
1908 *De Zuidwest Nieuw–Guinea–Expeditie 1904/5 van het Kon. Ned. Aardrijkskundig Genootschap.* Leiden.

Konrad, Gunter, und Yufentius Biakai
1987 Zur Kultur der Asmat: Mythe und Wirklichkeit. In: Mark Münzel (ed.), *Neuguinea. Nutzung und Deutung der Umwelt*, vol. 2 (2 vols.), 465–509. Frankfurt am Main.

Konrad, Gunter and Walter Böhning
1974 Asmat Shields from the Braza River: Weapons and Ancestors. *Sandoz Bulletin* 34:4–16.

Konrad, Gunter, Ursula Konrad and Tobias Schneebaum
1981 *Asmat. Leben mit den Ahnen: Steinzeitliche Holzschnitzer unserer Zeit / Asmat. Life with the Ancestors: Stone Age Woodcarvers in our Time.* Glashütten/Ts.

Kooijman, Simon
c.1955 *De kunst van Nieuw-Guinea.* Den Haag.
1956 Art of Southwestern New Guinea. A Preliminary Survey. *Antiquity and Survival* 5:343–372.
1961 The Art Areas of Western New Guinea. In: Hallam L. Movius, Jr., S. Kooijman and George Kubler, *Three Regions of Primitive Art*, pp. 41–59. New York.
1966 *Papoea-kunst in het Rijksmuseum / Papuan Art in the Rijksmuseum.* Amsterdam.
1977 Review of "Asmat Art. Seventy Years of Asmat Woodcarving. *Pacific Art Newsletter (PAN)* 4:9–11.
c.1984 *Nieuw-Guinea: Kunst, kunstvormen en stijlgebieden.* Leiden.

Korwa, A.Y.
1974 The Development of Asmat Art. *Asmat Papers 2, Research Report* 6.

Kuruwaip, Abraham
1974 The Asmat Bis Pole: Its Background and Meaning. *Irian. Bulletin of Irian Jaya Development* 3(2):32–78.

Lamme, Adriaan
1987 Van pioniers en koppensnellers. De militaire exploratie van de Zuidkust van Nieuw-Guinea, 1907/1908. Ms., Arnhem.

Lorentz, H.A.
1911 De tocht naar de eeuwige sneeuw van Nieuw–Guinea. *De aarde en haar volken* pp. 1–22.
1913 *Zwarte Menschen, witte bergen.* Leiden.

Mitton, Robert
1983 *The Lost World of Irian Jaya.* Melbourne and Bathurst.

Muller, Kal
1990 *Indonesian New Guinea, Irian Jaya.* Berkeley, California.

Nederlandsche Staatscourant
1919 No. 184, d.d. 25–08–1919.
1920 No. 11, d.d. 16/17–01–1920.

Newton, Douglas
1979 Continuities and Changes in Western Pacific Art. Catalogue: 21 The Southwest Coast. In: Peter Gathercole, Adrienne L. Kaeppler and Douglas Newton, *The Art of the Pacific Islands*, pp. 27–65; 288–293. Washington.

Nouhuys, J.W. van
1913 Der Bergstamm Pesegem im Innern von

Niederländisch-Neu-Guinea. *Nova Guinea* 7:1–36.

Phelps, Steven
1978 Oceanic Traditional Sculpture. In: Robert Sainsbury (ed.), *Robert and Lisa Sainsbury Collection. Sainsbury Centre for Visual Arts, University of East Anglia, Norwich, England*, pp. 137–163. Norwich.

Pionier [pseudonym of Antony Jan Gooszen]
1907–1908 Het exploreeren van Nieuw-Guinea. [First Series.] In: *Nieuwe Rotterdamsche Courant*, Newspaper

1914–1915 Het exploreeren van Nieuw–Guinea. [Second Series.] In: *Nieuwe Rotterdamsche Courant.*

Pollmann, Tessel
1987 Het Rijksmuseum voor Vokkenkunde, Leiden. In: Tessel Pollmann, Stof op het erfgoed. De kelders en zolders van de Rijksmusea. De depots van zes Rijksmusea. *Vrij Nederland* 28 maart 1987:13–15.

Rassers, W.H.
1937 *Overzicht van de geschiedenis van het Rijksmuseum voor Volkenkunde 1837–1937.* Leiden.

Rawson, Philip (ed.)
1973 *Primitive Erotic Art.* (In the series: World History of Erotic Art.) London.

Renselaar, H.C. van, and R.L. Mellema
1961 *Asmat. Art from Southwest New Guinea.* Royal Tropical Institute 121, Department of Cultural and Physical Anthropology 55. Amsterdam.

Rockefeller, Michael
1967 Atjametsj. In: Adrian A. Gerbrands (ed.), *The Asmat of New Guinea. The Journal of Michael Clark_Rockefeller*, pp. 158–168. New York.

Rockefeller, Nelson A.
1978 Michael C. Rockefeller. In: Douglas Newton and Lee Boltin, *Masterpieces of Primitive Art*, 10–13. New York. [Foreword by André Malraux, Introduction by Nelson A. Rockefeller.]

Rouffaer, G.P.
1908 De terugkeer en afloop der Lorentz-expeditie naar Centraal Nederlandsch Nieuw-Guinea. *Tijdschrift van het Koninklijk Nederlandsch Aardrijkskundig_Genootschap* 25:133–144.

Rubin, William (ed.)
1984 *"Primitivism" in 20th Century Art. Affinity of the Tribal and the Modern.* New York.

Ruinen, W.
1922 In memoriam A.J. Gooszen. *Tijdschrift van het Koninklijk Nederlandsch Aardrijkskundig Genootschap* 39:518–521.

Schlocker, Georges
1965 *Ozeanische Totenbeschwörung.* Frankfurt am Main.

Schneebaum, Tobias
1985 *Asmat Images: from the Collection of the Asmat Museum of Culture and Progress / Gambaran Asmat: dari koleksi Museum Kebudayaan dan Kemajuan.* Minneapolis.
1990a *Embodied Spirits. Ritual Carvings of the Asmat.* (A Travelling Exhibition from the Gajdusek Collection of the Peabody Museum of Salem and the Crosier Asmat Museum Collection of Hastings, Nebraska.) Salem, Massachusetts.
1990b The Areas of Asmat Artifacts. In: Allan Hanson and Louise Hanson (eds.), *Art and Identity in Oceania*, 36–43. Bathurst.
1991a Tourism and Art. *Pacific Arts. The Journal of the Pacific Arts Association* 3:27–28.
1991 Asmat. *Louisiana Revy* 32(1):22–37.

Schoot, H.A. van der
1969 *Het Mimika- en Asmatgebied (West-Irian) voor en na de openlegging. Beleidsaspekten van een overgangssituatie.* Ph. D. thesis. Tilburg. (With an English Summary.)

Simpelaere, Paul
1982 *Chez les Asmat: papous de Nouvelle-Guinée Occidentale.* Tielt. (Also published in Dutch: *Bij het volk van de Asmat. Papoea's van Nieuw-Guinea (Irian Jaya). Schetsen-vergelijkingen-herinneringen*, Tielt en Bussum, 1983.

Smidt, Dirk A.M.
1969 *Wow–Ipits. Mens en kunst bij de Papoea's. Uit de verzameling van het Rijksmuseum voor Volkenkunde, Leiden.* Antwerpen. (Exhibition catalogue Koninklijke Akademie voor schone kunsten, Antwerpen.)
1970 Voorouderpalen uit West Nieuw-Guinea. *Verre naasten naderbij* 4(3):86–100.
1987a Birth in New Guinea. In: *The Seasons of Humankind*, 17–24, Leiden.
1987b Death and the Asmat. In: *The Seasons of Humankind*, 73–80, Leiden.
1987c 115 Vrouwelijke voorouderfiguur / 115 Female ancestor figure; 116 Schild /116 Shield. In: Paul L.F. van Dongen, Matthi Forrer and Willem R. van Gulik (eds.), *Topstukken uit het Rijksmuseum voor Volkenkunde / Masterpieces from the National Museum of Ethnology*, 258–259; 260–261. Leiden.
1990a Het kunstenaarschap in Melanesië / The Artist in Melanesia. In: Toos van Kooten and Gerard van den Heuvel (eds.), *Sculptuur uit Afrika en Oceanië / Sculpture from Africa and Oceania*, 185–218. Otterlo.
1990b cat. nr. 124 Schild / Cat. no. 124 Shield; cat. nr. 125 Schild / Cat. no. 125 Shield; cat. nr. 126 Trom / Cat no. 126 Drum. In: Toos van Kooten and Gerard van den Heuvel (eds.), *Sculptuur uit Afrika en Oceanië / Sculpture from Africa and Oceania*, 334–342. Otterlo.

Spat, C.
1909 Koninklijke Militaire Academie. Ethnographische Verzameling. *Indisch Militair Tijdschrift* 40:1297–1298.

Stöhr, Waldemar
1971 *Melanesien. Schwarze Inseln der Südsee.*(Eine Ausstellung des Rautenstrauch-Joest-Museums für Völkerkunde der Stadt Köln, Kunsthalle Köln, 12. November 1971 bis 16. Januar 1972). Köln.

Sudarman, Dea
1984 *Asmat. Menyingkap Budaya Suku Pedalaman*

Irian Jaya. Jakarta.

Tigges, A.F.M.
1985a Analyse van een groep voorouderbeelden van de Asmat. In: Ad Boeren, Fransje Brinkgreve en Sandy Roels (eds.), *Teken van leven. Studies in Etnocommunicatie* (Liber amicorum bij het afscheid van Professor Dr. A.A. Gerbrands), 85–102. Leiden. [ICA Publicatie 71.]
1985b Stijlanalyse van 62 Asmatbeelden. Verslag van een stage in het Rijksmuseum voor Volkenkunde te Leiden in 1983. Ms., Leiden.

Van Amelsvoort (see: Amelsvoort, V.F.P.M. van)

Van Baal (see: Baal, J. van)

Van Nouhuys (see: Nouhuys, J.W. van)

Van Renselaar (see: Renselaar, H.C. van)

Voorhoeve, C.L.
1965 *The Flamingo Bay Dialect of the Asmat Language*. 's–Gravenhage. Ph. D. thesis.

Wassing, René S.
1977 *Asmat, een verdwijnende koppensnellerskultuur in Irian Jaya*. Delft.
1988 The Oceanic Collection. In: Suzanne Greub (ed.), *Expressions of Belief. Masterpieces of African, Oceanic, and Indonesian Art from the Museum voor Volkenkunde, Rotterdam*, 109–113. New York.

Zegwaard M.S.C., Gerard A.
1959 Headhunting Practices of the Asmat of Netherlands New Guinea. *American Anthropologist* 61(6):1020–1041.
1971 An Asmat Mission History. An Asmat Sketch Book 2:5–24. [Translation of: `De missie, geschiedenis Asmat missie' by Joseph de Louw osc].
1978b The Myth of Famiripitsj. *An Asmat Sketch Book* 6:100–103 [Translated by Jim Remmerswaal O.S.C.]

Acknowledgements

The editor extends his thanks to all who contributed texts to this volume. Several contributors provided field photographs as well. Field photographs were also received from Bishop Alphonse A. Sowada O.S.C., Tobias Schneebaum and A. van de Wouw M.S.C. The studio photographs of the Leiden collection were taken by Mr. Isaac C. Brussee of the Rijksmuseum voor Volkenkunde and Mr. Ben Grishaaver of the Audiovisual Centre of the State University of Leiden. Various people gave help in many ways towards the preparation of this book. The editor is grateful to Professor Adrian A. Gerbrands for his advice on various matters and for comments on an earlier draft of the manuscript. Dr. Simon Kooijman provided information on the context of the "Kooijman Shipment," a substantial Asmat collection acquired for the Leiden museum in 1953-1954 from various collectors in the field. Jac. Hoogerbrugge made helpful comments. Thanks are also due to C. Zwartenkot for his stimulating interest in the project and text commentary.

Kees van den Meiracker, Curator of the Department of Oceania, Museum voor Volkenkunde, Rotterdam, kindly provided information on Asmat pieces in the museum concerned. Peter Richardus translated the largest part of the manuscript from Dutch into English (with the exception of the chapters by Hoogerbrugge, Konrad and Wassing which were delivered in English).

Much support was received from people who are attached to the Rijksmuseum voor Volkenkunde. Ernst Storm, who as interim director of the museum asked me at short notice to prepare an exhibition, is indirectly responsible for the beginning of the project. At a later stage, he allowed an initially modest project to grow much larger than originally planned. In this context I also wish to acknowledge the encouragement I received from Agniet van der Sande and Frans Jehee, to carry on. J.A. Buijse commented on an earlier draft of the text. Paul Bijvoet gave valuable computer assistance in preparing the text. Nel van Hove and Berti van Woerden did some urgent typing work. Mrs. Alice Athmer and Angelique Jacobs of the branch museum in Breda facilitated the temporary removal of objects from the permanent exhibition in that museum to enable them to be photographed in Leiden. Last but not least, I wish to acknowledge the cooperation received from Jaap van der Burg in coordinating the movement of exhibits, from Th.P.M. Kop Jansen and Joop Gressie in careful packing and unpacking objects for the Asmat exhibitions in Leiden and Breda, and from Lex Verhey and Pieter Hazenberg in handling and mounting the woodcarvings for photographic purposes.

Index

Note:
Bold type indicates subjects found in chapter headings. Italic numerals indicate photograph or illustrations